Malise Ruthven is a writer and historian of the Islamic world. He has been a scriptwriter with the BBC Arabic and World Services and has taught Islamic Studies and Comparative Religion at the University of Aberdeen, the University of California and at Dartmouth College. He is a frequent contributor to the *New York Review of Books*, among other publications, and is the author of several books, including *Fury for God and Fundamentalism* and *Encounters with Islam* (I.B.Tauris, 2012).

'Over the last decade Malise Ruthven has consolidated his position as one of our most consistently stimulating and sophisticated writers on contemporary religion in general.... In a crowded field Ruthven remains way ahead of the pack.'   William Dalrymple

'A perfect and crazy concept... It's a rocking good read and something of a pocket guide to hell.'   *Time Out*

'This is a significant travel book... it has clear purpose and is not just a ramble through America. As Ruthven himself describes it, he set out to write "a kind of travel book: one that exposes the country's psyche as well as its social and physical landscapes." He is as good as his word.'   William Boyd

'Ruthven is a civilised man, sharp-witted and clever, with an impressive mastery of American social and cultural history and he has written a brilliant account of his travels in search of our spiritual byways and backwaters.'   *Los Angeles Times*

'Ruthven weaves accurate historical information with firsthand observations, interviews, and his own analysis. A readable book with some fresh insights. Recommended.'   *Library Journal*

Tauris Parke Paperbacks is an imprint of I.B.Tauris. It is dedicated to publishing books in accessible paperback editions for the serious general reader within a wide range of categories, including biography, history, travel and the ancient world. The list includes select, critically acclaimed works of top quality writing by distinguished authors that continue to challenge, to inform and to inspire. These are books that possess those subtle but intrinsic elements that mark them out as something exceptional.

The Colophon of Tauris Parke Paperbacks is a representation of the ancient Egyptian ibis, sacred to the god Thoth, who was himself often depicted in the form of this most elegant of birds. Thoth was credited in antiquity as the scribe of the ancient Egyptian gods and as the inventor of writing and was associated with many aspects of wisdom and learning.

THE DIVINE
SUPERMARKET

Travels in Search
of the Soul of America

Malise Ruthven

Foreword by Colin Thubron

TPP

TAURIS PARKE
PAPERBACKS

New paperback edition published in 2012 by Tauris Parke Paperbacks
An imprint of I.B.Tauris and Co Ltd
6 Salem Road, London W2 4BU
175 Fifth Avenue, New York NY 10010
www.ibtauris.com

Distributed in the United States and Canada Exclusively by Palgrave Macmillan
175 Fifth Avenue, New York NY 10010

First published in 1989 by Chatto & Windus Ltd

Cover image: 'St Paul, Minnesota, USA' © Simon Weller / Getty Images

ISBN: 978 1 78076 022 3

A full CIP record for this book is available from the British Library
A full CIP record is available from the Library of Congress

Library of Congress Catalog Card Number: available

Printed and bound in Great Britain by CPI Group (UK) Ltd, Croydon, CRO 4YY

To Wendy and Hughie

Contents

Acknowledgements

T his book could never have been written without the help of a great
many people.

First I would like to thank my brother Grey and my sister-in-law Neiti,
who not only let me stay in their flat in New York during the preparatory
stages of my journey; they also lent me their Welsh retreat where most of
the writing was done. Gail and Kevin Buckley were unstinting in providing
shelter and hospitality during a crucial and difficult time. My thanks to
both for their forbearance, and to Kevin for conscientiously forwarding my
mail to various parts of the world. Special thanks are also due to Barbara
Smith, who allowed me the use of her home near Washington D.C.; to
Marianne Spottiswoode, who had me to stay in Newport, Rhode Island; to
Joseph Michenfelder and Laurine Glynn, who entertained me in Brooklyn;
to Paul and Suzanne Slade, Frank and Rosemary Bleignier, Alan and Patricia
Hamilton and Fanny Howe Senna: all of them had me to stay and helped
open my eyes to the varieties of American religious experience.

I am especially indebted to Margaret Heffernan and Isabel Fonseca, who
read the whole book in manuscript and came up with useful suggestions for
improvements and omissions. I would also like to thank Nancy Ammerman,
of Emory University, Atlanta who read the chapters on fundamentalism and
Jan Shipps of Indiana University who read those dealing with Mormonism.
Both of them put me right on points of detail; neither is responsible for
errors of fact or emphasis that remain.

I am also grateful to Jeremy Lewis, my editor at Chatto and Windus,
who saw the book go through several drafts and made many useful and
constructive suggestions; and to Alan Williams and Andy Dutter of Arbor

House who also suggested useful improvements. I thank Carmen Callil for originally supporting this book, and for her patience in waiting for it.

Others to whom I would like to register my thanks include: Owen Allred, Lorrine Ardress, Paul Anderson, Leonard Arrington, Bronwen and Jenny Astor, Robert Balch, Wendel Bird, Davis Bitton, James Bradstock, Betty Brown, Alfred Bush, Jerry Cahill, Caroline Campbell, Kevin Cartwright, Robert Clarke, Ron Clarke, Tom Connolly, John Cooney, Henrietta Crampton, W. A. Criswell, Bill and Linda Custard, Caroline Dawnay, Margaret Douglas-Hamilton, Paul Edwards, Kirk Elifson, Frank and Gee Elliot, Frances FitzGerald, Cornelia and Lukas Foss, Duaine Gish, Angeline Goreau, Tom Green, John Grimond, Jeffrey Hadden, Paul and Mary Hambrecht, Susan Harding, Michael Hathaway, Loran Herbert, Christopher Hansen, Christopher and Eleni Hitchens, James Hunter, Love Israel, Wells Jakeman, Tim LaHaye, Alistair Lack, Don Lefevre, Austin Long, Guy Lytle, Ken Maley, Paul and Olivia Mason, Peter Matson, Dick Mercy, William Lee Miller, Bill Morlin, Margy and Tom Monante, Louis Moor, Fred Myrow, Linda Newell, Alfonzo Ortiz, Elbert Peck, Ellen Plunkett, Florence and Jack Phillips, Paul Quinn, Paul Richard, Alan Roberts, Jeff Rosenberg, Suzannah von der Schulenberg, Deborah Sharpe, Ted Shay, Barnard and Cherry Silvers, John Sorensen, Mark Strand, Richard H. Taber, Bill Wassmuth, Jack Welsh, Robert Wuthnow, Victoria Zinoviev.

John Buchanan and People for the American Way were unstinting in providing documentation, as was the Crystal Cathedral, Garden Grove, California; FARMS, Provo, Utah; the World University of America, Ojai; the Public Communications Department of the Church of Jesus Christ of Latter-day Saints, Salt Lake City; South-Western Theological Seminary, Fort Worth; the Southern Baptist Convention, Knoxville; and Liberty University, Lynchberg.

Katya Cruft, Jim Delaney and The Final Step provided useful secretarial help.

Some names have been changed in the text to protect the identities of the people concerned. To any who would have preferred anonymity, I offer my apologies.

I have tried to represent the views of my interviewees as accurately as possible. To err, however, is human. I beg forgiveness of any who feel themselves misrepresented, in the hope that I have not caused unintentional distress.

Finally, to Tiggy, Flocky and Fred I owe thanks for their companionship; for their patience during lengthy absences from home; and for their endurance during times of penury and upheaval necessitated by the demands of this book.

London, March 1989

Foreword
by Colin Thubron

The most influential thinkers of the nineteenth and early twentieth centuries – from Marx to Durkheim and Freud – postulated that religious faith would wither away in a post-industrial society; and this in time to many became conventional wisdom. Yet it is very different today. The more violent extremes of Islam, the rise of Hindu nationalism and the evangelism sweeping through Latin America have all run parallel with the collapse of the greatest atheist paradigm in history: the Communist Soviet Union. Cultic faiths have arisen even in China, and demographically the secular, urban populations of the West show a static growth-rate, while the poorer and traditionally religious peoples of the Third World multiply.

Western liberals may explain such manifestations as the vagaries of history or the vulnerability of the very poor. But there are other phenomena, closer to home, which cannot be so easily reasoned away. In the United States – the oldest secular polity on earth – religion is thriving: not by state fiat, but in a plethora of contending Christianities. Faith here is not the unique province of the underprivileged. It is a complex, multi-faceted phenomenon, liberated by a constitution that long ago sanctified independence of worship.

Malise Ruthven, in his remarkable book, *The Divine Supermarket*, has inquired into this kaleidoscopic world by means of a long and highly individual journey. From the lands of the Puritan founding fathers and the birthplace of Mormonism, he followed the famous trek of Brigham Young and the Latter-day Saints to Salt Lake Valley in Utah. From there, he moved on to encounter a bizarre neo-Nazi sect in Montana, the rituals of tribal remembrance among Native Americans, the remains of a sixties love-cult, and the estate of the controversial guru Bhagwan Shree Rajneesh. In California, heartland of the New Age, a melange of fantastical cults seemed to offer the bountiful variety of his eponymous supermarket; and in the unctuous 'theology of self-esteem', propagated by the televangelist Richard Schuller, Ruthven diagnoses the ultimate packaging of the Californian dream.

The marriage of religion and commerce haunts his journey. 'The Gospel was being marketed like soap powders:', he writes, 'the same product but with different packagings.' At a New Age exposition in Santa Barbara, the believers still slouched about in sandals and dungarees, but 'eyes that once gazed vacuously into psychedelic space or sought nirvanas beyond distant horizons had acquired a harder, more predatory gaze'. From the radio in his battered hybrid camper, the propositions pour out: "'Jesus has promised His presence in your life. Now's the time to take advantage of His Unique Offer"' And the multi-million dollar industry of television evangelism was headed by superstars whose lifestyle was indistinguishable from that of corporate tycoons.

Eastward into the Texas of the Southern Baptists, then the Georgia of Martin Luther King and of black converts to Islam, Ruthven reached Carolina just after scandal has broken out around the televangelist Jim Bakker. The trajectory of Bakker's career, in Ruthven's telling, is typical of many such leaders, from the Mormon founder Joseph Smith and before: a charismatic leader appears, huge followings gather, then something goes wrong. Their privileged lives start to separate them from their flock; sex scandals erupt, and there is a fall from grace.

As for Ruthven, he ends his journey, by a self-created irony, in a Trappist abbey in Kentucky, whose regime is one of merciful silence.

It is 25 years since Malise Ruthven undertook this mammoth journey. Yet markedly little has changed. Although the proportion of believers in some form of God has slid down from the 98 per cent that he reports, the United States still holds the largest Christian populace in the world. And much of its influence runs counter to the idea of a freedom-loving culture. When the World Trade Centre was brought down in September 2001, two of the evangelists deplored by Ruthven suggested that a nation corrupted by pagans, feminists, homosexuals and others was getting what it deserved.

The moments of benediction in Ruthven's narrative arise, in the main, from sources other than Christianity: the prelapsarian beauty of a Navajo valley, perhaps, or the splendour of the Grand Canyon, whose magisterial strata refute the Creationist myth. Even the comparatively impersonal

Islamic faith, of which Ruthven is a scholar, comes as a relief from the self-centred babble of the born again.

The demands of such a journey were formidable. In his ancient camper Ruthven travelled light, and his encounters were often chance ones. But if this is a travel book, its methods are barely typical. Ruthven does not engage in the ostensibly random wanderings of a Chatwin or Theroux. Rather, he works in the mode of V.S. Naipaul, moving from person to person on a paper-chase of understanding. His prose is lean and unpretentious. He has a lively eye and ear for the grotesque. But most remarkable are his powers of insight and dissection. From even the most garbled or complex expression of faith, the theological and psychological realities are beautifully – and sometimes mercilessly – laid bare. He writes with the lucidity of a sympathetic unbeliever; but there is no flaccid compassion. He is irritable sometimes, and occasionally angry: exasperation often touched with humour.

Tellingly, in this kaleidoscope of faiths, he finds patterns and ancestors. In Joseph Smith especially, the founder of Mormonism, he sees the link between the Puritan past, with its dream of a New Jerusalem on earth, and the New Age present. And the multiform flowering of religion he traces back to the Constitution itself: to a First Amendment, steered by Thomas Jefferson, that delivers faith from the shadow of national government, freeing it into unforeseen (and occasionally dangerous) forms, while protecting the state from its tyranny.

Preface
to this Edition

On September 11, 2001, more than a decade after I completed my journey, Armageddon happened – or so it must have seemed to many Americans when two high-jacked airliners hit the World Trade Center in downtown Manhattan, and another crashed into the Pentagon near Washington. The attacks, which completely demolished New York's landmark Twin Towers, killed nearly 3,000 people, maimed hundreds more, and exposed legions of people to toxic fumes released in the clouds of dust. Two of the preachers who feature in this book were quick to respond. Speaking with Pat Robertson on the 700 Club on September 12 Jerry Falwell saw the attacks as just retribution for America's moral failings:

> "I really believe that the pagans and the abortionists and the feminists and the gays and the lesbians who are actively trying to make that an alternative lifestyle, the ACLU, People for the American Way, all of them who have tried to secularize America, I point the finger in their face and say 'You helped this happen.'"

Robertson agreed:

> 'I totally concur. . . . It happened because people are evil. It also happened because God is lifting His protection from this nation and we must pray and ask Him for revival so that once again we will be His people, the planting of His righteousness, so that He will come to our defense and protect us as a nation. That is what I want to see and why we say we must have revival. We must have a spiritual revival.'

In the aftermath of the atrocity, Robertson's hoped-for spiritual revival, if it happened at all, took second place to the military response – the attack on Afghanistan, where the Taliban regime had been sheltering al-Qaeda and its leader, Osama bin Laden. Soon this initially successful campaign, which unseated the Taliban regime, at least temporarily, was upstaged by the war against Iraq, despite the absence of any convincing evidence linking Saddam Hussein's regime with the 9/11 attacks. Compared with the raging nights of bombardment, the destruction of bridges, hospitals, schools, power stations, and residential dwellings that preceded the land invasion, New York's Armageddon would have seemed a minor disturbance, a spike on the screen of normality. In Iraq and Afghanistan, by contrast, America's enraged response continues to exact an awesome toll. By the summer of 2011 civilian deaths in Iraq – the outcome of the violent sectarian and ethnic forces unleashed by the war as well as the bombing – had climbed to more than 100,000, while US military casualties were approaching the 5,000 mark. In Afghanistan, nearly 9,000 civilians have been killed, along with a similar number of Afghan troops. The estimates of peace activists – based on admittedly uncertain sources from countries suffering from chaotic conditions – put the toll of the dead in Iraq and Afghanistan at 300 times the figure for New York and Washington. In the calculus of death, America's God indulges in massive overkill: 600 eyes for 2.

In what US Defense Secretary Donald Rumsfeld dismissively called 'Old Europe,' divine intentions were perceived somewhat differently. Before the US-led attack on Iraq, Pope John Paul II sent his personal representative, Cardinal Pio Laghi (a friend of the Bush family) to try to persuade US President George W. Bush to avoid military conflict. Pio Laghi repeated the Pope's insistence that the war would be a defeat for humanity that could not be morally or legally justified. After hostilities had started, the Pope reiterated his message. 'When war, as in these days in Iraq, threatens the fate of humanity,' he told the Italian television channel Telespace, 'it is ever more urgent to proclaim, with a strong and decisive voice, that peace alone is the path to follow to construct a more just and united society.'

Despite the presence of millions of Catholics, who constitute about a quarter of the US population, the God in whom George W. Bush and his administration colleagues put their trust was a Protestant deity with strongly Old Testament leanings. Unlike Catholics, who are expected to follow the teachings of a Church that embodies centuries of accumulated wisdom, many Protestants communicate with God on their private hot-lines: 'God told me to strike at al-Qaeda and I struck them,' Bush told Mahmoud Abbas, the Palestinian Prime Minister in June 2003. 'Then he instructed me to strike at Saddam.' Bush, a reformed alcoholic, describes himself as a born-again Christian, so his sincerity in claiming divine approval can hardly be questioned. There were, however, important domestic political considerations in his choice of language. His principal adviser and deputy chief of staff, Karl Rove, a brilliant political strategist, had forged crucial links with the evangelical Christian Right, which, according to recent polls, represents a fluctuating constituency of between 40 and 75 million Americans. The groundwork had been laid in the 1990s, with Christian conservatives casting two out of every five Republican votes. As Joan Didion observes:

> 'By the time of the 2000 Republican convention, Christian conservatives had achieved a platform unswervingly tailored to their agenda, including the removal of language that could be interpreted as pro-choice, the removal of language that could suggest approval of civil rights for homosexuals, and the removal of language that could be seen to favor any form of sex education other than the teaching of abstinence.'

In the election that brought the junior Bush his second term in 2004 the Christian Right accounted for approximately 40 percent of the vote. In the face of the Pope's hostility, the leaders of this hawkish tendency argued the case for a 'Just War' in Iraq.

Richard Land, president of the Ethics and Religious Liberty Commission of the Southern Baptist Convention, organized a round-robin letter stating that a preemptive strike against Iraq would be legitimate under Just War Theory. It was co-signed by several influential evangelical leaders. These included Charles 'Chuck' Colson, a former Nixon aide and founder of the Prison Fellowship Ministries who found Jesus while serving a prison term for his part in the Watergate scandal; Bill Bright, founder and chair of the Campus Crusade for Christ; D. James Kennedy, president of the Coral Ridge Ministries Media; and Carl Herbster, president of the American Association of Christian Schools. These powerful voices were instrumental in securing initial 'Christian' support for the wars in Iraq and Afghanistan before the prospects for outright military victory began to fade.

Many commentators would see in the American response to 9/11 an example of imperial overreach, the hubris of a nation that had become the world's only superpower since the collapse of the Soviet Union in 1991. The Arab terrorists had tweaked the lion's tail, and the animal had responded with a combination of rage and greed. Michael Scheuer, a former CIA agent and special adviser to the Bin Laden unit, has argued presciently that war in Afghanistan is unwinnable. Sooner or later the Taliban will return to power. The attack on Iraq was even worse, morally and politically: it was 'an avaricious, premeditated, unprovoked war against a foe who posed no immediate threat but whose defeat did offer economic advantages.'

Rage and greed, however, were only a part of the story: a sizeable portion of America's response could be blamed on the Bible – or to be more precise, on the apocalyptic biblical visions dear to the Christian fundamentalists who Karl Rove had marshaled so successfully for the younger Bush in 2004.

One of the encounters I relate in this book (p. 190) gave me peculiar access to this vision. In 1987 I interviewed the evangelist Tim LaHaye for the BBC World Service. In his comfortable Washington suite, Mr LaHaye gave me a private sermon on his favorite subject, the doomsday events leading to Armageddon when the Antichrist will appear, Russia is destroyed supernaturally and 144,000 righteous Jews will convert to Christianity, while the remainder will perish miserably along with other recalcitrant nonbelievers, myself included. At that time, I was unaware of the extent to which Israeli politicians cynically exploited these eschatological fantasies in order to gain Congressional support for the colonization of Palestine and the illegal Jewish settlements that have long been the principal obstacles to the peace process between Israelis and Palestinians. Some of these settlements are funded by Christian sympathizers who believe, with Mr LaHaye, that the Jews must foregather in all of the historic Holy Land in order to bring about the eventual return of Christ. Contrary to much of the media analysis that focuses on the 'Jewish lobby,' these Christian Zionists have considerably more influence over US foreign policy than IAPAC (the Israeli-American Public Affairs Committee), not least because some 60 million or more evangelical Christians vastly outnumber America's five million Jews, a significant portion of whom are openly critical of Israeli settlement policies.

The 'wall of separation' between church and state that I commended (perhaps naively) in my Epilogue (see p. 296) may have protected American secularity at home by the encouraging denominational pluralism and church autonomy, limiting the seepage of religious dogmatisms into domestic policies. But in lending uncritical support for Israel as part of an eschatological agenda that sees Jews not so much as people with legitimate security needs but as ciphers in an unfolding cosmic drama in which Jesus completes Hitler's work, the impact of Mr LaHaye and his friends has been unfortunate, to say the least.

It would be going too far to suggest that the apocalyptic fantasies of pre-millennialists such as Mr LaHaye actually dictated US foreign policy during the Bush years – leaving his successor Barak Obama with a legacy of inextricable entanglements and unwinnable wars. Bush's policy toward Israel was characterized – like that of his successor – by a vacillating pragmatism that paid lip service to the international consensus of a two-state solution for Israel and Palestine (in violation of eschatological expectations), without pursuing it with the vigor that circumstances demanded and American leverage could make possible. The Christian Right, however, played an important part in softening public criticism of Israel's discriminatory policies (which for most Palestinians resemble those of the former white South Africa), and its vastly disproportionate response to amateur rocket attacks from Gaza. The Christian Zionist element ensured maximum congressional support for Israel's leaders, making it clear that for a president seeking a second term backing a legally mandated Palestinian state through the United Nations would be electoral suicide.

A more pervasive effect of the bizarre religiosity promoted by Mr LaHaye and his friends was the rhetorical process by which challenges to the New World Order, so confidently proclaimed by Bush Senior in 1991, were reduced to a simple war of 'us' against 'them,' of liberty against tyranny. The Manichean division of the world between 'good guys' and 'bad guys' featured in popular discourse – not to mention Westerns – long before Bush Junior launched his 'war on terror' declaring that those who are not with us are against us. But Bush Junior's speechwriters excelled in crafting a discourse that seamlessly conflated the aspirational language of liberalism with biblical tropes calculated to evoke a positive response among believers. The most blatant example of this conflationary rhetoric came in Bush's 2002 State of the Union address where three entirely disparate countries (two of which had fought a bitter, eight-year war against each other) were merged into a single 'axis of evil' embracing Iraq, Iran, and North Korea. But there were more subtle examples. In Bush's Second Inaugural Address – a speech that went through 21 drafts before being delivered – the President's speech writer Michael Gerson, himself a born-again Christian, waxed lyrical on the subject of freedom versus tyranny:

> 'We have seen our vulnerability – and we have seen its deepest source. For as long as whole regions of the world simmer in resentment and tyranny – prone to ideologies that feed hatred and excuse murder – violence will

gather, and multiply in destructive power, and cross the most defended borders, and raise a mortal threat. There is only one force of history that can break the reign of hatred and resentment, and expose the pretensions of tyrants, and reward the hopes of the decent and tolerant, and that is the force of human freedom. . . . Eventually the call of freedom comes to every mind and every soul.'

There are no explicitly biblical references here, but the tone is Manichean, juxtaposing good-guy America that stands for freedom against the bad-guy tyrannies feeding hatred and excusing murder. Actual US practices such as the targeted killing of enemies including US citizens, the use of unmanned aircraft or 'drones' to eliminate rebels or tribal chiefs who resist America or its allies, and the torture and 'rendition' to friendly dictatorships of 'enemy combatants' in violation of international agreements – all such practices of questionable legality are ignored or subsumed in the great global contest between 'freedom' and 'tyranny.' To the uninitiated, the concept of 'freedom' may appear pleasingly – even vapidly – secular, but for the born-again Christian the biblical resonances are strong and unmissable. Every true believer knows that 'freedom' means Jesus: the words are interchangeable. 'Ye shall know the truth, and the truth shall make you free' (John 8:32). 'If the Son therefore shall make you free, ye shall be free indeed' (John 8:36).

The religious enthusiasm evoked by the 'war on terror' soon ran into the sands of complexity, as the naive 'us-versus-them' mentality of the born-again right was forced to confront some harsh geopolitical realities. The most obvious place where the binary model of freedom versus tyranny broke down was in Afghanistan, where America found itself fighting tribally-based networks sustained by the intelligence service of its nominal ally, Pakistan. But many other contradictions would emerge as the war on terror progressed. In strategically important parts of the Arab world, the promise of freedom was suspended, with the US conniving at the brutal suppression of democratic forces by its long serving Saudi ally in Bahrain, while giving rhetorical and in the case of Libya some military support, to the movement for freedom that swept through the Arab world in the spring of 2011.

Faced with a world that is perversely resisting biblical expectations, the Christian right is finding new outlets for its energies. Tim LaHaye has quietly abandoned futurist prophecy for a highly lucrative career as a fiction writer. The *Left Behind* series of novels he co-authors with Jerry B. Jenkins provide graphic and detailed accounts of the Last Days, when Christians are miraculously raptured and planes flown by born-again pilots crash to earth. These books have sold upwards of 70 million copies to date. Their hermeneutic style remains as literalistic as their models in the Scofield Reference Bible and Hal Lindsay's *Late Great Planet Earth*. But the switch of genre from futurist prophecy to fantasy fiction is suggestive of a tacit recognition that these things may not be going to happen . . . just yet.

The promised millennium, endlessly deferred, remains integral to the story of the American Dream and Governor Winthrop's City on a Hill. The great Mormon narrative that lies at the core of this book charts one of its passages, from the catastrophic expectation of doom that fired the early Saints to the impressive feats of construction they created in the Utah desert. As I write, a Mormon stands – for the second time round – as a leading candidate for the Republican nomination. For true believers, a Mormon in the White House presents a theological obstacle, because Mormons, as 'Godmakers' or Pelagians who believe that men can aspire to divinity, transgress the boundary separating the Creator and his creatures, and cannot be regarded as Christians. But from a historical perspective such an eventuality would breach a significant threshold, with the first and most successful of the New World religions finally overcoming the stigma of an Old World heresy.

Saint Jacques de Néhou, France
April 2012

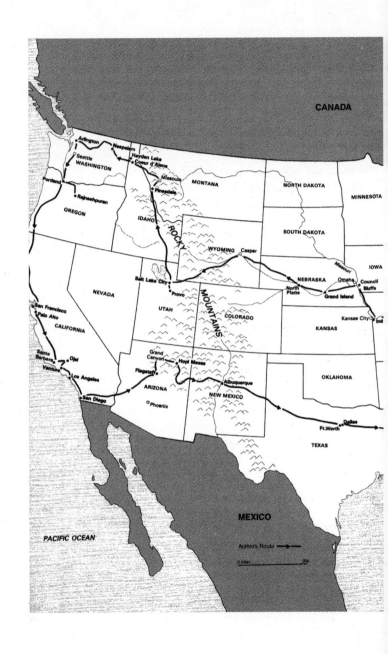

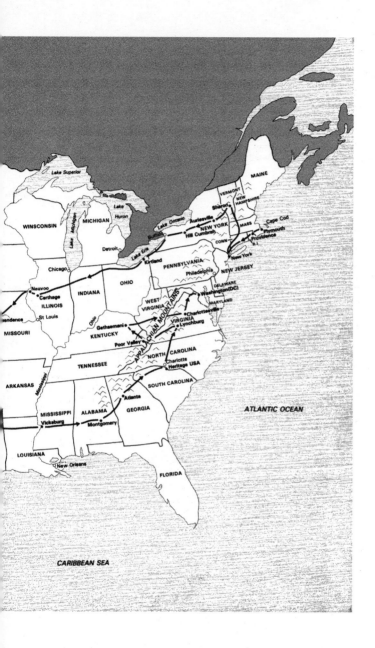

Prologue

The germ of this book came to me sometime during 1985. Having recently published a book about Islam, I was often asked questions like: 'Why are Muslims so fanatical? Why do they resort to violence? Why is Islam so politicised?'

I was never satisfied with my answers, which focused on the fact that unlike most religions, Islam began its career as a polity, and that politics, in one form or another, often entails violence. Sadat died violently; but so did Kennedy. Muslims have no monopoly of religious fanaticism – if by that we mean an excessive and seemingly irrational attachment to religious dogma. In discussions with colleagues I would sometimes air my misgivings.

'What about Jerry Falwell? Isn't he a fanatic? Have you seen Pat Robertson healing on television, or commanding hurricanes, in the name of the Lord, to leave America's shores? What about all those creationists who still insist that the world was created in six days a mere six thousand years ago?'

'OK,' said my colleagues. 'We all know Americans are crazy; but they don't mount suicide attacks in car bombs, expecting to be instantly transported to paradise.'

These remarks were said on the spur of the moment. But they set me thinking, raising a hundred questions in my mind. The United States, according to Sidney Mead, is a 'nation with the soul of a church' – the outstanding exception to the sociological truism that industrialism inevitably leads to secularisation. According to a Gallup survey taken in 1986, 81 per cent of the 166 million Americans over the age of seventeen described themselves as Christians; of these 62 per cent believed in the Second Coming; and while only 20 per cent of those polled belonged to evangelical churches, a remarkable 38 per cent (that is, 63 million people) claimed to have been 'born again'. 45 per cent of American adults claimed to worship at a church, synagogue or other religious meeting-place at least once a week. On this reckoning the only European country to exceed the United States in religiosity was Ireland, where under-development conspired with tribalism to produce a Sunday attendance figure of 82 per cent. By contrast, once-devout Spain could only produce a church attendance of only 41 per cent: while with only 14 per cent Great Britain, excluding Northern Ireland, was well down the league table of religious observance, far below Italy (36 per cent), Belgium (30 per cent), Netherlands (27 per cent) and West Germany (21 per cent).

What was the source of this religiosity? Why did Americans seem to need religion more than Italians, Belgians, Dutch and Germans – not to mention the British? On visits to New York I had been amazed and amused, like many British people, by the fare on television. Those channels that weren't showing five-year old British programmes like *Monty Python* seemed to be devoted either to pornography; or to preachers like Jerry Falwell, Pat Robertson, Robert Schuller and Jimmy Swaggart who promised heaven – or, rather, heaven-on-earth – in return for donations.

The Gospel was being marketed like soap powders: the same product with different packagings. Falwell was calm and avuncular, an old-time Baptist preacher with the reassuring manner of a friendly bank-manager; Robertson was smoother and more fluent – very much the professional TV chat-show host; Schuller was unctuous and slick – turning the Gospel into advertising slogans; and then there was Swaggart – aggressive and sexually powerful, something between a modern rock star and the hell-fire preachers of old. The radio preachers were no less varied and no less strident: the main difference was that they were less professional and more long-winded, numbing the mind with turgid and lengthy line-by-line biblical dissections.

Religion in America was a vast multi-billion dollar industry, employing thousands of men and women and attracting people of talent and ambition. The earnings of men like Swaggart, Falwell, Robertson and Schuller ran into millions of dollars. They flew around the world in private jets, breakfasted with presidents, rubbed shoulders with prime ministers, and to outward appearances were indistinguishable from the tycoons and corporate chiefs who headed other, secular, multinational corporations. Competing as they did for audiences, funds and 'souls' in a market that was not expanding as fast as their ambitions, rivalries had sharpened between them, creating a context in which minor peccadilloes were blown up into major national scandals.

After reports of a fifteen-minute sexual encounter between evangelist Jim Bakker and a church secretary had led to the collapse of the PTL ministry in 1987 – the initials stood for 'Praise the Lord' or 'People that Love', depending on one's choice – Jerry Falwell, who temporarily took over the ministry, estimated that church and church-related charities in the United States, including universities, schools, hostels and ministries, had lost about one-fifth of their financial support – approximately sixteen billion dollars out of eighty billion. Religion in America was very big business indeed.

It was a very far cry from the religion we had in Britain. Before the Salman Rushdie affair unleashed a wave of Islamic militancy, the only religious stories in the newspapers were either clichés about vicars and choir boys, or the pathetic tale of an Oxford don who committed suicide after being rumbled for making an anonymous attack on the Archbishop of Canterbury in *Crockford's Clerical Directory*. Tourism, not faith, kept our crumbling cathedrals from collapse; appeals for their preservation were made, not from godliness, but out of concern for the national heritage. Unlike their American counterparts, who earned 'executive' salaries, most of the Anglican clergy lived in genteel poverty, relics of a once-respectable profession that had seen itself overtaken by its secular progeny in advertising, the media and the academic world. Religion on radio and television was bland, patronising and dull – a sop to a dying tradition, an aspect, like the cathedrals, of Britain's 'museum culture'. The differences in style and content could only partly be attributed to differences between the deregulated American airwaves and those in Britain, which were still under strong public control. The media, however organised, could only reflect and project back onto society what was already there.

Why, despite the common language and a common Protestant legacy, were the American and British religious cultures so different? Was it simply due to the fact that American churches were disestablished? Or was it rather because the real religion of Britain lay not in the Church of England – that 'ingeniously contrived mechanism', in Bishop Charles Gore's pungent phrase, 'for defeating the object it is supposed to promote' – but the monarchy, which took control of the church more than three centuries ago, domesticating and emasculating it? I had on occasions observed the monarch in person. Grown men and women froze before her as in the physical presence of a deity, apparently terrified of losing control of themselves, of incontinently committing an act of sacrilege. Were not the royal festivals – the weddings and jubilees that permitted millions to congregate or dance in the streets, suspending class differences – the British equivalent of the great American revival meetings, where thousands jerked or danced for Jesus? Perhaps it was the absence of monarchy, of a socially-binding state cult, that encouraged the American mind to look for God, to seek, not so much immortality in the next world, but assurance of salvation in this.

Disgusted with a church that toadied so abjectly to the state, the Puritan founders of America had left England to create a new Church, a new Kingdom in the wilderness. The original messianic strain had persisted into a more secular age: it continued to find expression in the public, political realm – in grandiloquent phrases like 'manifest destiny', the 'American Dream', and in the idea of a nation, in Melville's phrase, 'predestinated at creation'. That primary biblical project, the Holy Commonwealth, had etched itself permanently on the American imagination, generating an optimism that seemed both inspiringly brave and exasperatingly simplistic; creating possibilities for real innovation and exciting social experiment, while offering *carte blanche* to rogues, megalomaniacs, frauds and impostors.

The central biblical myth informing the American self-image was the story of Exodus. In the Judaeo-Christian tradition, the myth of Exodus has always been a two-edged sword. Created by a pastoral people to chart their conquest of settled lands, it is both an ideology of deliverance and liberation, and of oppression and exclusion: a warrant for release, and a charter for conquest. Identifying themselves with the ancient Hebrews, the Puritans saw America as a new Land of Canaan, their passage across the Atlantic as another crossing of the Red Sea; so, perversely, did some African slaves who, adopting the religion of their enslavers, identified African paganism with Egyptian bondage, American slavery with Canaanite deliverance. Programmed into the American psyche, Exodus became the archetype of migration, the filter through which generations of newcomers viewed their experience. Its imagery became a metaphor not only for English Protestants and Russian Jews, but for Lithuanian peasants, Greek islanders, Irish navvies, German farmers, Swedish small-holders: virtually every migrant group or nationality excepting the Asians of the Pacific rim.

The Exodus motif was intimately bound up with millennialist eschatology: millennial expectations added urgency to the Exodus enterprise. 'We must hurry up and get to the Promised Land,' said the millennialists, 'before it is too late.' Far from inducing a mood of quietism and resignation, the imminence of the Messiah generated frenetic activity, encouraging formidable feats of construction.

Nowhere was the integrating, theologising power of this myth revealed more clearly than in the great Mormon migrations from New England and Europe to the American West. Here, under the inspiration of a Prophet who combined the types of Moses with Jesus, a people created itself using Exodus as a template. The genius of Joseph Smith was to have reconstructed the myth, combining the biblical narrative with a new Book of his own, one which reworked the Exodus motif in an American setting. The Book of Mormon has justly been described as America's religious Declaration of Independence: the first widely acknowledged text to have been 'revealed' in the Promised Land.

After Joseph Smith's death at the hands of a mob in 1844, his successor, Brigham Young, led the Latter-day Saints to Utah with Exodus in one hand and a frontier map in the other. Every step on the way was a literal re-enactment of the route taken by Moses and the Children of Israel. The unexpected freezing of the Mississippi which facilitated their passage was likened to the parting of the Red Sea; the sudden appearance of a flock of quails to the descent of manna from heaven.

But Joseph Smith, self-styled 'restorer' of Israel after centuries of apostasy, was also the first example of a distinctively modern type: the 'cult' leader who creates a new religious tradition by reworking and recycling older mythologies into a new synthesis. For an age that has seen a spectacular growth in 'new religious movements', Joseph Smith is a pivotal figure: he is the link which connects America's New England, Puritan past, with its New Age, Californian future. His Book is one of the most influential documents to have been produced on the western side of the Atlantic.

Like many people, I had first encountered Mormonism when approached by missionaries: two earnest young men with cropped hair, white shirts and black ties came to the door and left me with a lavishly illustrated paperback version of the Book of Mormon. I cannot believe this technique wins many converts: I myself forgot all about the book, which lay gathering dust on an inaccessible shelf for several years.

I became interested in Mormonism only after reading Richard Burton's account of his journey to Salt Lake City in 1854. Like Burton, I noted the parallels between Smith's religion and that of the Prophet Muhammad. I decided it would be fascinating to follow Burton's route to Salt Lake City, to see the New Zion a hundred and thirty years on. Did modern, educated Mormons really believe the fairy tales about the Golden Plates the angel Moroni gave Joseph, and the magic spectacles he used to 'translate' them?

Having got as far as Utah, it seemed a pity not to go on to the Pacific, in order to visit some of Smith's spiritual successors, the New Age cults. I knew people – ordinary, reasonable English people with privileged backgrounds like myself – who had suddenly abandoned families, sometimes fortunes, in order to join some cult or other. Some of them disappeared altogether; others re-emerged from time to time, bearing strange new names and even weirder clothes. The cults, widely regarded as 'fraudulent', raised interesting questions about religious truth. Most religions, after all, began their worldly careers as cults. The only qualititative difference between Christianity and Islam and modern cults like Rajneeshism or Scientology seemed to be in their antiquity. A cult becomes a religion when it gets older and bigger – when it is sanctified, not so much by God, as by history.

There remained the phenomenom of fundamentalism: although universal – there were plenty of fundamentalist churches in suburban New England – its greatest concentration, the source of so much power and money, lay in the South. To what extent, I wondered, did the new militant evangelism represent a return to Puritan values, a re-integration of the biblical past? How could prosperous, educated people still seriously insist that every word of Genesis be taken literally, that God created the world in six days a mere 6,000 years ago? What were the sub-texts behind this attachment to the Word? What were the fundamentalists really trying to say?

And so my American pilgrimage took shape. I would start in New England, with the Puritans. I would follow Joseph Smith and Brigham Young across the Adirondacks, into western New York; and on through Kirtland (Ohio), Nauvoo (Illinois) and Independence (Missouri). Then, like Burton, I would take the Mormon Trail across Nebraska and Wyoming, through the Rockies and into the Great Salt Lake valley. Leaving New York in late September, I would aim to reach Salt Lake City in time for the church's semi-annual conference, in the first week-end in October.

After that, I had an open agenda. I wanted to meet some American Indians, the survivors of that insidious genocide, the Silent Holocaust, which left no monuments. I had friends to stay with in San Francisco and Southern California; I aimed to 'do' the Grand Canyon, to explore the Hopi mesas, to visit Dallas and spend some time in the Bible Belt. I would end, as I began, in the East. Apart from that there was no definite shape to my journey: I would simply drive around in the camper I intended to buy, visit churches, see what happened.

The result, I hoped, would be a kind of travel book: one which explored a country's psyche as well as its social and physical landscapes, which sought explanations of why things were the way I found them to be. I do not claim to have been very successful in my endeavour, or to have found satisfactory answers to all the questions. My choice of subjects – in so vast an arena – has inevitably been somewhat arbitrary. I have deliberately selected subjects like Mormonism and fundamentalism, that seemed exotic and alien to my own way of thinking, to seek out differences rather than explore common ground. The mainstream, liberal Protestantism in which I was brought up contains no mystery for me, and therefore has no appeal.

The journey – whether successfully accomplished or not was immensely rewarding. Some of my prejudices and intuitions were confirmed. But I learned much more than I expected. The people I met were universally welcoming. They spoke with great candour about themselves, their beliefs and their hopes. Even though I remain unable to share these beliefs, many of which would tend to exclude each other, I never doubted the sincerity of those who held them. Even those preachers who seemed more intent on making money than alleviating human sorrows must be credited with sincerity: their material and moral interests are so obviously at one.

Did I feel a spark of faith myself? Did a chink of the divine light penetrate my intellectual scepticism, casting doubt upon my agnosticism? That I must leave for my readers to judge for themselves.

Part One

The Road to Zion

'And we Americans are the peculiar chosen people – the Israel of our time; we bear the ark of the liberties of the world.'

HERMAN MELVILLE

I

The Pilgrim Trail

'And I have also established my covenant with them, to give them the land
of Canaan, the land of the Pilgrimage, wherein. they were strangers.'

EXODUS 6: 4

'And where do you hail from, good master?' said the cockney-voiced wench,
displaying a fine cleavage beneath her shawl.

'From London town.'

'How fares the city?'

'Tis getting worse, headed for destruction.'

'Aye, so 'tis said.'

'Thou'rt better placed out here.'

'Hast had thy pocket cut?'

'Nay, praise the Lord, but a cutpurse, a young blackamoor, held a knife
at my goodwife's throat and took her money. 'Tis not safe for a woman to
walk the streets.'

A young Puritan, hatless but resplendent in buckled boots, drew me
aside to show me the flimsy wooden compartments on the Mayflower's
creaking lower deck.

'The shallop what we've been provided was all disassembled,' he said
in attempted seventeenth-century East Anglian. 'Some of the folk took to
sleeping atop the ship's hold. On the Cape o' Cod it took us sixteen or
seventeen days to put them together again.'

Like me, he had been mugging up on *Mourt's Relation*, the chronicle of the
Pilgrim landing. I wanted to know something the ancient chronicles never
tell you – nor, for that matter, do most newspaper reports of space-shots
or power failures in elevators and subways.

'Were there privvies, or did they just go over the edge?'

'Chamber-pots. But in truth there was no way of emptying them – so folks would just put the slops down through the ribs of the ship into the bilge. There was a fearsome stench down there.'

The thought was enough to send me back to the upper deck; relieved that the Plymouth Living Museum's passion for historic authenticity stopped short of the olfactory. I bade the mariners godspeed, and clunked through the turnstile back into the twentieth century.

I drove on towards Provincetown at the tip of Cape Cod, where America stretches a crooked finger into the Atlantic, beckoning voyagers to land, or wreck themselves, on sandy but treacherous shores. By the time I arrived at the Pilgrim Trail, tastefully marked but mercifully tourist-free, this being September, wet and windy, it was late afternoon. I entered the scrubby pine forest and followed a moss-flanked path which, my ears told me, must lead to the dunes and the ocean. It was the path the landing party led by Miles Standish and William Bradford had taken, stumbling through the brush with their leather boots and cumbersome armour.

They had spotted a group of Indians and wanted to contact them. But the natives took fright and, being more swift-footed, led the Pilgrims to stumble about for two days and a night, through boughs and brushes that 'tore their very armour in pieces'. At that season, in November 1620, the fall colours must have been at their brightest, just as Thoreau would find them two centuries later: bright red huckleberries, browner bayberries and the varied greens of pitch-pine, boxberry and plum mixed with fawn-coloured tints of birch, maple and aspen – an exotic carpet spread over the uneven surface of the sand which sometimes showed through, 'like the white floor seen through rents in the rug'.

But the Pilgrims didn't notice the foliage: their minds were firmly set on higher things. Their accounts are short on topography, long on religious symbolism. Typically, Bradford contrasted his own standing on the dunes of Cape Cod with Moses on Mount Pisgah. Unlike Moses, wrote Bradford, the Pilgrims could not

> as it were, go up to the top of Pisgah, to view from this wilderness a more goodly country to feed their hopes; for which way soever they turned their eyes (save upward to the heavens) they could have little solace or content in respect of any outward objects. For summer being done, all things stand upon them with a weatherbeaten face; and the whole country, full of woods and thickets, represented a wild and savage hew.

The Separatists who sailed in the *Mayflower* were not the rugged individualists who settled the new continent in later times. Their religious motives were paramount. Unlike the Presbyterians, who aimed to reform the church in England, submitting it to a more democratic form of governance, they had decided to start the world anew. Like the ancient Hebrews, with whom they identified themselves, they had put the 'bondage of Egypt' behind them; or, to use another of their favourite biblical analogies, they had abandoned the Whore of Babylon. Their original leader, pastor John Robinson (who succumbed to the plague before making the crossing) had explained their attitude in his manifesto, *A Justification of Separation from the Church of England*:

> Now as the people of God in old time were called out of Babylon civil, the place of their bodily bondage; and were to come to Jerusalem, and there to build the Lord's temple, or tabernacle, leaving Babylon to that destruction, which the Lord, by his servants, the prophets, had denounced against it . . . so are the people of God now to go out of Babylon spiritual to Jerusalem . . . and to build up themselves as lively stones unto a spiritual house, or temple for the Lord to dwell in, leaving Babylon to that destruction and desolation, yea furthering the same, to which she is devoted by the Lord.

Yet that 'spiritual house' would soon be fleshed in the material reality of a human community. The New Jerusalem they intended to build is described in Chapter 21 of the Book of Revelation – a city bathed in eternal light which would have 'no need of the sun, neither of the moon, to shine in it'. It would 'come down from God out of heaven, prepared as a bride adorned for her husband'. By preparing for it here on earth, the faithful would be bringing on the millennium which they knew to be imminent. From the moment of the Pilgrim landing, America's destiny became part of salvation history – the culmination and fulfilment of human life on earth.

The Pilgrims, of course, were not the first to arrive in the New World; and other people with different agendas, more opportunistic and less utopian, would follow. But the Puritans set a pattern that would prove remarkably persistent. Divine eschatology does not – except for small communities – form part of the political self-image of Canada, Brazil, or Australia. Yet in the United States it is central to the national mythology, embodied in such well-worn phrases as Manifest Destiny and the American Dream. The Pilgrims, steeped in their Biblical allegories, had *materialised* the Biblical myths, translating its allegories into symbols. Where Bunyan's City of Destruction, his 'wilderness of this world' were allegories of the moral and psychological states perceived, in traditional terms, by a protestant Christian sensibility, the American Pilgrim experienced them as concrete realities. The 'Christian' who arrived in the New World had physically abandoned the City of Destruction, be it Egypt or Babylon; he had literally 'crossed the Red Sea' – a terrifying and awesome experience in those leaky hulls – and had landed, by a miracle, as it were, in a real wilderness. In his famous sermon aboard the *Arbella* John Winthrop, first governor of Massachusetts Bay Colony, made this quite explicit. They had come, he said, to build that shining 'Citie upon a Hill' that would find the God of Israel among them, where 'ten of us shall be able to resist a thousand of our enemies, where He shall make us a praise and a glory, that men shall say of succeeding plantations: the Lord make it like that of New England!' Before he had set foot on land the heavenly Canaan, the New Jerusalem soon acquired a material dimension that was absent in Europe, except among extreme sects like the Levellers or the anabaptists of Munster.

To this day the Puritan project has replicated itself in all sorts of improbable, unexpected ways, from fundamentalist 'Christian' enclaves like Liberty University to San Francisco's 'gay republic'. Freed from the constraints of European society, generations of settlers and their descendants thought it perfectly feasible – in Frances FitzGerald's phrase – to 'start the world over', to build their 'Cities on a Hill' from scratch, as though no one had been there before. Utopia is as much part of the American agenda as is the Communist millennium in Russia.

The Housatonic is the most westerly of the great New England rivers that rise in the Appalachian ridge and disgorge themselves into the Atlantic's grey-green waters. Unlike its neighbours, the Naugatuck thirty miles east and the Hudson, forty miles west beyond the old colonial boundary in New York, the Housatonic has almost escaped the ravages of modern industry, meandering through lush pastures and tightly wooded hills, indifferent to the fact that a few miles either side lie some of the most developed and densely populated regions on earth. By American standards, it is an old landscape, moulded by more than three centuries of agricultural settlement. The pioneer snake fences that once surrounded the fields and homelots have been replaced by stone walls; the roads curve and undulate in an almost English regard for nature and private property, though the trees that line them, providing summer shade and winter windbreaks, remind one more of France.

The camper or 'RV' – recreational vehicle – I had bought, a sixteen-foot Dolphin mounted on a Toyota chassis, was no beauty. The heavy American coachwork did not seem to fit the sleek Japanese bonnet: it looked like a cow with a fox's face. Moreover, it was way past its first youth – with 72,000 miles on the clock, and spots of rust around the radiator. Still, it had obviously been well cared for by loving owners. Inside there were gilt Kleenex-holders and other peculiar nick-nacks, including a heavy iron match-dispenser that looked like something out of a German hunting-lodge. The mock-walnut interior, lined with capacious cupboards, had a rustic plaque with 'God Bless Our Camper, inscribed on it. It felt solid and dependable.

I drove up Connecticut Highway 7, joining the Housatonic Valley at New Milford. I was happy with the camper. It handled more like an ordinary car than I had expected. It was rather noisy, which didn't matter, as I was travelling alone and there was no one to talk to. I felt quite gleeful when passing trucks or other RVs – fat, complacent, overweight vehicles, much, I surmised, like their occupants. I had become obsessed with Obese Persons, who seemed to be everywhere, in and around New York, blocking supermarket checkouts, blocking escalators, elbowing one off sidewalks. They seemed to be constantly munching, licking, sucking, masticating: I felt no twinge of compassion for their offensive corpulence, only disgust at their ugliness and lack of self-restraint. It seemed a far cry from the Puritan virtues of moderation and self-denial that were supposed to have founded America.

The original Connecticut settlers had colonised the hills, clearing the rough fields and homelots out of the woods: the lush pastures that now flank the river were still swampy miasmas, infested with bears and wolves. Unlike later frontiersmen, the Puritans combined ruggedness with a strong sense of order and community. On board the *Arbella*, Winthrop had told his company they must be 'knit together in this work as one man'. Their commitment to strong civil government and strict control over personal behaviour had not been affected by the fact that in England they had found themselves in conflict with the crown. Their vision of the Holy Commonwealth or New Zion they aimed to establish was still quite medieval in its concern with hierarchy and order. The Chosen of God had yet to disintegrate into a babel of competing sects, each with its different mode of governance and interpretation of scripture. Nor had their civic consciousness yet been eroded by the free-wheeling individualism of the frontier. Puritan assemblies passed hundreds of ordinances punishing drunkenness, sabbath-breaking, gaming, singing and dancing in public, failure to attend worship, lax family discipline and sexual immorality. This concern with order was linked to a pessimistic theology inclined to believe the worst of fallen human nature. 'Pride, contradiction and rebellion', ministers reminded governors, had possessed the hearts of men 'since our corruption by the first unhappy apostasy'. The devil ruled the human will; as soon as they were free from restraints, people were automatically possessed by 'unlimited and insatiable lusts'.

Throughout New England the layouts of the small towns and villages, with their well-tended lawns adjoining the broad main street, their clapboard or shingled houses flanking the church or facing it across the village green, their meeting-houses, country stores, inns and burial grounds, suggested Puritan concern for order. Actually this spaciousness, so much better adapted to the needs of the automobile than the crooked English village, was dictated mainly by practical necessities. Cattle, pigs, sheep and other stock had to be defended against marauding Indians or wolves. The streets were arranged to enclose as much common land as possible; the houses were placed close enough together to permit a common system of defence. The early Puritan settlers in the Housatonic valley had good reason to fear the Indians, especially the warlike Pequots to the south and east and the Mohawks of the upper Hudson. They were still vastly outnumbered, and the balance of military power had not yet swung in their favour. Possibly for this reason, they generally behaved better towards the Indian population than later settlers further west.

In the majority of cases they acquired land by means that were legal under both English and Indian law. The prices paid, between one and ten cents an acre, in money, tools, weapons or blankets, was on the same scale that purchasers applied in subsequent transactions among themselves.

Beyond New Milford the country became wilder, the hillsides steeper. There were fewer fields and homelots. If one took away the asphalt road and the telephone wires, the countryside was much as it must have looked in the seventeenth century – if anything, less populated. The Indians, of course, had disappeared completely. The demise of their culture was, I suppose, inevitable.

The indigenous people of the valley were Mohegans, a branch of the great Algonquin nation. They were unwarlike and submissive. Before losing their lands to the whites in the lower part of the valley, they had constantly been kicked around by more powerful Indian neighbours, especially the Mohawks and the Pequots. They had a generally pessimistic outlook on life. When things went wrong, their maidens and warriors frequently resorted to suicide, jumping off cliffs into the arms of the Great Spirit, after singing hymns to warn him of their coming. However much the Mohegans may have hated and feared the English, they hated and feared the Pequots and Mohawks more. Both tribes had claims on their land and made sporadic raids to exact tribute. As a result many of the contracts of sale stipulated that the white purchasers would protect the sellers against these tribes.

The Connecticut English feared both tribes as well: the Mohawks were often in league with their rivals in the Hudson valley, the Dutch. In 1635 a party of Pequots led by their chief sachem Sadakus – 'a proud, cruel, unhappy and headstrong prince', according to one contemporary account – massacred more than a dozen Englishmen after laying siege to Saybrook fort at the mouth of the Connecticut River. They also attacked Westerfield, south of Hartford, where they took two young women hostage. New England was in uproar. The governor of Massachusetts sent a punitive expedition which killed about 400 Pequots near the Naragansett after setting their wigwams on fire. The whole country looked set for a war in which the English, and their Mohegan allies, could have been wiped out.

The situation was largely saved by Roger Williams, the founder of Providence, Rhode Island, and the most remarkable Puritan of his generation. Williams was one of those brilliant sturdy, maverick Englishmen, ruled by conscience and indifferent to personal ambition, whom one sometimes finds in the radical wings of politics. Among his many intellectual accomplishments, he made himself an expert in Indian culture and languages. After settling at Plymouth in 1631, he spent nearly two years lodging with them 'in their filthy, smoky holes . . . to gain their tongue'. Called to the church at Salem, he proved too radical in his separatist views for the Massachusetts congregationalists, who by now had imposed their own religious orthodoxy on the colony. He was expelled from Salem in 1635, but not before Governor John Winthrop had privately urged him to head for Naragansett Bay, which was free from English claims and patents. Here he lived by trading with the Indians, and eventually founded the Providence Plantation with a charter obtained in London.

When the Pequot crisis erupted, the Governor asked Williams to 'use his utmost and speediest endeavours to break and hinder the league laboured for by the Pequots against the Mohican and the English'. He set off, as he recalled many years later, in a 'poor canoe through a stormy wind with great seas, every minute a hazard of life'. For three days he stayed at a friendly sachem's house with the 'bloody Pequot ambassadors whose hands and arms, methought, reeked with the blood of my countrymen, murdered and massacred by them on the Connecticut river, and from whom I could but nightly look for their bloody knives at my own throat also'. His mission, however, was successful. The Pequots did not attack again for nearly half a century, by which time the settlers were strong enough to rout them completely.

Williams's interest in the Indians, most unusual for a man of his time, stemmed directly from his theology. Unlike most of his American contemporaries, he continued to interpret the Bible allegorically, according to a scheme of 'types' and 'anti-types' which stressed the discontinuity between Old and New Testaments. Christ, he believed, had abrogated the Covenant between God and Israel that the other Puritans had sought to restore in their Holy Commonwealth. With the Covenant no longer in force, magistrates (like those in Massachusetts) were wrong to try to enforce divine commands. Since everybody was outside the Covenant, no people could claim to have restored Israel. Therefore the Indians, though pagans, were on the same theological footing as the rest of mankind. They deserved to be accorded respect.

Williams, of course, is now celebrated as the first apostle of religious freedom in America, as well as the founder of its First Baptist Church at Providence, Rhode Island. His statue – a white limestone monolith done in the social realist style of the 1930s – stands on a hill near the campus of Brown University, gazing towards the Connecticut hills over a dead-beat area of rotting train sheds and empty shunting-yards.

The day I visited, the monument was defaced with graffiti: SLIM LOVES YOU NIKKI had been scrawled on the fascist-style arch which frames the statue. An inscription at the base reads: 'Here lies dust from the grave of Roger Williams.' This is probably mendacious: the local historian who escorted me round the nearby First Baptist Church – a magnificent edifice built around 1750 – assured me that Williams's grave had never been found, it being contrary to Puritan custom to erect tombstones. The church's own claim to Williams as its founder is itself pretty thin. He only stayed in the 'Baptist way' about three or four months, before moving on to become an independent preacher.

Eventually, after two or three years, he left the ministry altogether: the Church – any church – was irremediably corrupt. It could only be restored by a 'mighty interposition' by God Himself. Meanwhile, the spiritual life must be protected from contamination by the state. Williams was the first American to insist that a 'wall of separation' be erected between church and state – the formula adopted by Jeffersonians a century and a half later. But his world was poles apart from that of the Founding Fathers of the Republic. Whereas they, acting in the spirit of the Enlightenment, sought to preserve political freedom by protecting the state from religiously sanctioned tyranny, Williams's concern was for spiritual freedom as such. His belief in religious liberty, as enshrined in the Rhode Island charter, came, in the words of Perry Miller, 'as a consequence of the insight that freedom is a condition of the spirit . . . Out of the exercise of his imagination he perceived that no man can be so sure of any formulation of eternal truth as to have a right to impose on the mind and spirit of other men.'

At Falls Village I stopped for gas. I had spent the previous Easter staying with friends at Salisbury, a few miles away. I had attended the Easter service in the main Congregationalist church, an immaculate clapboard, porticoed building, which, like many American churches, combined the functions of church, offices, Sunday school and minister's residence in a way that made God seem like one of the family, a household patriarch. The congregation, young to middle-aged, was well dressed and, judging from the cars outside, affluent. It was culturally, but not racially, WASP, with a glimpse of Irish and even a hint of Latin or Hebrew among the complexions. I was slightly surprised to see a plain ungarnished cross above the Lord's table; even more so when the pastor, a trim, bearded man of thirty-five, preached an erudite sermon on the significance of the Cross in Western art.

Salisbury, it turned out, was not quite what it was dressed up to be Despite its classic New England elegance, its wide main street with freshly-painted wooden houses, its well-tended lawns reaching down to the road, it was far from being a time-warp from the Puritan past. In the late eighteenth century it had been the industrial capital of New England. Salisbury iron and steel were renowned the world over. Salisbury cannon won American independence from Britain, Salisbury muskets delivered Greece from the Unspeakable Turk. The iron ore in this part of the Housatonic valley was of the highest grade anywhere on earth outside Sweden. The charcoal-fed furnaces, fanned by giant water-powered bellows, glowed throughout the night.

Then the Bessemer process, a way of making steel from cheap-grade ores, priced Salisbury steel out of the market. The mines became lakes, the foundries were left to die by choking on their own solidified pig-iron 'salamanders'. But the valley's social composition had changed. The descendants of Irish navvies and Lithuanian colliers brought in a new blue-collar population, along with the Catholic Church. The Old Yankee yeomanry declined. Business arrived, with summer or retirement homes; week-end urbanites appeared, with polished BMWs and immaculate riding-boots. The Congregational Church, though formally disestablished like all other churches after the Revolution, kept faith with the new élite, becoming more and more ecumenical. Hence the Easter sermon, with its faint whiff of incense.

'Are there converts from Catholicism among your congregation?' I asked the pastor, Dick Taber, when I spoke with him after church.

'Quite a few,' he admitted. 'In this church you don't find many died-in-the-wool people who grew up in the Congregationalist tradition. There's quite a lot who started as Methodists and Catholics.'

'Is that why you put the Cross up there, and preached that sermon?'

'When I came here I was sitting in the sanctuary, and became particularly aware of the blankness on the wall. Of course, the decision to put it there was controversial. There are quite a few people from the old Yankee tradition which insists on the centrality of the Word who say: 'Well, it wasn't there in *my* church.' But we have to recognise that we're a church that draws people from a variety of traditions. For most of them its been normal to have the Cross in some form. But there has been a very interesting reaction on the other side, from Catholics' – he didn't say 'ex-Catholics' – 'for whom the Cross was a symbol of suffering, conveying the message that it was *good* to suffer. In my sermon I was trying to address people who did not want a cross because the message was suffering, not deliverance and the kingdom beyond . . . '

The Cross, it seemed, had travelled with the clientele, into an upwardly-mobile, optimistic mode. Congregationalism, the established church of colonial Connecticut and Massachusetts, had less and less to distinguish it socially from other establishments, including Presbyterian New York and Anglican Virginia. The hillbilly Yankees and other poor relics of bygone Connecticut had deserted to Methodism.

'Some farmers', explained Taber tactfully, 'found themselves more comfortable with the Methodists as our church began to attract wealthier folk and became more sophisticated.'

Taber's congregation, like that of neighbouring St John's Episcopalian, had attended the same schools and went to the same parties. The poorer Catholics, I presumed, remained with their suffering saviour, their guilt, and their Irish priests. I could see how the more rustic type of Yankee might feel uncomfortable in Taber's church. Whatever one's theology, church is a social occasion.

'The worship is certainly central,' he explained, 'but I consider coffee hour also very important, Being a church means being a community. We need to know each other.'

Was this where the Holy Commonwealth, Winthrop's shining 'City on a Hill' had ended up after three and a half centuries – a bland, agreeable blend of liberal theology, European culture and coffee hour? I thought of the freezing, windowless meeting-houses, the lengthy two-hour sermons of pastors like John Cotton, Increase Mather and Thomas Hooker: their obsession with Sin, and the pitiless clarity with which they exposed it – manipulating, as ever, the reins of sexual guilt. 'Now,' thundered Hooker, 'the affections of man are placed in loins, God tries the reins . . . a man may have many unruly affections, though he be paddling in the ways of Grace . . . the Grace of God yet comes so shallow in us, our passions are yet unmortified, so as we know not how to grieve in measure, our wrath is vehement and immoderate, you must wade until the *loins be girt with a golden girdle . . .* '

But Puritan guilt was much more than a neurotic fear of sexuality, although that was undoubtedly an important element. The thundering jeremiads of Cotton, Mather and Hooker were the obverse of a burgeoning worldliness, the compliment a sense of spiritual failure among the grandsons paid to the ideals of the Pilgrim Fathers. Just as their special covenant with God dealt not with the eternal salvation of the elect, but with their worldly mission of building the New Zion, so the success or failure of this mission would be rewarded not in the Hereafter, but in the here and now. If they kept to their covenant, God would bless New England, granting her 'peace and prosperity within, influence and praise without'. By the same token, betrayal would be met not with eternal fire, but with 'present visitations of God's wrath – with plagues and droughts, wars and rumours of wars, with scorn and laughter, derision and infamy'. Long before Arminian theology – which emphasised man's active co-operation in his redemption – became widespread, giving American Protestant values their formal ideological expression, the Puritans were quietly sliding away from strict Calvinist orthodoxy with its absolute insistence on man's depravity, salvation by Grace and the predestination of God's Elect. Their beliefs, located in the intellect, insisted that an omnipotent God could not be bound by human notions of justice. Their faith, rooted in the emotions, demanded that a beneficent deity would reward good and punish evil according to notions conveyed in the scriptures. For them, as for most of us, emotions were stronger than intellect, faith took precedence over belief. Calvin himself, no mean psychologist, understood the perils of theologising better than anyone: 'Puny man,' he wrote, magisterially, 'endeavours to penetrate the hidden recesses of the divine wisdom, and goes back even to the remotest eternity in order that he may understand what final determination God had made with regard to him. In this way he plunges headlong into an immense abyss, involves himself in numberless inextricable snares and buries himself in the thickest darkness . . . ' The Puritans continued to trust God in theory, while in practice relying on themselves.

As I crossed the Massachusetts state line, it began to drizzle. I passed through Great Barrington, the first major town in Massachusetts. Until the mid-eighteenth century this was still frontier territory; as earnest Puritan ideals declined, the motives for settlement changed from extending the frontiers of Zion to honest-to-Mammon land speculation. Already in 1744, two years after neighbouring Sheffield had been incorporated, all the land in its north parish, west of the Housatonic, had fallen into the hands of just three men – laying the foundations of the WASP aristocracy with which the Berkshires has since been associated.

The seeds of worldliness came from inside as well as outside the Holy Commonwealth. From the beginning, preachers had had to draw a fine distinction between lawful gain and covetousness. The saints must be industrious; they should seek wealth, but despise riches. Everyone must have a personal 'calling' to keep him out of trouble. 'A calling is not only our *duty*,' said Cotton Mather, 'but also our *safety*. Men will fall into horrible *Snares*, and infinite *Sins*, if they have not a *calling to be their preservative . . . The Temptations of the Devil* are best resisted by those that are least at leisure to receive them.'

Inevitably, the Calvinist work ethic inspired a desire for accumulation for its own sake, especially among the generations brought up in America, who gradually came to lack their parents' sense of divine mission. The first Puritans had, for the most part, been deeply spiritual people: though their theology denied them formal assurance of Grace, they experienced the divine in their everyday lives. Their very survival, against the perils of the North Atlantic, the harshness of the climate, the onslaught of disease and the depredations of Indians was evidence of God's special favour.

Few of the next generation which grew up in the church had this kind of experience. When required to produce proof of conversion as a condition of church membership they were annoyed, especially since without such proof their children were ineligible for baptism and they themselves could not vote in government elections. The issue led to a crisis, which was eventually solved by compromise. The 'Half-Way Covenant' provided that baptised infants could, on reaching the years of discretion, 'own the Covenant' without producing evidence of conversion. Moreover children could be baptised without their parents having to be communicants. The Half-Way Covenant admitted, by implication, that Zion had been postponed: the focus of the Holy Commonwealth was moving from earth back to heaven. The church doors were open for new members, including Citizen Mammon.

It was dark when I reached Stockbridge, the most celebrated of the Berkshire towns, with its main street of mansion-style dwellings and fine, well-tended lawns. It is unique among New England towns in having been founded as an Indian mission. In 1734 a young graduate of Yale, John Sergeant, arrived at what was then the Great Wigwam of the Houstunuck Indians to start a new mission funded by the Society for the Propagation of the Gospel in Foreign Parts. Sergeant, a fine linguist, immediately impressed the local chiefs, and persuaded them to build a church and school. The Indians cleared homelots, built houses on the English pattern, and were baptised as Christians. The scene was set for a peaceful transition that might have enabled the Indians to assimilate while avoiding the worst depredations of alcohol and white culture.

Unfortunately Sergeant tried to force the pace. He asked the Board of Indian Affairs to send him four English families, who would set an example of civilised living. The families which arrived, led by a scion of the formidable Williams clan, performed their duty much too well. Under rules agreed with the sachems, no more whites were supposed to be settled, beyond the original four families, and those of the missionary and school-teacher. The English planters were limited to owning one-sixth of the township (about 385 acres); the rest of the land (about 23,000 acres) was to be kept by the Indians, and the whites were strictly forbidden to buy it.

Within little more than a decade, by a series of devious manoeuvres on the part of Ephraim Williams, the Indian holdings had been reduced to around 4,000 acres. The rest had passed to the whites, a large portion of it to Williams himself. Sergeant's own hands – for all his good intentions – were tied. In 1739 he married Williams's ambitious daughter, Abigail. She refused to live in his humble mission house, insisting that he build her the miniature mansion that now graces Stockbridge as a museum. This house, with its magnificent front door and interior panelling specially hauled by ox-team from Connecticut, along with Abigail's other extravagances, contributed to the massive burden of debt Sergeant had to contend with until his premature death in 1749.

Not all the Williams clan were as worldly and unscrupulous as Ephraim. His cousins Solomon and Elisha were distinguished divines who taught at Yale. Another kinsman of his, Jonathan Edwards, finally put Stockbridge on the religious map. Edwards, probably the finest American mind of his generation, was one of that rarest of breeds: a mystic whose scholarship and intellectuality enabled him to organise his experience of the divine into orthodox religious categories. By the time he arrived in Stockbridge to take on Sergeant's mission in 1751 he had already acquired an international reputation as a preacher of 'hellfire' sermons, winning souls for Christ by terrorising his audiences. Tall, light-framed, with a high-pitched voice of compelling nervous intensity, Edwards warned his congregations of the tribulations to come, when the whole world would 'be converted into a great lake or liquid globe of fire, in which the wicked shall be overwhelmed [and] . . . their heads, their eyes, their tongues, their hands, their feet, their loins and their vitals shall for ever be full of glowing, melting fire, enough to melt the very rocks and elements'. They would be full of 'the most quick and lively sense to feel the torments, not for ten millions of ages, but for ever and ever without any end at all . . . ' The eternally damned would be 'tormented also in the presence of the glorified saints', who would thereby 'be made more sensible of how great their salvation is'. The sight of the misery of the damned would have the effect of doubling 'the ardour of the love and gratitude of the saints in heaven'.

Edwards greatly impressed his fellow-spiritual terrorist, George White-field, whose tours of the American colonies in 1739 and 1740 launched the period of revival known as the Great Awakening. Whitefield was also singularly taken by Mrs Edwards, mother of seven, whose 'meek and quiet' manner so impressed him during a visit to Northampton that he prayed to the Lord to send him an helpmeet just like her, from 'among the daughters of Abraham'. Like Whitefield and John Wesley in England, Edwards so terrified some of his hearers that they appear to have suffered nervous breakdowns, as attacks of 'melancholia' would be called today. One man was so overcome with guilt after hearing Edwards at Northampton that he went straight home and killed himself by slitting his throat with a knife.

Most people, however, were not quite so susceptible. The born-again convert usually went through three distinct phases: first apathy, then despair, and finally a state of euphoria after being shown that the terrors of hell could be avoided by the saving Grace of Jesus Christ. In his famous book *Battle for the Mind*, the psychologist William Sargant argued convincingly that the hellfire sermon had an impact on the brain similar to Stalin's brain-washing techniques and Pavlov's experiments with dogs. Edwards sincerely believed that such treatment was desirable and necessary for the salvation of souls. He defended himself by comparing his role to a surgeon's:

> Another thing that some ministers have been greatly blamed for, and I think unjustly, is speaking *terror* to those who are already under great terrors, instead of comforting them . . . To blame a minister for thus declaring the truth to those who are under awaking, and not immediately administering comfort to them, is like blaming a surgeon because, when he has begun to thrust in his lance, whereby he has already put his patient to great pain, and he shrinks and cries out with anguish, he is so cruel that he will not stay his hand, but goes on to thrust it further till he comes to the core of the wound.

Although Edwards brought many souls back to Christ, many of his Northampton congregation proved obdurate, and he was eventually ousted in a parish *putsch*. The problems began when Edwards tried to abandon the Half-Way Covenant by insisting the members of his church should show proof of positive conversion. Matters came to a head on the thorny question of sex. A number of young persons had been circulating what were coyly termed 'bad books' – manuals for midwives, the nearest thing to a sex magazine available in eighteenth-century Northampton. Edwards wanted to punish the children. The parents, who seem to have been extraordinarily enlightened for their day, thought otherwise, and in due course he was forced to resign. The Lord was evidently on Edwards's side. The day he left Northampton, his church was struck by lightning.

In Stockbridge the Edwardses were distinctly hard-up. The meek Mrs Edwards and her seven ebullient daughters duly set to work making fans and dress patterns from heavy paper. Edwards found the off-cuts useful for scribbling notes while returning from meetings in distant places. He used to stuff these scribblings into pockets, under the saddle, into his boots. When every cranny had been used up, he would start pinning them on his clothes. In due course, he would arrive home festooned in scraps of paper.

Edwards was not always lost in his thoughts as he rode through the Berkshire woods and hills, considering the great questions of sin, redemption, freedom of the will and the end for which God had created the world. He was unusual among his contemporaries, most of whom regarded the frontier as a 'howling wilderness', in having an almost Romantic feeling for nature, that was intimately bound up with his sense of the divine. He wrote in his Personal Narration that

> I walked alone in a solitary place in my father's pasture, for contemplation. And as I was . . . looking up on the sky and clouds, there came into my mind so sweet a sense of the Glorious Majesty and Grace of God, that I know not how to express . . . The appearance of everything was altered; there seemed to be, as it were, a calm, sweet cast, or appearance, of divine glory, in almost everything; in the sun and moon and stars; in the clouds and blue sky; in the grass, flowers, trees; in the water and all nature.

Only the direct experience of God made for true religion. Everything else was empty formalism. The convert had to be brought face-to-face with the terrors of hell before being able to experience the divine, or heaven-on-earth in this way. In today's terminology, he or she would have to engage in a period of 'de-programming' to shake the psyche free of blocks, in order to let a fuller consciousness flood in. The importance Edwards and other 'New Light' evangelists attached to personal experience makes them fundamentally modern, despite the biblical language they used to conjure up images of heaven and hell. Though they re-emphasised hardline Calvinist theology of depravity and grace, they opened the door to a new kind of freedom. They 'spiritualised' religion, taking it from the public realm to the innermost recesses of the human heart.

German and Catholic pietists and Wesleyans had, of course, done the same for religion in Europe, spiritualising both non-conformist and established churches. In America too the old denominations – Anglicanism, and Presbyterianism, as well as the classic Puritanism of the congregational churches – benefited for a time, having been infused with the awakening spirit. But things would never be the same for the churches of the colonial establishment. Although a majority of clergy – about three to one – had been in favour of the revival, ecclesiastical authority was undermined. Power was gradually transferred from pastor to people, as the former abandoned his ministerial powers. A born-again congregation, sanctified by grace, could be presumed to make the right decisions. In the long term, the established churches lost out in membership as well as authority. Emphasis on personal choice and experience led logically to adult baptism; and so the Baptist churches began to move from the Rhode Island fringe they occupied in Roger Williams's day towards the dominating position in American Protestantism they came to acquire after the Revolution.

The old political order lost out as well. The revivalists undermined it, as Richard Bushman observes, not by repudiating 'law and authority, but by denying them sanctifying power'. Neither obedience nor disobedience to the law were seen to bear on salvation any longer; men were freer to challenge their rulers without risking their immortal souls. The first phase in the American Experiment, the Holy Commonwealth, was finally over. The Puritans had been transformed into Yankees. But the vision of a restored Zion never disappeared completely. It would appear again in the nineteenth century, after another great revival, the Second Awakening, created a new wave of turbulence in American souls; and in numerous, strange modulations, it continues to exercise its sway over the American imagination.

I headed for October Mountain, where my road atlas told me I should find a camping place. The site, in a forest adjoining the old Whitney estate, was deserted, except for a man and a boy grilling meat by an open fire. The temperature was perfect. I lay in my bunk, the windows open, and drifted into sleep to the sound of crackling sticks, anonymous chirruping birds, chipmunks, squirrels, bats and other creatures of the night.

II

Prophets, Shakers and Martyrs

> We love to dance
> We love to sing
> We love to taste the living spring
> We love to feel our union flow
> While round and round and round we go.

MILLENNIAL PRAISES, 1813

In nineteenth-century America, conditions were ripe for Prophecy. As in Europe, old social structures were disintegrating, people were losing their moral and behavioural bearings in the changing historical landscape created by industrialism. At such times, universal dreams of brother- and sisterhood, of a united human family free from distinctions of class and wealth, where the individual finds his or her salvation by merging with the group, often come to the surface. In the ancient societies of Europe, however, such movements led to change in the existing social or political order: 'revolution', in its original meaning, means the turning over of something already there.

In the New World, the structures of government were relatively in-choate, unformed. Like the offspring of over-permissive parents, deprived of the need to rebel, the American mind turned in on itself, to the dreams and visions of charismatic individuals who identified their inner promptings with the voice of God. Jemima Wilkinson, Ann Lee, the Fox Sisters, Joseph Smith, Ellen G. White, Mary Baker Eddy, L. Ron Hubbard: none of these American prophets would have got off the ground in Europe, though once established, all successfully recruited converts there. America was the New Israel in more than the typological sense. It was the place where prophecy flourished, where the distressed, the gullible, the confused, the sick in mind or body sought out new panaceas, and found them in new, prophetic agendas. For the inspired seer or plausible impostor, America was a place where no claim to truth, however eccentric or bizarre, would be laughed out of court or would fail to find a dozen earnest seekers after certainty.

Of these prophets Mother Ann Lee of Manchester, founder of the Shakers, is probably the most bizarre. Having lost four children, the last after a horrendous forceps delivery, she became convinced that sexual intercourse was the root of all evil, the original sin which caused the Fall.

While detained in a 'house of correction' after disrupting a church service, she had a vision of Adam and Eve indulging in carnal union, followed by another in which Jesus appeared and ordered her to spread her new knowledge to the world. Taking charge of the small group of 'Shaking Quakers' to which she belonged, she crossed the Atlantic in 1774 after her associate, James Whitaker, had a vision of the Tree of Life with branches flourishing in America. Mother Ann expanded her attack on sexuality to include practically every branch of human activity. 'The deceitful wantonness of both male and female,' she preached, 'is at the root of hatred, envy, jealousy and murder among individuals and destruction, rapine and war among nations.' It brought distress and poverty, shame and disgrace upon families, filling the earth with 'wretchedness and misery'. The only hope of salvation lay in total abstinence from sex: her vision of hell was even worse than Jonathan Edwards's: sinners would be eternally 'bound and tormented in the same parts where they had taken their carnal pleasure'.

After Mother Ann's death in 1784, the Shakers grew from strength to strength. Since they abjured natural increase, they depended entirely on conversions. New recruits included people with children and orphans or strays who were adopted into the sect. At its peak in the 1850s there were about 6,000 Shakers living in eighteen prosperous colonies, most of them in New England and New York, with a scattering in the Mid West and South. The Shakers were organised into 'families' of about one hundred, males and females living together, like brothers and sisters.

I spent the morning at Shaker village of Hancock, near Pittsfield. The village had been wrecked by a highway running through its middle. But the buildings, in the plain warehouse style that reminded Charles Dickens of English factories, were impressive. In the kitchen of the principal dwelling-house I found a young woman wearing a Victorian pinafore, cooking pear butter on an ancient cast-iron range, using brightly-burnished copper pans. The smell of pears and spices reached to the upper, dormitory floor, mingling with beeswax and lavender polish. The bedchambers were similar:

the Shaker men and women had been separated only by the passageway. There were plain, built-in cupboards and chests with double rows of knobs like uniform buttons. Everything was clean, symmetrical, orderly. It felt oppressive and faintly surreal, like one of those dreams where you find yourself back at school and frustratingly subject to teachers who refuse to recognise that you are grown.

Shaker life was minutely regulated. The believers rose early (about 5 a.m.) to the sound of a bell. They said their prayers, made their beds, and set about their morning chores. Though sisters were spiritual and social equals of brethren, traditional Victorian sex-roles were maintained. The women did mainly domestic work – cooking, spinning, weaving, herbal gardening. The men managed the farms and workshops. Before each meal they gathered separately for a period of grace while awaiting the bell. In the refectory they sat at separate tables, eating in silence. According to Shaker theology, this routine represented a foretaste of Eternity. Shakerdom was already paradise on earth: the brethren and sisters were living a life free from sin.

Couples who fell in love were expelled, or returned voluntarily to the 'World' to get married. At least one sister, transferred to another village after forming a special attachment, is reported to have died of a broken heart. There were probably other cases which have not been recorded.

The faithful Shakers, however, worked out their frustrations in the famous Shaker Dance. This was a deliberate, conscious process. As early as 1812 Thomas Brown, an apostate, described how the dancers would mortify the flesh, believing that

> by the power of God they could labour completely out of their natural instinct implanted in mankind for the purpose of procreation . . . They often danced with vehemence through the greatest part of the night, and instead of reposing their heavy bodies upon a bed, they would by way of further penance lie down upon the floor on chains, ropes, sticks, in every humiliating and mortifying posture they could devise.

Such agonies appear to have induced ecstatic experiences, especially during a period of revival in the late 1830s and early 1840s known within the community as 'Mother's Work'. By now Mother Ann had been elevated to the ranks of deity: her ecstatic utterances, in which she had described herself as the 'Bride of Christ', with Jesus as her 'Lord and Lover', combined with the sects millennialist orientation to create a radical new theology. She was the Second Coming, the spirit of God incarnate in female flesh. She had the 'fullness of the Godhead bodily dwelling in her'. Through her Christ Himself was born again.

Young Shakers, often new recruits, began receiving 'gifts' or revelations from On High. These 'gifts' were often written down by their enraptured 'instruments' in messages for other believers 'some for consolation, some for mortification, and some for simplicity . . . ' The gifts which proved most durable, however, were the inspired drawings and paintings, like the tree 'received' by Sister Hannah Cahoon in 1854, which now hangs in the Hancock gallery. This highly geometric and stylised rendering of a perennial Shaker symbol, in which large, brightly-coloured fruit form contrasting patterns with diamond-shaped leaves on thin, vascular branches, creates an ethereal effect of weightless permanence – a fitting emblem of eternity.

'I entreated Mother Ann', reads the legend inscribed beneath, 'to tell me the name of this tree: which she did on October 1st 4th hour P.M. by moving the hand of a medium to write twice over Your Tree is the Tree of Life.'

Perhaps the grim, institutional, mechanistic and 'soulless' impression the Shakers made on their Victorian visitors was the obverse of the intense inner life they reserved for themselves, hiding its most perfectly realised manifestations from the World's People. The inspired paintings at Hancock were unknown to outsiders until the 1930s.

The Shakers may have inhabited a borderland between earth and heaven, but they excelled in practical work, especially the making of furniture. 'The peculiar grace of a Shaker chair,' wrote Thomas Merton, 'is due to the fact that it was made by someone capable of believing that an angel might come and sit on it.' I doubt, however, if their furniture (as distinct from the inspired paintings) owe as much to the possibilities of angelic visitation as they do to the practical needs of community life. Shaker chairs, like the modern steel and canvas chairs favoured by school halls, were easily carried around and could be hung upside down on pegs, allowing spaces to be cleared for the dance and other functions. The severe, linear simplicity which so displeased contemporaries and is so much admired today, was conditioned by another practical purpose – machine work. The Shakers were great inventors. They designed machines for turning broom handles, sizing brushes, filling seed bags and herb packets, cutting, splitting and twisting leather, making splints, weaving baskets and cutting boxes. Their artifacts, on general sale, were world-renowned, as was their industriousness: no lesser authority than Friedrich Engels, ignoring their peculiar religious beliefs, regarded them as a model socialist community.

They are credited with a wide range of inventions, very few of which were patented, because they regarded patents as immoral. These include screw propellers, rotary harrows, water turbines, mechanical threshers, circular saws, nail cutters, pipe-makers, pea-shellers, automatic cheese presses and butter churns, palm-leaf bonnet looms, revolving ovens, mechanical silk bobbins, a machine for peeling, coring and quartering apples: along with more mundane objects like metal pens and flat brooms. For a community of mystics, they had a remarkable grasp of the material. Perhaps there was something in Mother Ann's assertion that sex is the root of all human problems: economically and socially secure, they were free from the stultifying demands of biological necessity, which is the enemy of invention, not its mother.

I went back through Pittsfield, and headed north through the forested hills towards the Vermont state line. At North Adams I turned right for Readsboro and Whitingham, birthplace of Brigham Young.

Young's Mormon biographer, Leonard Arrington, called him the 'American Moses'. But this is misleading. Young was only a prophet in the titular sense established by the Mormon church, whose Presidents are deemed to be recipients of 'revelations'. If God spoke to Brigham, it was in the untranslatable language of glossolalia, 'speaking in tongues', a practice the otherwise down-to-earth Brigham indulged in during his youth. His only recorded 'revelation' in the Mormon scripture is an order of the day, couched in biblical language, concerning companies, horses and wagons. Unlike Moses, but like Joshua, Brigham was destined to reach the Promised Land, guiding his people across the prairies of Iowa and Nebraska and through the Rockies, to the Great Salt Valley. It was Joseph Smith, his martyred leader, who received messages direct from God – messages whose problematic nature would set Brigham's people apart.

The day brightened, revealing the dazzling colours of the maples and birches which grow promiscuously on the Green Mountain. The Brigham Young monument, a massive rectangle of polished granite carved with concave fluting, stood on a hill above the village, about 150 yards from the road. I spent an hour there, enjoying the September sunshine and listening

to the crickets. The inscription simply stated the date of Brigham's birth –
1 June 1801 – and gave the barest facts of his life:

> Leader of the Mormon pioneers from Nauvoo, Illinois to the Rocky Moun-
> tains arriving in the valley of the Great Salt Lake July 14th 1847. Became
> Second President of the Church of Jesus Christ of Latter-day Saints serving
> from December 27th 1847 until his death at Salt Lake City Utah August 29th
> 1877. His statue occupies a place in Statuary Hall, Ashmore Capital, Wash-
> ington D.C. This monument erected by descendents of Brigham Young in
> co-operation with the Church of Jesus Christ Latter-day Saints.

It did not tell you how many wives or children he had (16 wives, with whom
he had 57 children, plus 9 wives who were childless, plus 30-odd wives
to whom he was 'sealed for eternity'): nor did it say how much money he
made – an incalculable sum, since Brigham kept most church property in
his own name to stop the US government getting its hands on it. Nor did it
mention the institution for which he is probably known by the majority of
Americans – Brigham Young University, with its strict code of honour and
its famous football team. A previous monument erected by the citizens of
Whitingham was more succinct.

BRIGHAM YOUNG
Born on This Spot 1801
A Man of Much Courage
And Superb Equipment

Still, what the monument concealed about the man's achievements, it
revealed about the Mormon *zeitgeist*. It stood significantly apart from the
other, more rustic, Whitingham monuments made from rough-hewn local
stone – most notably the war memorials, which list the village's roll of
honour in two world wars, Korea, and Vietnam. Its expensive durable
materials and crisp carved lettering seem destined to endure when the
names of Whitingham's other heroes have crumbled to dust. While its
location suggested the idea of the Mormon leader as a person apart, not
wishing to socialise with the rest of Whitingham's deceased citizenry, it
nevertheless sought to advertise its commemoree's place in the pantheon
of the great in Washington. It looked like the Mormons all over – a people
apart, with a superiority complex, who still, rather desperately, sought the
rest of the world's approval.

Brigham did not stay long in Whitingham. His parents, with their eight older children, had moved from Hopkinton, Massachusetts, six months before his birth. But the fifty acres of land they bought for the same number of dollars proved too rough and toilsome to feed so large a family. Before he was four the family had made another great trek, this time to the West, across the Alleghenies, to richer lands in Sherburne, New York. Brigham absorbed trekking in the womb – and almost with his mother's milk.

The road became more twisted, and rougher from winter frosts. I passed several ski resorts, with forlorn cables and empty log cabins with steep, chalet-style eaves. The autumn foliage stretched forever: the only signs of humanity were occasional clapboard houses with perfect lawns cleared from the forest. There seemed nothing between wilderness and suburbia. I missed the tended, wrought landscapes of Europe, where every field or hedgerow testifies to generations of human effort.

Next morning, as I headed for Sharon, it was pouring with rain. An old New England gazetteer found by Fawn Brodie, Joseph Smith's biographer, remarked of Sharon: 'This is the birthplace of that infamous impostor, the Mormon Prophet Joseph Smith, a dubious honor Sharon would relinquish willingly to another town.' The citizens of Sharon who, despite the weather, were holding a Saturday market in the square, trading clothes and home-made cookies, seemed entirely unconcerned about the reputation of their native-born prophet, false or otherwise. There were no jangling bells, as in Bethlehem, no hordes of charabancs, no blare of loudspeakers, as at Mecca, ceaselessly relaying the Word of God. I was directed politely but indifferently to the memorial, which is about three miles up the river. I drove up a hill embellished with maple avenues and came to the monument, a stark granite obelisk set in a formal garden.

At the Visitors' Center an elderly man in a dapper brown suit, with a badge announcing his name to be Brother Orson, flashed a friendly greeting from behind his spectacles. His discourse sounded thoroughly rehearsed, as if I were a busload.

'You see that hole in that hedge?' he said, pointing to a gap in the shrubbery. 'It was a hundred and eighty-one years ago that Joseph Smith Junior was born in a little log cabin there . . . ' The monologue rambled on with synthetic enthusiasm. I thought the man might be a sophisticated device with a tape-deck inside. The monument was 50 feet high, weighed 100 tons, the polished shaft was 38 1/2 feet, one for each of Joseph Smith's years. It was dedicated on 23 September 1905, the centennial of his birth.

They got the granite at Barre, Vermont, and transported it by railroad to Royalton, where they loaded it onto a specially constructed wagon pulled by twenty-two horses, laying down planks for the wheels so they wouldn't sink into the mud . . .

The detail was soporific. My ears began to go numb. We went into the Visitors' Center. There were charts, blow-up photographs, models of the Golden Plates which Smith claimed to have been 'lent' by the angel, and from which he 'translated' the Book of Mormon. There were large paintings depicting Joseph at various stages of his career, done in bright acrylic colours: as a child, heroically refusing a shot of liquor while the surgeons operated on his leg; as a boy, buried in the Bible; as a youth, in the sacred grove near Palmyra, New York, where in a vision he saw the Father and Son (two clones with identical robes and beards, like a pair of heavenly twins); with the Angel Moroni and the Golden Plates on Hill Cumorah; at his desk 'translating' the Book of Mormon; with Oliver Cowdery undergoing mutual baptism in the Susquehanna River; as a prosperous figure with tail-coat and wing-collar surveying the city of Nauvoo; as Presidential candidate, festooned with blue and white rosettes; and finally, the martyrdom in Carthage Jail, where Joseph and his brother Hyrum were shot down by the mob.

I knew the story. I didn't believe the pictures. The literalistic detail with which they embellished the life of the Prophet rendered the whole thing much less credible than a few well-chosen relics would have done. It was part of the weft by which the church sought to stitch the prosperous material reality of its present to its mythical, though embarrassingly recent, past. Myths like those of Christianity or Buddhism become plausible when canonised by arts that penetrate the collective cultural psyche. But when rendered with literalism masquerading as fact, they lose their grip on the imagination, restoring disbelief.

Of the many extraordinary products of the American frontier, Joseph must be the most remarkable; he is still the most controversial. To his followers – who now number more than six million worldwide, and are growing apace – he was the man directed by God to 'translate' the Book of Mormon and restore the true Church of Jesus Christ after nearly two millennia of apostasy. To his critics, past and present, he was an impostor, a dabbler in freemasonry and the black arts, a seducer of women, a financial fraud – a man of almost insane ambition who sought to create a totalitarian theocracy, even to become President of the United States. What fascinated me about Joseph was not that the truth must lie somewhere between these two versions, the Mormon and the 'gentile' (as Mormons, conforming to their biblical vision of themselves as the children of Israel, refer to non-Mormons, including Jews); but that the truth must somehow encompass both versions.

Joseph was a visionary in the secular, if not necessarily the religious mode. In the Book of Mormon he created a whole mythology; in Doctrine and Covenants and in his Temple Ordinances a whole new religion; at Nauvoo on the Mississippi a thriving new city that rivalled Chicago in wealth and energy.

Under Brigham Young, Joseph's People founded an empire which, having exchanged territorial for corporate boundaries, prospers to this day. If this was imposture, it was an imposture so generous, so vast and so fleshed with substance as to lend the word a galaxy of new meanings. At the same time, even a cursory glance at Mormon history revealed that Joseph's claims to a virtuous prophethood were hopelessly flawed. He did dabble in magic, he did seduce women, he plagiarised masonic rituals and he was involved in fraudulent translations of ancient texts and bogus bank speculations.

Brother Orson pointed proudly to two newspaper extracts printed on blown-up placards. One, from the *New York Herald* of 1842, eulogised Joseph as 'one of the greatest characters of the age', comparable to 'Mahomet, or any of the great spirits that have hitherto produced revolutions of past ages'. The other, from the London *Morning Chronicle* of 1851 (seven years after the tragedy of Carthage Jail) described him as 'one of the most extraordinary persons of his time, a man of rude genius who accomplished a much greater work' than he knew'.

It seemed odd that a church which believed him to be the first authentic prophet since Jesus Christ should be so proud of approving comments by anonymous unbelievers, even if they were newspapermen. I asked the guide why they had chosen to display these statements.

'There were lots of others just as good,' he said. 'I guess they just went eeny, meeny, miney, mo . . . ' He began to sniff at my soul, like a dog inspecting its supper. 'We have lots of non-Mormons coming here,' he said, 'about as many as Mormons. Most times I don't know whether a person is a Mormon or a non-Mormon . . . but I would guess you're probably a Latter-day Saint because you seem to know quite a lot about it . . . '

'I'm interested in religious history, but I'm not a Church member.'

'Well, you're a good person: sometimes I get – what shall I say? – the wrong impression. But I do get the impression you're a very fine person.'

I edged away slightly. We came to a room with a painting of the scene in Fayette, New York, where Joseph, his elder brother Hyrum and Oliver Cowdery, the young schoolmaster to whom he dictated the Book of Mormon, organised the church. The guide switched on his implanted tape:

'In this room we talk about some of the accomplishments of Joseph Smith and things the Mormon church has which we think other churches lack. We think we are the only church that has this biblical organisation with a Prophet, Apostles, Seventies and other callings which the New Testament reveals about the Church which Christ Himself established.' He pointed to two managerial charts explaining the church's corporate structure, with passport-sized pictures of leaders, past and present. One showed Jesus, the twelve apostles and the leaders of the primitive church. The other showed Joseph Smith, with a line to his current successor as Prophet-President, Ezra Taft Benson, along with the Quorum of Twelve and the rest of the hierarchy – the Seventies, bishops, state presidents, ward presidents, down to the priesthood of adult, male believers. The charts suggested a corporate empire with Jesus as chairman, Joseph and his successors as chief executives, and the apostles as departmental heads.

'Compare the two charts,' said Brother Orson. 'You see what we have here is exactly like the church that Jesus established.'

'Weren't there some novel features in Joseph's church?' I asked. 'Surely the early Christians didn't practise polygamy?'

'That's right,' said the guide. 'You're perceptive. That's not in the New Testament, but in the Old.'

'So it's not so much the early church as a mixture of Old and New Testaments?'

'What we say is: this is the Dispensation of the Fullness of Times, when everything was brought back, including plural marriage. Of course, the US Congress made a law against plural marriage, and the Mormons quit it in 1890.'

He showed me another chart, with portraits of Presidents, past and present. It started with the handsome, beardless Joseph, through the whiskered patriarchs, Brigham Young, John Taylor, Wilford Woodruff, Joseph Fielding Smith, to the modern clean-shaven corporate heads like David O. McKay, Spencer Kimball and Benson, the current incumbent, an ageing relic of the Eisenhower administration.

'We claim they receive revelation,' said Brother Orson. 'It's interesting, too, how it worked. When I was in Germany in August 1939 we had a bike trip planned, but then our mission president told us: 'President Grant in Salt Lake has received a revelation that war will start in three days. He wants all of us out of Germany tonight. You're to catch the first train to Copenhagen.' When we got safely over the border, our mission president called the US consul in Frankfurt, who told him: 'You crazy Mormons, you're all alarmists. There isn't going to be any war. Come back and behave yourselves!' Well, three days later, the war started.'

'Perhaps it was a lucky guess: lots of people thought that war was going to break out.'

'The President knew what he was talking about, because God told him.'

'How can you be sure? God moves in mysterious ways. What about all those revelations of convenience – the one banning polygamy in 1890 because the US Congress banned it, and the one giving blacks the priesthood in 1974 because of all the fuss made by the Civil Rights movement?'

'OK. Some people think it's just a matter of convenience. Well, that's fine, they can think that if they want. But we believe they were revelations.'

'It's like the Golden Tablets – you have to believe it, otherwise your whole church collapses.'

'Well, I'll give you another example – the depression. F.D.R. had one idea of solving the depression, President Grant had another, and President Grant told it to the Mormons. Well, today the Mormon church is one of the most financially substantial in the world, and completely out of debt. The United States is over a trillion dollars in debt, following the politicians. So we feel like our president had help from God, and God knew ahead of time . . .'

'So what was Grant's policy for dealing with the depression?'

'Instead of getting on welfare, that people should be more frugal and thrifty, and save, and help each other find jobs, and stay employed, and stay fed and stay clothed. And it *worked*!'

'You mean there was no New Deal for the Mormons?'

'The New Deal made idlers out of millions of Americans, and today we have their descendants and their descendants, down to the fifth generation. Most people don't know how to work, they don't know how to economise. The government is making them big payments every month: well, you know what that does to any company or nation, it can get them deeper and deeper into debt . . . We Mormons believe we've got to work, earn our way and be independent, and at the same time be our neighbours' helpers, our brothers' keepers, when that needs to be done.'

It was a long way from Joseph and Brigham's theocracy, when Mormons had practised a form of socialism, sharing land, tools and merchandising outlets. The antagonism they had aroused had been partly due to their communalist impulses, which often gave them the advantage over their more individualistic competitors. They had abandoned socialism, like they abandoned polygamy, turning a full 180 degrees. When once they were reviled as socialists, they were now super-capitalists; when formerly detested as 'un-American', they were now super-Americans, and ultra-conformists to boot.

It was getting late. I wanted to cross the Hudson before dark. A camping spot near Moreau Lake looked suitable. I followed the White River valley to Royalton, and then headed west beyond Rutland, across the New York state line to Glen Falls, where I crossed the river. As I turned south, away from the Adirondacks, the country gradually opened up, yielding more agriculture and, judging from the forests of pylons and cables competing with the pine trees, more industrial wealth as well. The towns became less tidy: there were still suburban enclaves with clapboard houses in white and terracotta and perfectly trimmed lawns; but they were now hemmed in more intrusively by the agents of modernity – gas stations, shopping precincts, small factories, junk yards – scattered over the landscape without apparent reason other than the whims of property speculation. I found the campsite without difficulty, by a lake croaking with frogs. I was exhausted from the twisting roads and the visit to Sharon – from the psychic strain of defending my scepticism against the assaults of Mormonism. I couldn't even get my supper together before collapsing into sleep.

Next morning was Sunday, bright, sunny and warm. I got up late by force of habit: I drove towards Schenectady, through featureless towns – Wilton, Ballston Spa, Burnt Hills. To judge from the crowded parking lots of churches of every denomination, I thought the whole population must be at worship. I had already decided it was too late to make a morning service, when I found myself on Interstate 90, heading west.

As I drove up the gentle Mohawk Valley, the country became more generous, with undulating pastures, scattered clumps of trees and rocky outcrops spaced inconsequentially in the landscape. There is no better way to experience America than on a freeway heading west, the direction of opportunity, expansion, growth and optimism: I felt a sudden surge of excitement, a quickening of the blood. My irritation with Puritan narrowness and Mormon philistinism lifted, like the rain-clouds that had disappeared in the night. Perhaps I experienced an infinitesimal portion of that extraordinary surge of freedom that affected the whole country after the Revolution, when the new nation broke through its confines on the Atlantic seaboard and spilled over the mountains to the west.

I would have driven on blithely, for the sheer heaven of it; but suddenly I noticed a large circular building, set in a park with trees, crucifixes and statues. According to the map this was the Shrine of the North American Martyrs at Auriesville, New York. I turned off the freeway and was directed into a huge parking lot filled with buses.

Something important was happening. I walked to the Coliseum, where mass was being celebrated. It was a cheap and practical structure, made from brick with a minimum of embellishment. There was room, according to my leaflet, for 6,500 people on its hard wooden benches. Its most striking feature was the altar area. Instead of organ pipes there was an Indian-style stockade of plain pine stakes engraved with red crosses. It looked like the stage-set for a college miracle play, except that the lifesize polychrome statues of the martyrs and a huge nine-foot Christ, with a carved madonna of similar size holding an empty shroud, revealed that the fixtures were permanent. The altar was supposed to represent the Mohawk 'castle' in which three French Jesuits were tomahawked in the 1640s.

Outside, a large crowd had gathered at one corner of the park. It turned out to be a different kind of theatrical production: a large column of men, wearing cocked hats and brightly-coloured capes, were marching in ranks behind richly embroidered banners which proclaimed their membership of the New York chapters of the Knights of Columbus. They were mostly middle-aged and flabby. Few possessed the erect bearing or ascetic angularity of soldiers.

There were fiery Italian faces and melancholy Irish ones; faces that were strained with the burdens of guilt or office, or rendered rubicund from alcohol and good living. Blacks were conspicuously absent, as were men of Latin American or Indian origin. The knights looked overwhelmingly middle-class. Behind them was a motley rabble which I joined, consisting mainly of smartly dressed females and children in bright Sunday clothes and crisp white socks. At the head of the column walked a young priest, a tall imposing figure with a white gown, carrying a microphone. The dignity of his presence was somewhat lessened by his companion, to whom he was linked umbilically by a cable: this was a small round Sancho Panza of a man who walked backwards, bearing a large megaphone which relayed the priest's voice to the pilgrims.

We performed the Stations of the Cross on the hill where the Jesuit martyrs had been made to run the gauntlet between Indian clubs and rods. At each station there was a polychrome bas-relief mounted on a plain brick stela, where the procession would stop for a prayer and a homily. The priest's discourse was earnest and passionate, delivered with a ringing, high-pitched Bostonian accent, similar to Jack Kennedy's. He spoke about love and suffering, using images that conjured up the comfortable, if narrow way of life of his auditors.

'This is where Jesus stumbled and fell: the Lord teaches us to accept all our weaknesses, even alcoholism. Maybe we do love golf. There's nothing wrong in loving golf. But we should love confession more – and that means real repentance, offering up our sins to God, not just a few novenas and Hail Marys. God speaks to us in all sorts of unexpected ways. A priest was stopped for speeding: 'For God's sake, Father,' says the cop, 'slow down': God speaks even through a traffic cop. Malicious gossip is like cutting open a pillow: you can never put back the feathers, undo what you've done.'

Each homily concluded with a round of Hail Marys, mumbled automatically like some magical formula. The Knights looked hot and self-conscious. One had retired, sweating, to a bench by the wayside, attended by anxious relatives. Perhaps he was having a heart attack. Most of them looked uncomfortable in their outfits: aware, perhaps, of a certain incongruity about the occasion, in which a ritual born out of real torments had become an excuse for a display of fancy dress.

The sufferings of the martyrs were terrible. There were three of them at Auriesville, formerly Ossernenon, all of them French Jesuits, like the five martyrs of Canada canonised at the same time and also commemorated at the shrine. The Jesuits – 'Blackrobes', the Indians called them – arrived in Quebec in 1625 to evangelise the Indians. They had little success among the confederate tribes of the Iroquois, which included the Mohawks; however, they succeeded in establishing a mission among the rival Hurons at Georgian Bay, 800 miles further west on the north shore of what is now Lake Huron. In 1642 the Mohawks captured a party of Huron Christians which included two Jesuits, Father Isaac Jogues and his lay assistant or *donné*, René Goupil. After being flogged and having their thumbs cut off, the two men were assigned to different Mohawk families as their personal property. They were permitted to pray at some distance from the village, but not inside the

compound: the Mohawks regarded Christian prayer as evil magic. Father
Jogues kept a low profile; but his assistant, who seems to have been a
simple-minded fanatic, provoked his captors by making the sign of the cross
over the head of a four-year-old child, and was duly tomahawked. Jogues
eventually escaped and made his way back to France where he was treated
as a hero. Not to be out-martyred by his deputy, he returned to Quebec
with a new *donné*, Jean de la Lande.

Both men were tomahawked in 1646 by a party of Mohawks. Within
three years the Huron mission was wiped out by other Iroquois tribes,
creating five more martyrs, including the mission's founder, Father Jean de
Brebeuf.

The blood of the martyrs fell on fertile soil at Ossernenon: within a
generation, the Mohawks had produced a saint of their own, in the person
of Blessed Kateri Tekakwitha.

Kateri was born at Ossernenon in 1656, ten years after Jogues's martyrdom. Her father was a chief of the Turtle clan, her mother a captive
Algonquin convert to Christianity. When Kateri was four, her family was
wiped out in a smallpox epidemic. She herself was left permanently scarred
and myopic. She was adopted by an uncle, Onsegongo, and raised in some
seclusion because of her disfigurement.

By the time the French had finally defeated the Mohawks, Kateri and her
adopted family had moved a few miles west, to Cauhnawaga, near present-
day Fonda. A succession of Jesuits arrived, and about a fifth of the village –
some 400 people – were converted. The converts were bitterly resented
by the majority. To protect them from harassment, the Jesuits took them
to the Christianised town of Kahnawake on the St Lawrence, in what is now
Canada.

Kateri, we are told by the missionaries, was a faultless child, 'as good as
a well-bred French girl', with a cheerful disposition. But she had problems
with her uncle and aunts, who are described in the Catholic literature as
being 'very bigoted' because they resisted the Jesuit policy of resettling
Christian converts at Kahnawake (a policy, of course, that was sure to
undermine, and eventually destroy, the Indian social structure). She further
infuriated her uncle by refusing to marry. When she was about nineteen
Kateri was baptised at her own request.

Her uncle was furious, seeing the whole thing as a smear on his honour.
Kateri's aunts, we are told, wickedly cast slurs on her virtue; Onsegongo
even went so far as to urge drunken braves to molest her. Kateri remained

steadfast in her faith, and her virginity. Onsegongo, just as adamant, refused to let her go to the Christian settlement. Eventually, Kateri escaped to another Christian village at Sault St Louis, near Montreal. There she lived a life, according to the Jesuits, of irreproachable virtue and spirituality.

Kateri was permitted to take communion before other converts; she wore a blue, instead of the usual scarlet, blanket. In 1679 she took a vow of perpetual virginity, and 'with a heart on fire with love called on Him to be her unique spouse and to take herself as His spouse in return'. In April 1680 she finally succumbed to a fever which had been troubling her for a year. Her last words were 'Jesus, I love you!' Her face, ravaged by smallpox and further disfigured by penances, suddenly acquired a heavenly, transcendental glow. From the moment of her death the Indian Christians began venerating her as a saint.

The cult of the Jesuit martyrs began in the nineteenth century. In 1817 the governor of New York, De Witt Clinton, began constructing the Erie canal, employing thousands of Irish navvies, many of whom settled in the new cities in the brave new world of upstate New York. By the 1840s the Jesuits were back, with parishes in Buffalo and Troy as well as Quebec.

The Fathers began working on seventeenth-century history and archaeology. In 1884, on the basis of archaeological remains and Jogues's own descriptions, Auriesville was identified, as the site of Ossernenon, the place where Jogues and the two *donnés* were martyred, and the birthplace of Kateri Tekakwitha. The land was acquired and a shrine constructed, dedicated to Our Lady of Martyrs. Within a decade the canal and the railroad were bringing thousands of summer pilgrims. German-, Latin-, Lithuanian-, as well as Irish-Americans and French-Canadians flocked in as the shrine became a focus of an American-Catholic identity gradually breaking loose from its European hyphenations. Although the Irish came to dominate the hierarchy, causing considerable resentment among the Germans, Italians and Slavs, their fervent patriotism, forged in the same anti-British crucible as the Revolution itself, led their bishops to champion the 'Americanist' cause against Roman control – a factor which ultimately diminished 'nativist' Protestant hostility to both Irish and Catholic immigration. Auriesville became the Americanist shrine *par excellence*.

By 1905 the shrine was already receiving 12,000 pilgrims a year. The same year, the lengthy process of canonisation was begun. A tribunal was established to collect evidence. In 1925 the martyrs were beatified; in 1930 they were canonised. The celebrations at Auriesville created the largest traffic jams in the Mohawk valley's history. The Coliseum and its massive car parks were built to accommodate the swelling tide of pilgrims.

Kateri's elevation took longer, and is yet to be completed. In 1884 the archbishops and bishops of the Third Plenary Council of Baltimore petitioned the Holy See to institute a process of beatification, but formal proceedings did not begin until 1931. In 1939 Pope Pius XII formally introduced Kateri's 'cause'; in 1943 her virtues were officially declared 'heroic'. In 1976, as part of the Catholic Church's observance of the bicentennial, the US Conference of Catholic Bishops urged the Holy See to advance Kateri's cause. In 1980 she cleared the first hurdle on the path to sainthood when Pope John Paul II declared her beatification. The next stage is thought to be imminent. Her canonisation would be an event of great symbolic significance: a gesture of recognition towards Indian spirituality which would counterbalance the colonialist taint implicit in the canonisation of the Jesuits. Pope John Paul, who has experienced considerable difficulties in managing his American flock, disappointed Kateri's supporters by failing to announce the expected canonisation during his visit to the United States in 1987.

With or without canonisation, the Kateri cult has completely overtaken that of the Jesuit martyrs. The Lily of the Mohawks is immortalised in bronze on the doors of St Patrick's Cathedral, New York; the annual conference of American priests and laity is named after her. There are shrines at Fonda where she was baptised, and Kahnawake, in Canada, where she is buried; at Auriesville, at a stone's throw from the Coliseum there is now a full-blown National Kateri Center. As well as displaying wigwams, moccasins, beads, wampum belts and other familiar tokens of Indian culture, the centre is dedicated to celebrating the very spirituality the Jesuit martyrs gave their lives to destroying. The people whose souls were in bondage to Satan and had to be rescued and isolated if needs be by force, are now being commended for their special sensitivity to the numinous as manifested in nature. Pasted on one wall is a 'chief's prayer', whose pantheistic totemism must be causing Father Jogues a second martyrdom in whatever place his soul is currently residing.

> Great Spirit, hear me while I offer the united voice and devotion of my people as thanksgiving. For the sun that warms our earthhouse . . . For sleep that rides with the moon and stars, the rivers that flow from mountains of living waters. For healing herbs, nuts, fruits, grains, fish and meat . . . Teach us the patience of the turtle, give us the vision of the eagle, give us our

prophet's wisdom. Teach us to love our Mother Earth, with her dawn and evening light, dark clouds, mists, trees, flowers, seeds and corn . . .

The centre is, above all, an emporium for the Kateri industry. There are Kateri medals, Kateri chaplets, Kateri bracelets, Kateri statues, Kateri auto-plates, Kateri paper-holders, Kateri notepaper, Kateri beaded dolls, Kateri songbooks and a fine reproduction of the official Kateri portrait in which, as on all the other artifacts, her pockmarked features have not only been miraculously transformed, but completely Europeanised, so that she now looks like a typical Unesco kid – an even mix of Mediterranean and Nordic, with a hint of Afro-Asian – in pigtails and moccasins. There is a regular Kateri newspaper, *Lily of the Mohawks*, which among other things testifies to her remarkably wide range of intercessions. She is credited with halting brain tumours and other cancers, preventing seizures, headaches and dizzy spells, curing blindness, abscesses, skin rashes and allergies, silencing heart murmurs, preventing fires, bringing rain, getting people jobs, finding them spouses, preventing solvent and drug abuse and even helping with income tax payments. She unravels bureaucratic tangles, so that people can get the money due to them. Most importantly, she brings renegades back to the Church. There is a 'Special K club' which one may join, with a badge and regular outings; there are *pro-forma* prayers for her canonisation printed in seven different languages. But don't, warns the *Lily*, bother to collect signatures: they 'don't mean a thing in Rome'.

When I got back to the car park, the Knights were disrobing. Sashes and cocked hats were ranged in back windows, suspenders were exposed, even trousers removed, revealing striped undershorts and bulging bellies. Cans of beer were hissing amid sounds of general hilarity. The Hill of Torture was already forgotten.

I drove back to the freeway and on to Oneida, where I camped in a park by the lake.

I was now in the centre of the region known to the Methodist circuit-riders of the 1830s and 1840s as the 'burned-over district' – the region west of the Adirondacks where religious revivals had followed each other with such frequency that it was presumed to be suffering from spiritual exhaustion. In the view of the professionals, the evangelical pastures had become seriously over-grazed. 'I have visited and re-visited many of these fields,' wrote one of the preachers, 'and groaned in spirit to see the sad, frigid, casual and contentious state into which they had fallen . . . within three months after we left them.'

The most famous preacher of the day was Charles Grandison Finney, a former lawyer. After his own conversion, following an intense period of Bible study, Finney had become a freelance preacher with 'a retainer from the Lord Jesus Christ to plead his cause'. Like Jonathan Edwards, he was a master of the hell-fire sermon, with a commanding presence and hypnotic, theatrical manner. When he gesticulated, people in the audience would duck as if he were throwing things. In describing the fall of sinners, he would point to the ceiling, and as he gradually lowered his outstretched arm, people at the back of the hall would stand as if to watch the final entry through the gates of hell. Meetings would often go on all night. Unlike Edwards, who was concerned with essentially private conversions, Finney manipulated group psychology in order to achieve immediate results. Waverers were placed on an 'anxious bench' immediately in front of the pulpit: at the close of the lecture or sermon, he would demand their immediate conversions. His most important departure from Edwards, however, was not in style, but in theology: he put the final nails in the coffin of Calvinist determinism. 'God has made man a moral free agent,' he told his audiences. Evil was not the product of innate human depravity consequent on the Fall, but the result of individual choices made by selfish men and women.

'The sinner's *cannot* is his *will* not,' he declared. Sin and disorder would disappear if people chose good over evil, if they united and dedicated themselves to Christ, they could bring about the Second Coming in months. The efficacy of prayer, he was careful to add, was the change it wrought in human hearts, not in coercing God.

'I do not mean that God's mind is changed by prayer,' he said, 'but prayer produces a change *in* us as renders it consistent for him to do otherwise. What is that?' he asked, referring to Calvin's view of man's helplessness, 'but telling them to hold on to their rebellion against God . . . as though God were to blame for not converting them.'

Following the example of John Wesley, Finney reintroduced and made popular an idea that had hitherto been confined to the sectarian fringe communities like the Shakers: the idea of perfectionism. If sin were entirely voluntary and avoidable, perfect holiness or 'entire sanctification' was a human possibility. For the majority of Finney's auditors, this message had a liberating quality, consonant with the optimistic spirit of the Jacksonian age, a time of economic and geographical expansion, when the west was opening up. For one particular convert, John Humphrey Noyes, it had more radical implications.

Noyes was converted in the great revival of 1831, when Finney came to his home town of Putney, Vermont. An intellectual, he decided to take Finney's Arminianism to a logical conclusion: if the spirit and motivation were right, one's actions would be acceptable to God, regardless of the law. 'God tells me that he does not care so much what I do as how I do it,' wrote Noyes. 'The church and the world place men in a position of unnatural restraint . . . The abolition of law is an essential feature of the gospel and must not be kept back let the consequences be what they may.'

Foremost of the unnatural constraints imposed by the law of society was the institution of monogamous marriage. 'The law of marriage,' wrote Noyes,

> worketh wrath! It provokes to secret adultery, actual or of the heart. It ties together unnatural natures. It sunders matched natures. It gives to sexual appetite only a scanty and monotonous allowance and so produces the natural vices of poverty, contraction of taste and stinginess or jealousy. It makes no provision for sexual appetite at that very time when that appetite is strongest . . . This law of society bears hardest on females, because they have less opportunity of choosing their time of marriage than men. The discrepancy between the marriage system and nature is one of the principal sources of the peculiar diseases of women, of prostitution, masturbation, licentiousness in general.

This infamous law, stated Noyes, had only been applicable during the period of 'apostasy' prior to Christ's Second Coming – an event which he calculated had taken place at the time of the destruction of Jerusalem in 70 AD. The Kingdom of Heaven – where there was neither 'marriage nor giving in marriage' – was imminent. Noyes made an *a priori* distinction between marriage and sex. 'The outward act of sexual connection,' he wrote, 'is as innocent and comely as any other act, or rather, if there is any difference in the character of outward acts, that this is the most noble and comely of all.' 'When the will of God is done on earth as it is in Heaven, *then there will be no marriage*. The marriage feast of the Lamb is a feast at which *every dish is free to every guest*.' 'The true scheme of redemption,' Noyes concluded, 'begins with reconciliation with God, proceeds first to a restoration of true relations between the sexes, then to reform of the industrial system, and ends with victory over death . . . Holiness, free love, association in labor and immortality, constitute the chain of redemption and must come together in their true order . . . '

Being wealthy as well as serious, Noyes was in a position to put his theories to the test. In 1846 he introduced 'complex marriage' among his followers, making an agreement between himself, his wife and one other couple to allow 'full liberty' among themselves. The circle was then enlarged to include others, and eventually he announced that 'separate households' and 'property exclusiveness' had come to an end. The Kingdom, if not finally arrived, was definitely on the way.

Though everyone was sworn to secrecy about the details of the new arrangements, internal tensions led inevitably to leaks. Three young Putney girls had been drawn into Noyes's circle, creating anxiety among their families. Two dissidents, both of them men, went to the authorities. Noyes was indicted before a grand jury on two counts of adultery. There was a public outcry: and rather than face a trial whose outcome was certain conviction, Noyes left Putney, bringing the Kingdom and most of its subjects, to the shores of Lake Oneida.

Here at Oneida, at the heart of the 'burned-over district', the system of 'complex marriage' was institutionalised, to become one of history's most unusual sexual experiments. Like other modern cult leaders, Noyes ruled his community by controlling their sexual lives. Exclusive attachments were banned: couples found guilty of falling in love had their sexual privileges withdrawn, or were obliged to have children with different partners. The system hinged on an unusual form of birth control Noyes termed 'male continence', whereby the men made love without ejaculating, either during or after intercourse. The practice – known technically as *coitus reservatus* – was based on a blend of biblical with almost twentieth-century notions about sex. On the one hand Noyes – like Leviticus – regarded the expenditure of sperm without intent to procreate as a sinful waste of a man's seed and vital generative power; on the other he believed – in a remarkably modern way – that human nature demanded 'frequent congress of the sexes, not for propagative, but for social and spiritual purposes'. Just as exclusive attachments involved reprehensible possessiveness, so the goal of orgasm – at least in the man – diminished the spiritual benefits of intercourse. The method, of course, required a certain amount of skill. Young men were inducted into the system by older women who had passed the menopause; young women by older, more experienced men. The atmosphere at Oneida is described as having the quality of 'restrained, romantic excitement', where a pervasive feeling of 'continuous courtship' prevailed. As a method of birth control the system of male continence proved surprisingly successful. During the two decades between 1848 and 1869 that it was in force among the 200-strong community at Oneida, there were only thirty-one 'accidents'.

But the Oneida community was also an autocracy. Noyes's word, however benign, was law. Hinging as the community did upon the will of a single individual, it began to break up as its master became old and feeble. In 1879 the institution of complex marriage was formally abandoned.

Noyes's perfectionism was the most sophisticated of the movements which flourished in the 'burned-over district' during the mid-nineteenth century. But there were many others. In 1848 two young girls, Margaret and Katie Fox (aged twelve and fifteen) heard strange rappings in their home in Hydesville near Rochester – only a few miles from where Joseph Smith Jr claimed to have found the Golden Tablets inscribed with the Book of Mormon. Announcing that they were in touch with the spirit world, they became instant celebrities, holding public seances in which people paid to ask questions of the spirits and to hear their answers as relayed by the girls. The 'Rochester rappings' led to an epidemic of table-turning, slate-writing, glossolalia, automatic playing of musical instruments and other feats of clairvoyance, many of them transparently bogus. Within a decade there were more than seventy spiritualist mediums in New York State; by 1870 the spiritualist movement had acquired the status of a respectable denomination in cities like Boston, while claiming eleven million adherents worldwide.

No less spectacular was the rise and fall of Adventism in the same area. Its original adherents, like the Mormons, were millennialists: they believed that the Second Coming was imminent, when the faithful would be physically raptured or gathered up to heaven and the wicked sent to hell.

Their founder, William Miller (1782–1849) had originally been a deist, an enthusiastic supporter of Thomas Jefferson until his conversion in a local revival turned him into an earnest Bible student. In 1831, after a two-year study of the Bible using the chronology worked out in 1654 by Archbishop Ussher of Dublin (who counted all the 'begats' in Genesis and combined his results with other biblical hints, concluding that Creation began at 9 a.m. on 26 October 4004 BC), Miller announced that the Second Coming would happen between 21 March 1843 and 21 March 1844. As excitement mounted, huge tent meetings took place throughout the state, notably

Albany, Utica and in the Mohawk Valley. In Rochester the textile industry boomed in response to mass orders for ascension robes.

As the last date approached people gathered on hillsides outside their cities, waiting for Christ to descend. When 21 March 1844 passed without incident, Miller confessed himself mistaken; some of his disciples, however, insisted there had merely been an error of calculation, and fixed a final and certain date for 22 October; when that too passed without incident, a period known as the Great Disappointment ensued. Thousands of Adventists left the movement and Miller himself died, discredited and forgotten, in 1849.

A sizeable group of his followers, however, were not so easily discouraged. In 1844 one of them, Hiram Edson, a farmer from western New York, had a vision as he walked through a cornfield, in which he saw that the 'cleansing of the Temple' had occurred on the forecast date – but in heaven, not on earth. Under the guidance of the Prophetess Ellen G. White the residue of the movement developed its distinctive sabbatarian theology. Christ had decided not to come down because the world was still too sinful. The people must first purify themselves, spiritually by strict observance of the sabbath, physically by reducing their intake of meat. In 1855 the Seventh Day Adventists established their headquarters at Battle Creek, Michigan. While preparing for Christ's return, Mrs White's protégé, the nutritionist Dr John H. Kellogg, developed a special vegetarian diet of processed corn. Though Christ is still to come, Battle Creek remains the Breakfast Food Capital of the world.

How did three brand-new American religions – Mormonism, Spiritualism and Seventh Day Adventism – all originate within a few years of each other in the same few counties of upstate New York? During the mid-nineteenth century this was the fastest-growing agricultural region in the world, with immigrants, mostly Yankee New Englanders like the Smith and Young families, pouring across the Adirondacks. After the Erie Canal linked this part of the 'old' Mid West to the Atlantic coast, Rochester became a boom-town, with flourmills, workshops and factories springing up everywhere to satisfy the needs of the migrants. The old self-sufficient patriarchal Puritan family, in which several generations lived and worked together, often under the same roof, gave way to smaller family units in which the women took charge of the home. Correspondingly, the stern Calvinist faith with its emphasis on human depravity gave way to gentler more humanistic Arminian doctrine which saw that children could become instruments of their own salvation. At the same time, social disorder increased dramatically, as young people left home to work in the workshops and factories, living in rented lodgings. As Frances FitzGerald has observed, many were 'transients in the sense that they had no families, no land and no social context'. Young men spent their leisure hours drinking and fighting, and were often drunk at work.

At times of social and economic upheaval, people may react to emotional stress by withdrawing from ordinary life and seeking the guidance of some charismatic or prophetic figure. The mental processes of prophet-leaders are barely understood, having received surprisingly little attention from psychologists. The trances or mystic states in which they receive their 'revelations' appear to be very similar to states experienced by patients suffering from schizophrenia or other mental disorders. The prophet's acceptance or rejection, whether he is hailed as a saviour or locked up in a mental institution, seems to have less to do with the character of his message than with the condition of the surrounding society. In a stable, ordered society the prophet will probably be dismissed as mentally sick. In a society undergoing structural breakdown, he or she may find enough followers to form first a cult, then a sect, and finally a new denomination or religion, depending on how closely the new message conforms to the prevailing orthodoxies. So it was with the Jesus cult in Palestine during the first century AD; and so it still is in many parts of America, where charismatic preachers, prophets and cult leaders find their followings, especially among restless, confused, deracinated youth.

Into the socially turbulent 'burned-over district' the preachers and prophets introduced self-discipline and order from On High. According to the American historian Paul Johnson, the campaigns of Finney effected a radical transformation in social mores. First the upper ranks – the businessmen, professionals, skilled workmen and their women attended revival meetings; then the workers themselves joined in, partly because employers often made church membership a condition for obtaining jobs or promotion. Women participated as individuals, not as mere adjuncts to their husbands. The rewards for all were tangible: as so often in America, God and Mammon worked together.

Finney's revival, like other revivals, soon became absorbed into the mainstream: its very success led to a rapid accommodation with the existing churches – churches that had previously proved powerless to improve the social situation, because membership went through heads of families. The churches and their members rapidly adjusted to the new social situations and new hierarchies that came into being. A similar evolution took place in England, where the energies released by Methodism eventually ran into the sands of social and religious conformity. Unlike Europe, however – but like the Middle East, which harboured so many early Christian sects – America was a land of shifting frontiers, where the separatist impulse had every opportunity to maintain its momentum. Mormons could isolate themselves physically by moving further west, as did the Spiritualists and Adventists. In America the non-establishment clause in the Constitution protected heterodoxy from efforts to enforce religious conformity; by the same token it inhibited any hope the heterodox might have of conquering the state in the manner of early Christianity or Islam. Western New York in the nineteenth century was a microcosm of what the whole of America was said to be in the twentieth: a melting-pot where old allegiances and identities would dissolve and reconstitute themselves into new shapes or compounds.

III

The Golden Plates

For there shall arise false Christs, and false prophets, and shall shew great
signs and wonders; insomuch that, if it were possible, they shall deceive the
very elect.

MATTHEW 24:24

Hill Cumorah, where Joseph Smith claimed to have found the Golden
Plates, is the most prominent feature in the pleasing countryside
north of the Finger Lakes – a land of wooded hills and rolling pastures that
reminded me of parts of Burgundy; indeed the Finger Lake wineries are
said to be the best in America, outside California.

In the 1820s it was a booming region, with land prices soaring from the
expected gains of the Erie Canal. Joseph Smith Senior moved with his family
from Vermont because the land was so much better. He had to pay a top
price for his farm near Manchester, forcing his family to live under a heavy
burden of debt. Young Joseph appears to have been more personable and less
inclined to agricultural work than his elder brothers, Alvin and Hyrum. As a
teenager he spent much of his time with a gang of idlers digging for treasure.
This was not a particularly unusual activity, either in Vermont or Western
New York. Legends of Spanish gold attracted the greedy and credulous.
The Indian mounds yielded stone and copper artifacts, and sometimes
beaten silver. Magic and necromancy were tied up with the money-digging.
Joseph acquired a 'seer-stone' which, according to the sworn testimony
of a neighbour, enabled him to see 'ghosts, infernal spirits and mountains
of gold and silver'. Whether he believed in magic, or just 'talked big' to
impress people, cannot be known for certain. Magic often appeals to those
who feel themselves to be weak or powerless. As the cleverest child in the
family whose education was partly blighted by illness, Joseph could have
buttressed his self-esteem by pretending to achieve magical effects. But his

family appeared to have been convinced of his supernatural powers. Years later, without going into details, he would admit to having fallen into 'many vices and follies'.

Whatever the truth, the seer-stone brought both fame and notoriety.

Josiah Stowell, a farmer from southern New York, was so impressed by Joseph's alleged powers that he paid him $14 a month, plus board and lodging, to search for a disused Spanish silver mine in the Susquehanna valley. Nothing was found, however, and one of Stowell's neighbours took out a warrant against Joseph for disorderly conduct and being an 'impostor'.

While staying with the Stowells Joseph had courted the pretty, dark-eyed Emma Hale and had married her against her father Isaac's wishes. Mr Hale thoroughly disapproved of Joseph's interest in necromancy, and would never believe his claims to prophethood. A carrier hired to collect Emma's furniture reported finding Isaac Hale in tears.

'You have stolen my daughter,' he was saying to Joseph. 'I had much rather have followed her to her grave. You spend your time in digging for money – pretend to see in a stone, and thus try to deceive people.' According to the carrier, 'Joseph wept, and acknowledged he could not see in a stone now, nor ever could; and that his former pretensions in that respect were all false.' The same man testified that Joseph had revealed to him, on another occasion, that the story of the Golden Plates on which he claimed to have found the Book of Mormon was a practical joke he had played on his simple-minded family.

To the non-believer the story of the Golden Plates is frankly preposterous, though no less credible than the Virgin Birth and other biblical miracles. In the official version dictated years later by Joseph himself, young Joseph the farmhand had his first vision when he was fourteen. Two 'personages', later identified as God the Father and Son, whose 'brightness and glory' defied all description, appeared to him in a grove near his family's home. They warned him against joining any of the existing churches, since 'all their creeds were abominations'. Then on 21 September 1823, just before his eighteenth birthday, the angel Moroni appeared to him. Addressing him by name, he told Joseph about the Golden Plates which contained an account of the 'former inhabitants of this continent, and the source from whence they sprang'. The 'fulness of the everlasting gospel' was contained in the book, as delivered by Christ to America's ancient inhabitants. There would be two magic stones with the book, the Urim and Thummim, fastened to a breastplate, to enable Joseph to make the translation.

After telling his father, Joseph went to collect the plates from the designated hill, at a spot the angel had shown him in a vision. He tried to remove them but was forbidden by the angel: the time had not yet come. Every year just after his birthday he revisited the spot; every year he was given the same message.

Finally, in 1827, following his marriage to Emma Hale, he was allowed to collect the plates. He secretly took them home, with the Urim and Thummim, and began the translation. The greed of the neighbours, who had heard about the plates and wanted to steal them, forced Joseph to hide them and to take refuge with his wife's family near Harmony, Pennsylvania, just over the border from New York.

When Emma's father, Isaac Hale, heard about the plates he asked to see them. When Joseph refused, he ordered the couple to leave his house. But he relented sufficiently to allow Joseph and Emma to reside in the home of one of her brothers. It was here that the 'translation' was done. No one, apart from Joseph, appears to have seen the plates physically. Not even Emma was allowed to look at them. 'They lay in a box under our bed,' she stated in later years, 'but I never felt at liberty to look at them.'

Years later – long after she had left the Mormon church – Emma claimed to have handled them: 'The plates lay on the table without any attempt at concealment, wrapped in a small linen table cloth which I had given him to fold them in. I once felt the plates, as they lay on the table, tracing their outline and shape. They seemed to be pliable like thick paper, and would rustle with a metallic sound when the edges were moved by the thumb . . . '

The Smith farm, where Joseph is supposed to have brought the plates, has been somewhat over-restored, to accommodate, perhaps unconsciously, the image of affluence and respectability enjoyed by the modern Saints. But care has been taken to maintain historical authenticity, with the original furniture and chattels replaced by antiques of the period.

A smart, middle-aged female Saint in a calf-length skirt and a blouse of battle-ship grey which matched her hair and mother-of-pearl-framed spectacles showed me round the assembled Smithiana with well-rehearsed enthusiasm. The physical details of the house, so concrete and material, as revealed by this eminently sensible woman made the tale of the plates seem less implausible. She displayed the stove and the dishes, the pans and the bread-oven, the cast-iron sausage-makers, candle-moulds and butter-churns with the same relentless attention to details, explaining how here, on the frontier, the family had to make everything themselves.

I crossed the road and came by a footbridge to the wood, now owned by the Church, where Joseph is supposed to have had his first vision. The sun cast dappled shadows under the oak and cottonwood trees. The grove was empty, and for some moments I listened in silence to the scrabblings of squirrels and chipmunks and to the rustle of the breeze high in the branches above. There was a magic about the place, despite the paraphernalia of rest-rooms, prayer benches and loudspeakers with which the Church accommodated the requirements of its pilgrims. Perhaps young Joseph had really experienced a moment of special insight in this place; perhaps the grove had already been made sacred by generations of Indians who had frequented it for some religious purpose before the settlers arrived and pushed them out. It was even possible to believe that the vast edifice of theology, myth, power and money that makes up the Mormon church was founded on a moment of truth that once happened here.

Hill Cumorah itself is a steep wooded ridge about three miles from the farm, with a commanding view of the ragged fields the Smiths and their fellow-homesteaders once hacked out of the forest. The whole of its top has been decapitated to accommodate the monument to the Angel Moroni – a confection of sumptuous extravagance designed in 1935 by Torlief Knaphus. When the angel – a shining gilded figure standing eight foot tall on a square marble column with Mayan-Aztec motifs – gleams in the sun, it must be visible for miles around. At the base of the column, there are two bronze plaques bearing the Book of Mormon's official credentials: the statement of the Three Witnesses (Oliver Cowdery, Martin Harris and David Whitmer) and the statement of the Eight Witnesses (all of them members of the Smith or Whitmer families). It was on the authority of these eleven witnesses that Joseph based his claim that the Book of Mormon was an ancient text.

The testimony of the witnesses is very far from being conclusive. Martin Harris and David Whitmer were well-to-do farmers who came under Joseph's spell, and lent him money. Oliver Cowdery, the former schoolmaster, was his principal scribe. The Three Witnesses, according to their statement, were shown the plates not physically, but by an angel in a vision. Joseph, like L. Ron Hubbard, the founder of Scientology, seems to have had extraordinary powers of suggestion.

All Three Witnesses left the church after quarrelling with Joseph, though Whitmer later returned. Cowdery came near to reneging on his testimony altogether. The Eight Witnesses were all members of Joseph's immediate circle: Joseph Senior, his sons Samuel and Hiram, and five members of David

Whitmer's family – Christian, Jacob, Peter, John and David's son-in-law Hiram Page. As Mark Twain caustically observed, 'I could not feel more satisfied and at rest if the entire Whitmer family had testified.'

The Eight Witnesses stated, much more concretely than the Three, that 'We have seen and hefted [the plates which] we did handle with our hands.' According to several prominent Mormons who left the church in later years, the Eight were set to continual prayer and other spiritual exercises before Joseph showed them the box which contained, he said, the golden tablets. Seeing nothing inside, the witnesses protested 'But Brother Joseph, we do not see the plates!' Joseph vented the full heat of his prophetic wrath upon them: 'O ye of little faith! How long will God bear with this wicked and perverse generation? Down on your knees, brethren, every one of you, and pray God for the forgiveness of your sins, and for a holy and living faith which cometh down from heaven.' The eight disciples dropped to their knees, 'and began to pray in the fervency of their spirit, supplicating God for more than two hours with fanatical earnestness; at the end of which time, looking into the box, they were now persuaded that they saw the plates.'

Joseph, is supposed to have 'translated' the plates as directed by the angel, using the Urim and Thummim. He copied down the characters, then dictated the translation to his scribe who sat in the other half of the room, separated from Joseph and the plates by a blanket draped over a rope. His first scribe, after Emma herself, was Martin Harris, the farmer from Palmyra who had lent Joseph money to carry on the work.

However, it appears from Emma's testimony that Joseph did not need to refer to the plates when 'translating' the Book of Mormon. Her Last Testament described how she wrote at a table close to her husband while he dictated with his face 'buried in his hat, with the [seer] stone in it', just as he used to do when divining treasure during his earlier money-digging expeditions, without apparently consulting the plates at all. Her claim to the Book of Mormon's authenticity implicitly rests, not on the plates, but, like the Koran, on the sheer improbability that an unlettered man could have produced such a document so fluently. She told her son, Joseph III:

My belief is that the Book of Mormon is of divine authenticity, – I have not the slightest doubt about it. I am satisfied that no man could have dictated the writing of the manuscript unless he was inspired; for, when acting as his scribe, your father would dictate to me hour after hour; and when returning

> after meals, or after interruptions, he would at once begin where he had left off, without either seeing the manuscript or having any portion of it read to him . . . It would have been improbable that a learned man could do this; and for one so ignorant and unlearned as he was, it was simply impossible.

Once Oliver Cowdery became the scribe, the work proceeded at astonishing speed: the whole book was completed in about seventy-five working days. The theory that the book was a clever forgery or plagiarism has long been disproved: no scholar seriously disputes that the Book of Mormon was the work of Joseph Smith Jr. Even if the story of the plates is discounted as an imaginative device invented by Joseph to give his text authenticity, a considerable mystery remains. How could a semi-literate farmhand have produced such a document? On the one hand Mormons who do not swallow the story of the plates may continue to believe that Joseph received the text under divine inspiration; on the other, the sceptic may argue, with Smith's biographer Fawn Brodie, that it is the product of an exceptional, though obviously untutored, literary talent. Here the parallel with L. Ron Hubbard is most compelling. Before founding the cult of Scientology, Hubbard was a writer of science fiction who wrote complete books in two or three days, barely stopping for meals and never even looking at his typescripts before mailing them to the publishers. Under different circumstances, as Brodie suggests, Joseph might have been a highly successful novelist.

A third possibility – that the Book of Mormon was composed under some sort of trance – is suggested by the historian Lawrence Foster:

> . . . the evidence that the plates themselves (if they existed) were not even visible to Joseph Smith during much of the time he was 'translating' them, and the fact that Smith could engage in skillful dictation of a highly complex work for hours on end, suggest that Smith was acting as an unusually gifted trance figure, perhaps one of the most gifted such figures in the history of religion . . . From a non-Mormon view-point, it could be seen as an unusually sophisticated product of unconscious and little-known mental processes.

Later descriptions of Joseph's appearance while receiving 'revelations' certainly suggest an abnormal mental process. 'He got so white,' wrote one witness, 'that anyone who saw him would have thought he was transparent.' Other prophets and shamans have appeared in similar states while giving vent to 'divine' utterances: the Prophet Muhammad is said to have been seized with the shudders and to have lain for hours in a coma, bathed in sweat.

I left the monument, and took the path downhill through well-tended shrubs and flowering plants. On each side there were large wooden gantries with theatre lights connected by cables to a complex of wooden sheds and shelters set with rows of benches. In July and August the hillside is converted into a giant stage-set where the Mormons hold their pageant spectaculars depicting the seminal events in their history, including the 'sending down' of the plates. It is one of the world's largest theatrical events, with 15,000 spectators, a cast of 1,000 and a highly sophisticated audio system in which the voice of God is digitally processed to 15,000 megawatts. It is perhaps indicative of the Church's propagandist orientation and desire to live down its druidical origins that the pageants are held at the height of the tourist season and not on 22 September, the day I had deliberately chosen for my visit.

At the Visitors' Center I asked the brother-in-charge: 'Is there no special ceremony today?' His watery eyes looked at me blankly through thick rimless lenses.

'Nothing special,' he said. The date – the autumnal equinox, one of the most important in the occult calendar – obviously meant nothing to him, though this was the day when Joseph is supposed to have found the plates. 'But you can watch the videos if you wish' he went on.

A series of images flashed on the screen. Stout Cortez welcomed as a returning god by Montezuma and his Aztec warriors, Captain Cook receiving similar treatment from the Hawaiians. 'Why were the white men welcomed as gods?' asked the film. 'Was it because Jesus once visited the Americas?'

The story was familiar: I had already struggled through the Book of Mormon, desperately trying to resist the soporific effects of Joseph's neo-biblical prose – 'chloroform in print,' Mark Twain called it. The twenty-minute video, with split screens and stereophonic sound effects, was a lot more enjoyable than the book.

As biblical pastiche, the Book of Mormon does not seem especially impressive. As currently printed – though not as originally published – it is divided into books, chapters and verses exactly like the King James Bible, large chunks of which, including Isaiah Chapters 2 to 14 and Matthew 6 and 7, have been incorporated piecemeal into the text. The style is extremely repetitious: about half the sentences seem to begin with 'it came to pass . . . ', suggesting that the author was giving himself time to think up the next thing to say. (If all the instances of 'and it came to pass' were removed, said

Mark Twain, the Book of Mormon would be a pamphlet.) The command of the seventeenth-century English style which it tries to imitate is decidedly weak: 'And it came to pass that I did make tools of the ore which I did molten out of the rock' (1 Nephi 17:16) is a typical example. The sentences themselves are disjointed, resembling, as Brodie remarked, 'an earthworm hacked into segments that crawl away alive and whole'.

But despite the longueurs, repetitions, soporific homilies, cardboard kings, grotesque anachronisms and outrageous plagiarisms, the Book of Mormon is a remarkable work: a history of the Americas, couched in biblical style, which links its peoples and lands to the peoples and lands of the Old and New Testaments. It describes how the Americas were settled by the ancient Hebrews in two migrations. The first immigrants, the Jaredites, drifted to America under the Lord's guidance immediately after the destruction of the Tower of Babel. They came in barges 'built according to the instructions of the Lord' that were small and light

> even like unto the lightness of a fowl upon the water . . . and the bottom [sic] thereof was tight like unto a dish; and the sides thereof were tight like unto a dish; and the ends thereof were peaked; and the top thereof was tight like unto a dish; and the length thereof was the length of a tree; and the door thereof, when it was shut, was tight like unto a dish.

These hermetically sealed contraptions would clearly have been lethal but for the Lord's insistence on adequate ventilation:

> . . . And the Lord said unto the brother of Jared: Behold thou shalt make a hole in the top, and also in the bottom; and when thou shalt suffer for air thou shalt unstop the hole and receive air. And if it be so that the water come in upon thee, behold, ye shall stop the hole, that ye may not perish in the flood.

The Jaredites built a great civilisation in the New World, leaving their records on 'twenty and four plates' of brass to be discovered by the descendants of the second wave of immigrants, the Nephites. This group, led by Lehi of the tribe of Joseph (who else?), a prophet contemporary with King Zedekiah (*c.* 600 BC) arrives in proper sailing ships, guided by the Liahona, a kind of compass consisting of 'a brass ball of curious workmanship with two spindles'. Lehi's sons – and their progeny – soon set to quarrelling. The good guys, sired by Nephi and three of his brothers, are depicted as 'white and delightsome'. The bad guys, descended from Laman, the black sheep of the family, were 'cursed by the Lord' which explains the ugly dark hue of their skins. The Lamanites, in due course, become the Indian inhabitants of the continent.

In the struggle between Nephi and his brothers it is easy to discern the politics of the Smith household. In the second chapter of Nephi, for instance, Laman and Lemuel 'murmur against their father', while Nephi is obedient and prays in faith. When Nephi's wicked brothers tie him up during the voyage to America, the compass stops working; after Lehi's death in the New World, the other brothers rebel against Nephi, but Nephi, who has the Lord on his side, eventually triumphs, becoming the 'ruler and teacher' of his brothers.

Joseph's identification with Nephi is obvious – and explicit. Trained by the Lord, he is a smith by trade, teaching his people to work in copper and brass. Like Napoleon, Joseph, though not the eldest of the family, dominated his siblings. His eldest brother Alvin had died of a stomach disorder when Joseph was eighteen; his elder brother Hyrum, a gentle, self-effacing character, was utterly devoted to Joseph, and would eventually die at his side. Of his younger brothers, Samuel and Don Carlos were generally loyal subordinates, though sometimes they fell under the influence of the tiresome and truculent William – a gaunt, raw-boned, cadaverous youth possessed of none of his brothers' charm or gracious qualities. It is tempting to identify the wicked, rebellious Laman with William, and the vacillating Lemuel with Samuel Smith, whose loyalties were sometimes torn between Joseph and William.

Many modern editions of the Book of Mormon are enlivened by the colourful, literalistic illustrations of Arnold Friberg, the Mormon artist whose career included a spell as Cecil B. DeMille's chief designer. Several of these paintings appeared on the video, including one of Samuel the Lamanite, a Book of Mormon Prophet, preaching to the hostile Nephites atop the walls of Zarahelma – the Nephite Jerusalem. Friberg's walls are late Mayan (about 900 AD) although the official chronology contained in the Book of Mormon dates these supposed events to around 6 BC. The text contains many other anachronisms, such as references to horses, donkeys, pigs, sheep and cattle – animals that were not present in the Americas prior to the Spanish conquest.

'Did you enjoy the film?' asked the brother-on-duty as I left the theatre.

'Most interesting,' I said, not wanting to get into a discussion, 'but a bit hard to swallow.'

'I know,' he answered sweetly, eyes glinting ominously behind his lenses, like those of a predatory fish. 'Many people find the Book of Mormon difficult to accept at first. You have to be persistent – and pray.' He quoted James 1:5 at me, as if it dealt with everything: '*If any of you lack wisdom let him ask of God* . . . I myself have prayed to God about the Book of Mormon and He has revealed to my heart that it is true.'

The Visitors' Center annoyed me. It was full of misleading or tendentious items. There were blown-up photographs of Aztec and Mayan ruins dating from the second millennium AD, when the end of Nephite civilisation is supposed to have occurred in AD 421; pictures of Thor Heyerdahl's Atlantic crossing on an Egyptian raft, which 'proves', according to the Saints, that Mesoamerican civilisation originated in the Near East; displays of metal plates with cuneiform inscriptions as evidence that ancient peoples wrote on tablets of brass; pamphlets referring to un-named 'scholars' and 'archaeologists' as backing the Book of Mormon's claims. In fact no non-Mormon anthropologist or archaeologist of any standing has published a single scientific paper supporting these claims.

Back on the road I calmed down again: the problem facing the church was that which faced the defenders of all religions: they insisted on treating myths – in this case, myths which flowed from Joseph Smith's remarkably fertile imagination – as facts. What of the origins of Christianity, Islam and other world religions? None would stand up to inspection if we knew what really went into their making. Outside the Christian canon, there was precious little evidence of the life and career of Jesus of Nazareth, other than a brief reference or two in the writings of Josephus. If we ignored the pious accounts of the Prophet Muhammad's career as related by the early Muslim annalists, what would we know about the origins of Islam, beyond a few hints in the writings of Syrian monks? The history of most religions is written by the faithful. Independent or hostile accounts have either disappeared or been deliberately destroyed. It is the Mormons' misfortune that we know a lot more about the origins of their religion than we can ever know about the origins of older religions; because of this most of us who are not members of the Mormon church instinctively cry 'fraud!' But religion is not about historical truth, it is about creative myth-making. For all the obvious infelicities of style, Joseph Smith was a myth-maker of genius. The fact that the materials out of which he made his religion are known to us should increase, not diminish our admiration for his achievement.

Joseph's account of American origins was not particularly original. The discovery of the New World had sparked off a vigorous theological debate about the Indians. Assuming, as most people did, that the biblical account of creation was literally true, the key questions had to be: how were the native Americans descended from Adam and Eve? and how did they get to America? Each of these questions spawned a variety of theories. The learned disputed about whether the Indians arrived after the collapse of the Tower of Babel, or whether they were genuine Hebrews who came in a later migration. The argument centred on the problem of language: if the Indians came after Babel, their tongues did not need to belong to any recognised group. The proponents of Hebraic origins, who included Roger Williams and Jonathan Edwards, claimed that the Indian tongues belonged to the semitic family of languages. In the Book of Mormon Joseph Smith tried to have it both ways. The Jaredites arrived after the dispersion of Babel, but were succeeded by a people whose record was written in a Near Eastern script he called 'reformed Egyptian'.

The question of how the Indians got to the New World also gave rise to two alternative theories (with numerous variations), the second of which is now almost universally accepted. Either they crossed the ocean in vessels, or they crossed the Bering Strait by a land bridge, across the ice or in small boats. All these theories were still being debated in the 1820s, when Joseph was reaching maturity. The Babel theory went back at least to 1652, when the English theologian Sir Hamon L'Estrange argued that America's first settlers were descended from Noah's son, Shem. But the theory that the Indians belonged to the ten missing tribes of Israel was more popular. First mooted by Joannes Fredericus Lumnius in 1567, it gained renewed currency with the publication of the Reverend Ethan Smith's *View of the Hebrews* in 1823.

There is no proof that Joseph Smith read the *View of the Hebrews*, but a few sentences from it look like a synopsis of the Book of Mormon: 'Israel brought into this new continent a considerable degree of civilisation; and the better part of them long laboured to maintain it. But others fell into the hunting and consequent savage state; whose barbarous hordes invaded their more civilised brethren, and eventually annihilated most of them . . . '

The legend of Christ's visit to America is also of considerable antiquity. Early conquistadors, including Cortez, regarded the stone crosses they found in Central America as evidence that the Gospel had once been preached there. The myth of Quetzalcoatl, which so facilitated the conquest of Mexico, was taken to show that one or more of the Apostles – St Thomas, according to several accounts – had visited America after the Crucifixion. But at least one eighteenth-century writer, Chevalier Boturini, suggested that Quetzalcoatl might be Christ himself.

There are traces of other, more contemporary influences in Joseph's gospel. In 1826 a major anti-Masonry scare occurred in western New York following the disappearance of one William Morgan, who had written an exposé of the Freemasons and their rites. The acquittal at Canandaigua of five prominent Masons on murder charges inflamed public opinion. The issue became highly politicised, since President Andrew Jackson was known to occupy a high-ranking position in the Craft. Anti-Jacksonians exploited the wave of hysteria: soon every unexplained death or forgotten suicide was being raked up as proof of a diabolical conspiracy by the Masons to murder their enemies. The scare reached its climax in October 1827, when the bloated corpse of a man was washed up on the shores of Lake Ontario. Though the Masons later proved it to be the body of a hapless Canadian named Timothy Monroe, Morgan's widow (who later became a Mormon) identified it as that of her husband. A martyr's funeral in Batavia was attended by hundreds of thousands of people. As new trials produced more acquittals for lack of evidence, the sheriffs were accused of being Masons: throughout the state Masonry was attacked as a threat to free government and civil liberty.

The second half of the Book of Mormon contains a sustained attack on Freemasonry. In Joseph's gospel the democratic practices of the Nephites are undermined by a secret cabal, the robbers of Gadianton who receive instructions from the devil to 'carry on the work of darkness and of secret murder'. The Gadiantons obtain the 'sole management' of Nephite government, directly contributing to their eventual destruction by the Lamanites. But the New York hysteria was far from being the only aspect of Masonry to find its way into Joseph's fertile brain.

The whole subject fascinated him, and influenced him positively as well as negatively. The vision of buried treasure, the Golden Plates, the brass Liahona and the sacred Urim and Thummim – key elements in the Book of Mormon and the story of its discovery – are all to be found in the *Free Masons' Monitor* by Thomas Webb, a popular collection of Masonic legends published in 1802. After founding his church and building the Temple of Nauvoo, Joseph would incorporate the major Masonic rituals into his endowment ceremonies.

The Book of Mormon, however, is not just a hotch-potch of popular notions about Indian origins and Freemasonry woven into a biblical narrative: there are theological concerns as well, which Joseph placed in the mouths of his Nephite prophets. The prevalent theology is Arminian and perfectionist: men have free will and the power to choose or reject Christ's message; Calvinism is condemned as heresy and infant baptism, an 'evil abomination', is attacked on universalist grounds – 'Awful is the wickedness to suppose that God saveth one child because of baptism and the other must perish because he hath no baptism.'

But Joseph's theological enemies get a fair hearing, if not fair treatment. The anti-Christ Korihor makes a strong case for atheism before being struck dumb by the prophet Alma – suggesting that when argument fails, God fights dirty. The Christ who appears at the end of the book is punitive and denunciatory – a reincarnation of the Jehovah of the Old Testament rather than the Jesus of the New. Evangelicals who denounce Mormonism as 'un-Christian' (a charge hotly denied by the Church) are not to be lightly dismissed.

The facility with which Joseph could argue both sides of a theological debate suggests, as Fawn Brodie put it, an 'unusual plasticity' of mind. He knew the arguments 'as intimately as a bright child knows his catechism, but his use of them was utterly opportunistic'. Where he excelled was in his ability to weave the fabric of his fantasy into the structure of his own career: the Book of Mormon is not, like the Koran, a running commentary on the events of the Prophet's life, but an agenda for action. The Book not only foretells the coming of Joseph the Prophet: its coming forth will be a sign that the Lord has commenced the gathering of Israel under Joseph's leadership. The scale of Joseph's megalomania, which could well have led to insanity in other circumstances, was reinforced by the hold he exercised over his family, who were obviously less endowed intellectually than he was.

Joseph's preaching made little headway among his neighbours in Palmyra, where his reputation for necromancy told against him. But in southern New York, where he stayed near his wife's family, he was less well known. Here he was able to win a small nucleus of converts – enough to get his movement started.

By noon next day I was heading west for Cleveland, along Interstate 90. As I crossed the Ohio border, I felt a new surge of excitement. I was now approaching the Middle West. The dull grey blanket covering the sky had broken into fleecy Magritte clouds, revealing a day of sparkling sunshine which gave the trees and grasses their first autumnal tints. I switched on the radio. At first there was Mozart, which soon grew too crackly to hear as its transmitter went out of range. Instead a pleasant female voice came through. 'You may literally be making yourself sick because of your lack of faith in God. Speak to yourself as David did. With a little disciplined thinking and trust in God your life could be changed. Shalom.' What followed also became lost in the general electronic cacophany. I twisted the knob. Christian radio, inevitably, was louder and more durable.

'I want to bring you into Gaad's Presence and remain with you there,' said a youngish male voice in smooth, unctuous tones. 'Now that's a lofty goal, I grant you. But the Holy Spirit is our Helper. Hear the Music, and the Word. Stay tooned.' There followed a break for a Christian commercial. 'So nobody cares about you and your needs?' said a different, more businesslike voice. 'WRONG! If your house has plumbing problems . . . the Good Samaritan Sewer Service cares. Twenty-four-hour emergency service, seven days a week . . . '

A jingled version of the Hallelujah Chorus faded up, conjuring mental images of angels in bright blue overalls flying around with spanners, wrenches and celestial dyno-rods. Then the first voice came back.

'Because I live, ye shall live also,' it was saying. 'John 14:19. The Secret of Everything is living in Jesus Christ, being led by He-um, being trained by He-um. The powerful effect of spiritual conversion is that you get invaded from Beyond by the Bigness of Christ, your littleness by His Expansive Presence. A Tender Giant walks in your tiny footsteps, and you are no longer alone . . . '

There was more music, this time a maudlin song about Jesus delivered in saccharine tones by a crooner who sounded like Nat King Cole. Then the preacher's voice came back again, this time stronger and more assertive.

'Jesus has promised His Presence in your life. Now's the time to take advantage of His Unique Offer! It's not just a matter of refusing to do wrong. Oh no, no, no my friend. The Glory of the Presence of Jesus Himself within us is your real distinctiveness as a Christian.' The voice rose to a manic pitch: 'EMMANUEL – Gaad within you, SPIRITUS SANCTUS – Gaad within you. The Secret is the POWER-PACKED COMPANIONSHIP OF GAAD!' Finally, another more sober voice told me how I could get my own personal Jesus Power-Pack. 'Just send five dollars or call this number with your credit card . . . '

The Temple at Kirtland stands on a hill in what is now a pleasant dormitory suburb of Cleveland. It is an imposing three-storey building, very similar to the classic New England meeting-house, with a belfry at one end topped by a miniature steeple. It was built in 1833 after Joseph and his followers had moved from New York. Joseph's original plan had been to build the Temple in Jackson County, Missouri, on the borders of Indian territory. His idea of the restoration of Zion involved the re-conversion of the Lamanites, who would become a 'white and delightsome' people again. But his dreams of an empire on the Missouri foundered on the indifference of the Indians and hostility of the white settlers. The latter disliked the Mormon habit of voting for candidates *en bloc*, which they feared would give them the political advantage over other settlers.

The flourishing Mormon community at Kirtland was largely due to the presence there of Sidney Rigdon, a charismatic preacher gifted, it was said, with 'very fine powers of mind'. Rigdon had been a follower of Alexander Campbell, an evangelical reformer who, like Joseph, believed that the church could be restored to the conditions of the apostolic age. But the two men had quarrelled over Rigdon's insistence that the Disciples (as Campbell's followers called themselves) should hold all their property in common. On reading the Book of Mormon, Rigdon was immediately convinced that Joseph was the prophet whose coming would herald the millennium. He joined the Latter-day Saints, bringing with him his group of Christian communists.

At first Joseph and his New York followers treated Kirtland as a mere staging-post on the way to the Zion in the West. But after the Saints had been driven out of Jackson County by the burnings and lynchings of the mobs, and Joseph's efforts to rescue them had failed disastrously, Kirtland became his headquarters. The Temple was a half-way house, or 'Temple-in-Exile', which would have to make do until the Lord decided to allow the real Temple to be built in Zion.

In Kirtland the Church developed its characteristic organisation. At the top was the Prophet, whose word was final, governing as he did by 'revelation'. Whenever a decision was required, Joseph would pray and receive his instructions – as he claimed – directly from God. The revelations, canonised in the text of *Doctrine and Covenants*, are mostly discursive ramblings in the neo-biblical language of the Book of Mormon, though the style, with the frequent use of the phrase 'Verily I say unto you' recalls the New rather than the Old Testament. This highly authoritarian structure was balanced by the fact that every adult male had a share in the 'restored' priesthoods – the 'higher' or Melchizidech priesthood and the lesser Aaronic priesthood, now conferred exclusively on boys. (Later on women would be patronisingly relegated to the bizarrely-named Relief Society.) At the top of the priestly hierarchy, directly below the Prophet, stood the Quorum of Twelve Apostles; the rest were divided into bishops, seventies, elders and deacons – titles taken from the Apostolic church.

These priestly gradations were expressed architecturally in the triple tiers of rising pulpits at each end of the sanctuary and the school room which occupied the building's upper floor. The seating arrangements in both chambers was similar: there were stalls or box-pews in the traditional New England manner, but with movable benches so that people could sit facing either way. Each chamber had an ingenious system of curtains on pulleys that could be raised or lowered to screen different sections from each other.

In 1836 these screens or 'veils' were used to dramatic effect, during a period that became known as the 'Endowments'. The weeks following the Kirtland Temple's dedication saw scenes of religious enthusiasm unprecedented in Mormon history and never to be repeated. During the all-male priesthood session in the evening, according to Joseph's journal, the Temple was filled with the sound of a rushing mighty wind: 'All the congregation simultaneously arose, being moved upon by an invisible power; many men began to speak in tongues and prophesy; others saw glorious visions; and I beheld the temple was filled with angels, which fact I declared to the congregation.'

For two days and nights the men remained in the Temple, fasting and praying and speaking in tongues. Then on 3 April an even more remarkable manifestation occurred. After administering the Lord's Supper, Joseph and Oliver Cowdery, at that time his chief elders, mounted their pulpits. The screens were lowered, and for a while the pair remained invisible to the congregation. When the veils were raised again they were looking upward, lit by a deathly pallor: 'The vail was taken from their minds and the eyes of their understanding were opened,' says the minute dictated by Joseph in his diary:

They saw the Lord standing upon the breastwork of the pulpit before them and under his feet was a paved work of pure gold, in color like amber: his eyes were as a flame of fire, the hair of his head was like pure snow, his countenance shone above the brightness of the sun, and his voice was as the sound of the rushing of great waters, even the voice of Jehova saying: I am the first and the last.

Nor was this everything. After this vision, 'the Heavens were again opened unto them'. They saw Moses, who 'committed to them the keys of the gathering of Israel from the four parts of the Earth and the leading of the ten tribes from the Land of the North'. They saw Elias, who blessed their progeny, and they saw Elijah 'who was taken to heaven without tasting death' (without apparently being aware that these Old Testament prophets were one and the same).

Joseph claimed to have received the Temple's overall dimensions in a revelation: 'Verily I say unto you that it shall be built fifty-five by sixty-five feet in the width thereof, and in the length thereof, in the inner court; and there shall be a lower court, and a higher court, according to the pattern which shall be given unto you hereafter . . . '

The financing of the Kirtland Temple, which cost between $60,000 and $70,000 – equivalent to about ten million dollars in today's values – was made possible by the land speculation which was rampant at that time in the West. Real estate prices rose 800 per cent and more in a year. The Saints enjoyed the bonanza just like everybody else. In Kirtland itself lots that fetched $50 in the early 1830s had jumped to $2,000 by 1836. The city – according to the Mormon press – was 'all activity, all animation' with 'the starting up, as if by magic, of buildings in every direction', buoying up hopes that the 'days of pinching and adversity had passed by, and that the set time of the Lord to favor Zion had come.' The Prophet took the lead in land purchase and other speculations, borrowing massively. The Temple gave him excellent security, despite a $13,000 debt. He borrowed in Painsville, he borrowed in Cleveland, he borrowed in Buffalo, he even borrowed in New York City. He knew the day of reckoning was getting nearer, and that very soon he and his Church would have to liquidate their debts. In July 1836 President Jackson, in order to curb the land speculation, had issued his famous 'specie circular' ordering government agents only to accept payment for public lands in gold and silver. Faced with increasing pressure to settle his creditors, Joseph hit on a brilliant idea: he decided to start a bank.

In November 1836 he and Sidney Rigdon organised the Kirtland Safety Society Bank Company, with a capital stock of 'not less than four million dollars'. Most of the subscriptions to the capital stock was in land lots rated at five to six times their normal value. Joseph and Rigdon had thousands of bank notes printed. When they found out that the Ohio state legislature had refused to grant them a charter, they simply had the prefix 'anti-' stamped on their bank notes in an attempt to observe the letter of the law. For a fortnight, the ruse was a triumphant success. Local debts were paid off. The 'anti-bank' notes circulated freely among the Saints, who were convinced that God was behind the Society, which would become 'the greatest of all institutions on earth'. Doubters – according to several who apostasised later – were shown rows of boxes lining the bank vault, marked with '$1,000'. Each had a top layer of newly-minted fifty-cent silver coins. But all they contained underneath was 'sand, lead, old iron, stone and combustibles'. The story sounds plausibly similar to the box containing the Golden Plates which Emma felt and dusted, but never looked inside.

The crash when it came was more devastating to Mormon prestige than to actual Mormon fortunes: so much of the wealth had been spurious anyway. Joseph was fined $1,000 for operating a bank illegally; and in the next few months he was to face no less than seventeen court actions for debt. But far more serious than the debts, which amounted to about $150,000, was the damage done to Joseph's reputation. Between November 1837 and June 1838 some 300 Kirtland Saints left the church, about fifteen per cent of its membership, as well as a third of the leading officers, including – temporarily – all of the Three Witnesses and four of the Apostles. A dissident faction led by Warren Parrish, who had briefly headed the 'anti-bank' after Joseph and Rigdon resigned, tried to take control of the Temple by force. They did not succeed, but the attempt finally persuaded Joseph to cut his losses and head for Missouri. Parrish's comment to a local newspaper shortly after Joseph and Rigdon's departure was withering in its contempt: 'They lie by revelation, swindle by revelation, cheat and defraud by revelation, run away by revelation, and if they do not mend their ways, I fear that they will at last be damned by revelation!'

Financial fraud apart, the Kirtland period saw an important addition to the Mormon canon in the Book of Abraham. In 1835, two years before the results of Champollion's decyphering of the Egyptian hieroglyphics became available in English, a visitor brought Joseph Smith a number of papyri, one of which Joseph duly translated under 'divine' inspiration. The resulting text purports to be an account of early Israelite history, similar in content to the first two books of Genesis, but including theological and cosmological ideas culled from a contemporary dissertation, Thomas Dick's *Philosophy of a Future State*. The Book of Abraham, eventually published in 1842 along with facsimiles of the papyri, also contains the doctrine barring blacks from the priesthood on account of their descent from Ham and the 'daughter of Egyptus, which in the Chaldean signifies Egypt, which signifies that which is forbidden'. From Ham, said the Lord – speaking through the Book of Abraham, as translated by Joseph Smith Jr – 'sprang that race which preserved the curse in the land . . . ' Joseph's interpretation was first challenged in 1860 by a French traveller, who brought it to the attention of an expert in the Louvre. Later half a dozen leading Egyptologists examined the facsimiles and agreed that they came from ordinary funerary scrolls that said nothing about Israelites, Abraham or cosmology. The discovery of fragments of the original papyri in the 1960s confirmed these earlier appraisals. Three leading Egyptologists – John Wilson, Klaus Bauer and Richard Parker – concluded that the fragment originally reproduced in the Book of Abraham was a 'well-known scene from the Osiris mysteries' contained in Books of the Dead and other funerary texts found in thousands of Egyptian graves. Despite this embarrassing exposé, the text of the Book of Abraham continues to occupy a hallowed place in the Mormon canon alongside the Book of Mormon and Doctrines and Covenants. However, the notorious bar on black converts entering the otherwise universal male priesthood ended in 1974, with a 'revelation' vouchsafed to President Heber J. Kimball.

The controversy over the Book of Abraham lay safely in the future; the problem of polygamy – which began at Kirtland – had much more immediate and direful consequences, leading eventually to Joseph's martyrdom and the migration of his people to the West.

Joseph was a fine-looking man; his charisma was infectious. His revelations, when he took on the prophet's mantle, made him sound formidable and austere, but this only served to increase his approach-ability at other times. Many outside the church testified to his personal charm. Under any circumstances he would have been attractive to women. Within his own community it is probable that many, if not most of the women were in love with him. At the same time the Old Testament had plenty of examples of polygamy (or, to be precise, polygyny – one man with several wives) conducted with the Lord's approval.

Whether polygamy was institutionalised at Kirtland or not is hotly debated by historians. The question hinges in part on what the early Mormons meant by words like 'wife', 'marriage' and 'sealing' (a term used for two kinds of marriage in the Church: to be 'sealed for time' means to be married for life; to be 'sealed for eternity' means the marriage is supposed to continue into the afterlife).

At Kirtland Joseph was discovered *in flagrante* with a nineteen-year-old girl, Fanny Alger, whom Emma Smith had brought in to help in the house. According to one account Emma saw them together in a barn, through a crack in the door. She was furious, and when Fanny became pregnant drove her out of the house. The affair also enraged Oliver Cowdery, whose publicly-voiced criticisms led to his excommunication. Rumours of other affairs began to surface; but whenever Emma complained Joseph would simply 'shut himself up in a room and pray for a revelation . . . state it to her' and eventually bring her around.

None of this means, of course, that Joseph was necessarily fraudulent. In many cultures sexual and spiritual energies are perceived as the same. In North Africa there are holy men to whom husbands and fathers bring wives and daughters in the belief that sex with them will result in blessings. Among contemporary cults or 'new religious movements' it is not unusual for the charismatic leader to take the pick of the females for himself. Why should the woman who believes that a man speaks for God refuse him sexually? If God is life, then so is sex.

Joseph probably understood intuitively that the attraction he held for women, and the attraction he felt for them, derived from the same kind of energy that went into producing the Book of Mormon in seventy-five days. Expressing himself in the biblical language of his culture, he called that energy 'revelation', believing its source to be God. The non-believer will be more inclined to think that this energy came from his own unconscious. What is remarkable is not its sexual character, but that he was able to give it expression and institutionalise it in the puritanical milieu of lower middle-class white Anglo-Saxon Protestants, in mid-nineteenth-century America.

IV

The Holy Family

Behold David and Solomon truly had many wives and concubines, which thing was abominable before me, saith the Lord.

BOOK OF MORMON: JACOB 2:24

I arrived in Carthage on Sunday morning after a gruelling drive across the plains of Indiana and Illinois, which took the better part of a night and a day. It had been an endless, monotonous landscape of browning fields and telephone lines, relieved by the occasional giant silo that shimmered in the heat like some distant cathedral. There were no animals in sight, and the only humans were solitary males in checked shirts and baseball caps, hunched over the steering wheels of passing trucks. All the interest was in the sky, where the forces of nature were battling it out in thunderstorms that produced sudden, uncanny gusts of wind and hailstones the size of walnuts.

At nine in the morning Carthage was silent, neat and apparently dead. With its trimmed lawns and aura of respectability, it looked a desperate enough place for anyone under sixty-five. It was the last place you would associate with martyrdom, and the scenes of mayhem that led up to the death of the Mormon prophet and his brother.

The killing of Joseph and Hyrum was a tragedy of classical proportions. The Furies of prejudice – the irrational hatred of the mob, compounded by Governor Ford's Pilate-like complicity – played their part as agents of destiny. But it was Joseph's own hubris – his persistent womanising rationalised into a theological system – that really brought down the vengeful deities on his head.

After their expulsion from Missouri by the anti-Mormon governor, Lilburn Boggs, the saints had settled at Nauvoo on a bend in the Mississippi half-way up the Illinois shore, opposite the confluence of the Des Moines river. When Joseph arrived there in 1839, he found a wilderness covered with trees and bushes 'much of it so wet that it was with the utmost difficulty a footman could get through, and totally impossible for teams'. Within five years, by dint of the industriousness for which they became proverbial, the Mormons had drained the marshes and made it into a flourishing city of 12,000, which rivalled Chicago in prosperity.

Joseph was absolute ruler of this thriving domain, which was virtually an independent city-state within the state of Illinois. (There is even evidence that he had himself secretly crowned.) The charters he had obtained from an absent-minded state legislature almost guaranteed immunity from the law, since no Nauvoo citizen could be arrested without approval of the Mormon-controlled city council. The Nauvoo Legion, the city's 2,000 strong militia, became the largest military force in the state and was not subject to state military law. As Prophet, Seer and Revelator, the town's largest individual proprietor, owner of the hotel and store, Treasurer and Trustee-in-Trust for the Church, sometimes Mayor of Nauvoo and Lieutenant-General of the Nauvoo. Legion (a title he liked to celebrate by wearing a magnificent blue and white uniform) Joseph had concentrated a formidable amount of power in his hands.

As converts flooded into Nauvoo, mainly from England, non-Mormons became increasingly alarmed. The city state's legal privileges afforded a haven for pirates and renegades, who attacked non-Mormons and stole their stock with impunity; the Mormons attacked democracy by voting *en bloc* and maintaining a theocratic form of government that violated the principle of separation between church and state. Anti-Mormonism in Illinois was fuelled by ignorance and prejudice; but it was rooted in a genuine fear of despotism. To a great extent this fear was not justified: much of Joseph's behaviour was quixotic, an elaborate game of make-believe which he himself did not take too seriously. In general, he did not systematically abuse his power – unless one excepts the uses to which he put his prophetic role in obtaining sexual favours. As with other cult leaders, sex became the instrument which Joseph used to bind his followers to him. It also proved the weapon with which his enemies were able to destroy him.

Of the sixty-odd women to whom Joseph was 'sealed' during his lifetime, the account of one of them, Lucy Walker, has a special ring of authenticity. Lucy was sixteen when, following the death of her mother, she came to live with Joseph and Emma Smith, along with her two brothers. She helped with the housework, and attended school with the Smith children. 'In the year 1842,' she wrote many years later,

> President Joseph Smith sought an interview with me and said: 'I have a message for you. I have been commanded of God to take another wife, and you are the woman.' My astonishment knew no bounds. This was indeed a thunderbolt to me. He asked me if I believed him to be the Prophet of God. 'Most assuredly I do,' I replied. He fully explained to me the principle of plural or celestial marriage. Said this principle was again to be restored for the benefit of the human family. That it would prove an everlasting blessing to my father's house, and form a chain that could never be broken, worlds without end.

Joseph told Lucy that if she prayed hard enough she would receive a testimony of the 'correctness' of the principle. At first she thought she had prayed sincerely, 'but was so unwilling to consider the matter favourably that I fear I did not ask in faith for light . . . ' The Prophet saw how unhappy she was, and arranged another interview. This time he explained that though, for the present, he would not be able to acknowledge her as his wife, the time was near when they would cross the Rocky Mountains, and she would be fully acknowledged and honoured. He gave her until the following day to make her decision, and he added this warning: 'If you reject this message the gate will be closed forever against you.' Lucy continued to resist:

> For a few moments I stood fearless before him, and looked him in the eye. I felt at this moment that I was called to place myself upon the altar a living sacrifice – perhaps to brook the world in disgrace and incur the displeasure and contempt of my youthful companions . . . I had been speechless, but at last found utterance and said: 'Although you are a Prophet of God you could not induce me to take a step of so great importance, unless I knew that God approved my course. I would rather die . . . ' He walked across the room, returned and stood before me with the most beautiful expression of countenance, and said: 'God Almighty bless you. You shall have a manifestation of the will of God concerning you; a testimony that you can never deny. I will tell you what it shall be. It shall be that joy and peace that you never knew.'

Of course, the Prophet had his way. After another sleepless night of prayer, Lucy's room was 'lighted up by a heavenly influence . . . like the brilliant sun bursting through the darkest cloud'. Her soul was filled with a calm, sweet peace that 'I never knew'. Joseph's charismatic power is easier to describe than explain. It may be the stuff of prophethood, but does not necessarily bear any relationship to morality. Jesus certainly had it; but so apparently did Charles Manson, Jim Jones and L. Ron Hubbard.

Since polygamy at Nauvoo was confined to the inner circle of leaders, rumours about it not only fanned the flames of anti-Mormonism but threatened upheaval within the church.

The most serious exposure came from a wealthy businessman from Canada who had invested in Nauvoo and wanted to bring the Church back to its original apostolic principles. Unlike previous apostates, his group insisted on staying in Nauvoo, and with their own resources set up the press which printed the *Nauvoo Expositor*, an exposé of poly-gamy. Infuriated, Joseph ordered the Legion to destroy the press and burn its offices. His enemies now had a constitutional issue – freedom of the press – to add to the anti-Mormon crusade. The Prophet and the Nauvoo City Council were summoned to Carthage, the county capital, to face charges. They were released on bail of $500 – ten-times the normal bail for the charge – only to be re-arrested on a charge of treason issued by the Missouri governor Lilburn Boggs. (Boggs, the Mormons' most persistent persecutor, was subsequently assassinated – allegedly by Porter Rockwell, Joseph Smith's bodyguard.)

The jail in which Joseph and Hyrum were shot is an unpretentious two-storey house built of sandstone blocks in what is now a residential part of town. It makes an unlikely shrine. For decades after the murderous events of 1844 it was a family dwelling; and though the Utah church bought it around the turn of the century, nothing that has been done to the interior can bring back its former stench and squalor. The curtains are too fresh, the woodwork too polished, the straw mattresses too patently innocent of anything as unhygienic as real blood, sweat or tears.

I joined a party of visitors. They were mostly middle-aged couples, neat, silent and respectful, and without doubt – though I didn't actually ask – Latter-day Saints. Our guide, Sister Ethel, was a gentle brown-eyed creature of about sixty. She delivered her script, which sounded memorised, in a barely audible monotone. Not one of the visitors asked a question. Nor did anyone exhibit emotion beyond mild, polite curiosity as she related the story of Joseph's final hours.

Only Joseph and Hyrum were charged with treason; mindful, perhaps, of the story of Peter, Willard Richards, Joseph's secretary and John Taylor, editor of the *Nauvoo Neighbour* insisted on staying with their master. Sister Ethel took us into the dungeon, a cage of iron bars situated in an upstairs room because there was no cellar. She recalled the fateful kindness of the jailer who, seeing how hot they were in the cage, allowed them into the bedroom next door where there was more ventilation, but less protection from the mob. She described how the mob, ugly with blackened faces, advanced from the woods. One of the guards ran to the town centre to summon help. But the captain of the Carthage Greys, the local militia, who should have protected the prisoners, saw no reason to hurry. He got his 300 men up, made them stand to attention, inspected each of them individually, and stopped them three times on the road.

She showed us into the 'martyr room', where Joseph and Hyrum spent their final hours with John Taylor and Willard Richards. There were wax-work effigies of the four men grouped around the window. Joseph and Hyrum's features were taken from their death masks. If you looked closely enough you could see the bullet wound on the bridge of Hyrum's nose. The clothes were authentic 'period'; for men who had just spent three nights sleeping in them without washing facilities, they looked immaculate, especially John Taylor's white breeches and silk shirt.

Sister Ethel related how twice, at the Prophet's request, John Taylor sang the 'Poor Wayfaring Man of Grief' – a favourite Mormon hymn. After the second time, he turned to the window, and saw the blackened faces. The prisoners heard the men coming up the stairs; they put their shoulders to the door, then Hyrum fell to the ground, shot by a bullet through the door. 'I'm a dead man,' he said. Next to be hit was John Taylor, who tried to draw the fire away from the Prophet by going to the window. He was shot in the leg, but was saved from death by his pocket watch, which preserved the moment forever – 5.16 in the afternoon. Finally the Prophet, seeing the room was unsafe, made for the window: he had one foot on the sill when he was shot twice in the back, causing him to fall out of the window, then twice in the chest by the men outside, before finally hitting the ground. Then the assailants disappeared as silently as they had come. Word had got around that the Nauvoo Legion, Smith's 4,000 strong militia, was coming – which was how Willard Richards got away, while John Taylor, severely wounded, hid under the bed.

All this was related in the same dull dry monotone, as though any expression of feeling might invite the accusation of deviating from strict historical fact. In the end, however, Sister Ethel did permit a discernible bead of moisture to escape from one eye, which she carefully wiped away with a tissue.

'I have been a member of the Church of Jesus Christ of Latter-day Saints all my life,' she mumbled, in a voice that made it sound like a prison sentence, 'and I have never doubted that Joseph Smith was a prophet. But since coming here to Carthage, each time I come into this room, I have this very special feeling . . . And I do know that Joseph Smith is a Prophet of God, that he did restore the Church of Jesus Christ back again, and that here in this room he gave his life as a testimony for his work.'

I left Carthage and drove through sunlit woods down to the Mississippi, about ten miles away. Nauvoo lay a few more miles upstream, beyond the Keokuk dam. The river, which must have been at least a mile across, was both wider and deeper than in Joseph's time, when the Des Moines rapids made navigation impossible for large boats and difficult for small ones. On this still autumn day, with the trees just beginning to turn, it looked sluggish but menacing, like a sleepy alligator.

Joseph had named his city after a Hebrew word meaning 'beautiful plantation'. With its separate one-acre lots, each with a brick house, orchard and garden, it represented an idealised re-creation of the New England village; and, in the classic Puritan tradition, God and Mammon went hand-in-hand. Joseph had had to negotiate some expensive purchases to acquire the necessary land. He devised an ingenious system whereby new converts from the East swapped their properties for Nauvoo lots, with the Church taking the profit. These arrangements made Joseph the largest land speculator in Nauvoo, for which he was often attacked by anti-Mormons; but most of the profits went to paying off the large mortgages acquired by the Church. There were individual and communal land holdings outside the city limits as well; but since agriculture was inadequate to provide for the needs of the thousands of converts who flooded into the new Zion, most of them from England, Joseph persuaded Saints with capital to invest it in industrial projects such as saw mills, flour mills, workshops and tool factories.

Dominating the city on a bluff, with a splendid view of the river, stood the Temple. It had not quite been completed at the time of Joseph's death. The interior was similar to that at Kirtland, with two almost identical meeting-rooms on separate floors. But the exterior was more ostentatious and less elegant. It consisted of a massive box, based on a Greek temple but with pilasters instead of columns, surmounted by an incongruously large triple-tiered Georgian tower. It was here that the secret Masonic-style endowment ceremonies were first performed, which transformed Mormonism from an offshoot of Protestantism into something between a cult, an evangelical church and an initiatory sect.

After more than a century as a ghost town, Nauvoo is now a thriving centre for tourism and religious propaganda. Most of the houses fell down in the years following the Mormon exodus; a number have now been restored by the Utah and Reorganised churches, including the homes of Joseph Smith and Brigham Young, and some of the workshops and public buildings. There is discreet rivalry between the two churches: the Utah church can afford to spend more lavishly, but the Reorganites have the Smith family home and the graves of Joseph, Emma and Hyrum in their custody.

The division between the two leading Mormon churches is similar to the Sunni-Shi'a split in Islam. The Utah Mormons who, like the Sunnis, comprise the vast majority derive their legitimacy from the election of the Prophet's successor – in this case Brigham Young, Smith's colleague, but not a relative. The minority Reorganites – like the Shi'a – hold that leadership is vested in the Prophet's family. Like the split in Islam, the Mormon division can be traced back to the sexual politics of the Prophet's household: in this case to Emma's refusal to accept the legitimacy of polygamy. Insisting that Joseph had designated his son, Joseph III as his successor, Emma refused to leave Nauvoo with Brigham Young in 1847, preferring to bring up her child so he could come to his lawful inheritance as leader of the Church. In due course she fulfilled her sacred trust, though the Reorganized Church which was eventually established in Independence, Missouri, was only a rump, compared to that which flourished in Utah.

After the murder at Carthage the bodies of Joseph and Hyrum were brought back to Nauvoo in rough wooden coffins, covered with foliage to shield them from the heat. After a public lying in state, when the whole of Nauvoo filed past their caskets, Emma had the brothers buried secretly for fear that the bodies might be desecrated. Before her death in 1879 she instructed her sons to bury her in the same spot; in 1928 the three bodies were reburied under a plain marble slab near the Mansion House, with Joseph lying between Emma and Hyrum.

I visited the grave with a group of Utah Saints. They were large and blonde, probably of Scandinavian origin. There were no floral tributes or outward expressions of reverence. Instead, they stood around silently, shuffling their feet, looking more and more uncomfortable as the guide – a sprightly, petite young woman – explained how Emma had remained behind in Nauvoo, along with Mother Lucy Smith, after Brigham's great *hegira* to the west, to guard Joseph III's inheritance. I had the impression that they knew nothing about all this, and were deeply shocked to find the grave of their beloved Prophet in the custody of a rival church; perhaps they did not even know of the Reorganised Church's existence: many Utah Mormons are as ignorant about this most vital fact in their history as Soviet citizens used to be about Trotsky's role in the Bolshevik Revolution.

The tour of the Mansion House was subtly calculated to exacerbate any discomfort they might have felt. The theme was the Holy Family the dining-room table was laid out with cutlery and willow-pattern plates in a nice cosy circle, as if the Smiths were about to come in for supper. Young Joseph III's high chair was prominent: 'That chair was used by three Presidents of the Church,' said the guide casually.

We silently admired the secretaire from Kirtland, the betty lamp ('from the German *bette*, you know') the children took with them to bed; we felt the rope springs on the matrimonial bed; we gawped at the nursery with its assortment of dolls, tin drums and building blocks, even inspected a child's chamber-pot. Everything was calculated to reinforce the idea of a happy, healthy, loving nuclear household where Joseph, temporarily freed from the burdens of prophethood and cares of office, could relax in the warmth of his family and dandle his children – especially the dauphin, young Joseph III. It could not have been done better if Emma had arranged it herself.

History tells a different story. Although Emma was forced to live with her husband's 'plural marriages', she did everything she could to undermine them and would never admit, to the end of her life, that the doctrine was true. The Mansion House was a domestic nightmare. When she discovered that Joseph had married Eliza Snow, the young versifier who was one of her closest friends, she attacked Eliza with a broomstick (or threw her down the stairs, or out of the house, according to various accounts) causing Eliza to lose Joseph's child. But then, accepting the inevitable, she embarked on a programme of damage limitation: Joseph could have his wives, but she must choose them herself.

Emma picked two pairs of sisters who were living under her roof: Emily and Eliza Partridge, daughters of a prosperous Mormon bishop, and Maria and Sarah Lawrence, two young Canadian heiresses who had become Joseph's wards. Joseph had already married the Partridges, but did not want Emma to know, so they went through the 'sealing' ceremony a second time, with Emma as witness. According to Lucy Walker, Emma was fully aware that Joseph associated with these girls 'as wives within all the meaning of all that word implies. This [was] proved by the fact that she herself, on several occasions, kept guard at the door to prevent disinterested persons from intruding, when these ladies were in the house.'

Emma's grudging acquiescence, however, did not make life any easier for the girls. According to Emily – who would later become a wife of Brigham Young – Emma became 'our bitter enemy. We remained in the family several months after this, but things went from bad to worse until we were obliged to leave the house and find another home.'

In the nature of things, polygamy couldn't be kept secret. The families of girls who became pregnant with Joseph's children – there appear to have been at least four of them – had to be informed of the mysteries of celestial marriage. None of these children was ever formally acknowledged as the Prophet's. They were absorbed into families that went to Utah, which suggests that the women concerned were less proud of their association than some of them would claim in later years. No doubt Emma's resistance added to the general atmosphere of shame and furtiveness that surrounded the question. In July 1843 Joseph tried his strongest card. He announced the revelation inaugurating the 'new and everlasting covenant of marriage' which authorised polygyny in its most uncompromising, biblical form: '. . . if any man espouse a virgin, and desire to espouse another, and the first give her consent, and if he espouse the second, and they are virgins, and have vowed to no other man, then is he justified; he cannot commit adultery for they are given unto him; for he cannot commit adultery with what belongeth unto him and to no one else.'

In one paragraph, the Lord addressed Emma directly: 'And I command mine handmaid, Emma Smith, to abide and cleave unto my servant Joseph, and to none else. But if she will not abide this commandment she shall be destroyed, saith the Lord; for I am the Lord thy God, and will destroy her if she abide not in my law.'

Emma was not impressed. She teased and badgered Joseph so much that he allowed her to burn the text of the revelation – though not, evidently, before other copies had been made. To the end of her life she insisted that the revelation on polygamy did not come from God, though she continued, illogically, to believe that her husband was a prophet. For the benefit of her sons, especially Joseph III, she maintained the fiction that it was Brigham Young, not Joseph, who introduced the abominable practice of polygamy:

a position which, with minor modifications, the Reorganised Church holds to this day.

Joseph Smith was much more than the leader of a personality cult. With his highly creative imagination he was able to elaborate his own sexual promptings into a sophisticated theological system. To begin with, there were Old Testament rationalisations: Hebrew prophets, from Abraham to Solomon, had a plurality of wives with the Lord's approval. Therefore polygamy was permissible under the 'restoration' of the ancient order of things. Added to this there were practical, emotional, realities. Many people in Nauvoo, of both sexes, were widowed or separated from their spouses. The Apostles went on lengthy missions to England, leaving 'grass widows' at home; others had lost spouses permanently, through death or disease; others still had converted singly, having deserted or been left by spouses. There is evidence that in the early stages of 'plural marriage' Joseph had sexual relations with at least nine women who remained married to their husbands, though polyandry as such was never sanctioned. Then there was the problem of widowhood and remarriage – always a worry to those who believe in a personal afterlife. To which of one's spouses will one be married in the next world? This was of particular concern to Hyrum Smith and to Apostle Parley Pratt, both of whom had lost wives to whom they had been devoted, and remarried. Joseph told them not to worry. Provided the proper Temple ceremonies were observed, they could each have both of their wives in heaven.

Ad hoc answers, however, were not enough for someone of Joseph's intelligence. He had to work things out systematically. Heaven was already on the way at Nauvoo, in preparation for the millennium. The old contracts of marriage, whether single or polygamous, were in any case out of date since they were contracted during the Great Apostasy, before the True Church under Joseph's leadership had been restored. About 1842, when the new Masonic-style Temple ordinances were being introduced, the Saints were given to understand that their existing marriages were invalid, and that it was a sin for incompatible couples 'to live together and raise or beget children in alienation from each other'.

A new, more perfect order was coming into being. Celestial marriage not only allowed a plurality of wives: it was at the heart of a system that bound living and dead in a single continuum stretching from the here-and-now to eternity. The Saints were encouraged to baptise their dead relatives, using proxies, as well as to marry dead spouses if necessary, to guarantee them eternal life.

Spirit and matter were substantially the same in Joseph's new theology: 'All spirit is matter, but it is more fine and pure, and can only be discerned by purer eyes.' The notion sharply reduced the distance between God and man. 'God,' pronounced Joseph in one of his revelations, 'has a body of flesh and bones as tangible as a man's.' This extreme anthropomorphism led to the most radical of all Joseph's teachings: the idea of progressive 'godhood'. Man, by following the ordinances, could eventually become God. The Apostle Lorenzo Snow summarised this doctrine in a well-known aphorism: 'As man is, God once was; as God is, man may become.' To achieve godhood a man must marry for 'time and eternity'; those who only married for 'time', without the full Temple ordinances, would have their marriages dissolved at death. In heaven they would be reduced to a class of 'ministering angels', to wait upon the more fortunate ones who had entered the state of celestial marriage. And just as those who had been 'sealed for eternity' with one person could climb on the ladder of eventual godhood, so those who entered into plural marriage in this life and the next would have the process accelerated. Like Abraham, their substance would be increased by children, grandchildren, great-grandchildren down to the umpteenth generation, till their seed was as plentiful as the sands on the sea shore.

As a vision it was stern, patriarchal, authoritarian, expansionist and highly materialistic. Culturally it harked back to the Puritan past – with its emphasis on family, order, social discipline and civic virtue, tied to the notion of a chosen people making their destiny manifest under covenant with God. But there was no Calvinism in this theology, no insistence that the enormous gulf between God and His creatures could only be bridged by the workings of divine grace. Mormonism was strictly, radically perfectionist, dedicated to material advancement and the attainment of collectivist social ideal. Like Marxist-Leninism it combined collectivism (the People of Israel = the Working Class) with a hierarchical, authoritarian structure (the Higher Priesthood = the Communist Party) in a manner that ran directly counter to the individualistic American Way. This was instantly perceived by its enemies, whose hatred of Mormonism acquired the same virulence that socialism excites among so many Americans today.

Yet it was also quintessentially American. The Book of Mormon had been a religious Declaration of Independence, combining the idea of biblical legitimacy with a scenario of events, past and future, that linked the Gospel message with the American continent and its peoples. Not only did Christ visit America: the People to whom He had manifested Himself in the New World were capable of becoming gods, recreating the world in their image. Not only had they ceased to be religious colonials; they could now aspire to the godhead, appropriating His power for themselves.

The home of Brigham Young was about half a mile from the Mansion House, at the other end of the settlement. It is a small, ramshackle construction of brick, more homely and less elegant than the Mansion House. Brigham built it himself in 1843 for his wife Mary Ann and five of their seven children, adding bits as the need arose and money became available. The main downstairs room has an open hearth with black pots and kettles, like an English farmhouse kitchen. The rustic image it presents contrasts strikingly with a painting of the Youngs done in 1843, where the family and their lap dogs are shown in a semi-formal, bourgeois group against a palatial background with pleasing sunlit avenues.

At the time when this picture of complacent Victorian domesticity was made, Brigham had already married – with Mary Ann's agreement – his first plural wife: Lucy Ann, a widow who lived a few blocks away. His initial sense of horror over the new and everlasting order of marriage seems to have disappeared remarkably quickly. By the time he left Nauvoo he had married eleven women, in addition to Mary Ann. Two of them had already given him children; altogether the plural wives he married in Nauvoo would provide him with forty-two of his fifty-seven progeny. None of this, of course, was mentioned by the tour guide, a frail-looking Sister with a quavering, almost inaudible, voice. But she did quote a remark of Brigham's which somewhat modifies the conventional idea of the stern, puritanical bewhiskered patriarch: 'To sleep in our beds, that is the height of joy. But the next is to sleep with a babe in arms.'

A photograph of Brigham, dating from the early 1840s, reveals more of his personality than the official portraits. Clean-shaven in a top hat, frock coat and carrying a cane, he wears his stock at a raffish angle beneath a thin, determined mouth, a handsome, regular nose and eyes that still shine through the old scratched negative as brilliant, appraising and shrewd. It is the face of a man who knows very well what he wants, and how to get it; it belies the idea that he embarked on plural marriage solely out of a sense of religious duty. Where Joseph seems to have stumbled into polygamy as a result of his susceptibility to female charms, through an understandable weakness for women who found him irresistible, Brigham saw immediately that plural marriage gave him power, binding his community with ties of kinship and making apostasy difficult, especially for women. Once they were tied to the leaders of the church in polygamous unions, and had children by them, the women had nowhere else to go. By entering into unorthodox sexual relations, they cut themselves off for ever from 'respectable' society.

No love was lost between Emma Smith and Brigham Young. When Joseph and Hyrum were murdered Brigham, the senior Apostle was, like most of the Twelve, abroad on mission. On his return he immediately immersed himself in the manoeuvres that were to make him President of the Church. For more than a month he was too 'busy' to call on the Prophet's widow. The differences between them were both personal and political. He knew that her fierce opposition to polygamy had almost persuaded Joseph to abandon the practice. This would have been even more disastrous than its original adoption, calling into the question Joseph's pretensions to Prophethood. He blamed her for persuading Joseph and Hyrum to give themselves up to the law. If the Apostles had been there, he argued, this would never have been allowed to happen.

In the struggle over the succession, Emma put her weight behind Sidney Rigdon, Joseph's senior counsellor in the First Presidency, and William Marks, President of the Nauvoo Stake (parish) both of whom were fiercely opposed to polygamy. Rigdon, who had been in Pittsburgh, claimed that he had received a 'revelation' on the day of Joseph's death appointing him 'guardian' of the Church. Brigham represented this as a kind of sacrilege. Playing on the Saints' sense of insecurity and despair after the assassinations, he argued that leadership must be vested in the Twelve collectively. At first, he was careful not to push himself forward as caliph or Prophet's successor: 'No man or set of men,' he said, 'can get between Joseph and the Twelve in this world or in the world to come.' But when he addressed an open-air meeting of 5,000 people, Brigham, who was an able mimic and delighted in theatre, spoke with the accent and mannerisms of Joseph himself, to such effect that many of the Saints present thought they saw the prophet's mantle fall upon him. Wilford Woodruff, a future President of the Church, later recorded that 'If I had not seen him with my own eyes, there is no one that could have convinced me that it was not Joseph Smith.'

Caliphs often have more power than prophets, as charisma routinised and rendered predictable acquires the regularity of law. Brigham was greatly helped in his consolidation of power by the gentiles, who forced Nauvoo to become what it had never quite been in Joseph's day, a full-blooded theocracy. Joseph's secular authority had derived, not from prophethood, but from the Nauvoo Charter. In January 1845, against Governor Ford's advice, the Illinois legislature revoked the Nauvoo charter, leaving the city without a legal government. Rather than let anarchy take over, Brigham adapted the machinery of the church to rule the city. The priesthood of believers became a self-governing republic, with lay bishops responsible for law and order in their wards, and deacons as watchmen. This only served to further inflame the feelings of those who had hoped that the removal of the Charter would lead to Mormon dispersion. As the pressure mounted, attacks on Mormons in outlying districts grew more severe. Governor Ford advised the Saints to head west, beyond the boundaries of the United States.

The idea was not new. Before his death Joseph, who knew that the Saints would never be allowed to practise polygamy openly in Illinois, had considered migrations to Texas, Vancouver Island, California and the Great Basin in the Rocky Mountains. In the winter of 1845 Brigham and the majority of the Twelve settled on the last of these possibilities as being the one most likely to guarantee independence from other settlers. Like California, the territory was part of Mexico; but unlike California, it was empty and beyond the reach of government.

Brigham made his preparations with military precision. He announced that the Saints would be leaving in the spring of 1846, when there would be enough grass on the prairies to feed the cattle and ox teams. As an earnest of their intentions, the Saints stopped sowing winter wheat. Every family was put to work to make the 2,000 wagons that would be needed for the journey.

At the Nauvoo blacksmith's shop, which has now been restored, they show you how it was done. A cheerful old man in a straw hat and bright yellow shirt, with the craggy face of a German peasant, wielded adzes and bellows, hammers and lathes with missionary vigour, talking the while to a group of us who sat on schoolroom benches. His body was lean and wiry and tense with energy as he darted about the workshop, showing how everything worked.

'Now we all know you can't have a wagon without wheels,' he said. 'In 1845 it took a skilled wheelwright approximately forty hours to make each wheel, and they just didn't have enough wheelwrights in Nauvoo to make all them wheels in time.'

I took out my pocket calculator. What he said must be true. Even with 100 wheelwrights working an eighty-hour week it would have taken nearly a year to make all those wagon wheels. Then there was the problem of finding seasoned hardwood. It takes years for fresh-cut timber to harden sufficiently to prevent warping. So they cut fresh hardwood, boiled it in salt water, and took it to the brick-kilns to be dried – inventing, in effect, a brand-new process. Then they sent the sections to be roughly fashioned by the men, women and children in their homes, before being finished and assembled in the workshops. As with the wheels, so with the shafts, the bodies and coverings.

In the winter of 1845–6 the cottages of Nauvoo barely slept for the ringing of hammers and the rasping of saws and the chatter of candle-lit women sewing leather and sailcloth with restless, competent hands. It was a mighty communal effort, enlisting the skills and devotion of the whole society. Brigham's practical spirit reigned in the workshop. Joseph would have been out of place there. Yet they made a perfect combination, one that was truly American: Joseph, the magician, conjured visions out of the air, allowing his people to dream dreams and seek out their fantasies; Brigham, the iron-willed administrator and practical entrepreneur, created the organisation that enabled them to realise their dreams in the world. It was Moses and Joshua, Hollywood and Henry Ford.

Before leaving Nauvoo I drove up the hill to the site of the Temple, now an open square which doubles as a public garden. Within months of the Mormon exodus it was burned down by an arsonist. A severe thunderstorm, perhaps expressing divine displeasure at the arcane uses to which the building had been put, did the rest. For the Saints, however, it had served an essential purpose during its short career. Only in the Temple could the endowments be performed which would make them a saved and covenanted people; without them, their departure from Nauvoo would have been ignominious flight.

As thousands of the faithful flocked into the city to receive the keys of salvation from the Twelve, Brigham became impatient: the attacks on Mormons in outlying areas increased, fuelled by gentile suspicions that the influx of newcomers meant the Mormons intended to stay. In the end Brigham decided to leave earlier than announced, without waiting for the 'grass to grow and the water to run'. There were rumours that the Twelve were about to be arrested. Lynch mobs were gathering, daubing themselves like Indians. The priests worked overtime, baptising, sealing, washing, and anointing the living and dead. Even before this essential 'Temple work' was finally completed, Brigham decided to move. Early in February during an unusually mild spell, the first wagons and their teams were loaded into the flatboats. Then the river unexpectedly froze over, enabling some to cross on foot.

All that remains of the Temple is a group of capitals from the pilasters. They are carved in the shape of sunstones, with strange cyclopean faces which glower at you through unseeing eyes. Back in 1843 a visitor to Nauvoo, Josiah Quincy, was being shown round the uncompleted Temple by the Prophet, when they passed a mason working on one of these enormous grotesques.

'"General Smith," said the man, looking up from his task, 'is this like the face you saw in vision?' 'Very near it,' answered the Prophet, 'except' – this was added with an air of careful connoisseurship that was quite over-powering – "except that the nose is just a thought too broad."'

His tone, wrote Quincy, was 'half-way between jest and earnest . . . which might have been taken for either at the option of the hearer . . . ' That was Joseph Smith all over, and that is how he still remains for posterity. A prophet to his people, a joker – perhaps the greatest in history – to the rest.

V

The Camp of Israel

Although in woods and tents we dwell Shout, shout, O Camp of Israel! No Christian mob on earth can bind Our thoughts, or steal our peace of mind.

ELIZA SNOW

A s I left Nauvoo the shadows were lengthening, making dappled patterns on the lawns of comfortable villas. I crossed the Mississippi at Keokuk, and found myself in country that immediately seemed more wild and less ordered than Illinois. The roads were rougher, the villages less kempt. The gas stations sold fireworks and liquor. With the coming of night, the rain began to pour down in sheets of water so dense that at times I was forced to slow to a walking pace. I wanted to rest but had to press on in order to make a morning appointment in Independence, 250 miles west of Nauvoo. Towns whose lights swam briefly between the windscreen blades – Withers Mill, Monroe City, Lakenan, Clarence, Macon – are still only names on a map. For a hundred miles or more I followed the same eighteen-wheel truck, which forged a path through the wetness at a speed I would never have dared by myself. Eventually I retired exhausted into a picnic area and snatched a few hours fitful sleep before rising at dawn to continue the journey.

Independence, Missouri, is now a suburb of Kansas City. It stands on the bluffs south of the Missouri river, meshed in the grid of freeways and boulevards that surround the downtown area, where the same rectangular geometry is pushed vertically into the sky. Many of its prominent buildings are named after its most famous citizen: in addition to the Harry S. Truman library and Museum, where the presidential bucks have their last resting place, the city has its Harry S. Truman National Historical Site, its Harry S. Truman Sports Complex, and its Harry S. Truman Children's Neurological Center, not to mention the name of its principal street.

Most Independence-dwellers – I suspect – are sublimely indifferent to the Latter-day Saints' belief that their city, near to the original site of the Garden of Eden, will be at the centre of the millennial events announced in the Book of Daniel; that Far West, near Kingston, about forty miles north, is the exact spot where Cain killed Abel; and that a deserted field near the Grand River, a few miles beyond, is the place where Adam blessed his children after his expulsion from Eden, whither he shall return as the Ancient of Days, seated upon a fiery throne, to accept the homage of his people 'with thousand thousands ministering unto him and ten thousand times ten thousand standing before him'.

The Temple Lot in Independence is the most august of the shrines that commemorate these future events: it is the place where the Lord announced to Joseph, in July 1831, that the temple of the city of Zion would be built. At that time Independence was a frontier village, only four years old, consisting of a dozen log cabins, three stores, a school house and a brick courthouse. It was near the centre of the North American continent, on the borders of Indian territory and 250 miles west from St Louis – a journey that usually had to be taken on foot. All roads ended there, except for the deep dark trail leading to Santa Fé, eight hundred miles to the south-west. But it was already a boom town, furnishing supplies for the Santa Fé caravans and providing a market for the Indians who lived on its borders or streamed through the town as they headed towards the plains, displaced by white settlers in the East.

Joseph never built his Temple here in Independence. He merely dedicated the plot of land, which he bought for two dollars an acre. Like the rest of his legacy, the plot is the subject of bitter disputes between his successors, who re-purchased the hallowed ground years after the Missouri expulsions. They now occupy positions in inverse proportion to their wealth or their numbers. The Utah church is marginalised to the fringes of the area, its centre dwarfed by the enormous auditorium which serves as cathedral, temple and world headquarters of the Reorganized Church. But the prime spot, where the Prophet stood at the time of dedication and where, according to my Mormon guide book, the Temple will 'probably' be built when Zion is finally restored, is in the custody of a tiny splinter faction, the Church of Christ Temple Lot.

My appointment at the auditorium had been postponed as the person I was due to meet, the principal of the Temple School, had been unexpectedly summoned by the President, Wallace B. Smith. With an hour to fill I wandered over the grassy patch, about the size of a football field, which makes the Temple Lot, and banged on the door of the Church of Christ. It is a diminutive clapboard building, about the size of a New England village meeting-house, and I expected to find it closed. But after a few minutes a tall, lean, elderly man arrived at the door. He took me into the lower chamber – a room without furniture, with plain, white-washed walls – and showed me the building's *raison d'être*, the Temple foundation stone.

'Is this where the Temple will finally be rebuilt?' I asked stupidly, knowing the answer already.

'It'll be built right here, beginning at the Temple Lot,' he said. 'That's what the Scripture tells us. The Lord's going to do something about it one of these days,' he added, with the resigned but loyal tone of a retainer describing the rarely executed intentions of an absentee landlord. 'He's going to bring about one People, with One Heart and One Mind.'

'Wasn't this also the Garden of Eden?'

His answer came as a shock. 'That's a load of hooey. Wait till I tell you, sir. That story's just pitiful. This supposed to be the Garden of Eden!' He chuckled, spluttered, coughed and lapsed into a chesty wheeze at the sheer absurdity of the idea. 'The Garden of Eden was over on the other side of the world, everyone knows that! Adamondi-Ahman – where they tell you Adam first sacrificed after leaving the Garden of Eden – SHOOT!' He doubled up laughing again.

'But didn't the Prophet Joseph say it . . . ?' I asked tentatively.

'Yes, sir. But he was way off his rocker.'

'You mean, he sometimes said things that were untrue?' I said, stunned at the blasphemy.

'Absolutely, absolutely.'

'But what about the Book of Mormon: do you accept that as holy writ?'

'Oh, yes, sir. Definitely. But that other stuff didn't come in till after the Book of Mormon was printed, even till after they set up the Church.' He showed me an early edition of Joseph's revelations, stabbing at various verses with gnarled, bony fingers to prove that the First Presidency, and other Mormon institutions, were unscriptural. Joseph, Brigham and company had adjusted things to suit their requirements, abandoning the Word of the Lord. The rot went back to Freemasonry. The Book of Mormon condemned it as the work of darkness. Yet they let Masonry, with all its hocus pocus, infiltrate the Church, rotting it from within.

'But surely that doesn't apply to the Reorganized Church,' I said. 'They haven't got any Masonry in their rituals?'

'I know what they're doing.' His voice was quivering with indignation. 'They're doing away with the Book of Mormon. Wallace Smith, he said: Nuts, he don't believe it.'

'He said that in public?'

'Yes, sir. There's been several come in here and said he's told them he don't believe the Book of Mormon.'

I asked which of the two bigger churches threatened him most. It was clearly the RLDS. They had sued the Church of Christ in 1891 and 1893 – he made it sound like yesterday – but his church had won on appeal. Was that, I asked, because the RLDS inherited all property belonging to the Smith family? His voice rose to an even higher pitch on the scale of rage before reciting a litany of briberies, forged documents and other skulduggeries.

'What about the Utah church?' I asked him. 'Do you have any problems with them?'

'The only trouble we've had with them is: "Whadya take for it?"'

'They have tried to buy you out?'

'They were told they could buy the Temple Lot as quickly with a postage stamp as with a billion dollars. We're just custodians for the Lord.'

I thanked him, and left him to rage alone.

Paul Edwards, principal of the Temple School, is widely regarded as the RLDS Church's leading intellectual. He was friendly, about forty, with an honest, open manner. I felt immediately at ease with him. We talked about differences between the RLDS and the Utah Church. The Reorganized Church had a saying: 'Utah has the kingdom, we've got the king.' It brought to mind the anthropological distinction between the cult of the person and the cult of the text: Catholics, Shi'as and Reorganites are person-oriented, Protestants, Sunnis and Utah Mormons are peoples of the book. This, rather than Masonic infiltration, would explain Wallace Smith's alleged disbelief in the Book of Mormon. So long as the RLDS had the Holy Family, they didn't need Joseph's Golden Bible. I steered towards the question, without putting it directly.

'Family legitimacy was crucial up to 1915,' said Paul. 'After that the Reorganization became protestantised. I think it has enough identity now to survive without a Smith at its head.'

Paul went on to elaborate. The Utah people had managed to establish their church without the legitimacy of the Prophet's family, enabling them to expand at an unbelievable rate. Although the RLDS had the Family, they had never managed to establish the same sense of legitimacy for their church. They remained a comparatively small, élitist group of about quarter of a million. Most of them lived in the Independence area, and could trace their membership back two or three generations.

'Our church is an aristocracy,' said Paul. 'We've got the princes and princesses of the blood royal; but we also have a whole range of dukes and duchesses, lords and ladies whose fathers or grandfathers held important positions in the church. So while there's a lot of loyalty to the Smith family, I think there's even more to their predecessors at court. Most of the members of our Joint Council had fathers or grandfathers on the Council; some even go back to the fourth generation. My impression is that the family aristocracy is a much stronger source of allegiance than any particular religious belief. From the theological point of view, most of our people would be quite satisfied with Methodism or Baptism, though their style is probably closer to the Quakers.'

I asked how big a part the Book of Mormon played in the teachings of the Reorganized Church.

'My guess would be that it constitutes less than ten per cent of our scriptural readings. We don't teach it much in our schools. Our people believe *in* it, but they don't believe it. It's important as a symbol.'

'Is it an intellectual encumbrance, then, an obstacle to faith?'

'Well, how would you describe the Book of Mormon?'

'Mark Twain did it better than I could,' I said.

'That's true,' Paul chuckled. 'I think the Book of Mormon is something we've got to live with. It's a story, a myth, who knows what? For most people I know it's got nothing to do with anything. It's the way we explain ourselves. But whenever possible, I avoid bringing it up. If somebody else brings it up I squirm. If somebody wants to know what I think I usually lie.'

How, I asked, could someone like him remain in the Church?

'The Church has some social and I think, in a very small sense, some religious meaning, and I don't want to see it destroyed. I'm a member of the Church despite the Book of Mormon, not because of it. I don't think that's an unusual position for people in the RLDS, but it's totally unacceptable to announce it . . . '

'And Wallace B. Smith: hasn't he announced it?' I asked, thinking of what the Temple Lot elder had said. Paul brushed my question aside.

'. . . it's equally true of the Utah Saints,' he continued. 'Except that their evangelism is much more committed to the Book of Mormon. It's more difficult for them because they have a less élitist organisation. For some of them the Book of Mormon is a positive attraction. The church tells them what to believe, they're not allowed a lot of questions. So you get the impression that the LDS are a bunch of happy, content, people, whose questions have been answered. But if you actually know any Mormons, you know better than that.'

'How do the two churches get on?'

'The Presidents of the Churches don't talk. The two groups of Apostles don't talk. But the rest of us, the division heads like myself who run fairly significant divisions but don't have the power to affect theology, we get along great. We talk all the time, we inter-relate, we exchange information and material. But if you get above that level, or too far below it, our people don't get along. A lot of the Utah Saints don't know we exist. It comes as a great shock to them to discover that a quarter of a million people use the same scripture as they do, but don't think Brigham Young is a prophet.'

On the way out, I looked into the auditorium, where the lights had been switched on. The vast circular conference chamber, with seats for nearly six thousand arranged in concentric segments, was empty. The ceiling lights gleamed like distant stars in the great vaulted dome, the organ pipes glistened in silence, a riot of brilliant fountains turned to ice. Above the platform, a dozen sound reflectors floated like a squadron of flying saucers from a remote galaxy. It was the Celestial Kingdom, as seen through the lens of the 1950s. It brought me back to the *Eagle*, comic of my boyhood. The platform was arranged with chairs, around the circular rostrum. But instead of human dignitaries with grey heads and dark suits, one expected the green-skulled Mekon, with his army of ant-like Treens.

I set off northwards, towards St Joseph. If western Missouri had once been the Garden of Eden, it had gone to seed since the Fall. The fields had a scrubby neglected look, with thistles their principal crop. The fences were broken, which cannot have bothered the farmers much, since the few animals I saw looked far too depressed to escape. The weather was warm and muggy, with a fine, continuous drizzle. The whole lacklustre scene reminded me of damp, twilight evenings in the west of Ireland, where the spirit gets caught in a geophysical oubliette, trapped between the mists and the hills. The only signs of humanity were occasional shacks of corrugated iron and mortuaries of decomposing cars. By the time I reached the turning for Adam-ondi-Ahman it was almost dark, and the drizzle had turned to rain. I abandoned my plan of visiting the Ancient of Days, and headed for Nebraska.

I arrived in Florence, Nebraska – which faces Council Bluffs, Iowa across the Missouri – on a Tuesday morning, after spending the night in an empty apple yard near Nebraska City. The rain had given way to sunshine that sparkled like cider with crisp autumnal gold. The city, now the northernmost suburb of Omaha, is the site of Winter Quarters, where the Saints gathered in 1846-7 before making their great trek to the Rocky Mountains. Apart from the inevitable Visitors' Center, with its relics and replicas, slides and video shows, there is only the cemetery to commemorate the brief but thriving Mormon settlement on what was then a grove by the river in Indian lands.

After their expulsion from Nauvoo, Brigham had wanted to take the Saints straight to the Rocky Mountains, beyond the United States and gentile interference. But the crossing of Iowa had drastically weakened the Saints through malaria, tuberculosis, scurvy and other ills, especially the women and children.

The weather that March and April had been appalling, with almost incessant rain. The teams and wagons became bogged down in the mud, clothes were permanently sodden, children caught colds and died. Between a third and a half of the dead were children under five, many of them less than fifteen months old. The diaries record several births that happened en route. One of Brigham's plural wives, Zina Huntington Jacobs, was delivered of a son, with only one other woman attending her. She named him Chariton after the creek they were camped on. Another woman, according to Eliza Snow, gave birth in a crude hut made from blankets stuck to poles fastened in the ground, with leaky roof made from bark. 'Kind sisters held dishes and caught the water,' she wrote, 'thus protecting the mother and her little darling from a shower-bath on its entrance to the stage of human existence.'

By the late 1850s the railway had reached Iowa City, and Brigham Young, then ensconced in Salt Lake City, hit on the idea of building handcarts so that the rest of the 1400-mile journey could be completed on foot. Many of the migrants came from England and Wales, the fruit of Mormon evangelism in the depressed industrial cities. Converts were offered assisted passages to the Promised Land under the well-organised auspices of the Perpetual Emigration Fund, whose ships were a model of cleanliness and sobriety.

The migrants were the cream of the skilled working class. Most of them had come in search of a better life. Not all conversions were sincere, and Brigham well knew that the migrants must be brought to Zion as quickly as possible if backsliding was to be avoided. They piled their belongings on the carts, which were really flimsy boxes with enormous wagon-style wheels designed to fit the usual five-foot track.

'Fifteen miles a day will bring them through in 70 days, and after they get accustomed to it they will travel 20, 25 and even 30 with all ease . . . The little ones and sick, if there are any, can be carried on the carts, but there will be none sick in a little time after they get started,' wrote Brigham confidently. By now he had had himself elected Prophet, Seer, Revelator and President of the Church: no one was going to tell him the scheme was crazy. But many of those – especially children – who survived the thunderstorms, rattlesnakes, insect bites and other natural hazards, succumbed to ordinary diseases. Influenza, asthma, whooping cough, pleurisy, and malaria swept through the camps, not to mention such local complaints as 'black canker', 'cholera morbus' or the 'American fever'.

The Mormon cemetery is more like a war memorial than a graveyard. Situated on a grassy slope some way above the river, it contains no individual headstones. But the names of some of the 600 or more who died on the Iowa trail are engraved on the monument, a life-size Rodinesque bronze portraying a couple looking tragically into the grave of their child.

Life at Winter Quarters was far from salubrious. Along with carpenter-sized tooth-pincers, heavy metal horse-hobbles, ox-yokes and other instruments of animal or human torture, the Visitors' Center displays a full-size replica of one of the sod-huts used by the Saints at Winter Quarters. Constructed from blocks of prairie grass cut out of the ground and used for both walls and roof, it must have been draughty, dirty and damp, and infested with every kind of vermin, from bugs and fleas to mice and snakes. Despite these obvious privations, contemporaries were impressed by Mormon energy and *joie de vivre*. A gentile sympathiser, Colonel Thomas Kane, who watched them camp in Iowa, described how the wagons

> took their positions in double rows so as to leave a roomy street or passageway between them. The tents were dispersed also in rows at intervals between the wagons. The cattle were in yards outside, the quadrangle inside left

vacant for the sake of ventilation. The streets, covered with leafy arbor work and kept scrupulously clean, formed a shady place to walk. This was a place of exercise for slowly recovering invalids, the daytime home of the infants, the evening promenade of all. From the first formation of the camp all its inhabitants were constantly and laboriously occupied. Many of them were highly educated mechanics and seemed only to need a day's anticipated rest to engage them at the forge, the loom, the turning lathe.

At Winter Quarters they even constructed a water-mill which – after successive reincarnations using coal and electricity – is still in use. Nor was all this work undertaken in a spirit of joyless duty or drudgery. Freed from the fear of gentile oppression, as well as the guilts and conflicts that beset them in Nauvoo, they came into the fullness of life, a happy people who lived for each other. Before their departure from Winter Quarters, the Saints threw a ball for the Mormon Battalion. The party, Kane observed, revealed that they had known better times: their jewellery had been sold, their stockings were darned, their lawn or gingham gowns had faded with washing. But

. . . they did dance! None of your minuets or other mortuary processions of gentles in etiquette, tight shoes and pinching gloves, but . . . French fours, Copenhagen jigs, Virginia reels, and the like forgotten figures executed with the spirit of people too happy to be slow, or bashful or constrained. Light hearts, lithe figures, and light feet, had it their own way from an early hour till after the sun had dipped behind the sharp skyline of the Omaha hills.

'Man is, that he might have joy,' said Joseph.

Nebraska, 'Shallow Waters', takes its beautiful Indian name from the river now called the Platte which flows through a thousand miles of arid grasslands between the Rockies and the Missouri. It must be one of the dullest rivers in the world: for mile upon mile it follows the same miasmic course, choking itself with reeds and willows and cottonwoods, creating tufted islets, shallow lakes and swamps between the low bluffs – around a mile apart – containing its floodwaters. Before the railroads and highways the Platte valley – especially its northern fork – was the major route to the West, presenting travellers for more than 600 miles with a gently graded surface, a constant source of water, timber and food, with no greater obstacle than the occasional swamp or quicksand that could be overcome fairly easily by climbing over the bluffs. But for all its apparent placidity, it had to be treated with respect. Unnavigable except by canoe, its quicksands were dangerous.

The Pioneers were organised, military style, into companies of hundreds, fifties and tens, just like the Children of Israel in the Book of Exodus. Their instructions had come directly from the Lord, as transmitted by Brother Brigham in the only revelation he ever claimed to have received: 'Let each company, with their captains and presidents, decide how many can go next spring; then choose out a sufficient number of able-bodied and expert men, to take teams, seeds, and farming utensils, to go as pioneers to prepare for putting in spring crops . . . '

The Lord continues for a total of forty-two verses, but in a language less grandiloquent, and considerably more to the point, than Brother Joseph's revelations.

In fact, the pioneer party was considerably smaller than the host commanded by revelation. It consisted of 143 men, three women (including one of Brigham's plural wives) and two children. They had with them 72 wagons, 93 horses, 52 mules, 66 oxen, 19 cows, 17 dogs and some chickens. The men included six of the Twelve Apostles, two of Joseph's secretaries, Thomas Bullock and William Clayton, and the legendary Porter Rockwell, Joseph's former bodyguard and alleged assassin of Governor Boggs.

I picked up their trail near Fremont, about forty miles west of Omaha, beyond the Elkhorn river. The seemingly eternal, gently undulating steppe that the pioneers would have seen stretching before them was the same, except that the delicate grasses had been replaced by sturdier corn and soya, now brown and ready for harvesting. The buffalo had gone, driven to the brink of extinction by greedy hunters and sharp-shooting Indians. Instead the evolutionary clock seemed to have been put back. Giant tractors and harvesting machines roamed the fields, gobbling their produce and spewing it out through massive orifices, as if biology had finally given up the ghost and handed the earth back to a race of dinosaurs newly fashioned out of rubber and steel. This impression, of a world taken over by fleshless reptilians, was reinforced by the sloughed-off fragments of tyre that lay coiled by the roadside; while the towering silos that gleamed in the distance had a faintly menacing quality, like bastions of some futurist order run by aliens.

The distance from Fremont to Columbus is about fifty miles, which took me a little more than an hour. The weather was cool, but sunny. A steady breeze was pushing clouds across the sky that were perfect, fleecy and separate, as in a child's painting. The landscape began to seem correspondingly naïf: everything was clearly demarcated from everything else. The monotony of the fields was occasionally interrupted by bungalows with neat lawns and wagon-wheel gates. They drew attention to themselves by the height of their TV aerials and the span of their satellite dishes. Factories and car lots appeared suddenly among the fields, for no very obvious reason. River, road and railway ran on parallel courses, as did the telephone lines, which were mounted on unusually low wooden posts – a precaution, I supposed, against high winds. Like graves in a military cemetery, they marched forever, a cruciform file leading towards a perfectly ordered eternity beyond the horizon.

At Columbus I crossed the Loup River, which joins the Platte from the north. After the long dry summer the river was running low and sluggish between muddy borders. To follow the Pioneers correctly, I should have gone north and west to Genoa and Fullerton: but the country looked all the same, and I doubted if anything would be gained by spending an extra two hours on the road. It was Wednesday, and the Mormon conference in Salt Lake City began on Saturday. There were only three more days travelling, and I wanted to spend what time I could in the mountains where the pioneer track would be more interesting, and harder to find.

Grand Island announced itself with a riotous display of illuminated signs, making its streets seem eternally festive. Most of them advertised fuel or food, without any obvious distinction: Hardees, MacDonalds, Dennys and Burger King mingled promiscuously with Texaco, Getty and Shell, the needs of human and machine accorded equal prominence and served by staff in liveries of similar hue and style. Here in the West the garishness of Lollipopland seemed almost welcome after the loneliness of the prairies. In any case there was nothing of architectural merit – no clapboard churches, Federal-style public buildings or pretty Victorian terraces – to disfigure. The eclectic assemblage of glass and plastic and electricity, so offensive when competing with the now respectable vulgarities of earlier times, were here doing their thing, shamelessly, unobserved by the past. Their excess carried conviction.

Mormon Island, where the Saints used to camp, is now a state park, linked by a bridge to the freeway. I ate my lunch there and strolled around it for an hour, grateful for an opportunity to stretch my legs after so many hours cramped at the wheel. The river was low but swift, its banks littered with rotting branches. The water was creamy blue, producing a whitish scum at the edges – first evidence, perhaps, of the bitter cattle-poisoning alkalis that the Saints encountered further west. The pioneers had cooked and warmed themselves on dried buffalo dung or 'buffalo chips' which, they discovered, made excellent fuel. Soon afterwards they came upon the animals themselves, at first in twos and threes, then in a herd of a hundred or more. Porter Rockwell, Joseph's Smith's bodyguard, led the hunt on horseback. They killed a bull, three cows and six calves. The meat, cooked over the buffalo chips, 'tasted sweet and tender as veal'.

Grand Island is close to the 98th parallel, 'that all-but-mystical line' which Wallace Stegner sees as beginning 'another climate, another flora and fauna, another ecology, another light, another palette, another air, another order of being'. The Saints encountered increasing numbers of snakes and lizards, antelopes and prairie dogs. Clayton complained that the dry wind made him feel 'parched up and feverish'. The prairie grass had become short and curly, like buffalo hair.

Cruising along Highway 80 at a steady 60 m.p.h., I noted few of these changes. The difference in fauna could hardly be inferred from the bits of squashed animals that lay flattened or dismembered on the road. Beef cattle grazed in unfenced contentment along the banks of the river, oblivious of their destiny as T-bones or porterhouse steaks. The trees had all but disappeared, reduced to bushes in the islets made by the river. By the time it got dark, I had reached the city of North Platte. I stopped at a camp site at the edge of town and sniffed the night air. There was a faint, pleasant whiff of cow dung mixed with the sounds of dogs barking in the distance. For a moment I imagined myself on a high plateau somewhere in Asia. The air, the smell, the dryness, the sounds and the brilliant moonlight were the same as I had known in the deserts of the Levant, as was that indefinable sense of freedom one experiences in flat, wide, open spaces.

At North Platte the river divides into two almost symmetrical forks. The southern prong reaches south-west, through the Pawnee grasslands and into central Colorado. The North Platte River stretches north-west into Wyoming, before turning due south at Casper to find its source in the Colorado Rockies near Steamboat Springs. The old Oregon Trail, which ran from Independence to the Pacific, met the North Platte on its south bank at Ash Hollow, thirty miles west of modern Ogallala. Although the buffalo had eaten most of the grass, and the Indians had burned the rest, the Mormon decided against joining the Oregon Trail, preferring to continue separately, making a new trail of their own, along the northern bank. Brigham did not want his Saints contaminated by unnecessary contacts with the gentile companies. Godliness came before fodder.

In the circumstances, he may have been right. The earlier discipline was breaking down. The country was now alive with buffalo. They had to be chased away from the camp so the Mormon stock would not get mixed up with them. Their numbers were uncountable: 50,000, 100,000, even 150,000 are mentioned in the diaries. The brethren were so profligate in slaughtering these animals that Brigham called the captains of tens to his wagon for a serious dressing-down. Some brethren left meat on the ground because it was not hindquarter, he said. Others were complaining because they only got meat from the forelegs. This was not right, because God had commanded them not to waste meat and not to take life unnecessarily. They were wantonly wasting ammunition as well, shooting at everything on sight. Some men would continue firing at a rabbit thirty times. Instead of helping the elders look out for the best road, all they seemed to care about was what they would be getting for breakfast. All this had to stop. They must accept their meat 'as a blessing from God, not as a stink offering from the devil'.

I turned off the highway at Ogallala, taking Route 26 to Scottsbluff. The road was pitted and bump-ridden, evidently due to neglect. I encountered at most a dozen vehicles in a hundred and twenty miles. The river was becoming more shoaly and sandy, a dark green smudge of bushes, reeds and marshes, pushing itself through small lakes and tufted isles in its relentless pilgrimage towards the Mexican Gulf. To the north and west the country was becoming increasingly rugged, with clumps of cedars nestling in shallow canyons and occasional green squares where irrigated fields had been planted with winter crops. In a few fields hay had been cut and stacked in piles that looked warm and inviting, like shaggy teddy bears. The giant silos and mechanised dinosaurs had gone, at least for the present. Small farmsteads, with windbreaks and water-pumps, were the only evidence of human settlement.

Near Ash Hollow I stopped and climbed up Windlass Hill, a notorious spot on the Oregon Trail where the gradient was so steep, according to legend, that a ship's windlass had to be used to steady the wagons. A notice placed by the State Historical Commission spoiled a good story by insisting that it could not be substantiated by any historical or archaeological evidence. However, a small ravine crossed by a footbridge provided real testimony of the difficulties of the Trail. The gorge, too steep to climb down with any hope of getting up again, had been entirely created by wagons, the deep ruts of which were clearly visible under the grass. At the top of the hill the Trail could be clearly seen winding its way towards Missouri, a curving line of dark green against the paler undulations of the prairie.

The Mormon pioneers spotted Ash Hollow, a mile or two upstream beyond Windlass Hill, from the north bank. A handful of the brethren crossed the river by boat to check the place out and test the accuracy of their maps. The current was too strong for the oarsmen, so one of them jumped overboard, and pulled them across with a rope. Satisfied that this was indeed the right place, they gathered wild cherry blossoms and 'rambled about' for a while before returning to camp. I parked the camper by an empty wooden schoolhouse, relic of a later era when the school marms brought such civilisation as was available to the West. I too began rambling about, until I saw a notice announcing that rattlesnakes were common. That kept me rooted to the asphalt.

A few miles further on, the road crossed the river onto the northern, Mormon, shore. Despite the choking rushes and reeds along its banks the current was swift and turbulent. Everything – cattle, river, field and haystack, bluff and prairie – was bathed in the same transcendent light, with angular shadows radiating from a sun that was soon to be extinguished by massive storm clouds building in the west. Ahead of me, the fantastic castle-like formations of Courthouse and Jailhouse rocks – named, I expect, by men with guilty consciences – began to appear beneath the glowering sky. A similar scene in the spring of 1847 sent William Clayton plodding towards ecstasy.

> The scenery . . . was indeed sublime, the sun peering out from under the heavy clouds reflecting long rays upwards which were imitated in the east. The romantic bluffs on the north and the lightning playing in the south-east all tended to fill my mind with pleasant reflections, on the goodness and majesty of the Creator and Governor of the universe, and the beauty of the works of his hands.

But it was the works of man, rather than those of the Lord, that made me ecstatic. Between the road and the river, on a single track, were the longest freight trains I had ever seen. They followed each other from west to east, headlamps blazing, piled with even stacks of coal, or trailing freight cars inscribed with the magic words Union Pacific Railway – a name that conjured up all the excitement I used to feel as a child when being taken to the cinema. The moans of their sirens were as evocative of distant, unspecified yearnings as the curlew cry. Their sheer length was fascinating. I counted fifty-two cars on one train, 115 shorter ones on another.

About twenty miles upriver, Chimney Rock, a solitary limestone pinnacle set on a pyramid-sized mound, shimmered into view. Its height, greatly reduced by lightning and erosion, has diminished in proportion to its usefulness as a landmark. Early travellers estimated the shaft at 500 feet or more; by the 1850s when Burton passed by it was already down to thirty-five feet. Beyond it lay the majestic cliffs of Scott's Bluff, dominating the valley like the castle of a forgotten race of giants. Nature compensates for the lack of antiquities in North America by supplying megalithic ruins of her own. Every traveller on the Trail, like every visitor to Arizona, comments on the architectonic character of the cliffs, the bluffs and the canyons, as though these features can be experienced only as categories of human culture. Perhaps only the Indians who live without folk memories of man-made monuments can appreciate these things as natural objects, invested with spirits of their own.

For the Saints, the dry, high purity of the air, along with an excessive diet of meat, produced a mood of general lightness and euphoria. The tight discipline of earlier days had disappeared completely. Card games, dancing, horseplay, mock trials and wild hunting parties had replaced the solemnities of prayer and constant vigil against private sin and public enemies. Near Scott's Bluff Brigham read the riot act for a second time. In a Sunday sermon he harangued the Saints for succumbing to a 'mean, low, grovelling, covetous, quarrelsome spirit'. 'When I wake in the morning,' he intoned,

> the first thing I hear is some of the brethren jawing each other and quarrelling because a horse has got loose in the night. I have let the brethren dance and fiddle and act the nigger night after night to see what they will do, and what extremes they would go to, if suffered to go as they would . . . Help your teams over mud holes and bad places instead of lounging in your wagons, and that will give you exercise enough without dancing.

Then he solemnly called the High Priests out in front of the wagons, followed by the bishops, and the seventies, and the elders, all of them in their priestly robes and made each rank of the hierarchy swear to turn to the Lord with their hearts, to repent of all their follies, to cease from all their evils, and serve God according to his laws'.

Elders Pratt and Woodruff reinforced the message. Many of the brethren 'were in tears and felt humbled . . . No loud laughter was heard,' noted Clayton, 'no swearing, no quarrelling, no profane language, no hard speeches to man or beast, and it truly seemed as though the cloud had burst and we had emerged into a new element, a new atmosphere and a new society.'

That night I crossed into Wyoming and slept in a park in Torrington. The next morning was laden with sleet, with visibility down to twenty-five yards. I cursed the weather. I had only two days left on the trail, and had been particularly looking forward to this part of the journey. I had planned to trace it along the Sweetwater and over the 7,500-foot South Pass into Utah, crossing the Continental Divide, that imaginary line where streams only yards apart opt for separate destinies in the Atlantic or Pacific.

From what little I could see the country was getting hillier and obviously more difficult. From Guernsey – where the road, like the Mormons, crossed to the south bank of the Platte, joining the Oregon Trail – they had seen their first serious mountain, the 10,000-foot Laramie Peak. The ground got rougher, the bluffs steeper, the corners sharper. A cart overturned, and one of the women got run over (though without being seriously hurt). Brother Heber gave George Billings a wigging for abusing his team. But the fresh mountain air, perfumed with sage and wild mint and alive with birdsong and crickets, entranced William Clayton, reminding him of his native Lancashire.

As I approached Casper, the sleet turned to wet, sludgy snow. The highway, which I had joined near Guernsey, was now laden with jeeps and ranch wagons, cattle trucks and horse carriers. Despite the weather the Wyomingers seemed to be blooming. At a filling station I watched as two young men, dressed in jeans, stetson hats and cowboy boots, reorganised the occupants of a pony truck – a pair of spirited Arabians with delicious curves and sleek well-tended coats. With their snake-hips and hint of devil-may-care arrogance, the minders looked as aristocratic as their charges. The young woman at the till seemed equally brimming in health and good looks. Wyoming was stylish and sexy: forget the mountains – it seemed to be telling me – and watch the people. There was liquor and 'soft' pornography on sale; in the men's room a vending machine offered a whole range of condoms, with notices advertising their powers. 'If she's a moaner,' warned one of them, 'this'll make her a screamer. If she's a screamer, this'll get you arrested.'

Modern Casper was the last crossing of the Platte on the old Mormon Trail. Using their leather boat, the *Revenue Cutter,* the pioneers set up a ferry service, charging gentile passengers $1.50 per load, payable in flour. The empty wagons had to be brought across, one by one, on rafts. The whole operation took three days, with the men standing up to their armpits in icy water. The stock had to be driven across on the hoof. After they had completed the crossing, Brigham left a team to operate the ferry. The revenue would be useful in supplying the other companies that were to follow.

The pioneers found the Sweetwater at Independence Rock, after a fifty-mile trek marred by poisoned, alkaline water, mosquitoes and a shortage of timber for fuel, as well as the harassment of a company of jeering Missourians who stopped them making camp by pretending to be Indians. A huge, domed-shaped outcrop of granite, about a mile in circumference, Independence Rock lies in a flat basin surrounded by mountains, a Kraken half-submerged beneath the sands. For decades it became the custom for pioneers and travellers to paint their names on the rock, using powdered pigments and buffalo glue. It is thought to have been named by William Sublette, leader of the first wagon train to cross the continent, who came upon it on 4 July 1830. By the time the Mormon pioneers reached it several hundred names had already appeared; eventually there would be 40,000 of them. Nearly all have now disappeared, eaten by the lichens that are remorselessly turning the rock into sand.

During a break in the snowstorm I walked up the rock. A notice at its base urged me to trust in Jesus, which seemed a sensible precaution as the granite surface was frozen and it was extremely difficult to get a foothold. The wind seared through my jacket, and I bitterly regretted not having any gloves. On the fissured, craggy surface near the top I took out a penny to scratch my own name, but the granite proved much too hard. For a few moments, the swirling clouds cleared, revealing the snow-sprinkled mountains surrounding the basin. I briefly spotted Devil's Gate, where the Sweetwater cuts a jagged gap in the solid limestone barrier of the Rattlesname Mountains. The roar of the waters funnelling through Devil's Gate could be heard from the pioneer camp; and when the brethren fired their guns, the echoes made them sound like cannon shot.

Back on terra firma, I encountered two young electricians with three vans, one of them on tow. I asked them about doing the South Pass.

'I wouldn't in this weather,' they said. 'Not without a four-wheeler.'

'Any chance of the weather getting better?' I asked.

'Only three kinds of people predict the weather in Wyoming. God, fools and tourists.'

Abandoning the South Pass, I made for Rawlins. It was now snowing again, much harder, and getting dark. After an hour, the snowstorm turned to a blizzard. The fat white flakes bombarded my retinas with light from the headlamps. Great gusts of wind buffeted the camper's sides, making it difficult to hold the road. I slowed to a crawl. Occasionally a truck would appear out of the whiteness and bear down on me at what seemed terrifying speed. I felt like a tiny skiff in a fog, surrounded by unknown ships.

The treacherousness of these mountains was proverbial. Men holed up at Devil's Gate had been reduced to chewing raw hide and pelts for months before being rescued. In November 1856 more than a hundred men, women and children belonging to the handcart companies froze to death in the snows round Devil's Gate. Borne up by Brigham's optimism, they had set out from Florence, Nebraska in August, too late for safety. By the time they had reached the Sweetwater, they were already beyond exhaustion, frozen to the skin having crossed the Platte on foot. Faced with the prospect of several more weeks of struggle through the winter mountains, they threw away their 'excess' clothes and bedding to lighten the load on the handcarts. Many had already drowned in the Platte, or fallen by the wayside to die unburied, meat for the wolves. A rescue mission from Salt Lake arrived too late for more than a quarter of the 800 who originally set out from Florence. Brigham, whose power by now as absolute, blamed his subordinate, Franklin Richards, for the disaster, though he himself was clearly responsible, having thought up the whole idea and grossly underestimated the difficulties.

At last, after what seemed like one of those nightmares one tries to shake off, the lights of Rawlins gleamed feebly into my vision. Never have I been so relieved to see the hoardings announcing a city. I checked into the first motel, and collapsed, exhausted and supperless, into oblivion.

By morning, the blizzard had abated, and the snow had turned to drizzle. As I approached Rock Springs on US 80, the clouds began to break up, revealing tantalising glimpses of a landscape partially wrapped in sinewy mists. The mountains seemed to be constructed out of horizontal layers, like patisseries, with snowy dusting and ragged gaps where geological mouthfuls had been torn away by wind and weather. Bizarrely familiar shapes – elephant legs, dinosaur backs, or great craggy molars – appeared from nowhere, fragments of cosmic scrap strewn around aimlessly by the Creator in a childish tantrum. Human artifacts were similarly surreal. I almost drove off the road watching a train that coiled round a canyon with neither front nor rear, a segmented worm in perpetual motion. The city of Green River flashed past – a dismal collection of huts that looked more like a camp than a town, scattered haphazardly round a shoulder above a jade-green torrent. Then I was on the high plateau again, prairie grass speckled with sage-brush and juniper, an arid empty land with no visible features save a distant oil refinery.

The final descent to the Valley came just after Evanston, across the Utah state line. This was really a frontier: I was entering another country. The outrageous lunar rock formations gave way to real mountains, with classical shapes and vertical slopes. They rose majestically to heights – not peaks – above intimate valleys where sheep grazed contentedly among cottonwoods and willows. The sun suddenly came through its veil of cloud, showering the valley with divine beneficence. I knew I was entering the Kingdom. My excitement was childish and palpable. It was singing in my ears and thumping through my veins.

Actually, this was the Weber, not the Salt Lake Valley, the antechamber, not the temple. The pioneers had entered their promised land by this self-same route, through Echo Canyon. Then they turned right, following the Weber River for a while before taking the trail broken previously by the Donner-Reed party down to the Great Salt Lake.

Brigham, as every Latter-day Saint knows, was not with them, having being struck down by a dose of 'mountain fever' near Fort Bridger. The honour of being the first to enter the valley went to Orson Pratt and his advance party of forty-two. The last part of the journey was the worst, as they had to cross and re-cross the creeks and canyons, fighting their way over boulders and through willows 'thick as porcupine quills'. When they eventually came to the hill whence they could see the whole valley spread beneath them, with the lake shining silver against the dark blue of the Oquirrh Mountains, they stopped and waved their hats in the air and cried 'Hosannah!' three times. The canonised version has upstaged this exclamation with the official – if pedestrian – 'This is the Place!' supposedly uttered by Brigham from his sick bed in Wilford Woodruff's carriage. The original record, in Woodruff's diary, is even more prosaic: 'The President expressed his full satisfaction in the appearance of the valley as a resting place for the Saints and was amply repaid for his journey.'

As for me, I had no desire to leave the enchanted Weber valley during what was left of the day. I turned south, and then made a detour up a small valley to my left that opened to the west and was now filled with evening sun. I passed by small farms with well-drained fields, wooden fences and neat piles of wood. There were Dutch barns and tidy wooden houses, all freshly painted in bright colours, with edges picked out in white. There were horses, ducks and poultry, just as in a book about the country for children. It was reassuringly familiar yet delightfully different. It all seemed essentially European, with Swiss, Dutch, Scandinavian and English overtones. But it was also somehow American, in the old New England, colonial way.

And then, for the first time, I really *believed* in the Saints – not in their bizarre religion, but in what they represented: a collection of European townsfolk and villagers, who arrived in groups, not individually; who came not to escape, but to build.

VI

Unease in Zion

Fear not, little flock, the kingdom is yours until I come. Behold, I come
quickly . . .

DOCTRINES AND COVENANTS

The semi-annual conference of the Church of Jesus Christ of Latter-day
Saints was held in the Tabernacle, the large turtle-shaped assembly
hall next to the Salt Lake City Temple. Like the Kaba at Mecca, the Temple is
the focal point of the city, its *raison d'être* and the centre of its consciousness.
The streets are not numbered conventionally: instead addresses are given
as coordinates with the Temple as zero. 2215 South 1600 East means that
the place you want is number 15 on a street 22 blocks south from Temple
Square on a line 16 blocks to the east. Not being good at geometry, it took
me ages to work this out, and I was constantly late for appointments.

Having time to spare before the opening session, I walked from my hotel
to Temple Square, a distance of about ten blocks. The downtown area of
Salt Lake City is almost unique for an American city. Much of it belongs to
the Church: in addition to the Temple complex and the Church offices and
museums, the Church owns the Hotel Utah – now an office building – and
ZCMI – Zion's Commercial and Mercantile Institution, the city's largest
department store – and several office buildings. The city centre is clean
and well-kept. The almost antiseptic Swiss atmosphere is enhanced by the
bracing altitude of more than 6,000 feet, the pine-clad mountains and the
recorded bird songs – including cuckoos, pigeons, and nightingales – which
accompany the WALK signs at pedestrian crossings to inform the blind that
they may proceed in safety.

The Church office building is a tall modern tower with wings and a
piazza adorned with fountains and statues, right next to the Temple. I
doubt if Brigham would have allowed the tower to dominate the Temple,

staring down, like Big Brother, at its crenellated walls and pinnacles. The relationship between the buildings, however, is not at all inappropriate, since nowadays the Church Corporate is much more powerful than the Church Spiritual. The priests and elders who move sveltely through the carpeted corridors of the Church offices, or glide in and out of its elevators, are primarily executives of a giant, corporate empire, which controls untold investments in uncounted enterprises. The Church owns farm lands and urban properties, not just in Utah, but all over the United States. It controls a dozen radio and TV stations, four insurance companies, a newspaper, clothing mills and department stores, as well as investment portfolios worth billions. The full extent of its income is never divulged; but it is thought that its earnings from tithings – from the 25 to 40 per cent of 'good' Mormons who pay a tenth of their salaries to the Church – runs to almost a billion dollars a year.

The Temple, though not beautiful, is extraordinarily impressive. It admirably reflects the eclectic blend of rationality and atavism that made up Joseph's religion. The meeting halls of Kirtland and Nauvoo are turned inside out. The tiered pulpits of the two priest-hoods are transformed into two triple banks of castellated towers, surmounted by pyramids and encrusted with pinnacles, which soar from Zion to heaven, six quivers aiming at the sky. The body of the building has circular and arched windows alternating on different levels and framed by pilasters that extend above the roof like miniature buttresses. The grey granite walls are decorated with symbols borrowed from Freemasonry: sun-stones, clouds, the north star, earth, bread, clasped hands, bee hives, the all-seeing eye. The effect is a bizarre combination of nineteenth-century gothic and baroque styles.

The ordinances that take place inside are mostly derived from Freemasonry. They are supposed to be kept secret, but have been widely publicised by Mormon apostates who have made careers out of exposing what they regard as the frauds, fictions and falsehoods of the Church. Though only Mormons of good standing with a Temple Recommend are allowed inside, there are also films and photographs which the Church uses in its evangelism.

As the sacred space where the divine encounters the human, the Temple is organised as a progression from earth to heaven. In a chamber below ground level, in 'similitude of the grave', stands the baptismal font, a tank for total immersion supported by twelve sculpted oxen, symbolising the tribes of Israel. This is dedicated mainly to baptisms for the dead, for whom living friends or descendants stand proxy. New converts and children over eight are baptised in the Tabernacle, or in their ward chapels. When postulants for entry into the Temple – known as patrons – arrive they are stripped of their clothes, ritually washed and anointed. They must now put on their secret Temple garments, consisting of a kind of bodystocking stretching from below the neck to above the knee and embroidered with cabbalistic symbols. They are required to wear these garments, which represent the clothing given to Adam when he was found naked in the Garden of Eden, for the rest of their lives.

'Inasmuch as you do not defile [the garment],' the patron is told, 'but are true and faithful to your covenants, it will be a shield and a protection to you against the power of the destroyer until you have finished your work here on earth.' The patrons are given secret names and shown the secret signs and handshakes adopted from the Masons in Nauvoo. They watch a dramatic enactment of the Creation of the world by Elohim, the expulsion of Adam and Eve from paradise, the Atonement, the Apostasy, the Restoration and the Grand Plan of Redemption spearheaded by the Church. The rooms through which they must pass are lavishly decorated with murals depicting the same scenes. The climax is the ritual passing through the Veil and entry into the Celestial Kingdom. The patron is met on the other side of the veil by a Temple Worker. Reaching through the veil, they assume the five postures of Masonic fellowship (foot to foot, knee to knee, breast to breast, hand to back and mouth to ear) while the patron repeats a solemn formula: 'Health in the navel, marrow in the bones, strength in the loins and in the sinews, power in the Priesthood be upon me and upon my posterity through all generations of time throughout all eternity.'

Of all the rooms through which they must pass, the Celestial is the grandest, with thick pile carpets, Second Empire furniture, gilded rococo plaster-work, mirrors and chandeliers. Heaven – as conceived by the saints of Brigham's day – lay somewhere between the Ritz and Ludwig of Bavaria's palace of Chiemsee.

Outside the entrance to the Tabernacle area a young man was handing out leaflets. He was thin and dark with a wispy beard, and a long-suffering air that reminded me of Donatello's John the Baptist. He wasn't having much success with his leaflets. Most of the people ignored him; those who accepted a leaflet took one look and threw it on the ground. I took one and glanced at it. 'Grace plus Works is dead,' it announced, 'being meaningless.' A short tract, peppered with citations from Romans and Galatians, insisted that salvation was a free gift that could not be earned.

'Do you really think you're going to get many converts at a gathering like this?' I asked him.

'I don't know. That's up to God.'

'What about Joseph Smith: what's wrong with his teaching?'

'I honestly and truly believe,' he said, making it sound like a credo, 'that Joseph Smith is burning in hell right this minute.'

Hostility to Mormonism no longer takes the form of lynch mobs: the Church is too powerful to let that happen. But prejudice is still strong among 'born-again' Christians of several denominations. This is surprising, since sectarian intolerance is uncharacteristic of the born-again movement as a whole: rabid anti-Catholicism has long been out of fashion. A great deal of this hostility is fuelled by ex-Mormons who have established various organisations, such as the Utah Lighthouse Ministry and 'Saints Alive', with the sole purpose of attacking the Church and its doctrines. In modern America anti-Mormonism has to wear a theological guise: to attack the Church from a secular or humanistic viewpoint would be to risk the charge of atheism – or even Communism. The pamphlets are unanimous in condemning the Arminianism in Mormon theology – the idea that salvation can be 'earned' through 'works'. Yet both Arminian and Calvinist doctrines can be found co-existing in other churches – for example, among the Baptists – without generating anything like the same amount of controversy.

The underlying reasons are psychological: Mormonism, like Moonieism and other more recently established cults, is a 'high demand' religion, that requires a total commitment from its adherents. It is intimately bound up with a person's social and family ties. To break with the Church, especially in Utah, risks the loss of family, of friends and the whole network of communal ties through which the Saints have their being. Rational scepticism or liberal agnosticism are too negative to supply the ideology for apostates, who will almost certainly have left the Church for complex personal reasons. Only another shibboleth – 'salvation by Grace alone through Jesus Christ', and the new solidarity of anti-Mormon Born-again Believers – can deliver the ex-Mormon from the chains of his or her upbringing.

The Tabernacle was full to capacity. From my seat in the press gallery I observed the crowd of faces below. They were overwhelmingly white male and clean-shaven. All wore suits with sober neckties. Hair was invariably neat, trimmed and businesslike. They looked like a gathering of insurance or banking executives, which many of them probably were. On the raised benches to my left, flanking the mighty Tabernacle organ with its massive pipes and mahogany hats, the famous Tabernacle choir was seated. The men looked like waiters, with tuxedos and clip-on bow ties. The youths among them were young and clean and quiffed, like high-school kids in movies made in the 1950s. The women wore Grecian-style dresses, which concealed a variety of shapes from the matron to the nymphet. Hair-dos were immaculate, with a preponderance of Princess Diana's. A few were strikingly beautiful, though to the gentile unalluring. Their sights would be set on a Temple wedding, Family Home Evening, and a year's supply of food in the cellar.

On the platform, facing the audience, seated in comfortably upholstered chairs, sat the General Authorities – the President and his two counsellors, the Quorum of the Twelve, the First Quorum of the Seventy and the Presiding Bishopric. Many were ancient to the point of incapacity, like the old pre-Gorbachev Politburo. A defensive, almost paranoid tone was set by President Benson in his opening address. The Book of Mormon, he said, that precious gift of God to mankind, of greater value than all the modern industrial and technological revolutions put together, was under attack by the enemies of the Church. They must hold on to it, and let its power flow into their lives. It was the keystone of their testimony: and just as the arch crumbles if the keystone is removed, so would the Church stand or fall with the truthfulness of the Book of Mormon: 'Do eternal consequences rest upon our responses to this book? Yes, either to our blessing or our condemnation. Every Latter-day Saint should make the study of this book a lifetime pursuit. Otherwise he is placing his soul in jeopardy . . . '

Other speakers lectured in laboured metaphors about the importance of family life, the dangers of drugs and alcohol, the evils of child abuse, the virtues of thrift and honest labour. They lauded the devotion of wives and mothers, waxed lyrical about departed grandparents. They lingered over the hardships of their youths on remote farms, and celebrated the joys and sacrifices of missionising. The audience listened attentively, but without much show of emotion. Again and again I was reminded of the old pre-*glasnost* Soviet party congress, where everything was managed and no one spoke out of turn. This was literally true: every address had been submitted and approved beforehand, for we in the press gallery had been presented with advance copies, some of which were clearly marked 'revised'.

At times this docility was comical, as when votes were taken on the re-election of officers or the appointment of new ones. Since God nominates the officers – through the Prophet President – the outcome can hardly be

in doubt. Yet every officer, from the President down, had to be approved
by a vote, expressed in a one hundred per cent show of hands: there was no
visible evidence even of the 1.5 per cent negative vote admitted in Soviet
elections or Middle East plebiscites. Even the Saints in the press gallery –
oblivious of any distinction between their roles as participants and observers,
let their hands shoot up, like Pavlov's dogs, whenever votes were called
for. Burton regarded this peculiar blend of democracy and autocracy as

> the perfection of government. 'It is the universal suffrage of the American
> States, tempered by the despotism of France and Russia . . . Every adult male
> has a vote, and all live under an iron sway. His poor single vote – from which
> even the sting of ballot has been drawn – gratifies the dignity of the man,
> and satisfies him in the autocracy which directs him in the way he should go.
> He thus has all the pleasure of voting, without the danger of injuring himself
> by his vote.

All was not blandness and nostalgia, however. The President's embattled,
Manichean themes recurred in several of the addresses. The Saints were still
engaged in the eternal struggle of good against evil, of the people of Israel
against their gentile enemies. There could be no relaxing of the guard: the
enemy was cunning and ruthless, and would use every trick to weaken and
undermine the faith.

One of the Pavlovian arms in the press gallery belonged to a tall, dark-
suited man in his thirties. He had an open countenance, intelligent yet
guileless, of a kind that one often sees in America, but rarely anywhere else.
Saint first and journalist second, he was representing *Sunstone* magazine, an
intellectual monthly of which he had recently been appointed editor. His
name was Elbert Peck.

At lunch the next day he told me about the Hofmann affair and the famous
salamander letter. Mark Hofmann, a dealer in early Mormon documents,
had persuaded a number of wealthy Mormon businessmen to buy sensitive
papers which they would present to the church where – the assumption was –
they would disappear into the vaults of the First Presidency, safe from prying
eyes. All of these documents turned out to be forgeries. They had included
a letter from Martin Harris to W. W. Phelps which contained an account
of Joseph's finding of the plates, according to which, instead of an angel, a
'spirit' showed Joseph the plates, taking the form of a white salamander.

The whole affair came to light when Hofmann was indicted for murder after a series of explosions in Salt Lake City in 1985, in which Hofmann himself was seriously injured. To pre-empt an exposure that would ruin his career, Hofmann – whose skills evidently extended beyond forgery – had delivered a parcel bomb to the office of the man who had acted as go-between; he was killed while opening his parcel; another was delivered to the go-between's business partner. It was opened by his wife, who was also blown to bits.

Hofmann had evidently intended a third bomb for someone else, but had managed to blow himself up instead. He was now in a wheelchair, awaiting trial. The affair had focused the unwelcome attentions of the national press on the Church and its archives. It also made it necessary for the Church to come clean about magic. The fact that the General Authorities had fallen for Hofmann's forgeries suggested that they now accepted the early accounts of the Smith family's involvement in magic and money-digging, no longer dismissing them as the slanderous inventions of anti-Mormons. Magic became the most fashionable topic for scholarly research at Brigham Young University.

Elbert explained that the *cognoscenti* no longer took Joseph's story of the Golden Plates very seriously. 'He didn't use them to translate in terms of how we think of translation, looking at the characters and recording them in the English language. He looked at the stones in his hat.'

'And the Church now accepts this?'

'It's accepted, but not canonised. The General Authorities don't deny it, but they don't like to talk about it, because it sounds really hokey to the twentieth-century mind . . . Finding stones in the bottom of wells and putting them in hats and looking into them all day long, that sounds just a bit too superstitious for most people. Their concern is to defend the 'weaker Saints' – to use their phrase. So they would rather just stick to the story we have in the official *History of the Church*. Their attitude is "Why are people placing all this emphasis on the environment and the way the Book of Mormon came forth? – when the important thing is to talk about its spiritual message."'

This hardly satisfied my curiosity. No one had been attacking the Book of Mormon's 'spiritual message' – whatever that was – except the anti-Mormon Evangelicals. I doubted if that was what was worrying President Benson either.

The attacks on the Book of Mormon about which he was understandably concerned came from within the scholarly community – from the Mormon and non-Mormon academics who wrote about magic and Masonry; in particular the historians and anthropologists who were bound, from the professional point of view, to have questions not only about the book's origins, but about its claim to be a factual account of pre-Columbian American history. Whereas I could understand how semi-literate people of Joseph's time might have believed his imaginative fantasies about the ancient Americas (and you had only to look at Brigham Young's spelling to know how uneducated they were), there remained the question of how educated, sophisticated modern Americans, people with professional backgrounds and interests, could still accept the Book of Mormon in the late twentieth century, when archaeology and anthropology had totally failed to substantiate any of its claims? My inquiries took me fifty miles south, to Provo, seat of Brigham Young University and intellectual bastion of the faith.

Mormonism tried to defend itself on the basis of four disciplines – history, archaeology, anthropology and textual analysis. The first of my interviewees, who did not want to be mentioned by name, was a distinguished historian. To begin with he was somewhat defensive; but our discussion became warmer and more friendly as it progressed. I began by raising the questions of magic, Masonry, and Indian origins. Every day new material was being published about early nineteenth-century American culture which threw the composition or 'translation' of the Book of Mormon into greater relief (I picked my words cautiously). Was this not making it more and more difficult to sustain the official version, that there was a 1500-year gap between the Book's original composition and its 'discovery' by Joseph Smith?

'I have two comments to make,' said the historian, carefully. 'First, I have never had anything presented that would cause me to lose my faith or abandon the Church. The second is this. Having grown up in non-Mormon country, in another state, separate and apart from Mormon culture, my religious beliefs and my faith have always been separate from my learning. So the faith – the whole thing is a kind of religious narrative, a sacred history – is quite separate from the history I studied in school and that was a part of my life.'

'So you read the Book of Mormon right from the start as 'sacred history', separate and distinct from the kind of history you teach at university?'

'I do. What the Church tells us is sacred history, and somehow it doesn't bother me that what I'm doing down here – the study of people, and places and events – appears different. I don't expect them to merge together. When I was a student I read George Santayana's *Reason and Religion* in which he discusses the difference between myth or sacred history and actual history. He presents the idea that there is a sacred epic for Christians, Muslims and practically every other people . . . '

' . . . like national epics?'

'Exactly. So at an early stage I came to accept the idea that there is a truth which does not rest upon historical narrative, but comes under the heading of faith, belief or religion. Nothing that has come up, in the form of new historical data, has ever bothered me. The story, the way that it's told, is something that's in your heart. When you hear songs sung, or poems read, or see pictures that show these things, whether it's Christian history, or Mormon history, or whatever, it stirs you inside. But it does not affect what you're writing professionally. Protestant, Catholic, Jewish and Muslim historians have found ways of pursuing their work and displaying their integrity while maintaining their faith. Why shouldn't Mormons do the same?'

'It's easier for historians in older traditions,' I said, 'since so much contemporary material has disappeared. The only non-Christian sources about Christian origins are in the writings of Josephus; the Muslims have not had to contend with the equivalent of E. B. Howe, the anti-Mormon polemicist. How can the Church respond to the duty of enshrining, encoding and preserving its foundation myth, while at the same time operating as an institution in the real world? How can it avoid appearing ridiculous when it has to be seen insisting on impossible and incredible ideas?'

'The Church will absolutely insist on preserving certain things. There's Joseph Smith's First Vision, and the visit of the Angel Moroni; the Book of Mormon, however you understand it, and whatever it means, still exists. These things represent the intervention of God, as has happened on a number of occasions, throughout history. They have been preserved in song and drama, in works of art. I don't think our Church has anything to fear. The role of these stories is the same as the Virgin Birth, the Resurrection of Jesus, even the Immaculate Conception, in mainstream Christian tradition.

'Of course the Catholic Church has its periodic skirmishes with theologians and historians, but it emerges just as strong. I don't see any problem, because the so-called myth, the sacred narrative, is preserved in a whole group of things – in poetry, songs, plays, sermons, testimony meetings, family histories. We have our own little skirmishes, of course. Over questions like why did the Saints practise plural marriage? Or what is the exact origin of the Word of Wisdom, which forbids alcohol, tobacco, tea and coffee? Our historians will write about them. Some will take the primitivist view, saying 'Well, the Lord spoke to the people.' Others can say 'Well, it was part of the culture of the time.' And the more studious can say 'That's the way the Lord had it prepared so he could get the people to do what he wanted them to do.'

'I really don't see any problem. *The scholar can be bilingual.* He can speak as a scholar, and he can speak as a member of the Church. That does not mean he's a divided personality; he's just speaking to different people in the languages they understand.'

My next interviewee, an archaeologist, did not need to be asked any questions. His lecture was given with the polished professionalism of one who had done it many times before. It was detailed, technical and delivered with the conviction of a sermon – which, in effect, is what it was. Its language was uncompromisingly monolingual: there was no suggestion here that faith and science must run on separate tracks, to meet only somewhere beyond infinity, like parallel lines in geometry.

It was a sophisticated version of the message in the Visitors' Centers. New discoveries in Mesoamerican studies, deciphered from bark leaf codices, genealogical histories and dynastic records, had produced some remarkable, inexplicable parallels between the civilisations of the Ancient Americas and those of the Near East. Some of these parallels were so striking, and arbitrary, that we had to consider the possibility of transoceanic migrations. Early chronicles, translated by Spanish priests, spoke of a highly civilised people of unusually tall stature who had built great temples and practised a form of monotheism. There were traditions according to which these people had arrived from across the ocean. Even more remarkably, it appeared that they may have come in two groups, separated by hundreds of years. One tradition spoke of a great hurricane and earthquake, followed by an era of internecine wars, in which one of the groups in question had been forced to migrate northwards, abandoning its city.

It might be inconceivable to most people that the Book of Mormon could actually be an authentic historical record of Mesoamerica, but that was the inescapable conclusion compelled by the evidence. They had found in that record, said the archaeologist, a very long and often detailed account of ancient people in this same Mesoamerican area, leading back to the time of the unidentified ancestors of the Toltecs. The location was the same, the time was the same. But parallels and correspondences, however arbitrary, were not in themselves decisive proof. More positive, literary, evidence was needed.

The archaeologist paused, as if for drum rolls. His son, a swarthy, dark youth appeared from the neighbouring room, apparently on cue. He was carrying a large piece of polystyrene carved into bas-relief. The design was a cluttered confusion of animal and human forms of different shapes and sizes, distributed around an eight-branched object that looked like a sea anemone, but was probably a tree, judging from the leaves which sprouted, flame-like, from its branches. The central figures, which seemed to be wearing animal masks, looked as if they were meant to be gods; the human figures resembled gnomes with beards and hats. One of them was seated under an umbrella, held by a foetoid creature that could have been a newt. At the base of the relief were a series of stylised waves which curved round the lower edges, forming a rhythmic pattern of spirals.

'Here,' said the archaeologist, 'is the portrayal by an ancient artist of an episode recorded in the First Book of Nephi, in which the prophet Lehi has a vision of the Tree of Life, and gathers his wife and four sons around him.'

The polystyrene plaque was a miniaturised reproduction of a well-known pre-Mayan carving, the fifth stela at Izapa, on the Pacific coast of Mexico.

'See that young man with the short beard? He's gesticulating and saying something to the others. See? There are the four sons, one of them holding an umbrella, ancient symbol of ancestry in Asia. See that staff there? That turns out to the head of a crocodile in profile. Umbrella = ancestry; crocodile = jaws: that's what the Hebrew name Lehi means. So there we have a name-glyph: a quite remarkable correspondence.'

It all sounded too good to be true, like the theories of those venturesome writers who, also taking their cue from pre-Columbian artifacts, argue that God was an astronaut. Unfortunately no non-Mormon archaeologist subscribes to the theory, widespread among the Saints, that the Izapa Stela represents Lehi's dream of the Tree of Life.

The archaeologist found correspondences where the rest of his profession saw mere coincidences. Spiral patterning, for example, may exist on objects as diverse as a Mycenaean gold ring and a canoe from New Guinea: yet no one claims that the doomed house of Atreus sailed to the Antipodes. But the archaeologist's presentation was a lot more convincing than anything I had seen or heard in the LDS visitors' centres.

The anthropologist wanted to talk about the tree of knowledge, something he did not believe existed in Mormondom.

'You have leaves of knowledge,' he said, 'but the tree isn't there: there's no structure, no experience, no politics. This is a fragmented country. Most people just don't understand the conceptual framework of Mormonism. They only understand the experience, and that experience focuses heavily on obedience. People are more concerned to be obedient than the general authorities are to make them so. If the authorities refuse to give an answer, the people will insist on one. They depend on authority for the psychological organisation of their lives.'

I asked him how he viewed the Book of Mormon. He said that at an early age he had received a spiritual testimony as to its truth. For him the historical authenticity of the Book was beyond question. He could not analyse, or even describe, his experience of testimony: 'It's like the taste of lemon: how can one discuss it?' But he conceded – to my probings – that it was connected with the need for roots.

'Here,' he said, referring I think to America, not just Mormondom, 'there's a lusting for ancestors. I do not myself know about my English, Danish and Swedish ancestors. In their absence I identify with Lehi and Nephi – I know a lot more about them. In any case, my concern is not *whether* the events described in the Book of Mormon took place, but *how*. Assuming that there *was* a migration, assuming that there was an ancient people, the questions are: what kind of people were they? How were they organised? What were their beliefs? What sort of rites did they have? Where did they actually live? Which pieces of territory – given the transport available to them – did they occupy?'

'So is your work science, or textual exegesis?' I asked him'

'This, I guess, is where I wonder what science is,' he replied. 'As scientists we do not invest in activities in which we are not enthusiastically interested. It takes a great exercise in myth-making to maintain that science is an objective activity.'

'Once you get to that position,' I said, 'you may as well choose any myth you like.'

'What do you want? I know from my anthropology that we all live on myths. I cannot imagine people being otherwise. So the issue then is: which set of myths? I have a set which is rewarding to me, which I believe in deeply. I can bear my testimony that God has told me – has communicated with me – that it is true.

'This does not rule out what He – or She – might have said to someone else. But for me, this is my bedrock. The steam-hammer drives piles far enough down into the swamp to fall on what feels like solid ground – for the present. Is my work science? I believe that other scientists, if they are honest, will look at my work and say: yes, that is science in generally the same way that we do it. But it's not Science with a capital 'S'. I don't believe in that.'

The lawyer was courteous and elegantly dressed. He was younger than the others and seemed formidably clever. He belonged to the type of neo-conservative, in manners, ideology and dress, that in Britain is called a 'young fogey': a type I instinctively dislike, and which instinctively dislikes me. Despite this, I found his earnestness winning. His specialty – or rather, obsession – was *chiasmus*, a form of inverted parallelism found in Hebrew and other ancient literatures. Joseph Smith could not have known about chiasmi. Their occurrence in the Book of Mormon was evidence that it could indeed be an ancient Semitic text. The lawyer discoursed on chiasmi with the eloquence that lesser, British, fogeys devote to good Chablis, or other pleasures of the table. Chiasmi were the very stuff of ancient poetry, balanced as Shakespeare sonnets, elegant as Bach fugues. Our meeting turned into a crash course in chiasmus-spotting. He inducted me with nursery rhymes:'

Old King Cole	was	a Merry Old Soul	a Merry Old Soul	Was	He
A	B	C	C	B	A

(ABC CBA)

He made them sound like literary truffles, to be snuffled out by discerning connoisseurs. They nestled among the Ugaritic epics, grew fat on Homer and Lucretius, sprouted in the Psalms:'

Save me / O my God / for thou hast smitten / all my enemy / on the cheekbone'

The teeth / of the wicked / thou hast broken / to Jehovah / the salvation.

(ABCDE EDCBA)

In the Book of Mormon they appeared in profusion,'

'Yes,' I said, determined to be unimpressed. 'Joseph got them straight from King James.'

'In most cases,' said the lawyer, with a hint of pedantry, 'the King James translators avoided the inverted word orders' – a point I was forced to concede in the case of the psalm just quoted. The King James version reads, asymmetrically: 'Save me, O my God: for thou hast smitten all mine enemies upon the cheek bone; thou hast broken the teeth of the ungodly.' (Psalms 3, 7–8)

(ABCDE CEDAB)

'What about Doctrine and Covenants?' I said, knowing that some bright young saboteur had done a thesis on this subject at Brigham Young University. If the Prophet's modern utterances could be shown to sometimes take the chiastic form, that would surely knock on the head the conclusion that the chiasmus-riddled Book of Mormon must be an ancient text of semitic origin.

'There have been some people who have tried to find chiasmus in Doctrine and Covenants,' he said, guardedly. 'I have not been persuaded that the examples I have seen are of the same quality in terms of length, precision, meaning and uniqueness. Take the 36th chapter of Alma. That is a very extensive, elegant, and precise chiastic pattern which manifests a level of artistic achievement you find in something like the Parthenon . . . The chiastic patterns in the Book of Mormon really bring the text alive, enabling its meanings to come out, due to the focusing and contrasting capabilities of this particular structural device.' It sounded less like a truffle-hunt now, more like a sales pitch for a piece of photographic equipment. But his argument impressed me. My scepticism began to wobble.

Later, in the privacy of my hotel, I did some chiasmus spotting on my own. The best of the Book of Mormon chiasmi he had shown me came in Alma 41: 13 and 14.

O, my son, this is not the case: but the meaning of the word *restoration* is to bring back again evil for evil, or carnal for carnal, or devlish for devlish – *good* for that which is good; *righteous* for that which is righteous; *just* for that which is just; *merciful* for that which is merciful.

Therefore, my son, see that you are *merciful* unto your brethren; deal *justly*, judge *righteously*, and do *good* continually; and if ye do all these things then shall ye receive your reward; yea, ye shall have mercy restored unto you again.

(ABCDE EDCBA)

But the great Parthenon chiasmus, which extended over thirty verses of Alma, while it got you from A to N and back again, seemed to leave a lot of spare masonry lying around. Looking for chiasmi became addictive, like crosswords or Scrabble. After an hour or two one began to see chiasmi everywhere, in the newspaper, the phone book, learned sociological texts. Yet there was obviously more to the Book of Mormon than met the eye – at least, the eye unendowed with faith. As the lawyer had said, 'I wouldn't say the Book of Mormon's an open and shut case. We're talking, as always in a court of law, as in any science concerned with human affairs, with *degrees* of certitude, *degrees* of probability. We're not dealing with deductive logic . . . '

Although I remained sceptical, the Mormon intellectuals had been persuasive ambassadors for the faith. Even if one didn't accept their arguments, it became possible to begin to see things from their point of view. Mormonism was more than a book: it was an experience of being in the world, in particular, a way of being American. Other American cultures – Catholics, Episcopalians, Lutherans, even Baptists, held on to a Cross and a Bible forged in another hemisphere in alien contexts.

For all the apparent charlatanry surrounding the origins of Joseph's text, the Mormon prophet had created a mythological edifice that rooted his people in the heart of their own continent – no longer marginal to Europe, but centred on themselves.

It had shifted the locus of mystery that lies buried at the heart of every culture from the crypt at Bethlehem to an undiscovered spot in the heart of the jungles of Mexico or Guatemala. What did it matter if the archaeologists never found Zarahelma? Physical evidences – like the fragments of the True Cross or the *saint prépuce*, with all their fraudulent possibilities – belonged to the literalism of the medieval mind. What mattered was that Zarahelma existed in Mormon hearts, a hidden, sacred region where the soul could take its refuge, protected from the harsh banalities of the world.

Religion is a by-product of human biochemistry that, like other cultures in the organic realm, has the ability to transform or modify the substances upon which it feeds. What Mormondom had created out of the repetitive flights of Joseph's fancy, his improvised romancing, was no less impressive in its way than those much vaster edifices of myth, theology, mystery and drama that Christianity had built out of the bleeding, tortured corpse of its founder. In Provo the quest for truth about Mormon origins became meaningless. The truth was plain enough, in the passion with which the scholars, like early Christian fathers, defended the impossible and then, by trimming its more preposterous edges, gradually negotiated its acceptance in the wider world.

As I walked past the administration building I paused by the lifesize bronze statue of Brigham Young. He would have been proud of the university which has made his name familiar in every American household, less from academic distinction than its famous football team.

In its crisp alpine setting among the Wasatch mountains, the campus belonged to a world that came near perfection. Around the fountain a group of students were sunning themselves. They looked well on the way to becoming the gods their theology told them to be. They were clean, healthy, wholesome and mostly fair. They looked happy and animated, but not quite real, like people in an advertisement for deodorants. If any were suffering from the absence of alcohol, tobacco, sex or caffeine, they did not show it. Brigham's paternal gaze was stern but kind. Happiness, it seemed to say, consists in having life's ordinary temptations placed out of bounds.

I lunched with Rachel Murdoch, a neat, trim blonde from North Carolina who worked for the student newspaper. The canteen strictly upheld the Word of Wisdom: they didn't even serve iced tea. Rachel explained the famous BYU Code of Honor. Before enrolling every student had to sign a statement pledging them to observe a code of dress and behaviour. Shorts and 'riding' jeans were forbidden for women, hair below the collar for men. Alcohol, tobacco, tea, coffee, drugs and sex outside marriage were also forbidden. Most of the students had lived in this way all their lives, so the code did not pose much of a problem for them. But some of the athletes – brought in from outside to bolster the school's reputation – found it tiresome. There had been problems with marijuana: about sixty students had been expelled the previous year.

'Why did you come here?' I asked.

'I grew up in North Carolina, where there aren't many Mormons. I wanted to be in a Mormon college.' She would not admit that she had come to look for a husband, like many Mormon girls from the diaspora. But she ended up marrying all the same. Her husband, who had been on mission in Fiji, was in statistics.

'Are many students married?' I asked.

'About 29 per cent – nearly four times the national average.' I supposed that helped deal with the problem of sex. But did the marriages last?

'There's a bit of a phenomenon,' she said. 'They get married and the wife goes to work, sees the guy through graduate school. Then after he graduates they get divorced – he leaves her, or something like that.'

Perhaps the answer was polygamy. I asked if there were polygamists on campus.

'Anyone who practises polygamy isn't a member of the Church any more,' she said, somewhat primly, as though that were the end of the story.

It wasn't, of course. For the proverbial forty years that the Saints remained in the Great Salt Lake wilderness, plural marriage became institutionalised, although it was only practised by a minority (about twenty per cent.) A whole generation was raised in the system and in turn began rearing polygamous children. The sacrifices polygamy demanded of both men and women were made possible – and justified – by theological principles presumed to have been revealed directly by God. Yet under judicial pressure from the United States expediency took precedence over faith or commitment. The pressure was perhaps severe in the context of American history, but not by standards of religious persecution anywhere else in the world.

In 1882 the Edmunds Act provided severe penalties for polygamy and 'unlawful cohabitation'. Polygamists were liable to fines, five years in prison, and were debarred from jury service, the right to vote or hold public office. Most of the Mormon leaders went 'underground', relying on traditional Mormon solidarity and a network of 'safe houses' to escape the raids of federal marshals. When these measures failed to persuade the Church to give up polygamy, Congress in 1887 passed the Edmunds-Tucker Act which officially dissolved the Church as a legal corporation and required it to forfeit all its property in excess of $50,000. In the face of this threat to its material assets, the Church leadership collapsed. In September 1890 President Wilford Woodruff issued the famous Manifesto, in which he stated that the Church had stopped teaching plural marriage and was not allowing anyone else to enter into the practice. The Manifesto was reluctantly endorsed by the General Conference a few days later.

Church leaders, however, continued to practise polygamy surreptitiously, and ensured that selected members of the priesthood were endowed with the necessary authority to perform polygamous weddings in Mexico, where a number of Mormon colonies had been established to keep plural marriage alive. In 1904, in order to quell rumours that were threatening to unseat a Mormon Senator in Washington, the President of the Church, Joseph Fielding Smith (son of Hyrum and nephew of the Prophet) issued an even more categorical denial of polygamy, and announced that any member of the church continuing the practice would be excommunicated.

This document, known as the Second Manifesto, set the Church on an anti-polygamy course, despite the fact that President Smith himself had actively encouraged plural marriages in the years after the original Manifesto, both as an Apostle and as President. To preserve what he regarded as a sacred institution, Smith had even perjured himself, under oath, before the Senate Committee.

Thereafter the polygamists were progressively cut off, and persecuted, by the Church. Two Apostles, Matthias F. Cowley and John W. Taylor (son of the Carthage survivor and polygamous Church-president) refused to denounce the 'Principle' and were eventually excommunicated. Polygamist groups, claiming legitimacy from Taylor or his father, proliferated in Mexico and Arizona, where state authorities were less liable to prosecute them. With the zeal of converts, official Mormons became ultra-monogamous and ultra-American, adopting a way of life that identified them aggressively with the majoritarian culture they had previously despised and rejected. Yet the theology that had made plural marriage an integral part of Mormonism was never formally abandoned. The line of preexisting spirit-babies waiting in what Joseph had called the Telestial Kingdom continued to rely on the faithful to bring them into the world. A man's exaltation still depended on the number of children he fathered.

With the changing sexual climate of the twentieth century, an ironic situation developed. Only Utah, with its Latter-day Saint majority (around 72 per cent), its Mormon governors, senators and congressmen, persisted in persecuting polygamists.

In the 1930s, 1940s and 1950s the Church instigated and actively co-operated with federal and state raids on polygamous communities – raids which, as in the nineteenth century, fell most harshly on women and children. Fortunately, in the increasingly secular climate of the post-war era, a live and let live attitude developed out of necessity as state authorities became increasingly reluctant to connive what was really an attempt by the Church to exorcise the ghosts of its past. It was difficult to defend the prosecution of one set of citizens for illegal sexual acts committed openly, when adultery, which was still a crime on the statute books of many American states, remained unpunished. In recent years, apart from occasional sackings in sensitive jobs, Utah polygamists have been left in comparative peace. There are said to be between ten and twenty-thousand of them, with a smaller number in the neighbouring states of Idaho, Arizona and Montana.

After discreet enquiries and an expensive evening when I found myself buying dinner for a polygamist and three of his wives – including a mother and daughter – I took the road to Pinesdale, Montana, to meet Owen Allred, leader of one of the polygamous churches, the Apostolic United Brethren. As my visit had been arranged at short notice, I had to drive the 500 miles through part of the night, missing some beautiful country. By the time I had reached the Lemhi range, just west of the Continental Divide in Idaho, it was almost dark, and I could only just make out the shapes of the snow-covered mountains looming out of the mists. The road was one of the emptiest I had ever been on: mile upon mile without a vehicle, except for occasional hunters with slide-on campers and deer-carcasses strapped to their pick-ups.

I camped by the Salmon river and slept to the music of its waters. The morning was brilliant and sunny. The hunters woke me at dawn, punctuating the valleys with the crack of rifles. At Deep Creek, near Gibbonsville, the road crossed the Lewis and Clark trail. The mountains became stonier, the trees thinner. The explorers had had to cut their way through the rocky outcrops and lost several horses on the steep shaly slopes. The area had once been the territory of the Blackfoot Indians; the only visible reminder of their presence was a plastic wigwam with life-size human dummies garbed in chiefly regalia and aimed, I presumed, at some kind of tourist promotion. I wondered what other exterminating nation would celebrate the culture of its victims for commercial ends: would the Third Reich, a hundred years on, have displayed full-size plastic models of rabbis or frock-coated merchants with fur-trimmed hats?

The patriarch received me with suitable *gravitas*. He was a large, handsome granite-hewn man, vigorous for his seventy-two years. He confessed to having forty-three children, twenty-three of them his own. The rest were step-children. I asked him how many women he had been sealed to.

'Enough so I leave my neighbour's wife alone,' he chuckled. 'I will admit that I have a plurality of wives, and they are the most wonderful girls on earth. They are not just women, they are administrators and counsellors. How they do help me with all my responsibilities. I do not know what

I would do without the love and concern of these precious women.' He paused, overcome with gratitude for the female sex.

'You know, there isn't any place in the world where women are more honoured than among our people. I do not have one child,' he added proudly, 'that's revolted against their parents.'

He drove me in a large four-wheeler up a forestry road to have a better look at the kingdom. The houses were distributed randomly among the fields and pine forests. There was a school on two floors that doubled as a meeting-hall, some farm buildings and numerous private dwellings, many of them unfinished. There were several clearings among the trees, where cattle were grazing. Behind us the steep craggy tops of the Bitterroot mountains rose in crests with forests lining their leeward slopes, like hairs on a gorilla's arm.

'We started with three families, twenty-seven years ago. Now there are seventy-six, about 600 people,' he said. 'See through the brush down there' – he pointed like Moses surveying the Promised Land – 'and that fence running up the hill, and those farm buildings, and up there to the county road? That's all our land.'

'Do the cattle belong to your church?'

'The cattle belong to the community. We do not call ourselves a church, but the state does, and so does the Federal Government, and we're even a tax-exempt corporation. AUB: Apostolic United Brethren, or as we sometimes call ourselves, All Us Boys. The cattle man and the schoolteacher are paid out of community funds – they get their expenses and some spending money out of the tithes. But not one of our offices in the religious organisation is paid. I don't receive a dime for all the work I do. All I have is my pension – I was thirty-six years with the American Oil Company in Salt Lake City and I'll say I was treated wonderfully by them.'

We drove back through the village along muddy, unpaved roads. Every once in a while Brother Owen would stop the car and introduce me to a group of people. Most of them were young and enviably healthy. Otherwise they did not look much different from other American children, except that they were extremely polite, and many of the girls wore long dresses. Some were strikingly beautiful.

'I may be prejudiced,' said Brother Owen, picking up my thoughts, 'but I think we've got some of the most beautiful girls in the world. There'll probably be a youth meeting tonight, and it won't make me feel a bit bad when I get a dozen of these lovely young girls putting their arms around me.'

We visited the ward bishop, to pick up a two-way radio set. The house was a bungalow, no bigger than the standard dwelling you find in any American suburb. The bishop lived there with his three wives and eighteen children. None of the wives was visible. But the garden was amok with children, shouting and playing and tripping one up, a human cabbage-patch gone to seed. The bishop – a lean, youngish man, probably under forty – looked utterly overwhelmed.

'How do you all fit in?' I asked.

'We don't,' was all the bishop would say.

Brother Owen waxed indignant against the Utah church and its compromises.

'A lot of Mormons today say they believe in the principle of plural marriage, but that they're not supposed to live it today. Well, if that's the case, the Prophet Joseph is a false prophet. Because he said that the ordinances and principles of the Gospel were restored never to be taken from the earth again. If the modern leaders of the Church say these principles have been taken away, then Joseph Smith was wrong, Brigham Young was wrong, John Taylor was wrong . . . They say: 'Well, plural marriage will come back during the Millennium.' But we say, it takes a mortal being to administer mortal ordinances. Who is going to administer the ordinances when the Millennium comes? We may be a tiny little minority, but we're keeping the Principle alive so as the prophecy can be fulfilled.'

The logic was undeniable. How could the modern church change what Joseph and Brigham had laid down? Joseph's theology had been literal and materialistic: if polygamy were abandoned altogether, not only would his prophecies prove false. The Millennium might never come.

Part Two

The Rim of the World

'Here individuals of all nations are melted into a new race of men whose labours and posterity will one day cause great changes in the world'
HECTOR DE CRÈVECOEUR

VII

Purity and Danger

'And I looked, and, behold, a pale horse: and his name that Sat on him was Death, and Hell followed with him.'

REVELATION 6:8

A map of the USA showing only interstate highways, state and county lines looks like a Christmas stocking pulled unevenly over bulging parcels. East of the Mississippi the mesh is dense and tight: less than one third of the country's geographical area contains almost two-thirds of its states and a similar proportion of counties, while more than one hundred major cities are connected by a dense network of roads. The further west, the fewer the cities and roads, the larger the states and the counties. While the frontier may now officially be 'closed', it is in these geographical and administrative interstices, where the gaps in the mesh are largest, that utopian dreams are still most prone to flourish.

'All Utopian visions,' writes Sacvan Bercovitch, 'pastoral, matriarchal, millennial, whatever – express powerful feelings of social discontent.' In settled polities like Britain or France, they form part of a subculture that may surface in the political mainstream, to be co-opted into the system, whether by evolutionary or revolutionary means. In America, however, the gaps in the geographical and administrative mesh permit utopian projects, however bizarre, to establish themselves as viable organisms, to acquire a tangible reality of their own, or at least a period of independence before being swallowed into the wider culture. Indeed, it is the diversity of lifestyles so engendered that makes the United States so much more fascinating than other societies initiated by Anglo-Saxon settlement, such as Canada or Australia. The deadening effect of homogenisation – the standardisation of roads, the awful sameness of cities (with a few striking exceptions), the identical hamburger purlieus and Lolliplands, the rectangular downtown blocks and the limitless replication of suburban townships – all these are mitigated by the diversity of social landscapes.

The Mormon Zion – after the original Massachusetts commonwealth – was the most impressive and durable of the American utopias; but there were many others as well. The West, between the mountains and the Pacific, was host to a great variety of 'mini-Zions', from fearsome survivalist communities who lived in daily expectation of nuclear armageddon, to free-love communes populated by ex-hippies, devoted to vegetarianism, sunshine, sex and personal growth. The West – particularly California – was to late twentieth-century America what the 'burned-over district' of New York had been to the early nineteenth: a region of rapid urbanisation and population growth, where a second industrial revolution – the shift from manufacturing to high-tech service industry – caused similar social disruptions.

As in the past, traditional churches had difficulty in coping with the speed of change. Church membership, which reached its peak in 1960, began to fall; church attendance, which reached a height of 49 per cent in 1958, had dropped by 1971 to the steady 40 per cent where it remains today. The slack, however, was taken up by the great variety of new religious movements that grew up especially among the young and in the west. According to Melton's authoritative *Encyclopedia of American Religions* (1978) at least 184 new religions were founded during the Sixties, compared with sixty-eight in the previous decade. Like their forbears Americans rebelled, not by trying to overturn the social or religious order, but by rebuilding the world from scratch, by creating new religions and theocracies. Each had its shibboleth, its own special interest. Racism, homosexuality, drugs, detoxification, psychotherapy, yoga, personal growth: attitudes and activities that may occur anywhere acquired in North America an added enthusiasm, a *theological* dimension.

After leaving Pinesdale I drove through the beautiful Bitterroot Valley, where the November mists were clinging to the meadows like spiders' webs caught in the sun. At Missoula I joined the same Interstate 90 that I had left, about 2,000 miles to the east, in northern Ohio. At Lookout Pass the road crosses the Continental Divide and traverses the pleasing pine forests of northern Idaho before skirting the northern tip of Lake Coeur d'Alene, whose mirror-calm waters flawlessly reflected the surrounding mountains.

Coeur d'Alene was a prosperous tourist colony, where expensive new hotels and marinas were pushing out piers and buttresses into the lake. The newspapers were full of stories about the Church of Jesus Christ Christian–Aryan Nations, at Hayden Lake, a few miles to the north, near the Canadian border. Members of the church – a front for the Nazi party and other white supremacist groups – had recently murdered a dozen people, including a Jewish radio announcer in Denver, Colorado, who had been particularly outspoken in his verbal attacks on them.

They had 'declared war' on the US Government, planting bombs in various federal offices. It was only luck – or divine grace – that had saved a local Catholic priest, Father Bill Wassmuth, from a pipe bomb in his porch. A black man – of whom there are very few in northern Idaho – found himself assaulted in a local supermarket for simply being black: his assailant, a member of the Church, had migrated from another part of the country in order to live in what he had been told was a 'whites only' region. The sight of the black man calmly buying his groceries was evidently too much for him, and he set upon the bemused fellow with his fists before being dragged away kicking and screaming by management and police.

'Please don't try and see those people,' my wife Tiggy had pleaded on the telephone, after seeing an article in the *Sunday Times*. 'They're completely crazy. They might shoot you and dump you in the lake.'

The church was situated deep in a pine forest, up a remote dirt road a few miles from the airport. Everything about it reinforced the image of the Nazi party at prayer. The first thing I saw as I drove up the dirt track leading off the road was the flag with its swastika-type emblem; then came a checkpoint complete with sentry-box and barrier and a hand-painted notice saying WHITES ONLY. After passing through the checkpoint, which was open and unmanned, I came to a collection of wooden buildings just like an army camp. One of them, with a small wooden cross above the door, was evidently the chapel; the others were offices and refectories, with tables and benches laid out under the pine trees. Brooding above the whole complex was a grim wooden watch-tower with authentic Auschwitz-style roof. It was more real than a movie set, and it sent a shudder up my back. The fact that it seemed deserted only increased my unease.

I was early for my appointment, and had time to brood on Tiggy's words. As I sat in the camper eating a sandwich, a large German Shepherd wandered over and started sniffing round the doors. A cold panic gripped me: the dog was obviously trained to kill on sight. Party members would be exempted, since he would know them by their smell (beer, sweat and wurst). The polite lady who answered my phone call had said she'd be happy to see me at half-past two: she was obviously a lure, like the witch in *Hansel and Gretel*. My name, which sounds like Reuben, would have alerted her. After being mauled by the dog, I would be subjected to the anatomical examination which would definitely seal my fate.

I got a grip on myself. I must plan a diversionary tactic, like Richard Burton the actor in *Where Eagles Dare*. Not having any fire-crackers, I tried a piece of chocolate, which I threw as far as I could, to lure the animal away – long enough, I hoped, to enable me to sprint the fifty yards to the office. At that moment the Nazis, however inhuman, seemed less menacing than the dog. But the beast, addicted as it obviously was to human flesh, was quite uninterested in chocolate, and continued to guard my egress relentlessly. I was planning my next move – preparing to sacrifice the steak I had bought for supper – when a car drew up. The dog bounded over to inspect this newer, more interesting meal. A very un-Nazi looking man in a raincoat got out and calmly walked to the office, barely noticing the dog, which was by now wagging its tail sociably. Emboldened I followed him, swallowing what was left of my fear.

There were two people in the office, a man and a woman, plus the newcomer I had just seen entering. The woman was a slim well-kempt blonde with a pleasant, quite pretty face, and an air of clerkly efficiency: she might have been a secretary, or perhaps a schoolmistress. The man, who sat at another table, was clean-shaven with short hair and ruddy features. He wore a dark suit, and did not surprise me when he said he was a Mormon. The newcomer, Chris Hansen, was a journalist from Reuters in Washington. I have never been so happy to meet a colleague.

The man, who introduced himself as Richard, did most of the talking. 'I'm not a member of the Aryan Nations,' he said. 'I'm just visiting here doing research on conspiratology. I don't want my name used. I refuse to have my photograph taken. I represent an organisation – the International Conspiratological Association – that strikes at the very heart of the conspirators, and I'm constantly placing myself in jeopardy.'

'Is this association a large body of specialists?' I asked.

'We have interests all over the world.'

'Did you start it yourself?' asked Chris, who obviously knew a paranoid delusion when he saw one.

'Yes, I did.'

'How many people belong to your Association?' I asked for the record, knowing full well what the answer would be.

'I'm not at liberty to tell you . . . Conspiratology is a new concept, using the latest scientific methodology to uncover the international conspiracies in order to warn people of the perils involved.'

Scientific methodology had done nothing to modernise the conspiracy theories. They were the same ones that sent Jews to the gas chamber. International Zionist-Bolshevist capitalists secretly pulled the strings, while the visible rulers, the Gorbachevs, Thatchers and Reagans, danced to their tune. Scratch hard enough, and you will find the Rockefellers and General Motors were all tools of the same Communist-capitalist Jews. The apparent conflict between the superpowers was just a sham to deceive the people, from whom the real truth was being kept by the Jewish-controlled media. The final object of the International Chosen was to make planet earth a vast concentration camp, a world Gulag controlled by the Soviets.

A few embellishments had been added to keep up with events. The Holocaust, of course, had never really happened: all those corpses you saw in the pictures were a vaudeville act put on by Hollywood. Civil rights, affirmative action, immigration and pornography were part of the same scheme aimed at subverting the race. The whites had lost the Eastern seaboard, southern California, the Mid-Western cities and the whole of the South. All that was left was the Teutonic Triangle comprising the north-western states, where whites were still a massive majority. The whites must be indoctrinated with 'mythos', taught proper pride in their race. Then, when they saw what was happening, they would secede, declare the new republic.

Richard denied, predictably, that the Church had anything to do with the murders, the bombings and other terrorist activities reported in the press: that was all part of the media bias against the white supremacists put out by the Jews. If a Mormon happened to machine-gun a dozen people, no one would take the LDS Church to task: yet in this case, just because someone might have worshipped here, the Church was held accountable for their actions.

The woman showed us the chapel. It was a plain meeting hall, with chairs instead of pews. The flags of the white nations were draped above the platform. There were crude paintings and drawings and bits of embroidery, mostly the work of imprisoned comrades, celebrating neo-Nazi themes: St George, dressed as a Teutonic knight, slaying the Jewish-Bolshevist dragon;

heroic young warriors from Valhalla; a portrait of the Führer which, even here, seemed oddly out of place. I had never expected to see Hitler in a church.

With the conspiratologist out of earshot, the woman – her name was Betty Tait – told us about her son, David. He was serving two life sentences in Missouri for killing one state trooper and wounding another. She referred to these murders as an 'accident', as though David had been the victim.

'Why did he shoot?' I asked.

'Because he was stopped,' said Betty. 'He knew the arms he was carrying would not go down well. I believe he was protecting others. If the troopers had been honest with him, the accident needn't have happened. But I feel David is as strong a Christian today, living in the evil prison system, as he was back at home . . .' There was something chilling about this woman, so gentle, polite and pleasant.

I wasn't satisfied with the interview. Richard's presentation, fluent to the point of glibness, did not reveal how Nazism, still the purest manifestation of evil the world has seen, could be sanctified in Christian worship. We had our Nazis in Britain, marginal elements dedicated to racism and violence. But they did not attend church services and had not, so far as I knew, provided themselves with a theology of hate.

I attended the church the next Sunday, after a few days spent camping by the southern shore of Lake Coeur d'Alene. I felt strengthened by my solitary sojourn in the wilderness, with no one for company except the bears who came by night and upset the garbage bins. The place was more beautiful than anywhere I had been outside the west of Ireland. The lake was absolutely flat, reflecting gentle shapes of wooded hills surrounding its shores. The stillness amplified the sounds of the air: you could hear the ducks quacking from half a mile away. In the distance I could see the shadowy St Joe River plying through the lake between banks of cottonwoods. A day in that place, in that light, was worth a thousand sermons.

The congregation was small: about fifteen men and women. They were unpretentiously dressed, in cotton frocks and open shirts. The only uniform belonged to a small boy in battle fatigues. No one was armed, as I had been led to expect from the press. Pastor Butler had hooded eyes and creases that flowed like rivulets down his cheeks. It was the embattled, worn face of a lion that had seen many kills and fought many battles. His delivery was tired and lacked fluency.

He began the service by praying for the brothers in bondage, naming them individually. The congregation remained seated, raising their right arms in the Nazi salute.

I sat alone at the back, to avoid taking part. But after a whispered briefing from one of the ushers, the pastor welcomed me by name. 'We thank Mr Reuben in the last row for coming to our message this day,' he said. Everybody looked round and stared. When it was time for the collection a tall, handsome man with a Zapata mustache came up to me with the tray. When I shook my head he turned on his heel and walked stiffly back to the platform. I was later told that he had just come out of prison, after serving a sentence for murder.

The pastor's 'sermon' was the same message of hate I had heard from Richard, except it was peppered with biblical quotations. The Bible had been revealed exclusively to the white race. It was 'unto that race that the Word and the Law was given', not unto the world. The biblical Jews had sought to crush out all knowledge of the Word in the past, just as they were doing today. The time would come when they would be punished for their arrogance.

'When victory comes, I can tell you this. It's going to be a capital offence to be a live Jew or a race traitor in the Kingdom of God.' I wouldn't say I was shocked, because by now I more or less knew what to expect. But I could not quite believe that I was hearing a warrant for genocide issued from the pulpit.

The wall of separation erected by the Founding Fathers had removed the state's ideological underpinnings, leaving religion to thrive in privileged enclaves, immune from legal control. The result was that any ideology, however hare-brained or evil, could find a protected platform so long as it dressed itself in religious garb. The situation favoured the left as well as the right: progressive churches gave sanctuary to political refugees from Latin American dictatorships.

Here, in Hayden Lake, Nazis could preach the most virulent forms of anti-semitism, unmolested by the law. As long as the message was delivered in the sanctuary of a 'church', the state was powerless to interfere. Later, Pastor Butler and several of his associates would be arrested for terrorist offences. But that did not affect the principle. What they said in church was protected by the Constitution. It was a grotesque abuse of the idea of freedom of conscience. In Britain, where the church had long ceded its privileged position to the state, these people would have been silenced by the civil law, and rightly so. Freedom of speech stops short of incitement to murder.

The rest of Pastor Butler's sermon was devoted to AIDS. Thank God for AIDS, he said. It would punish the Judaised minds of the sodomites for all their vile abominations, their depraved animal acts. The Jews had been laughing to watch so many of the *goyim* reduced to the level of the beasts. AIDS was also punishing the Africans for what they had done to Rhodesia and were now trying to do in South Africa. 'The pestilence will purify,' predicted the pastor.

There came more prayers and another hymn. Afterwards I asked the pastor how he could have fought in World War Two when he so admired Hitler. It did not come up, he said, because he was in the Pacific, fighting the Japanese, an inferior race. And what if he had been sent to Europe? He shrugged: the question was hypothetical.

A wiry little man called Chuck introduced himself and attempted to answer my questions. Surely, I said, Jesus was Jewish. How could they call themselves Christians and be so virulently anti-semitic? He delivered a long rambling, incoherent account of 'Identity' theology. It all went back, it seemed, to Jacob and Esau. Adam was white, Abraham was white, and so was Jacob. Esau had married out of his race, destroying his lineage. The true Hebrews were pure white Aryans. During the Babylonian captivity the Edomites, Esau's bastardised descendants, had infiltrated Jerusalem. Thereafter the Israelites became infected with impure blood. But pockets of racial purity remained, in places like Nazareth. Jesus had come to restore the one true race: that's what the Gospel had all been about . . .

Chuck's discourse concluded with another anti-semitic diatribe. 'Do you start to get the picture?' he said. 'The Jew today is a parasite. To make money, he just has to latch onto the white man. Heard of Einstein, the 'brilliant Jew'? Where do you think he got all his theories from? He was a professor in college. The students who were working for the masters and doctorates had to go through him, show him their papers. He was leaching all that stuff off them. Made himself famous by it. That's typical Jew.'

'Do you know many Jews?' I asked him. 'Have you met many?'

'You meet them everywhere,' he said.

'But how do you know if someone's Jewish? Can you tell just by looking at them?'

'No, you can't,' he said. 'There's a saying 'By their fruits ye shall know them.' You tell a Jew by what he does.'

A priest had suggested that I should meet some Indians on the Colville Reservation in central Washington, north-west of Spokane. The drive was magnificent but somewhat daunting. The day was dull and overcast. The black volcanic cliffs abutting the artificial lakes made by the damming of the Columbia River created a world of seamless monotones, where nature had been taken over by geology and engineering. The cottonwoods and willows that grew in strips in the valleys looked precarious and vulnerable. I came upon Nespelem with relief. The landscape became more gentle, with pine forests and open, rolling pasture. Around the village human sovereignty – of the careless untidy variety one finds in Ireland or the Middle East – had reasserted itself. There were horses, dogs and battered cars wandering around the streets with no obvious purpose in mind. The houses, built by the government, had the cheap, standardised look of an army camp, but there was no hint of military order.

Father Dick Mercy wore the jeans, beard, open shirt and sneakers which seemed to be *de rigueur* among the Jesuits I had met. His manner was gentle and self-effacing. The Mission of the Sacred Heart was a modest building on two floors, with the chapel and vestibule downstairs, Father Dick's quarters and offices above. The chapel was uncontaminated by the beauty of holiness: its walls were as plain as any Puritan meeting house.

At mass the next day, it being the Feast of All Saints, Father Dick spoke on the subject of death. He saw its heavy hand throughout American society – in the court system which passed death sentences on the poor, but never the rich; in the poverty and lack of opportunity which afflicted the blacks, Hispanics and Indians; in the perfectionist pressures that compounded failure with guilt. The Resurrection confronted the world with the spirit of life, the promise that death would be overcome.

'The heavy hand of death keeps trying to push us around,' he said. 'Jesus keeps filling us up with hope. In some ways it's not the kind of hope I would like, because He keeps saying: "If you stand up you're going to suffer. But together, given the spirit and promise of resurrection we can confront the oppressors."'

The congregation sat passively through this exposition of liberation theology. I wondered how much of it sank in. Most of them, I thought, would derive more comfort from Father Dick's concluding remarks: 'Jesus tells us it's OK to drift, OK to fail, OK to be not perfect, to simply be as we are.' Jesus was the friendly psychiatrist: 'Relax,' He said. 'Bring Me your problems and I'll make you feel better.' It was the opposite pole from the stern, strenuous, perfectionist Jesus of the Puritan fathers and Mormondom. It was the Jesus with whom I, a sinning agnostic, could personally identify. For the first time on my journey I felt a breath of spiritual fresh air.

After Mass, Father Dick took me to the Nez Percé Longhouse, about a mile from the village.

The Nez Percé group at Nespelem are the descendants of Chief Joseph's band who were forcibly settled there after their defeat in the Nez Percé war of 1877. Refusing to give up their tribal lands in Idaho, the non-treaty Nez Percés had fought a brilliant campaign, under Joseph's leadership, which inflicted several humiliating defeats on the US Army. Chief Joseph's courage and the chivalrous way he conducted the war, as well as the shabby circumstances of his final capture near the Canadian border in violation of a truce, made him a hero among white settlers as well as Indians. He was fêted by the citizens of Bismarck, Missouri, and received in the nation's capital by President Hayes. None of this popularity enabled him to regain his people's ancestral hunting grounds from the entrenched white settlers. But he did win his plea for exile in the same region after the government had tried to settle him and his people in the southern plains, where many of them died from the unaccustomed heat.

The Nez Percé revolt had been fuelled ideologically by the Dreamer religion, a messianic faith taught by the hunchback Prophet Smohallah in the middle of the last century. Though influenced by elements of Christian liturgy – particularly the Lord's Supper – the Smohallah cult was radically traditionalist and anti-white.

The dreamers taught that Mother Earth, having been created perfect, should not be disturbed by man. Cultivation, or any other improvement of the soil, must be avoided. Everything that human beings ate must grow by itself. Any form of submission to white authority, in government, school or church, was sinful. If the Indians remained steadfast to these teachings and performed the appropriate rituals, a leader would arise in the east who would revive all their dead, expel the whites and restore them to their ancestral lands.

Some of the ritual, if not the teachings, survived in the Seven Drum religion as practised by the Nez Percés. Their longhouse, a large utilitarian square building with room for several hundred people, was divided into two rectangular halves, one for worship and the other for feasting. The former had an earth-covered floor at its centre, where the dancing took place.

The seven drummers were ranged in front of a stone fireplace where logs were blazing in accordance with the ritual. At one end, next to the bell boy, sat Joe Red Thunder, the current chief, a short, sturdily built man with short grey hair that stuck out from his head like the bristles of a boar. The other drummers looked stern and dignified, with portly figures and noble, craggy countenances. They wore jeans and embroidered jerkins bearing tribal emblems or totems. From above the mantel the handsome face of Chief Joseph presided over his people, with pleated locks, massive silver earrings and a proud, sardonic expression that testified to years of struggle and bitterness.

I took my place on the men's side of the room; the seating opposite was gradually filling up with women and children. Nearly all were dressed 'traditionally' in cotton prints, moccasin boots and brightly-coloured shawls with tassels. Their shapes were matronly, but never obese. At a sign from the chief, the drumming began – a slow steady beat of even minims, like the opening bar of Beethoven's Violin Concerto. The tempo was absolutely constant; only the volume increased, as the dancing progressed.

The dance began with the children, who remained on the floor throughout the ceremony. On one side half a dozen boys were ranged in order of height, from a tallish teenager down to a boy of six. All wore coloured shirts, jeans and moccasin slippers. Facing them opposite were two little girls of about ten and eight, exquisitely dressed in tasselled shawls and knee-length moccasin boots. The taller girl was thin and aquiline. I named her Little Horse. The younger was a moon-faced beauty with two sunflowers in her hair, white boots and silver tassels on her bright green shawl. I named her Sea Wind, though her given name, I learned, was Camille.

The children jumped up and down to the drum-beats, with the springy gait of colts or lambs. The girls were perfectly tuned to the rhythm: Little Horse, especially, had a way of fractionally anticipating the beat which gave an eager fluidity to her movements, a gazelle ever poised for flight. The boys were much more ragged, the elder concentrating on their movements, the younger frequently bouncing out of step. Masculine gaucheness was ranged against feminine grace, compensating with superior numbers for its lack of skill.

For two hours the children danced, forming and re-forming on the earthen floor, the girls always leading, the boys never catching up. Sometimes they were joined by two or three matrons who would decorously circle the floor and salute the drummers, lending solidity to the dance, like posts supporting a trellis. Then the drumming would stop and a person from the audience, bereaved, crippled or just unhappy would deliver a tearful, halting testimony, invoking our prayers for an aunt or child, living or dead, an ailment or some other complaint.

After more drumming Chief Red Thunder halted the proceedings and made invocations in the Nez Percé language, which he translated into English for the children. But it was not the Almighty, or some remote, abstract Great Spirit, that made its presence felt; rather it was the spirit of the community itself which the drumming called up, creating a link with a past now lost beyond retrieval. There was no theology, and little moralising apart from the occasional enjoining of youngsters to keep the faith of their forefathers. It was tribal group therapy, a ritualised invocation of its collective childhood made with actual children as its focus, closing the generations in a single act of devotion, the tribe worshipping itself.

At the feast in the next room, Chief Red Thunder placed me opposite the drummers who had brought their instruments with them. The drumming continued for half an hour while the food was served by the women and girls. The boys sat next to me on the bench, learning to be waited upon. First the sacramental foods – water, salmon, elk meat, camas roots and huckleberries – were placed in disposable cups and bowls on the table. Then the other foods were ranged around them – cassoulets, hams, chicken, turkey, jellies, sweets, cakes and every other kind of supermarket junk piled into plastic bowls and paper plates till they occupied every inch of space on the table.

As our gastric juices began to work, the drumming continued, mocking the cavernous hollows of our stomachs. When – after what seemed an age – the drumming finally stopped, the chief gave the order to begin. '*Water*,' he intoned, and we drank our ceremonial cup of water; '*Salmon*,' and we reached for fragments of dried salmon from a small plastic bowl; followed by the commands for meat, roots, and berries. The sacramental foods, originally placed in small dishes in front of us, had become overwhelmed by the more substantial offerings, and we were hard put to dig them out. The fare seemed to mirror the gastronomic progression of the Nez Percé Indians from hunter-gathering to supermarkets and welfare stamps, from leathery, sinuous men and nymphlike squaws to the stout, overfed and under-exercised elders and matriarchs who filled the dining-hall.

After we had gorged ourselves awhile the speeches began. A little girl whose sixth birthday it was smiled ecstatically when the cake – a giant confection of sponge with jello filling – was paraded around the hall. Following Chief Red Thunder's lead, we all relieved ourselves of dollar bills into a plastic bag the little girl carried for the purpose. I was introduced, and made a short speech of thanks. Then Virginia, a handsome matron with swept-back silvery hair, made a testimony, saying how good it felt to be at the longhouse among her people, despite the poor health she had suffered that morning.

'I want you young ones to know that whatever you think about it now, you must carry on our religion, you must preserve it, for that's what will give you strength.'

A thousand elders in a thousand American churches were probably delivering exactly the same message that very Sunday morning, using more or less the same words. But in this case, I knew she was absolutely right. It was not in the abstruse realms of theological discourse, the ambiguous truths of the Bible or in sanctimonious appeals to moral rectitude that the truth of her statement resided, but in the deep vibrations of the drums which from infancy must penetrate every ganglion of the Nez Percé child's nervous system, every fibre of its being. The Seven Drum Religion found the parts that hymnals, liturgies, bible-sermons and even sacraments could never reach in the deracinated post-industrial world.

After the feast was over, there was more drumming and dancing, and then it was time to go home. One of the drummers gave me a ride in his truck back to the Mission. He had exchanged his tribal jerkin for a parka and had put on an ordinary baseball cap. I asked him how he would be spending the rest of his Sunday.

'Watching the ball game on TV, just like everybody else,' he said.

Sunday was Sunday, even for pagans.

VIII

Love is God

If any man come to me and hate not his father, and mother, and wife, and children, and brethren, and sisters, yea, and his own life also, he cannot be my disciple.

LUKE 14:26

Paul Erdman, alias Love Israel, was one of the more engaging Sixties characters I have met. A tall man in his forties with a commanding presence, he was, if not a reincarnation of Joseph Smith, in several ways his twentieth-century counterpart. In his hippie days, when his hair was long and he wore embroidered robes, he had resembled the Nordic Christ of Mormon iconography. In later years his fondness for cocaine and good living had lent a discreet portliness to his figure. Having cut his hair and shorn his beard, he looked less like Jesus, more like a Prussian junker.

I visited the Love Family – or what remained of it – on their ranch near Arlington, north of Seattle, after driving from Nespelem over the North Cascades. It was exhilarating to be in the mountains again after the deserts south of Colville. After climbing up the 5,000-foot Rainy Pass where the snow lay on the ground, I came down through the thick evergreen forests of the western side where the lakes were so green they seemed to be made of pine essence. When I got to Arlington it was pouring. The 300-acre ranch was situated in what was probably a beautiful clearing on the edge of the forest. Unfortunately nothing was visible beyond some sodden crops and puddles that formed in ruts in the road.

The King of Israel received me in his yurt, a cunning adaptation of the circular dwellings, half hut and half tent, favoured by the horse nomads of Central Asia. The original yurt was designed to be transportable while standing up to Siberian winters. It has a wooden frame and a thick horsehair superstructure and may be lined with carpets and kelims to add beauty and warmth. The Washington Israelite yurt is a much flimsier structure made from plywood and plastic sheeting, designed to circumvent city zoning laws which forbid the building of permanent dwellings on agricultural land. Nevertheless the royal yurt was comfortably appointed inside, with a kitchen, a bar and a spiral stairway leading to an upper floor, most of which was occupied by His Majesty's bed. The wall above the bed was adorned with a bow, arrows and a harp. Whether these objects represented the royal insignia (love's food and love's weapons) or were merely decorative I forgot to ask.

We had lunch – freshly baked bread, imported cheeses, beans and carrots and celery with avocado dips – sitting at the bar. Love's wife Honesty, a fair, good-looking woman, busied herself with our needs. A small balding gnome-like creature tinkered with a wood-burning stove which appeared to have abandoned its task of producing hot water. We were joined by Mikhail, a large bearded Israeli who taught Hebrew at the Family school and at a nearby US army base. His manner seemed odd: I thought he might be high on dope. He contributed nothing to the conversation, but every now and then would quake with manic giggles, causing his whole frame to shake.

Love Israel told me how he found Jesus and founded the Kingdom of Love. A television salesman by training, he had left Seattle in the early Sixties and migrated to San Francisco's Haight Ashbury district, then the centre of hippie culture. His First Vision – as I was later informed, though he was reticent about this – occurred while he was on an 'acid trip' with his friend, Brian Allen, son of Steve Allen, a television personality. As is well known, LSD acts on the sensory part of the brain in such a way as to reduce, or even abolish, the relation between subject and object, I and Thou. Users become part of what they are looking at. Some become insects, or bits of orange peel, or get distressingly trapped in the wallpaper. Paul Erdman and his friend Brian became each other. This was a narco–mystical, not a sexual experience.

'All of a sudden we looked at each other and saw that we were One Person,' said Love. 'We were both very embarrassed. I was standing out there naked, like I was exposed to the whole world, to everyone that had ever lived, and everyone knew what a jerk I really was. Then I saw Jesus Christ.'

'How did you know it was Jesus?' I asked, remembering how Joseph Smith had got into a theological fix over his First Vision.

'I recognised Him. I'd always known Him. It was like the face of all of us put together as One. That's what I saw.'

The visions, with or without the help of LSD, came thick and fast. He had dreams of heaven where green was really green and blue really blue, he saw the world as a vast insane asylum where the bureaucrats and rulers were pitting people against each other, individual against individual, group against group, religion against religion; and he saw in his dream that all these people were powerless, because in reality Everybody was One. Doubtless many people had the same vision, induced by acid, magic mushrooms, marijuana and love, during the Sixties. But unlike the average acid-head, Erdman the salesman knew about marketing.

He turned to the Bible, which 'put Jesus in my mind'. He read the Old Testament which revealed to him the law and the prophets. Like Joseph Smith he muddled the wine and the bottles, though as a child of the Sixties his mixture was the opposite way round. Where Joseph had put the New Testament wine in the Old Testament bottles, subjecting the antinomian effervescence of Christianity to the sterner dictates of Judaism, Paul brought Israel into the kingdom of love. As he contemplated Haight Ashbury and its flower children, he saw an ancient people emerging out of the past with long, flowing dresses and gorgeous apparel: the People of Israel. He rechristened himself Love; Brian became Logic, Israel their surname. Returning to Seattle, they bought an old gabled house on Queen Anne's Hill above the port. It became a utopian hippie commune, with a distinctive biblical flavour of its own. Following Love and Logic, the robed and bearded elders were given 'virtue' names like Strength, Willing, Helpful, Meekness, Courage. Narcotics – including LSD, marijuana, and 'magic mushrooms' picked in a nearby cemetery – were taken as aids to enlightenment. Toluene, a paint solvent – the Family called it 'tell-you-all' – was used in sacramental breathing sessions. As all were One in love, mirrors were forbidden: Family members were expected to see their own reflections in each other's faces. They lived apart from the rest of society, rejecting newspapers, telephones, radios, television and the US Postal Service. Letters from parents were returned unopened, stamped with the message: 'eye to eye, hand to hand, we'd love to see you in our land'. Where letters had to be sent, they were delivered in person, even when this required travelling thousands of miles.

As they were parts of the same Eternal Being, Family members refused to divulge their individual birth dates, making it impossible for them to acquire social security numbers or driving licences. These practices, inevitably, brought confrontation with the authorities. Several did time in prison for driving illegally, or for refusing to register their dates of birth when booked for traffic violations. A much more serious incident involved the deaths of two men, Reverence and Solidity, from the effects of toluene. The Family prayed over the bodies for three days, expecting them to return to life, before the police removed them. Like Christian Scientists, the Love Family refused all medical treatment, believing in the healing properties of herbs and faith alone. Serious illnesses went untreated. One woman almost died of a brain tumour before Love would allow her to have surgery.

Members were strongly encouraged to 'merge' their egos. Anyone who disagreed with the group was criticised for thinking with the 'small I' instead of the 'big I', the separate as distinct from the collective ego under the control of Christ. Not surprisingly, parents regarded the Love Family as a 'cult' using techniques of 'brainwashing' and 'mind control'. At least two Family members were 'kidnapped' on behalf of their parents, one of them in full view of the nation's television cameras. Another, Sure Israel, was brought back to his home in suburban Boston, where he was deprived of sleep, food and subjected to constant harassment. After escaping to the Family ranch in Alaska he was captured again, and interned in a psychiatric ward, but released under a court order that found him religiously eccentric but not insane.

Though all were One, some were more so than others. By virtue of his vision, Love identified himself with God. It was a benign, loving deity, not the jealous and punitive Jehovah of the Old Testament.

'The God I saw was really nice,' Love told me, 'and He was Me . . . without my misconceptions. It was Me simply knowing I was One with everybody. It was Me having created the world to keep Me company. He was totally kind, totally forgiving, totally merciful, totally understanding. If I was going to be like Him at all, I had to be the same.'

Love's followers accepted this, and did everything they could to keep him loving and merciful. For them he was the representation of God, holding the keys to paradise. In 1971 they anointed him their king, as Joseph had been anointed in Nauvoo. Members of the Family were expected to have 'no thoughts but Love's'. Like Joseph, he ruled by divine authority, and was accorded special privileges in recognition of his superior spirituality. He ate better food, helped himself to the women he fancied and determined who coupled with whom. In the early days, the differences in lifestyle were marginal. The commune was desperately poor, relying on small charitable contributions, leftover foods from friendly supermarkets, and occasional payments for unskilled work – such as cherry-picking – where no one asked for social security numbers. But then several massive windfalls arrived. In 1973 a middle-aged widow donated $120,000 worth of cash and assets. The same year a young millionaire from a wealthy family in Idaho, David Gruener (alias Richness Israel) joined the Family. His contribution over the next ten years amounted to more than $2,000,000, including trust funds, a clothing store, and the 160-acre farm in Alaska.

God told Love it was time to expand and acquire another house for the Family. For this a legal entity was necessary. The family became incorporated under the name of 'Jesus Christ: The Chief Administrator for the Church of Jesus Christ at Armageddon.' It meant that Love Israel was empowered to buy and sell property on behalf of the Family without having to consult anyone else at all.

With the wealth now at his sole disposal, the gap between Love and the majority of his followers began to widen. They continued to eke out a meagre living on carrots and porridge and whatever else the supermarket workers were kind enough to contribute. Love ate in expensive restaurants with whomever he chose for company. The Family acquired a home in Hawaii where Love was called to minister during Seattle's cold, damp winters. Those lucky enough to be invited arrived back with healthy-looking tans. Those who remained in Seattle, or on the ranch at Arlington, developed colds and 'flu – especially when they were detailed to repair an ageing fishing vessel with rotten spots on its hull that Love had bought.

Soon the Family began working on a sumptuous three-storey home for Love's exclusive use. It had the best furnishings, secret passageways, beautifully-tended gardens and a private sauna adjoining the bedroom. An élite group of priests served as domestics. There was excellent food, fine wine and beautiful women. To be in Love's proximity and favour was to enjoy a millionaire's way of life. To be in disfavour, or simply out of view, was to shiver and practically to starve.

Despite the glaring disparities, very few members complained at first. When confronted by outsiders, they would argue that Love deserved and justified his privileges. Spiritually he was always at their disposal, 'raising them up' to a higher level of consciousness. Like people stuck in a hole, they had to get behind him and push him up so he in turn would be able to help them out. Materially they argued that Love required his privileges for the sake of the whole community. He needed his aircraft to 'stay connected' with the Family members in Hawaii and eastern Washington; his superior house on Queen Anne Hill was necessary so he could entertain church leaders and other local dignitaries whose co-operation was essential for the good of the Family.

The first serious rumblings of discontent came from women with children. Despite the Family's hippie origins, the role accorded to women was strictly traditional, confined mainly to cooking, cleaning and child-care. Love himself had two permanent wives, Honesty and Bliss, with whom he had nine children; but most of the other women elders – those with 'virtue names' – had had sexual relationships with him at one time or other, and most of the male elders had affairs with women in addition to their regular wives. The inevitable jealousies were resolved by appealing to faith: people who had their feelings hurt – the women were told – did not believe in Christ. Despite the plurality of partnerships, it was not a 'free love' community. Sex was a privilege reserved for the committed, and new members were expected to abstain from sex for at least a year after joining. All relationships had to be sanctioned by Love, who could also separate couples if he thought it desirable for the good of the Family.

Although Love opposed birth control on biblical grounds, he was not inordinately fond of children. Infants who cried were locked in cupboards or had rags stuffed in their mouths. If they gobbled their food they were made to fast. A number of children were severely beaten. By the end of the Seventies there had been fifty-five births within the Family, and children accounted for more than a third of the membership. The differences between Love's lifestyle and that of the majority grated on mothers whose children were short of essentials like milk or shoes.

In 1981 the Family received the last of its major legacies from the Greuner estate, an inheritance worth more than one million dollars. But the Family scarcely benefited, and within six months most of its members were all but destitute, scratching around for work. Love's lifestyle had not only become increasingly ostentatious, with credit cards, expensive suits and Cuban cigars; he was becoming increasingly addicted to cocaine which was costing between $200 and $2,000 a day, depending on how many people were with him.

The showdown finally came at a meeting of the elders' council in July 1983, when a flood of pent-up resentment was unleashed. A dissident majority presented a petition in which they demanded that Love apologise for his 'gross self-indulgence' and relinquish authority to the council. Love tore the letter up, accusing the council of being controlled by Satan. The dissidents left; and by the end of the year all but a handful of members – around 85 per cent – had followed them out of the Family. They included Richness Israel, now David Greuner again, who had most of his remaining property returned under the terms of a settlement reached out of court. Love and his dwindling band of loyalists were left with the Arlington ranch and their yurts.

Love's version of these events was predictably vague and benign. 'Sure, we went through a kinda shake-up,' he said, 'some of it my fault, some other people's. We were getting to forty and nobody owned anything yet. You know, in American society you have to own something by the time you're forty.' Not yet having the full picture I asked him if the problem had been shortage of cash. With hindsight, his answer was barefaced.

'There didn't have to be . . . I didn't like us just to sell everything and spend money. I preferred to just buy land and continue living the way we always did, so we wouldn't get too spoilt. I never saw life as being that difficult. When times were hard we dug carrots. We all turned orange. I had carrot juice, baked carrot, sliced carrot, carrot cake and carrot soup every day.'

At this point Mikhail became convulsed with one of his maniacal fits of giggles. I suspected that the joke might be on me, without knowing what it was. Later, when I knew more of the facts, I thought perhaps that Mikhail's laughter came from a scholarly appreciation of Love's use of grammar. His 'I' was the first person universal – the 'I' of the Family, not the little particular 'I' which tucked into *filet de bœuf en croûte* while the big 'I' was having its carrots.

Something had happened to Love's digestion. He retired to the water closet, whence erupted a series of stupendous explosions that caused the whole fragile structure of the yurt to quake. He apologised noisily from the loo.

'Man, my stomach's really giving me trouble,' he told us. Then he emerged to take me on a tour of the estate. He talked incessantly about himself and his experiences, occasionally punctuating his discourse with a fart. After trudging through sodden fields and dripping woodlands we came upon a tractor in difficulties. A group of hirsute men in boots and anoraks were trying to remove the caterpillar tracks. They came up to Love and explained the problem: 'We have to glue the plates,' they said.

Their manner was easygoing, but definitely tinged with deference. It started raining harder.

'Malise, you need a hat,' said Love. He beckoned to the balding, gnome-like individual and asked if I could use his hat. The man seemed honoured by the request, as though I were visiting royalty. 'Sure,' he said, 'I'm going in anyway' – which didn't sound true.

We came upon another yurt, one of several distributed in the woods around the lake. Love knocked on the door. A buxom young woman emerged, wearing a bright yellow parachute suit. On seeing us she coloured slightly and smilingly showed us inside. There was a solid wooden floor, but scarcely any furniture. A five-year old child was playing with bricks on the floor. Love barely noticed them, preferring to talk about himself.

'You know those dreams when you're supposed to wake up when you die?' he said. 'I don't wake up. I die.' There followed a noisy report, as the soul escaped from another Pythagorean bean in his stomach. The woman said nothing, and this time Love did not bother to apologise. I felt obscurely complimented, included in the Family.

Before leaving, I asked about zoning laws. Some of the yurts looked pretty permanent. Was there trouble from the authorities?

'They don't bother us much,' said Love. 'We've been around for ten years. Our sword is beauty, not fear: we avoid antagonising the community.'

It was a classic evolution, the Mormon saga in miniature, speeded up in accordance with the accelerating dynamics of the twentieth century. Most of the basic elements were there: the original vision, the charismatic prophet, the radical antinomianism which refused to conform to the rules of the greater society, the scandals over money and sex, the gradual, and ultimately successful, accommodation to the ways of the world. True the Love family, unlike the Mormons, had employed the modern short-cut to spiritual enlightenment, using narcotics and other toxins to reach in minutes those rarefied states of consciousness that the Saints had achieved by days of prayer and fasting. There were other, qualitative differences as well: Smith had originally entranced his followers with his magic and his Book; Erdman, a far less talented individual, gave them only the Bible and the benefits of his home-spun platitudes. But these were details: the wider social realities were similar. The Pacific coast was to the continent what upstate New York had been to the former colonies: a frontier territory, a land of opportunity for people with the will and the necessary luck, a social disaster area for the less fortunate. To the homeless, the uprooted, the urban nomads and adolescent victims of parental repression or neglect, Love offered a kind of warmth, a casualty ward for damaged psyches. To dismiss him as an impostor would be to make an arbitrary and unsustainable distinction between different versions of the utopian myth represented by the Kingdom of God. If Love was a fraud, so was Joseph Smith and so, in the final analysis, was Christ Himself. There are no grounds, outside theology, for distinguishing between 'true' and 'false' prophets. 'Cults' are simply religions in fluid stage of their infancy, before the elaboration of organisation and belief become encrusted with tradition. Christianity was once a cult, subversive of the state, which tore children from parents and urged its adherents to make martyrs of themselves under circumstances that made martyrdom virtually indistinguishable from suicide.

When I left the Family it was still raining hard. Although Love asked me to come back, I decided I had seen enough. Friends were expecting me in San Francisco; I was getting lonely, and tired of being among strangers whose ways of seeing the world were so very different from mine.

The evening traffic was building up, as commuters flowed out of Seattle's downtown area, past the sanitised factories where the Boeing giants, cruise missiles and myriads of components were manufactured under the silvery skies of the Pacific north-west.

At Portland I hit a serious traffic jam, the only one I encountered in some 12,000 miles of motoring. The previous spring, I had flown there from New York to visit the ranch of Bhagwan Shree Rajneesh, who had recently been expelled from the United States.

Like most other people I had heard about Bhagwan. People I knew, or whose families were known to mine, had gone to his famous ashram at Poona near Bombay, whence they returned wearing bright red clothes and *malas*, beaded necklaces bearing his smiling, bearded face with its bulging, frog-like eyes. Wealthy and beautiful women I had glimpsed in my youth had abandoned lovers, husbands and children to follow him. It was not difficult to see why: Bhagwan was the only Enlightened Master among Indian gurus who taught that, in order to arrive at the truth, you did not have to give up sex.

It was not surprising to hear that, faced with an attempt on his life and a massive tax bill from the Indian authorities, Bhagwan decided to move to the United States. The great majority of his neo-sannyasins ('seekers') were westerners, with a preponderance of Anglo-Saxons and Germans. (The French, it was said, were too free from sexual hang-ups to find his message appealing.) Free sex, with or without yoga, meditation, encounter-therapy or any other of the 'personal growth' techniques developed at Poona, seemed likely to do better in the American West than in spiritually advanced but sexually retrograde India. Tales from Oregon began to appear in the British press. Bhagwan's wealthy disciples had bought him an 80,000-acre ranch in the middle of nowhere. Here a theocratic paradise was being built, where meditation, macrobiotic food and organic waste disposal would be combined with a leisurely, hi-tech, affluent lifestyle. It sounded like a twentieth-century version of Nauvoo, but wealthier and more sophisticated.

A higher than average proportion of the commune's residents were graduates, with many having advanced degrees. While the faithful toiled ceaselessly to create this Buddhist Zion, the Enlightened One became increasingly wealthy, as befitting the self-styled 'Guru to the Rich'. How could the poor, Bhagwan asked, breaking with millennia of eastern asceticism, become enlightened when they are overwhelmed with the struggle for survival? The disciples expressed their devotion by presenting the Master with brand-new Silver Shadow Rolls-Royces. The Ranch was eventually said to have nearly a hundred of these vehicles: a much higher density *per capita* than Beverly Hills or Kuwait.

Later, there came reports about sinister goings-on, inside and outside the Ranch. The red-clad acolytes had taken over a local town against the wishes of its inhabitants. There had been demonstrations led by a fundamentalist clergyman: stones and mud had been thrown at the guru in his Rolls-Royce. Car stickers appeared bearing messages such as 'Better Dead than Red'. Oregonians began sporting T-shirts emblazoned with Bhagwan's head, framed in the sights of a rifle. An explosion damaged a hotel owned by the group in Portland. Security at the Ranch was tightened: watch towers appeared, a two-metre electrified fence was built. Rajneeshees, male and female, were filmed undergoing weapon training with sub-machine guns and semi-automatic rifles. The Rajneesh 'Peace Force' was reported to have as much advanced weaponry as all the other Oregon forces combined. Again, the parallels with Nauvoo and its famous Legion were compelling.

From April 1981, before he arrived at the Ranch, the guru had gone into a period of silence, or mystic withdrawal from the world. His appearance at gatherings of Rajneeshees, or at the daily drive-by in one of the Silver Shadows, had not been accompanied by any inspired utterance. He communicated only with his housekeeper, his personal physician and Sheela, his secretary.

As the only channel of communication between Bhagwan and his followers, Sheela became the Ranch's organiser, manager and eventually, dictator. A dynamic Indian woman in her early thirties, Sheela and her 'gang' had operated a reign of terror. Hotel rooms and telephones were bugged with highly sophisticated equipment. Anyone who crossed Sheela, or threatened her position in any way, was put on to menial jobs, like driving trucks or manning the all-night switchboard. Her power was enormous. It was Sheela who made the key appointments to the fifteen or so Rajneesh corporations which controlled the labyrinthine financial operators by which the movement sought to protect its assets. It was Sheela who organised the Stakhanovite work schedules, the twelve- to fifteen-hour day by means of which the sannyasins sought to 'worship' the Master (the word 'work' was never used); who arranged the Summer Festivals when thousands of sannyasins would flock in from abroad, to drink His spirit and commune in His silence, make love and eat vegetables.

Then, quite suddenly, Sheela and her cronies disappeared. They resigned their positions and left for Germany. Bhagwan abandoned his silence. He accused Sheela of embezzling millions of dollars, transferring them to secret bank accounts. He called in the FBI and the state police to investigate allegations of attempted murder by poisoning and telephone tapping. Sheela and her associates were extradited from Germany. Among the charges against them was the arrangement of marriages between American and foreign sannyasins with the aim of circumventing the country's immigration laws. All received jail sentences.

Bhagwan, however, did not get away with blaming everything on Sheela and her 'fascist gang'. The INS (the federal immigration and naturalisation service) had long kept a watchful eye on the guru. They had extended his original visitor's permit, but had refused to grant him the coveted green card to allow him to reside permanently in the United States. The charges against Sheela gave the INS the opportunity for which they had been waiting. On 28 October 1985, the same day that Sheela and her gang were arrested in Germany, the guru was himself arrested, after landing at Charlotte, North Carolina in a private jet. Police claimed that he was about to leave the country, to avoid prosecution on thirty-five counts of immigration violations handed down by a federal grand jury in Portland four days earlier. After a period spent in various US jails, the guru pleaded guilty to two of the charges involving arranged marriages. He was given a suspended ten-year sentence, fined $400,000, and ordered to leave the United States. Within weeks most of the Rajneeshees were leaving Oregon. The Ranch was up for sale.

A few weeks later, I decided to visit the Ranch before it was all sold up. I telephoned from New York and spoke to Sarita, the public relations person in charge. She had a soft, lilting Californian voice. Sure I could come up and spend a day or two. She would find time to show me round. I flew to Portland, rented a car and headed east on Interstate 84.

By the time I had reached the Dalles, the long narrows at the centre of the Columbia River gorge which have given their name to the capital of Wasco county, it was already dark. At Biggs, I turned south along Route 97. The road was empty, except for the lights of an occasional long-distance truck heading God knows where. The country seemed utterly desolate. After what seemed like hours I arrived at Antelope, the small town – really no more than a crossroads with a church, a school, a store or two and half a dozen wooden houses – that the Rajneeshees had taken over after they bought the Ranch. A bid by the Antelopians to commit municipal suicide by voting to disincorporate themselves came too late, and was narrowly defeated at a meeting reported nationwide on television. The Rajneeshees, moreover, clearly had bigger ambitions. After gaining permission from the Wasco County commissioners, 154 of them – all Americans – voted to incorporate a city of their own on the Ranch. They claimed they needed it in order to obtain vital municipal services. The move, however, was challenged by the Thousand Friends of Oregon, an environmental protection group. The incorporation of a new city outside existing urban boundaries, they said, violated Oregon's strict land use laws which had been carefully designed to prevent 'Californication' – the kind of haphazard development which prevailed in the next-door state.

A sign pointed me towards Rajneeshpuram, nineteen miles away. It seemed reassuring: but I soon became lost in the dark among muddy pot-holed tracks that went on forever. Exhausted and bewildered, I doubled back to Antelope – more than thirty miles on the clock – where, miracu-lously, I found a telephone which worked. I called the Ranch. A disinterested American voice informed me that I had been on the right road all along: only the local rednecks had taken down all the signs. I retraced my tracks once more, and then spotted a sign I had missed, which would have told me I was heading in the right direction: 'Jesus Christ died to save us sinners!' it defiantly proclaimed – obviously a 'redneck' slogan to bait the Rajneeshees. I followed the dirt road which led off opposite the sign. Sure enough, after what seemed like a century of bumping and boring, I came upon a row of orange street lights glaring behind a high wire fence. It looked more like a prison camp than a place of pilgrimage. But the guard at the gate – bearded, beaded and dressed in red – didn't even ask for any identification. Yes, this was Rajneeshpuram. Yes, I was expected. 'Turn left, past the Mall, and you'll find the hotel.'

At reception I was presented with a key attached to a laminated card marked 'ultimate accident'. It showed a woman with a broken pail of water reflecting the fragmenting image of the moon. I went, as bidden, to the door marked with the same picture, and opened it with my key. Inside a young woman was getting undressed. Visions of instant sex, purged of preliminaries, rushed to my mind. I retreated, bemused and slightly alarmed. Was I being 'set up' with one of the famous Twinkies (the P R persons, selected for their beauty, who used to escort visitors around the Ranch) to enlist my silence, sympathy or even – God forbid! – conversion? I checked with reception, and found, to my relief, that it was just an ordinary mix-up. My room – with the same key and picture – was in a different courtyard. I entered the room, which was spotlessly clean and empty. It had two large, circular double-beds.

In the bathroom there was a plastic bin, marked 'Contaminated Waste' in which I was invited, by a series of graphic but crude illustrations, to dispose of my used condoms and latex gloves. Earlier visitors, I learned later, had been presented with sex-kits consisting of condoms, gloves, and spermicidal jelly, with instructions for use. The gloves were supposed to be worn during foreplay. Bhagwan had announced, through Sheela, that AIDS was the plague predicted by Nostradamus, destined to wipe out two-thirds of humanity. Everyone on the Ranch had been obliged to take the AIDS test. Anyone whose test showed positive was put in a special isolation unit, far removed from the rest of the Ranch. Sheela and Puja allegedly faked some of the results – people Sheela wanted to get rid of were told their tests had shown 'positive'. If you hadn't got AIDS already, you now stood a better chance of getting it.

Fortunately the bin was empty. It sounded as if any contents must be destined for some nuclear reprocessing plant. Outside the bullfrogs were croaking. There were noises upstairs as well: someone was having what sounded like an orgasm. My sleep was exhausted, fitful and filled with nightmare images: I was caught in endless, bumpy tracks, unable to find my way; there were buckets filled to the brim with contaminated waste, spilling their lethal contents under shattering moons.

Sarita was everything her voice had promised. She was lithe and trim with cascading chestnut hair. Though Californian by birth her features, pointed with slightly slanting eyes, suggested that she belonged to an ancient race, perhaps Indian or Egyptian. Her movements were light and springy: in one of her previous incarnations, she had definitely been a cat.

The 'city' of Rajneeshpuram consisted of a few dozen timber or metal-roofed buildings scattered along a canyon surrounded by steep, scrubby hills. The day was bright, fresh and clear. With its slightly abandoned look, the Ranch reminded me of a ski-resort in summer. Sarita showed me a five-acre vegetable farm – 'all one hundred per cent organic' – set with rows of polythene drip-fed cloches.

'We can grow vegetables throughout the winter' – she used the present tense – 'so there are plenty for the July Festival when we might be harvesting three or four tons a day. When we came here this was all just desert. The first year we just planted sunflowers which we turned back into the soil as green manure so we could plant proper vegetables the following spring.'

Had there been experienced vegetable-growers at the ranch to give expert advice?

'Intelligent people are attracted to Bhagwan, not necessarily people skilled in any area. We learn fast because we are intelligent, dedicated and enthusiastic, and we have the juice for life.'

'Does Bhagwan insist on vegetarianism?'

'What He has said on the subject is this. If people meditate, they become more and more sensitive to different life-forms, and it becomes quite difficult to actually eat flesh' (she enunciated the last word with subtle, onomatopoeic disgust) 'because it's like eating your own brothers and sisters. But He never orders us to do or not to do anything. He just speaks from His own experience. What I've found from my own experience is that I'm so sensitive to the *smell* that I can immediately tell if a person's been eating meat. It's disgusting, the smell of dead flesh. What's more, people start resembling what they eat. If they eat too much pork, like Americans tend to, they start looking like pigs . . . '

I edged away slightly, as the spectre of a hot-dog eaten the day before rose before me, like Banquo's ghost.

We passed the Rabiya Dairy, the Omar Khayyam vineyard, the Rumi housing estate and Jesus Grove, a complex of three de-luxe mobile homes where Sheela had had her headquarters. Under Sheela and the 'Moms' – as her cronies were known – Rajneeshees considered too influential or potentially 'disloyal' would be summoned to Jesus Grove for a 'chat', which acquired all the dreaded significance of a visit to the headmaster's study.

I marvelled politely at the organic (uncontaminated) waste recycling system with its series of solar ponds set at different levels, and was genuinely impressed by a holiday village of A-shaped wooden huts set on a hillside among fragrant juniper trees. We went past the airstrip where two planes bearing the Air Rajneesh livery were parked on the runway. One of them, a Convair, had formerly belonged to the reclusive Howard Hughes. We passed by the Rajneesh Buddhafield garage, once home to the world's most celebrated fleet of Rolls-Royces, now sold to a Texan dealer. The Californian distributors of this most expensive car had capitalised on the publicity. The Rolls's unique hydrolastic suspension, they announced, compared favourably with the 'endless peace discovered by the Buddhas'.

What was the point of all those Rolls's, I asked. She replied with the fluency of an Intourist guide showing a visitor round a model shoe factory. 'The point, of course, is that the material and spiritual dimensions should go together. The New Man, Zorba and Buddha, contains the two different poles of humanity – Zorba the Greek, a totally sensuous being seeking enjoyment and pleasure, and Buddha the Transcendent One. Bhagwan's trying to bring these two poles together, to erase the schizophrenic attitude that's created so much poverty in the world. It really short circuits people's brains to find a mystic driving a Rolls-Royce. And that sets them thinking. Bhagwan's view is that if you change man's consciousness, then the physical world will also change as well. It's not a belief, it's not a dogma, it's not a creed,' said Sarita, 'it's more like a love affair – that's how sannyasins will experience it.'

'Sannyas,' says Bhagwan, 'is falling in love with existence.' Love is the only commandment: 'The whole of religion is nothing but a commentary on love.' Christian love, however, is centred on a transcendent father-creator on the one hand and one's human neighbour on the other. Bhagwan departs from Christianity, setting a high value on sexuality. Only through sex, he believes, are people really connected with the world. Thus he urges his sannyasins to celebrate the orgiastic in sex with all the enthusiasm of a counsellor in a 'girlie' magazine. 'Next time you make love, hum together, or dance, shriek, go wild, jump around, jog in the room, do absurd things. Do anything new.' The faithful had taken him at his word. Reports out of Poona had spoken of sexual group therapies, orgies, even gang rapes.

His attitude towards sex derived from Tantrism. 'Sex is a function of bio-electricity,' he said. 'Men and women are polar opposites. Homosexuality is like trying to create electricity without positive and negative. Every time you make love, just pray together. Pray to God to take possession of you and to do whatever He pleases – "Thy will be done."' Sex led up towards love, love towards prayer. 'You can fall down and become sexual, or you can rise and become religious.' But there was no discontinuity between these different states. Bhagwan's 'new man', Zorba the Buddha, encompassed both divine and animal: 'To become God one has to pass through animality.'

Bhagwan's attitude towards God was Eastern and Sufic, not Western and instrumental. As in the Sufi rituals, it involved the disinterested celebration of the divine, not a request for divine intervention. 'Prayer is not to ask anything from God, rather it is to give.' Such giving however, did not necessarily apply to other human beings. 'Never try to be unselfish, never try to show that you are unselfish. That is one of the dangerous cancer-like diseases. Unselfishness kills people, it is poison.' He viciously attacked 'do-gooders', whether political activists or philanthropists like Mother Theresa of Calcutta.

'If everybody is selfish, the world will be very, very beautiful . . . ' In deliberate contrast to the Christian gospel, he proclaimed that 'God is not going to ask you "Why was someone else a beggar, and somebody poor, and somebody dying?" – no. He will ask you "What have you done with your self? I have given you an opportunity, has your seed sprouted? Have you flowered? Has your life been a fulfilment? Have you *lived*?"'

It was hardly surprising that Bhagwan was popular in the narcissistic culture of the West Coast – especially with therapists and other psychiatric professionals. But in enjoining his followers to 'selfishness', Bhagwan made a crucial distinction between the self and the ego. 'By self is meant your innermost core which is absolutely egoless – your pure self uncontaminated by the idea of 'I'. First the selfishness, then altruism will come of its own accord.'

It was through meditation that the ego was transcended. Meditation was feeling as distinct from thought: 'Thought is individual, feeling is universal,' he said, 'feeling is cosmic.' Knowledge and thought reinforce the ego, feeling and meditation dissolved it. The ego was only a label for social use. It intervened between the individual self and cosmic reality. It created its own shadow, guilt. There was nothing spiritual about guilt. It was simply 'part of the egoistic mind' exploited by religions. The ego was the bucket which separated the water from the ocean.

Bhagwan had borrowed eclectically from many spiritual traditions. 'I have been like a bee going from one flower to another, gathering many fragrances,' he said. His discourses were replete with references to and quotations from Christian, Judaic, Islamic, Taoist, and Hindu mystical traditions. But the techniques of 'dynamic' therapy applied at Poona and later in Rajneeshpuram were really Western, similar to those employed at the Esalen institute at Big Sur, California. They owed as much to Abraham Maslow, Gestalt and the 'personal growth' movement as to any Eastern tradition. Bhagwan's originality lay in placing Western 'growth' therapy in a broader Hindu-Buddhist religious framework. He thus provided Westerners steeped in guilt and repression with both the religious justification for 'doing their own thing' and the means of overcoming their inhibitions. He made the self-indulgent individualism of the hippie generation respectable. Instead of drugs, he gave them meditation. Instead of mindless sexual promiscuity, he offered enlightenment through tantric ecstasy.

I drove Sarita up Yoga Drive, where Bhagwan used to exercise his Rolls-Royces. We passed Pythagoras Medical Centre, through arid, conical hills sparsely covered with sage brush and juniper trees. The road, built entirely by the Rajneeshees, had been finished to a standard worthy of the Enlightened One's Silver Shadows. In one or two places it had been washed away by torrential rains during the winter. Great piles of stone chippings, quarried and crushed on the ranch, testified to the community's unfulfilled ambitions. We drove for six or seven miles along the canyon, snaking round fantastic lunar outcrops of terracotta rock. Then we turned off the road, and drove up a track to a lake whose surface, unflawed by the wind, reflected the shapes of the hills. For a while we stood together, in silence.

Why, I asked Sarita, did Bhagwan choose Sheela as his personal secretary?

'He chose her because she was very practically-minded, because she's a good organiser and could get things done. She's not a great meditator: meditators tend to be very preoccupied with their inner development as human beings. They don't have much energy left for practical things. But she was, I guess, in love with Bhagwan, though they never had a physical affair. It had been her dream, I think, to find a place, and then to invite Him there.'

Sheela's father, a Gujerati landowner, had been wealthy enough to educate her at a private college in New Jersey. In Poona her knowledge of English made her the ideal secretary for a community that was being taken over by increasing numbers of Westerners. She was instrumental in persuading Bhagwan, when things got tough in India, to move to the United States. At first they rented a nineteenth-century castellated mansion near Montclair, New Jersey, where Sheela had been at school. Later she acquired the ranch, with the help of her brother, a Chicago businessman. They paid more than six million dollars for it, more than twice its current worth, with funds loaned by wealthy sannyasins. Throughout these negotiations, as well as the development of the commune, Bhagwan maintained his silence. Was he, I asked Sarita, giving her enough rope to hang herself with?

'It's strange,' she said, 'I remember seeing Sheela after one private session with Bhagwan. She was very excited. I asked 'What happened?' She said: "You know, He said something so funny to me. He said: 'Sheela, I can't help you go through the front door to enlightenment. I have to sneak you in through the back door. That's the only way to help you get enlightened.'"'

'You mean, the whole of this commune was just the 'back door' for Sheela?'

'I think so . . . She couldn't do it by meditation, through introspection. She just didn't have it in her. Yet somehow all her energy could be used for His work. She wanted to offer herself for Him. She was totally devoted to Him. She had tremendous energy, but a very raw type of energy. And somehow all her energy could be used for His work. And somehow He really poured Himself into her, and she absorbed what she could. Maybe it won't be manifested right now. But later, perhaps, it will begin to show. And perhaps she'll be transformed through it – I hope so. Maybe jail will be really beneficial for her – because she'll be forced into that introspection.'

The Eastern masters used to enlighten their pupils by literally smashing their egos. One of them had forced a pupil to build and re-build a house for him, seven times. Each time it was ready he found fault with it, and ordered the disciple to pull it down and start again. Only when the disciple had given up trying to please his master was he ready for enlightenment. By then his ego had been crushed completely.

The lesson of the commune, of course, wasn't just for Sheela. Everyone's ego had been totally involved – the female 'moms' who lorded it over all the others, the dozens of able and creative people who were put onto menial tasks. The individual egos merged into the commune's collective ego: it was totalitarianism all right, a corporate mini-state ruled by a single authoritarian leader. And in four and a half brief years, it had run the full gamut, from redemption-through-labour, via confrontation with the rest of the world, to eventual destruction. But there was also a difference. All along, the Führer of this miniature Reich had been silent. His charismatic hold had been exercised at second-hand. When the time came, he had no hesitation in chopping that hand and consigning it to darkness. Political expediency, or spiritual inoculation? A manoeuvre to try to escape responsibility for what had happened, or the massive wielding of a giant 260 million-dollar Zen stick?

The next day was the thirty-first anniversary of Bhagwan's enlightenment in India, at the age of twenty-one. It was the first time Enlightenment Day – the most important event in the Rajneeshee calendar outside the July Festival – had been celebrated without His presence. Before breakfast we did *gachchmis*, a communal meditation adapted from Buddhism. We sat cross-legged on foam-rubber cushions in the downstairs room normally used for discos and barbecues. In front of us was a large photograph of Bhagwan, to which the sannyasins offered greetings, Indian-style, with the palms pressed together. Everybody chanted Hindi words which meant something like 'I go to the feet of the Awakened One.' At the back of the room three musicians – a pianist, a guitarist and a flautist – played languid melodies which blended the repetitive patterns of Eric Satie with the meandering harmonies of Ravi Shanker. We swayed gently before the Master's portrait. Doped by the music, I became lost in the myriad threads of His beard, the crow-foot creases of His eternally laughing, protruding eyes. I felt almost at One with the worshippers, almost in love with Big Brother Bhagwan. What would have happened – I thought afterwards – if he had been there in the flesh?

That evening they put on a show which Sarita produced. She placed me at a table right by the stage. There was food and wine, there were children. The whole community was gathered – about a hundred people in all. A lanky American began with a solemn statement about his 'strong but fragile' relationship with Bhagwan. After reading a Sufi tale from one of the Master's discourses, he delivered this message: 'Be playful and transcend all seriousness.' It was said in a tone more suitable for a funeral oration. Life was a purposeless, festive game, with nowhere to go. Heaven and hell were within us, said Bhagwan. Genghiz, Tamerlane and Hitler were there, along with Buddha, Muhammad, Lao Tzu. Only through the anguish of Auschwitz and Hiroshima could life be renewed on earth. To live intensely, in every moment, that was Sannyas. Life, its joy and its beauty, was insecurity. To be locked in security was suicide.

We sang a song specially written for the occasion:

> 'Sweet taste of Your Higher Love,
> Sweet taste of Your Being,
> No, No, No, have no fear,
> It's just the lions roaring out Your song, it's clear,
> Now the lions' hearts are growing strong, no fear!'

The show began: 'Bhagwan's World Tour.' Each of the countries where he had been thrown out – India, Greece, Ireland – was satirised in brilliantly executed song and dance routines. The tunes were clever, the lyrics hilarious. The Pope and Mother Theresa, Bhagwan's chief tormentors, wandered over the earth in pursuit of the Enlightened One, but finally drowned in the Caribbean. On reaching the shores of Paradise, they peeled off their white garments to reveal the orange robes of the sannyasins. We all ended up dancing on stage.

They were still dancing when I drove into the night.

IX

Cosmic Biz

God is the Iz-ness of the Is,
The One-ness of our Cosmic Biz;
The high, the low, the near, the far,
The atom and the evening star;
The lark, the shark, the cloud, the clod,
The whole darned Universe – that's God.

ROBERT SERVICE

I took the coast road to San Francisco. The weather was disastrous. The persistent Pacific mists kept most of the famous coastline with its rocky headlands and its black volcanic sands out of view. My knowledge of whales, giant sequoias, sea birds and what was termed the 'eternal contest of ocean and continent' had to be gleaned from fading tourist notices placed at scenic stops along the route. South of Florence, however, the mists parted for a few hours, revealing a thin, watery sun. I walked for several miles along a dune-flanked beach, watching small waders scudding mechanically before the waves and admiring a forest of ancient tree stumps that the ocean had sculpted into fantastically beautiful shapes. There was not a human in sight.

I spent one night at a campsite in a giant redwood grove south of Eureka. It was late and the few weekend campers were already asleep, except for a group of discreet revellers ensconced around a fire. There was a primeval, magical quality to the glow of faces under the massive, receding trunks, a distant echo of some ancestral memory of the forest. Too tired, and timid, to seek inclusion, I found a secluded lot at the edge of the ground. I switched off the lights and the engine, and was startled by muffled cries of a woman followed by what sounded like the heavy grunts of a bear. Alarmed, I got out of the camper and flashed a torch through the trees. The beam revealed a tiny canvas tent that was heaving and palpitating like a sackful of piglets: a couple, evidently in the throes of passion.

This had to be California.

Ivan had been recommended to me as the man with his finger on the city's pulse. I met him next day at his home on Liberty street, at the top of a very steep hill with a magnificent view of the Bay. Above us a tall three-pronged radio mast skewered the mist, a diabolic symbol towering over the City of Sin. The neat painted rows of houses fell below in semi-circular rows, like seats in a Greek theatre. The house – really a cottage – was furnished with oriental rugs and kelims, Indian carvings, house plants and other organic things. The stereo was playing a version of the Beethoven Violin Concerto adapted for piano and orchestra. It seemed an appropriate theme for San Francisco: familiar yet somehow outrageous, like the carved and gabled 'Victorian' houses that people painted in over-bright colours.

When I commented on the music Ivan threw back his blonde Slavonic head and laughed at my purism. 'I guess there's a market for everything in this town,' he said.

He was a fine-looking man, tall with piercing blue eyes and an infective exuberance. Over coffee and salad he launched straight into his sex life, relieving me of the need to phrase carefully probing questions.

'I occasionally get involved with women. I suppose I've had twenty women over the last twenty years, compared with two thousand men. I enjoy firmer bodies. I find most women very flaccid. I used to go to the bath-houses three to five times a month. We celebrated the absolute glory of physicality. We touched manhood *per se* in all its original forms.' He paused, munching his salad. 'But now I'm forty-five, and unless there's something rather special, I don't get involved any more. I'm with a new man now. I'm astonished that it's still fresh all over.'

'But doesn't AIDS cast a shadow over new relationships?'

'There was a time when I used to think about it a lot. But right away I knew that the real issue was fear. Spirit informs matter, the sickness is in the soul. Of the two people I know who have been most paralysed by fear, one is a friend who goes to bed with a new man at most once or twice a year, which in the gay community is very conservative; the other is a straight, married friend who tortured himself with guilt about an extra-marital affair. My own feeling is this: I'm doing some very valuable things in life. It isn't appropriate for me to die yet. If I were to come down with AIDS it would be to reveal some larger truth in the world . . . '

'Have you taken the test?' I asked him.

'No. There isn't any point. Everyone uses rubbers now, so there isn't much danger of getting it any more. If you're positive, you're psychologically better off not knowing.'

We talked about the churches. Despite the existence of gay clergy in all the mainstream denominations, as well as one fully-fledged gay church, the Metropolitan Community Church, Ivan felt that Christianity had little or nothing to offer him or his friends. They were far beyond the reach of a conventionally-organised faith. Ivan found his spiritual nourishment in the gay festivals that took place in San Francisco or the surrounding countryside, or in activities like channelling, a comparatively new craze that was sweeping the West Coast.

'What's channelling?' I asked.

'Come at six this evening and I'll take you along,' said Ivan.

I turned up as arranged, and followed Ivan and two of his friends down the freeway to Palo Alto. Our venue, the Women's Club, was already crowded when we arrived. The cars outside were Volvos, Volkswagens and BMWs, hallmarks of an intelligentsia which rejects the lumpenbourgeois vulgarity of the American automobile. Inside, every chair was taken, and many people were standing or sitting on the floor. There must have been at least four hundred people there. At fifteen dollars a head, that represented quite a healthy box office – even before the sale of the books and tapes. Two performances a week must bring in a tidy income.

We were there to hear Emmanuel, a being from an outer galaxy. He spoke through his 'channel', Pat Rodegast, an attractive woman of about forty. Ms Rodegast, casually dressed in brown slacks and a white jumper, sat demurely on stage, while her two female companions did the introductory honours. Then the lights were lowered, Albinoni came on tape, and we did our meditations. Our instructions were to get in touch with the Emmanuel inside our own rememberings and experience the wonders of unfoldment.

Emmanuel had a soft, gentle voice which accorded well with his/her soft, gentle message. The burden of this was a kind of spiritual Panglossianism: all was for the best in the best of all possible cosmoses. Don't worry about anything, s/he said. Just relax and get in touch with your innermost isness, and everything'll be OK. Trust the heart, not the intellect, and do what feels right: God's right there inside you, you and God are One. Nothing exists in the human world that is not godly: evil is simply a manifestation of ignorance, a necessary part of our pre-school education.

'Murder, violence, cruelty, viciousness, wickedness – yes, this all exists, just as kindergarten exists before first grade,' said Emmanuel. Even pride and vanity, those deadliest of sins, were OK when you got to the bottom of them. Those who felt pride should seek the Isness that lurked behind its wall. There they would find 'a most beautiful blossoming consciousness that, in order to survive, put on the armour of pride'.

Don't even worry about the victims of Hitler and Stalin, s/he said: 'Remember, this is a schoolroom and . . . some of the lessons need to be written across the heavens in order for them to be heard and understood.' The souls of the Holocaust victims sacrificed their lives in a 'tremendous gift of love', just as others were sacrificing themselves today. No need to worry about stopping these horrors: the souls would come back in new karmas. Same with torture and child abuse; they also could be learning experiences, for the victims as well as the perpetrators. Suicide? Nothing to worry about: same as dropping out from school; the only problem was the governors and teachers of Karma College would insist on you making you come back to make up your credits: 'It is clear that when one chooses to quit school,' said Emmanuel in his/her meandering monotone, 'it is necessary to come back again and learn what could not be learned at that time. I speak to you from eternity. There is no limit to the number of lives one can have.'

If Joseph Smith had been around today, I mused, he would definitely be a channeller. Our less materialistic, more information-oriented age would have suited him admirably. Channellers don't have to mess around with cumbersome artifacts like peep-stones and golden plates. All they have to do is get in touch with their innermost isnesses and spout – in seminars, on stage, in private counsellings or radio phone-ins. The top spirit guide Ramtha earns his channeller, a husky-voiced blonde with an upturned nose known terrestrially as Mrs J. Z. Knight, up to $400 *per head* for an evening session, or $1,500 for a week-end seminar. Shirley MacLaine, despite having won an Oscar, is somewhat lower on the astro-dollar scale, charging $300 per person for a week-end seminar on how to get in touch with your Higher Self. Still, Shirley makes up for this by doing it on television. Her friend, blue-eyed Kevin Ryerson, channels for 'John', a contemporary of Jesus who speaks English – not Aramaic – in a slow, deliberate manner with lots of Smithian ye's and thou's. Today's channellers, however, do not require the biblical legitimacy demanded by nineteenth-century audiences: the invasion of Eastern mysticisms pioneered in the Twenties by Annie Besant, Madame Blatavski, Krishnamurti, and other forerunners of the New Age, has made karma a familiar part of the culture.

Karma is free-flowing where the Gospel (even a brand-new one, like Joseph's) ties you to a text. The Gospel only allows one Incarnation – which means that everybody, whether they want to or not, has to be saved through Jesus. Karma allows for an infinite number of incarnations, reincarnations and cosmic recyclings, endless permutations in the lottery of life.

I looked around the room, at the audience. They were overwhelmingly white and middle-class. The women were mostly dressed casually with a hint of chic, without being ostentatious. The men were in their thirties and forties, with keen, observant looks on their faces. Their questions – passed anonymously to the medium on pieces of paper – reflected the concerns and guilts of high achievers. 'My daughter's on drugs, what do I do? Are we not destroying the planet? Is having money not a spiritual "downer"? Is it OK to get divorced?'

Emmanuel's answers were uniformly reassuring. What appeared physically harmful was not, in the cosmic order of things, ultimately so. Judgements were valueless, they simply closed the door more tightly to healing. Trust the earth, and trust the universe: in man's belief that he had within himself the capacity to obliterate the world there was a 'sense of grandiosity that borders on the infantile'. Don't worry about money: 'If you can release your guilt about money and accept it as part of the Divine Universe and the physical reality of your earth, you will see that it has no more or less power than you give it. It is a necessity. You hold the sense of money too tightly.' Divorce was all right. Souls came together, not to remain together but to grow. When this had happened, and the gifts had been given and the lessons learned, it was time to move on. 'The gifts have been given. Do not be alarmed by change.'

Underpinning the whole sense of karmic reassurance there lay a positive, affirmative, vision of death. The process of dying was always joyous, once fear had been overcome. Death itself was insignificant: a pleasant release from mortality, 'like taking off a tight shoe, or leaving a smoke-filled room'.

There was a suffocating complacency about Emmanuel's message. Reincarnation, karma and other vedantic ideas were illuminating when applied to metaphysics, or to the teeming poor of India, who had no hope of escaping from their condition except into the fantasy of other, better incarnations. Among the affluent denizens of Palo Alto the teachings took on a much more dubious meaning: since everyone gets another chance anyway, we might as well make the best of it this time around, enjoying guilt-free rides in our Volvos and BMWs without worrying about pollution, the poor, the sick, the hispanics and the blacks. No wonder channels were so popular: they told you everything you wanted to hear.

The session closed with another meditation, and then the audience began to drift away – those, at least, who declined to queue for tapes at fifteen dollars each. At the back of the hall Ivan and his friends were holding a hug-in, standing in a circle with their arms clasped around each other, locked in silent communion.

I signalled goodbye, and drove on south to Ventura, where my cousin Delia lived, taking the inland route. After the cool mists of San Francisco, the Salinas Valley was dusty and hot: it was like motoring from England to Provence in under two hours. Everywhere Mexican workers were harvesting vegetables, piling up green cascades into trucks that crawled along the furrowed fields, groaning with abundance.

Santa Barbara, where I rejoined the coast, was hot and windless, but the air was fresh. I welcomed its civilised precincts, its outdoor cafés – so inexplicably rare in California. It almost felt like southern France or Italy.

A New Age Exposition was being held in a large yellow geodesic dome a few blocks away from the town centre. The theme was set in the parking lot outside. Along with a predictable array of Beetles, 2 CV's and other ecologically acceptable vehicles with life-affirming slogans and anti-nuclear stickers, I saw the most perfect exemplar of the Rustic Camper I have yet encountered: a Volkswagen van completely dressed in shingles, with latticed cottage-style windows and potted geraniums – a product of air-polluting Wolfsburg that tried to insist, against all evidence, that it was an innocent woodland hut.

The harsher facts of life and death were absent in the exhibition hall, where the New Age practitioners displayed themselves, their skills and their wares. Every stall had its panacea, its guaranteed solution to life's riddles, its answer to the problems of body and soul. Each excluded the others; all cost money. The wide-eyed idealism of the Sixties had hitched itself to Eighties commercialism: New Age personhood, hirsute, bewhiskered, or ostentatiously pregnant, still slouched about in sandals and shapeless dungarees, but eyes that once gazed vacuously into psychedelic space or sought nirvanas beyond distant horizons had acquired a harder, more predatory glaze.

A young man was offering healing for a modest dollar a minute. I asked him if he could cure the allergic rhinitis which constantly plagues me. 'We heal,' he said 'but that doesn't always mean that we cure. Healing means "to make sound or whole", according to the dictionary. That can help the curing process, by making you more relaxed, calmer and clearer-thinking.'

'So does a glass of wine,' I said, 'which costs a lot less than a dollar a minute.'

The New Age movement, of course, had spread far beyond its Californian motherland: every city now had its gurus and swamis, its psychic healers, its palm-readers, crystal-gazers, astrologers or spiritualists. There was no shortage of such activity in Britain, either: a similar repertoire of home-brewed panaceas could be found at the Mind and Body Exhibition held in London every year. But in California, unlike other regions, these things no longer seemed part of a heterodox fringe or subculture that merged into personal eccentricity, like the spiritualism or table-turning indulged in by elderly spinsters in Brighton or Bournemouth. Here, on the fringes of the Pacific, the Sixties, and decades of spiritual radicalism preceding them, had become one of life's permanent features: it came as no surprise to learn, after my return to England, that Ronald Reagan, ex-Governor of California, and his wife had brought astrology into the White House. Rampant individualism and personal insecurity had conspired to make heterodoxy quite normal.

Where other religious movements dried into the brittle twigs of bureaucracy or ossified into institutions, New Age, that dawn of a new, more spiritual consciousness heralded by the hippies in the Sixties, seemed to have run into sands of utility and commercialism. Like everything else, it was something to be packaged and marketed: channelling, the music of Steve Halpern, subliminal tapes, divination, astrology, arithomancy, crystal healing, runic reading, psychometry and the myriad styles of meditation were all for sale at a price, supporting an army of mediums, counsellors, therapists, consultants and practitioners. Yet no one seemed necessarily healthier, happier or more relaxed as a result of these inner explorations. If some Californians looked bronzed and carefree, like the surfers I watched deafly avoiding the rocks at Ventura Point, it was probably because they enjoyed sunshine, good health and plenty of exercise. New Age culture wasn't changing the world: it was making it run more smoothly, like alcohol, exercise, sunshine, money and sex.

By the time I reached my cousin Delia's, it had long been dark. Despite her careful instructions, I had got lost in the network of boulevards and shopping malls that people called a city, but seemed only a glorified suburb without centre or personality. After an hour of frustration, I fetched up in the Hilton Hotel, and asked for directions. The house was in a place called Runnymead Park. The doorman hadn't heard of it.

'Isn't that the mobile home place across the road?' said the concierge, his voice containing the faintest hint of disparagement.

'I doubt it,' said I. 'I don't think my cousin lives in a mobile home park.'

I barely knew my father's first cousin, but imagined her to be more than comfortably off. Her father – a German of Jewish origin from Dresden – had been a banker. Her mother – my grandmother's younger sister – had been a grand, somewhat formidable lady of whom I had been in considerable awe as a child. They had lived in a magnificent Jacobean house, with fine paintings, gloomy furniture and a home farm endowed with a prize Jersey herd that provided thick jugs of cream at a time of post-war austerity when cream was almost unknown. Cousin Delia – I had assumed – would have a luxurious condominium overlooking a private beach, or in one of those exclusive enclaves built in the Spanish style. Nonplussed, I telephoned. She sent her husband Ted to rescue me.

I had been wrong. It was the mobile home park after all. Next morning Delia and Ted showed me round. There were tidy prefabricated bungalows with verandas and garages grouped round a pond with ducks and goldfish. The houses had neat, symmetrical gardens with miniature cypresses, flawless lawns and little brightly-coloured paths surfaced with marble chips or crushed quartz of the kind you find on modern graves. Several had gnomes or plastic animals on their lawns.

The inhabitants were white, elderly couples living on pensions and their savings. Dogs or young families were not allowed, though grandchildren were permitted at week-ends. You rented the space and bought the mobile home yourself from a number of models approved by the property company that owned the park. The house arrived on a truck. It only took a day to erect. There was a clubhouse with swimming pool and tennis courts, a bar and video room. It was a safe, self-contained island of modest prosperity in the midst of a chaotic urban sprawl, a refuge where like-minded people could congregate in their declining years, enjoying each other's company and the sun which shone – comfortably removed from the Los Angeles smog – for three hundred days in the year.

Delia's home looked different from the others. She had inherited the passion for gardening that ran in my grandmother's family. Her little house was festooned with bougainvillaeas and jasmine. Its exterior had been meta-morphosed into something inviting and almost familiar, a Wiltshire cottage garden translated to the riotous subtropics where blue hibiscus, trumpet vines and flaming poinsettias reigned instead of lobelia, clematis and roses.

'The manager disapproves,' said Delia. 'He told me I'd get termites if I let creepers grow on my roof. I said that was my problem, not his.' Ted and Delia, as the park's longest-established residents and most senior citizens, enjoyed a special status in the community. They formed the welcoming committee for newcomers – arriving at each house with a pot of honey and a bouquet picked from Delia's garden. Appearances favoured them. Ted was tall and lean, with a long white Santa Claus beard that made him much in demand at Christmas. Delia had my grandmother's white hair and Red Indian features; but unlike my grandmother, who had always worn well-cut suits and hats (with ornithological embellishments kept in crisp condition by a lady's lady who devoted the best part of her life to this purpose), Delia shuffled around her garden in sandals and flowing Indian robes, wearing a benign otherworldly smile.

This strange yet familiar conundrum continued indoors. Despite its spacious interior ('It's a double-truck-width home,' said my cousin proudly) it was dark and gloomy, with a thick patterned carpet of ochre and brown, composition walls of imitation oak panelling and cheap-looking furniture of the kind one finds in inexpensive motels. The paintings and bibelots reflected a bizarre confusion of tastes. There were Woolworth reproductions of large-eyed Spanish children and clowns, butterflies made out of Tiffany glass, modern electrified knick-knacks that made coloured patterns. Yet, with a sense of shock, I also recognised items from my great-aunt's house – a carved oak Jacobean chest, a painting of Bacchus by Jordaens, and Sargent's fine charcoal sketch of my great-aunt as a black-eyed Edwardian beauty about to be launched on London society.

The garage, with its beam-operated, sliding door, was a shrine to its occupant, a 1970 Oldsmobile Convertible named Emily. Every surface, including the ceiling, was covered with posters, magazine photographs, brightly coloured prints, French impressionists, decorous nudes, blown up menus, traffic reflectors and other icons culled from Ted's career as a truck-driver, bricolage merchant, decorator and general handyman. The car with its white-walled tyres with matching canvas roof and expensive leather upholstery, was the most substantial and valued thing in this world of disposables and movables. Its owners invariably referred to it by name, a mark of affection and respect never accorded to the house itself.

During dinner they asked me about my travels. Naïvely assuming myself to be among expatriate kin, I began to relate stories that would have appealed to my grandmother's impish sense of fun; but then to my slight consternation I began to realise I was among true believers. Fortunately they were not evangelicals, like cousins on my grandfather's side of the family who were joylessly seeking to morally re-arm the world by abolishing alcohol and communism. Delia and Ted were at the other end of the spectrum. They had been through spiritualism and were now beyond theosophy, into an ecumenical ministry which sought out the mystic common grounds between all the religions. They had been up there in the New Age, before the hippies and their gurus, when I had still been in adolescence, struggling with Marx, Freud and Nietzsche.

Next day they took me to see their mentor in Ojai, the celebrated Dr Benito Reyes. I assumed he was celebrated: the back cover of a book Delia showed me described him as the author of more than twenty works of philosophy, psychology, religious studies, poetry and Oriental culture; the holder of two Fulbright professorships, founder of two universities as well as the World Congress of University Presidents, and also founder of the Ecumenical Ministry of the Unity of All Religions.

'Philosopher, teacher, lecturer, educator, Orientalist, general semanticist, poet, author, clinical psychologist, therapist, ecumenical minister and lover of humanity,' said the blurb, 'Dr Reyes is a modern example of the Renaissance idea of the *uomo universale . . .* '

As I had suspected, the World University of America was in inverse size to the grandiloquence of its title. It consisted of a whitewashed one-storey building enclosing a small courtyard. There were two classrooms, half a dozen offices and a meditation hall, where Dr Reyes held his ecumenical services. When we arrived the great man was busy, but his wife, the university's Vice-President, graciously received us in her office. A small Filipino lady of about sixty, she had an animated face and eyes that sparkled behind her spectacles. My cousin introduced me as a visitor from London.

'Have you met Benjamin Creme?' asked Mrs Reyes. 'The gentleman who make such a noise about the coming of Christ.'

'I'm afraid not.'

'He says Christ has already come, and is living in London. You know, I believe that. I know from my studies that Christ is supposed to be of Celtic origin.'

'You mean when Jesus comes back he'll be an Irishman?' I said chauvinistically.

'No, no, no,' said Mrs Reyes, looking annoyed at my ignorance. 'Not Jesus, Christ. The two are not the same. There's the Black Nazarene – that's Jesus; and the White Christ. Surely you've heard of the Black Nazarene?'

'No. Who was the Black Nazarene?'

'Jesus.'

'Was he black?'

'No, not in that sense. He's like a Jew who lived in the south – a dark Jew, not a Negro type.'

'And Christ?'

But before she had time to explain, we were summoned to the lecture. There were a dozen people in the classroom in addition to Delia, Ted and myself. Most were middle-aged and female; there were two youngish men, one of whom was introduced to me as a teacher at the university. The other was protecting a blonde girl in her twenties with the marketable face of a model. There were various charts in the classroom, and a large-scale geological map of the world showing the earthquake zones. Fissures in the earth's crust, including the San Andreas Fault, were studded with symbols representing explosions, along with dates, most of which lay in the future.

Dr Reyes was small and neat-looking, like his wife. Like many south-east Asians he appeared ageless. He wore a microphone affixed to his tie: every word of *uomo universale* was being preserved for posterity.

The subject of his lecture was 'Scientific Evidence of the Existence of the Soul'. I found it very difficult to follow. Dr Reyes enjoyed using long, unfamiliar words like 'thanatological and soteriological phenomenology' and 'epiphenomenalism' – his favourite term of abuse. His mode of delivery was even more forbidding than his vocabulary: his discourse seemed to wind itself round and round in circles, like a spacecraft in orbit, never quite escaping from the gravitational field into which it had been trapped by the epiphenomalists, materialists and other negative forces.

Nevertheless, his argument sounded impressive. It was based on empirical data from the testimonies of people who had had 'near-death experiences' (NDEs) and 'out-of-body experiences' (OBEs). In both cases people had felt themselves leaving their bodies while remaining, so they claimed, fully conscious. The NDEs were particularly interesting; not only did they correspond to ancient Egyptian, Tibetan and other accounts of souls leaving bodies; some of these experiences – for example in the case of the victims of accidents or heart attacks – had occurred while the patients' activity was being monitored on an electro-encephalogram (EEG). The experience of lucidity, being 'out of one's body' while apparently fully conscious, coincided with the total absence of EEG activity – a state of 'brain death' which, in the case of the witnesses, proved to be reversible.

The implications were heartening for believers in the soul, immortality and reincarnation, suggesting that consciousness could exist (even if only for a split second) while the brain had ceased to function. If consciousness existed independently of the brain, then what the religions taught about immortality might be true after all, and scientists who took the view that consciousness was merely an 'epiphenomenon' or by-product of brain activity, could be wrong. The conventional scientific wisdom could be turned on its head. Instead of being a by-product of brain activity, consciousness could, in fact, be the 'user' of the brain, the musician, as it were, behind the instrument. According to this theory, loss of consciousness was not the result of death, but its cause: the brain ceased to function because consciousness had withdrawn from it, had ceased to use it in order to manifest itself.

Buried in the thickets of Reyes's discourse, there seemed a plausible case for immortality. I wanted to believe in it, to share my cousins' enthusiasms.

He talked about his out-of-body experiences, claiming he could induce them at will: 'By the way,' he added, 'that is not a gift that I alone have – everybody has it. As a matter of fact, many of you have experienced it. This lady experienced it,' he said, pointing to one of the women, 'so I asked her: "Where are you?" "I am in the oak tree," she said. "What oak tree?" "The oak tree in front of the building here." "What do you mean, you're sitting under the oak tree?" "No, I'm inside the oak tree." "What are you doing there?" "I'm studying the cells."'

The woman, pleased to be singled out, nodded her assent. Dr Reyes rambled on about genes and DNA, the pineal gland and how consciousness was the same as energy. God was the only reality, he said, citing the Eastern mystics: 'We are not really ever separate from God, the Universe, and everything else, for Life is One and God is Omnipresent and Reality is a Continuum, the Theanthropokosmic Continuum or God-Man-Universe

Continuum . . . We are Unconditional Bliss, Unlimited Energy; we are, as a matter of fact, $E = MC2$'.

Then somebody asked a question: 'Tell us about the Great White Brotherhood.'

'The Great White Brotherhood,' said Dr Reyes, 'refers to a group of teachers of humanity who decided to form a school to liberate mankind. They came from the planet Venus – 108 of them, about 80 million years ago. Before that there were human beings on earth, but they had no cerebellums. They trained the leaders of humanity through a system of five initiations. To be able to go out of the body is the hallmark of the first initiation . . . '

My mind began to wander. We were back in the realms of channelling, L. Ron Hubbard, Shirley MacLaine and other New Age enthusiasts. After the lecture my cousin introduced me to Dr Reyes.

'How did you come to Ojai?' I asked.

'He called us,' said Dr Reyes. 'I was scheduled to become Minister of Education. At first I was reluctant.'

'Who called you?' I asked.

'The One who guides me, outside and inside.'

'One of the White Brothers? Is he still on the earth?'

'He materialises in different places.'

'Is he the person who trained you?'

'I've been training with Him in quite a few lives,' said Dr Reyes. 'He took me over at the age of sixteen and let me go out of my body. All my life I've been guided by Him. That's why I came to Ojai. It's where the new advanced inhabitants of the earth will gather: that's why we're building the World Ecumenical University here. A new kind of humanity will be born here.'

No reasonable person could object to research into NDEs and OBEs; or to an ecumenical ministry that sought to break down sectarian prejudices and barriers. What was curious, but somehow typically Californian, was the manner in which several activities that elsewhere would have remained separate were merging synthetically around the person of this diminutive Filipino, in a penumbra of semi-occultism. Here in the new Far West the old pre-millennial fantasies had been reconstituted, with karma and brain-death research instead of the Books of Daniel and Revelation, a mystery Indian guru in place of the Christ, and Dr Benito Reyes playing the part of the Prophet Joseph Smith. The utopian thread in American culture that linked Governor Winthrop to Joseph, ran from Massachusetts Bay to Nauvoo and from Nauvoo to California like a subterranean cable, conveying messages from the past. Just as for the English Puritans America was the New Israel, so California was America's America: a haven for new utopias, the venue for great millennial events, where history would achieve its final denouement, where the nation's, nay the world's destiny would finally be manifest.

Christmas was now approaching. I flew home to London, leaving the camper with my cousins. I returned to California the following April. Nothing had changed. The flowers were the same as when I left. The sun shone with identical intensity. Only the days were longer, allowing more time for exploration. After collecting the camper I spent my first night at Malibu, in the RV park overlooking the beach. For a place that has given its charming name to cocktails, cigarettes, surf boards, male deodorants and automobiles, it was disappointing. The better part of the beach had been privatised, with wire fences and threatening notices denying general access to part of what I had always considered my birthright. The sea was cold; the sun refused to unwind itself from a shroud of morning mist. Disgruntled, I abandoned my plan for a day on the beach and headed for downtown LA.

Los Angeles has been described as 'forty suburbs in search of a city'. This, of course, is an essentially urbanite view. There is a city downtown – or rather, there are two; a yuppie metropolis of tall buildings with underground car parks and plexiglass cladding, and a Hispano-Afro-Asian casbah where English is never heard and barely understood. Occasionally these two, mutually antagonistic worlds have to meet. The doorman at the Biltmore Hotel in Pershing Square earns his keep by carefully discriminating between who should be allowed in and who kept out. This is no easy task in a country where formal rules of race segregation have been abandoned, and where the affluent may appear unshaven, wearing washed out denims or loose-fitting, shapeless dungarees with designer-patches on their legs. The square was once an elegant arrangement of palm trees and lawn done, like the Biltmore itself, in an art-deco style that still whispers Bugatti and Hispano-Suiza, conjuring visions of ladies with straw hats, white skins and chic chiffon dresses. Now it is a dumping ground for down-and-outs, and addicts who rifle the litter-bins and do drug deals behind the trees.

Mexico is quietly reconquering California. It has nearly taken over LA. I went by myself to cash some travellers' cheques near the Times-Mirror building. The street was alive with small brown people jostling each other on the pavements. The shops were scruffy but buzzing with activity, as in Cairo. The only smart-looking stores sold wedding outfits – elaborate confections of chiffon muslin, satin and taffeta with their polyester imitations that tempted poor peasants to dreams of purity and affluence. A would-be mugger, vomiting Spanish expletives, lunged at me with a knife. Fortunately, he was so drunk he would have missed an elephant.

The sense of being in a Third World city was confirmed when a man came up and asked if I wanted to change travellers' cheques. But the rate he offered was robbery, so I headed east towards the office district. The girls in the bank were all brown or black, but exquisitely dressed. White Americans were evidently expelled to the suburbs, or confined to the gleaming high-rises that towered over the city like a medieval castle. LA was a twenty-first-century Carcassonne, where corporate barons and knights lived in magnificent air-conditioned isolation ruling the world with money, while far below the peasants, shopkeepers, helots and rentiers struggled against violence, grime and squalor for their living.

I lunched at a Mexican diner for $2.50, taking on a leaden belly-full of beans and tortilla and a scraggy something that might have been chicken before heading south for San Diego. By the time I reached Orange County, it was beginning to get dark. A vast unplanned grid of suburban banality superimposed on what had once been a lovely Mediterranean landscape of gardens, vines and orange groves, Orange County is best experienced at night, when the lights transform its emptiness. The dismal utilitarian shops lining the boulevards are suddenly dancing with neon; the freeway becomes a necklace of rubies and diamonds that recede towards invisible horizons, merging with the galaxy. As I passed Orange County airport I saw another chain of lights slung over the dark form of the mountains as the aircraft came into land, a stately school of whale-finned silhouettes swimming out of the firmament. The banality of this world, the chaotic desecration it had wrought upon the land, the rape of nature's continent by concrete, metal, glass and human greed had gone with the sun. What was left was suddenly, inspiringly beautiful: a universe of illuminated dots and flashing signals to be decoded by the human brain, which alone could distinguish between what was terrestrial and what belonged to the sky.

The most arresting landmark in this lightscape was the huge plain neon cross, a hundred foot tall, that stands above Robert Schuller's Crystal Cathedral. This magnificent structure of tubular steel and glass, designed by Philip Johnson, I had visited before, when I went to see the Christmas show, a lavishly-produced pageant, with live sheep, donkeys and camels, flying angels, kings in Rembrandt costumes and shepherds dressed as Arabs – a Christmas card brought to life by a thousand Hollywood extras and a battery of special effects. The production was flawless: the only anachronistic note was struck by an 'Arab' who followed the animals around with a 'pooper-scooper', to collect their droppings as soon as they hit the stage.

I had also watched Schuller on television. He is a smooth, silver-haired man of sixty with regular features, sunken brown eyes hiding behind steel-rimmed spectacles, a tight, unfurrowed skin and a taut, rictus-like smile. His *Hour of Power*, beamed into three million American, Canadian and Australian homes every week, is something between a service and a chat-show. It is less liturgical than Jerry Falwell's *Old Time Gospel Hour*, but more so than Pat Robertson's magazine-style *700 Club*. Schuller is the only widely-viewed television preacher who belongs to one of the mainstream churches and is not a fundamentalist. Founded by Dutch settlers in the seventeenth-century, his church, the Reformed Church of America, is one of the oldest in North America. Though liberal theologically, Schuller's style is evangelical: like the fundamentalists he sermonises, pontificates, harangues and urges the unsaved to give themselves to Christ. But the content of his message is world-affirming, hedonistic, and unabashedly Californian.

'Before thou cans't love thy neighbour,' he says (I paraphrase: these are not his actual words) 'thou must first love thyself.' Since most of us get stuck at the first stage of any endeavour, 'Love Thyself' is the message which really comes across. Schuller is, not surprisingly, very popular and immensely rich. The twenty-five-odd books he has published consist mainly of his sermons recycled and packaged into marketable nuggets. These include catchy phrases like: 'There is no gain without pain.' 'The Cross sanctifies the ego trip,' 'Make your scars into stars, your tears into pearls, your pain into gain,' 'Tough times never last, but tough people do.' Schuller says that Jesus has addressed him personally at least five times. He claims that his cheer-leading jingles and mnemonics, which doubtless would have brought him success on Madison Avenue, are inspired, if not actually dictated, by God.

Schuller describes his message as a 'theology of self-esteem', designed to bring about a 'new reformation'. Luther and Calvin erred in placing too much stress on human depravity and its corollary, divine grace. The 'dignity of the person' he says, should become the 'new theological bench-mark'. Once the church teaches people to value themselves fully as Children of God, the energy and creativity will be released that will enable them to help others: 'Where the sixteenth-century Reformation returned our focus to sacred Scriptures as the only infallible rule for faith and practice, the new reformation will return our focus to the sacred right of every person to self-esteem! The fact is, the church will never succeed until it satisfies the human being's hunger for self-value.'

Though he rather glibly condemns Freud's pleasure principle, Schuller draws on Freudian concepts. The Fatherhood of God – he says – is built into the human subconscious: 'until we experience reconciliation with God, we are the victims of an inferiority complex'. Only conversion through Christ can give us a true sense of our own significance. To be born again means changing from a negative to a positive self-image. Once that has been achieved, and only then, will we be able to help our fellow human beings. 'A theology of self-esteem sets the stage where a theology of social ethics will evolve naturally, unavoidably, beautifully.'

Schuller employs scripture to buttress his arguments in a selective and tortuous way. His favourites are the Lord's Prayer ('a classic timeless therapy') and the Beatitudes ('The Be-Happy Attitudes'). According to Schuller, 'blessed are the meek' really means 'blessed are the mighty'; and while he is clearly referring to moral fortitude here, his principles explicitly favour the rich above the poor. He ignores Christ's condemnations of wealth completely, stating instead that 'untold numbers of Christians have remained at poverty level because the pursuit of wealth was always proclaimed to be sinful and materialistic'. He even goes so far as to condemn those who criticise wealth as 'cynical have-nots' who persecute the rich, assuming that anyone who is wealthy must either be a 'crook or a swindler'.

In essence Schuller's doctrine is a liberation theology of the right, a form of spiritual Thatcherism that endows wealth with respectability, equating success with virtue. 'Every competitor is a winner,' said Schuller in one of his crasser statements: 'The losers never tried.'

There are two undeclared assumptions in Schuller's theology. One is a radical individualism, which always puts personal above social achievement. The other is that market forces – those forces which govern the 'world' – are invariably benign. The systemic poverty that condemns whole groups, minorities, even nations to spiritual and material oppression are not addressed at all seriously.

For him the needle's eye appears to be large enough to admit two houses, several cars, an ocean-going yacht – the whole American dream. The Christian doctrines of service and self-sacrifice – too difficult for most people to live by – get only perfunctory attention. Christianity as moral standard, the Gospels as a set of criteria by which God judges the motives and actions of humankind, is transformed, none too subtly, into a cosy ethic of personal reassurance. 'God loves you and so do I!' is Schuller's favourite slogan – the sign-off he uses in all his correspondence.

Few would deny that true self-esteem is essential for human health and well-being: medical science confirms the obvious fact that people with low self-esteem are more prone than others to suffer depression and related disorders. Psychotherapy rightly concerns itself with making individuals 'feel good about themselves', assuaging guilts and anxieties – feelings which all too often have been promoted or exacerbated by religious zealots.

As an honest-to-the-devil agnostic, I am inclined to admire Schuller's efforts to undo the centuries of damage pastors, priests and nuns have inflicted on the human psyche by their obsession with sin, with fallen human nature. Were I Christian, however, I would have very serious doubts: for his weapons of redress are concepts forged outside the structures of Judaeo-Christianity, by people who were mostly antagonistic towards organised religion. Schuller's critics are probably right in seeing the 'theology of self-esteem' as a strategy according to which – whether consciously or otherwise – secular values inform, and eventually replace, religious ones. I suspect that Schuller is really a secular-humanist wolf in shepherd's clothing. It does not take much reflection to realise that his 'theology of self-esteem' leaves little or no room for God as traditionally perceived or understood. His reinvented God is the mirror image of humanistic modern man.

Meditating on Schuller, as I drove past Garden Grove, I was again reminded of Joseph Smith, archetypical American genius and prophet of dreams. Like Joseph, Schuller preaches a perfectionist Arminian doctrine of material achievement, of justification by wealth. Like Joseph, he is a brilliant showman and entrepreneur who builds his city on a swamp, his cathedral in a dismal suburb. Like Joseph, he fills his followers with faith, tapping their energies and shoring up their hopes. His achievements may prove more durable than Joseph's. His Cathedral is no less a monument to 'possibility thinking' than was Joseph's Temple at Nauvoo: costing three times its original estimates' Schuller completed it by sheer *chutzpah*, browbeating his congregation into making contributions, cajoling larger donations out of sympathetic tycoons. Like Joseph, he claims that God has spoken to him – telling him and his audience what they most want to hear. His divinely-revealed message contains a mishmash of contemporary cultural values, much as did the teachings of Joseph Smith. Where the Prophet Joseph took magic, Freemasonry and popular myth about Indian origins, mixing them with a traditional biblical brew, Schuller achieves the same with the nostrums of the 'me decade' – self-improvement and psycho-therapy. He makes the new narcissism respectable to Christian conservatives bewildered by Californian hedonism, Californian excess.

I found an almost deserted beach under crumbling cliffs at San Onofre, the only part of the coast south of LA that had not been built upon. The reason for this oversight soon appeared out of the sky, where giant military helicopters chased each other in and out of the mists. The hard chop of their blades ricocheted off the cliffs, cutting through the dull roar of the ocean. The whole area, apparently, was a US Marine Corps base. Walking for miles along the almost deserted beach, glimpsing the odd couple sunbathing nude above the tide-line, I came across some soldiers in a half-track who scared me out of my wits by appearing suddenly from behind a rock. At first they seemed to follow me, but instead of stopping, cheerfully waved as they passed in a churn of sand, cannon unsheathed, pennants flapping on the radio mast. The faces under the menacing camouflaged helmets looked much too young and harmless for battle, even in practice.

Returning I saw a young man uncouple from a girl. Pink, blond, gaunt and utterly naked, he displayed his hairless body, sporting a long, thin, upwardly curving penis with which he saluted the sun, as if participating in some neolithic rite. His gesture mocked the war games around us, as if to tell the Marines: 'Make love not war!'

In Britain I would have been shocked at this exposure. Here, on the eastern rim of the Pacific it left me quite unembarrassed. As I walked along the beach everything seemed equally valid, equally plausible, without fixed moral reference points, like the lights that spun along the freeway and the waves that pounded evenly upon the shore.

Part Three

People of the Book

'Consider the Dictionary: scarcely a word in the language has a single, fixed, determinate meaning'

JOSEPH HOPKINSON

X

Genesis

Of old hast thou laid the foundation of the earth:
And the heavens are the work of thy hands
They shall perish, but thou shalt endure . . .

PSALM 103

If America's West Coast was the Brave New World, where cults and new religions flourished in a climate that encouraged hedonism and social experiment, it was also a place – especially in the southern counties – where the most strident versions of Christian evangelical conservatism took root. We owe the word *fundamentalism* indirectly to two Los Angeles businessmen, Lyman and Milton Stewart. In 1910, desiring to advance the cause of true religion, they created a $250,000 fund in order that 'every pastor, evangelist, minister, theology professor, theology student, Sunday schools superintendent, YMCA and YWCA in the English speaking world' might be given twelve volumes in which the theological issues of the day would be addressed. Within three years three million copies of *The Fundamentals*, containing some ninety articles in twelve separate booklets, had been distributed. The word 'fundamentalist' first appeared in 1919.

The enterprise, a major ecumenical triumph on the right, was a response to what conservatives saw as the abandonment of Christian essentials by liberal theologians in élitist divinity schools like Harvard, Yale and Union Theological Seminary, New York. The adoption of higher critical methods – which sought new understandings of scripture in the light of modern science and modern techniques of textual analysis – had according to their critics led the modernists or liberals to virtually redefine Christianity. It became a purely ethical system, sometimes (but not necessarily) charged with a current of mystical pantheism which placed God inside, but not above, the natural order.

The activist wing of liberalism found its expression in the Social Gospel, a movement in the same tradition as the great abolitionist crusade that had split the churches over slavery. Drawing on the social sciences as well as liberal theology, advocates of the Social Gospel repudiated the traditional view that moral and social ills could be solved by individual conversions. Instead, they put forward the essentially secular argument that evil could only be dealt with by changing the larger social structures over which the individual had no control. An important feature of liberalism was the movement towards greater ecumenicism and inter-denominational co-operation: since salvation depended on social and political action, the theologies dividing the churches became less important.

The reaction against the worldliness of the New Christianity took the form of a conservative theology that laid particular stress on the Bible as the divinely-revealed, infallible Word of God. The new fundamentalism combined several strands of tradition in a new theological synthesis. Its social strength derived from the popular reverence for the Bible which was very widespread in America, especially in rural areas. It also drew heavily on millennial expectations.

The least biblically-oriented fundamentalists in America belong to the Pentacostalist and Holiness churches, whose roots are in eighteenth-century Methodism. John Wesley's theology, heavily influenced by mystical German pietism, contained two distinctive notions of 'grace'. To the assurance of salvation, as preached by other churches, he added a second 'experience of sanctification' or Christian perfection. The theology was strongly Arminian: God's grace was free for all, but men were free to accept or reject it. The 'justified' sinner must seek the goal of perfection – that is to say, freedom from wilful sin. In addition to the traditional Puritan virtues like chastity and moderation, early Methodists prohibited slavery and alcohol. Later, like other denominations, they split over the issue of slavery. The secessionist Methodist Episcopal Church became the leading ecclesiastical supporter of the Confederacy.

Methodist organisation, which combined powerful elected bishops with populist 'circuit riders' – itinerant evangelists who spoke the language of the people – made it ideally suited to frontier conditions, and by 1844, when the church divided, it was the largest Protestant denomination. Its appeal for mostly poor settlers lay in simplicity of doctrine and above all in the emotional catharsis that accompanied the experience of 'sanctification'. The great revival meetings of the 1840s and 1850s saw many examples of holy extravagance, including dancing, jerking, and faith healing. However, as the century wore on and Methodism became more respectable, the leadership became increasingly alarmed at such vulgar excesses, and began suppressing them. In the resulting schisms the Holiness enthusiasts left to form their own churches, accentuating their charismatic practices. Their memberships swelled further when, towards the turn of the century, the liberal leadership increasingly began looking to the Social Gospel for salvation. Many of the Holiness churches remained as small, independent sects, since, by definition, perfectionists are censorious of the worldliness of others. But two groupings eventually solidified into denominations: the more sedate Church of the Nazarene, and the more radical Assemblies of God.

Most Pentecostalists are fundamentalist in doctrine, though it is experience, rather than doctrine, that mainly concerns them. All fundamentalists, whether Baptist or Pentecostalists, are biblical inerrantists: the Bible, for them (to quote the creedal statement of the Southern Baptists), 'has God for its author . . . and truth without any mixture of error for its matter' Most interpret the text literally – which means giving 'every word the same meaning it would have in normal usage, whether employed in writing, speech or thinking'.

This literalism is at the heart of fundamentalist thinking. Logically it leads to pre-millennialism, the belief that the Second Coming of Christ is due at any moment. Other schools of interpretation have to choose uneasily between metaphorical and literalistic modes, which opens their adherents to the charge of inconsistency: for example, if the stories of Adam and Eve are regarded as metaphorical, why not the Resurrection and Virgin Birth? The key passages for the pre-millennialists are the prophetic verses in the Books of Ezekiel, Daniel and Revelation: if these are literally true – as they must be – they can only refer to future events – the coming battle of Armageddon and the return of Christ to rule the earth.

Pre-millennialist ideas have long taken hold in the evangelical wings of most American protestant denominations. They are disseminated by the numerous Bible colleges and Bible conferences established by the defenders of inerrancy. The knowledge that the world is about to end lends urgency to evangelical efforts: it becomes a philanthropic duty to save as many souls as possible before the millennium, when all the unsaved will go to hell.

Pre-millennialism is very far from being an esoteric doctrine espoused by a fringe of deluded scholars. A popularised version of the scenario developed by John Nelson Darby in the nineteenth century, and his disciple Cyrus Ignatius Scofield, who died in 1921 – Hal Lindsay's *The Late Great Planet Earth*, published in 1970 – has, according to its publishers, sold more than eighteen million copies: after the Scofield Bible it is probably the most influential text in the bibliography of the Christian right. Lindsay's book is a mixture of biblical epic, science fiction and disaster movie. The first requirement for the fulfilment of the prophesies is already being fulfilled: 'the Jewish people reestablish their nation in the ancient homeland of Palestine' an act accomplished by 'unbelieving Jews through human effort' After the restoration of the Temple the seven-year 'countdown' to Armageddon will begin. It will be 'marked by the greatest devastation that man has ever brought upon himself. Mankind will be on the brink of self-annihilation when Christ suddenly returns to put an end to the war of wars called Armageddon.' There will follow the reign of anti-Christ, a European dictator who 'will make the regimes of Hitler, Mao and Stalin look like girl scouts wearing a daisy chain by comparison'. The anti-Christ will be given 'absolute authority to act with the power of Satan'. The anti-Christ will make war on the 144,000 Jews, who will be converted to the belief that Jesus is the Messiah. 'There are going to be 144,000 Jewish Billy Grahams turned loose on the earth,' writes Lindsay. 'The earth will never know a period of evangelism like this.' The born-again Christians will already have disappeared, having been 'raptured' or physically transported into the air. 'Without benefit of science, space-suits or inter-planetary rockets, there will be those who are transported into a glorious place more beautiful, more awesome, than we can possibly comprehend.' He puts a description of this amazing event in the mouth of a reporter: 'There I was, driving down the freeway and all of a sudden the place went crazy . . . cars going in all directions . . . and not one of them had a driver. I mean it was wild. I think we've got an invasion from outer space.' Car stickers in Dallas and other southern cities often have messages like 'IN CASE OF RAPTURE DRIVER WILL DISAPPEAR'.

One of the foremost exponents of Armageddon theology – apart from Hal Lindsay – is the Reverend Tim LaHaye. When I interviewed him for the BBC World Service in December 1987, Mr LaHaye had just left his Baptist church in San Diego for an office in Washington DC in order, I presumed, to be nearer the centre of power. He was a sober, dignified man in a brown suit. His office, on the eighth floor of a modern building on 'C' street, with deep pile carpets and well-coiffed secretaries, was the last place you would associate with religious extremism. Mr LaHaye himself seemed anything but a crank. He appeared like any efficient sensible executive who spends the day at his desk making 'phone calls and dictating letters and memoranda. As well as being the author of numerous books, he heads the American Coalition for Traditional Values, one of the largest umbrella groups on the religious right. His wife Beverly shares his work, being chair of Concerned Women of America, a national anti-feminist, anti-abortion movement. After Jerry Falwell, the LaHayes are probably the most influential figures in the new, politicised fundamentalist movement.

'The Bible says "No man knows the day or the hour,"' said LaHaye. 'But we can know the season. What I'm trying to be is a season-projector, and the indications are that this could be the season. One of the most important signs is that Israel and Russia are both dominant players on the world scene, just as the prophets said they would be 2,500 years ago. Russia was just a nothing power till our generation, and Israel was not even in the land.' He went on to quote a passage from Ezekiel about the invasion of Israel from the north.

'In that passage,' he explained, 'the Bible says that God will supernaturally intervene to destroy Russia in the midst of its attack on Israel. Then Israel, the Jews, will burn the implements of war. Well, how in the world are they going to burn metal, fabrics, plastics and all that? I'll tell you: they'll do it with lasers.'

Was there not a danger, I asked, that an American President might take it upon himself to do God's work, by trying to destroy Russia using nuclear weapons? The Armageddon scenario might encourage such a development – especially with a fundamentalist President like Pat Robertson, who at that moment was campaigning for the Republican nomination. Mr LaHaye was emphatic in his efforts to reassure me. 'Quite the contrary,' he said. 'There are at least eight references where God makes it clear that he's going to destroy Russia supernaturally, so that all the world will know that He is Lord Part of the purpose is to demonstrate his supernatural power. For more than 1950 years God has chosen to be pretty much silent. He expects people to believe in Him and accept His Son through the teachings of the Bible. But today people yearn for Him to demonstrate His supernaturalness, because there are so many sceptics about. Of course, I believe that God can perform miracles today. But they're not Grade-A test-tube type miracles that I can take to my secular-humanist friends and say "Look, here is irrefutable evidence that God exists." But when He destroys Russia supernaturally, it's going to demonstrate to the whole world, by way of satellite and television, that there's a Supernatural God Who has at last demonstrated His existence. The aftermath of that will be a great turning to God on the part of millions.'

The interview took place on the day Mikhail Gorbachev visited Washington to sign the treaty reducing intermediate nuclear weapons.

If the pre-millennialist doomsday scenario is the first pillar of fundamentalist wisdom, creationism is the second. The two positions complement each other – concerned as they are with Genesis and Revelation, first and last books of the Bible, First and Last Things. Since becoming objects of national ridicule at the famous 'Monkey Trial' in 1927, biblical creationists have developed a sophisticated strategy. Instead of demanding that the teaching of evolution be banned in schools, they ask instead that 'creationism' be given equal time. Evolution, they say, is only a theory. So, they claim, is creationism, which is just as plausible, if not more so. Since neither theory is susceptible to final proof, let the schools teach both, so children – and their parents – can choose. The argument appeals to a natural American sense of fairness. It makes the evolutionists – who reject it – look like doctrinaire spoilsports. The creationists are also careful to conceal their religious motives, which would rule out their agenda as violating separation of church and state. Creationism, they say, is a scientific theory that fits the facts according to purely scientific criteria. That it happens to conform to biblical teaching is purely coincidental.

One of the leading lights in the creationist movement is Duane Gish, of the Institute of Creation Research. After two days on the beach at San Onofre, I drove to the Institute which is situated in El Cajon, an up-and-coming township in the valley east of San Diego where prosperity seemed to be spreading like a cancer, with new roads, homes and small factories gobbling up what had once been lush and fertile land. A small friendly man in a cream shirt and neat brown suit, Gish reminded me irresistibly of a Capuchin monkey, no doubt because I knew that, according to his lights, the very thought must be anathema. He was jolly and cheerful and adored his subject. Facts and arguments cascaded out of his head with the fluency of the accomplished polemicist. Not being a scientist, I did not try to argue with him. I was more interested in finding out why he thought the way he did.

Because their religious agenda is hidden, creationists devote more of their energies to attacking scientific orthodoxy than to putting forward a coherent alternative of their own. The truth, as they see it, has already been revealed in the Bible, but they are careful not to make this too obvious when pleading for 'equal time' in schools Members of the Creation Research Society have to sign the following statement:

1 The Bible is the written Word of God and because we believe it to be inspired throughout, all of its assertions are historically and scientifically true in all of the original autographs. To the student of nature this means that the account of origins in Genesis is a factual presentation of simple historical truths.
2 All basic types of living things, including man, were made by direct creative acts of God during Creation Week as described in Genesis. Whatever biological changes have occurred since Creation have accomplished changes only within the original created kinds.

Creationists differ about the details. 'Progressive creationists' are prepared to accept that the earth may be millions, even billions of years old: for them the six days of Genesis may refer to aeons. Most creationists, however, including Dr Gish, are 'Young Earthers' who put the upper limit of the world's age at around 10,000 years. That is a good 4,000 years more than the date given by Archbishop Ussher.

To the argument that a 10,000-year-old earth flies in the face of the geological evidence the creationists reply 'What evidence?' The standard geological column – the sequence of rocks with the oldest lying at the bottom – says nothing about their age. The creationists insist that sedimentary rock formations, which scientific orthodoxy regards as having been built up by particles deposited by rivers over millions of years, are a consequence of the Flood.

'Take the Grand Canyon,' said Dr Gish. 'If you try to reconstruct its supposed gradual formation over millions of years you come up against insoluble problems. The geologists claim that the Kaibab Plateau was uplifted 65 million years ago; however they date the beginning of what they believe to be the delta of the Colorado river at 5 1/2 million years – that's 60 million years too late. The Colorado River could not have cut that canyon and deposited its contents in the delta. What's more, to make the Grand Canyon you would have to remove a thousand cubic miles of sediment. There just isn't a thousand cubic miles of sediment down there in the delta.

As you read the geologists' theories, you find that all of them have fatal flaws.'

Creationists are just as dismissive about the radiometric dating of rocks, the technique whereby age is estimated by measuring radioactive isotopes. No one was around to take measurements 3.8 billion years ago, when the 'parent' isotopes are supposed to have begun their half-lives. Decay rates, they say, are only 'statistical averages', not 'deterministic constants'.

But it is evolution, rather than the age of the earth, that really exercises the creationists. The fossil record, they say, far from proving evolution, simply demonstrates that there were a lot of life forms prior to the Flood. The Noachian Deluge, as they prefer to call it, explains just about everything, from the arrangement of fossils in the geological column to the extinction of the dinosaurs. The reptiles were evidently too large to make it into Noah's Ark.

'We believe that the fossil record is a record of mass death and destruction resulting from a wide-world flood,' said Dr Gish. 'This was a great cataclysm on a massive scale, not just an aqueous catastrophe. There were unprecedented techtonic movements and volcanic upheavals as well. It is described not just in the Bible, but in stories from numerous other peoples, including North American and South American Indians, Chinese, Polynesians, Babylonians, to mention just a few of them . . . '

The fossils, say the creationists, are arranged hydrodynamically, not chronologically, as the evolutionists think. The simplest creatures appear near the bottom of the geological column, like trilobites, brachiopods and other invertebrates, either because they were already living at the bottom of the sea, or because they tended to sink faster. The more complex life forms – amphibians, reptiles, birds and mammals – were buried later by the Flood, which is why they appear higher up in the rock record. The cleverer animals were better at swimming or making for higher ground, which is why they appear near the top . . .

The strongest creationist weapon in their war against the evolutionists is the existence of gaps in the fossil record: in particular the absence of the transitional forms we would expect to find if all species had really evolved from common ancestors.

'Now if you can find fossils of bacteria in algae,' said Dr Gish, 'you should have no trouble finding everything intermediate between them and the complex invertebrates. There's hundreds of millions of years of evolution supposedly in between, yet we find no ancestors for sponges, jellyfish, sea cucumbers and so on. In each case they appear fully-formed. That's a gap of immense proportions. The second gap is between invertebrates and fish. Since our museums have thousands of fish fossils, they should have hundreds of thousands of examples of the intermediate stage, showing which invertebrates evolved into fish, and how it happened. Yet we don't have a single one.'

These gaps, of course, have been the subject of lively debate among scientists who do not question overall evolutionary theory – the notion that all organisms past and present are interrelated by ancestry and descent. Evolutionists now talk about 'quantum leaps' when new species rapidly appear in the record. But this does not overturn the sequence of evolution from simpler to more developed forms, or the notion that all life is linked up in a hierarchy of similarities. Creationists do not have an alternative theory that operates within the paradigms of scientific inquiry. The sum of exceptions, variables, errors or gaps in knowledge does not amount to a system. The alternative, they postulate is not science, but religious dogma: the creationist 'model' requires a Creator who operates supernaturally, by divine fiat, and then sets in motion a world which is supposed to function according to an entirely different set of 'natural laws'. Thus within the limits of the observable – as with genetic experiments with fruit flies, or changes in the population of peppered moths – creationists admit that natural selection occurs: they call it micro-evolution. But they refuse to accept that the same principles apply – on a much larger scale – between species. Their definitions as to what constitutes a species or 'kind', the subject of special, separate creations, are quite arbitrary. *Homo sapiens* is a 'kind' par excellence, whose creation is quite distinct from that of other primates; but they are quite prepared to lump together huge invertebrate groups, such 'worms', which include at least five different phyla or species as defined by other biologists.

Dr Gish wanted a supernatural deity who created man in His own image. 'Evolution is contrary to the attributes of God,' he told me. 'If God is omniscient and omnipotent, the One who knows the End from the Beginning, why would He use such a wasteful, inefficient process to create man in three billion years, when He could have created us instantaneously? Mutations are genetic mistakes – they are random, accidental changes in genetic material. All mutations are harmful. Look at all the fuss about the damage being done to the ozone layer: scientists are saying it will increase the incidents of radiation, mutations.

'If you teach young people that everything started out as hydrogen gas, they will soon conclude that their ultimate destiny is a pile of dust. It's hard to convince youngsters that God is meaningful, that there is a relationship between creator and created if we see ourselves, with our twelve billion brain cells and their hundred million million connections, as no more than the product of properties inherent in matter. Evolution is a twentieth-century myth that man has invented to explain his origin without God. God would not have created us and left us in darkness!'

Gish wanted his God to be orderly as well as powerful. Such a deity would never permit something as apparently random, or accidental, as mutation to be the mechanism of change and adaptation. In a similar vein, he argued in favour of 'special creation' for different 'kinds' including man, while acknowledging the necessity for a common biochemistry.

'Supposing God had created plants with one type of amino acids, proteins and sugars, animals with another and humans with a third? What then could we eat? We couldn't eat plants, we couldn't eat animals, the only thing we could eat would be each other. In other words God created the world with the same types of chemicals in plants, animals and man so we could have the food chain, the food supply . . . '

But this seemed tantamount to admitting that God was subject to the laws of nature, a view which the whole creationist project seemed designed to oppose. Gish's scientific training demanded a Newtonian, eighteenth-century deity who upheld the universe, the God whom William Paley saw as manifesting Himself through the natural order. Yet his theology required a jealous, Old Testament God who disobeyed his own rules and arbitrarily intervened with special creations, catastrophes and ready-made canyons.

At first I thought these two views irreconcilable. But then I remembered what I would have said if my wits had been about me: 'Jesus loves sinners. Therefore, God loves the mutant.' What looks bad from the human perspective may, in the divine order of things, be good. The trouble with Dr Gish and his kind was not just that they didn't understand science: they appeared not to understand Christianity either.

I got up at six the next morning and headed towards Arizona. The freeway undulated through pleasing valleys of virgin grass before plunging down through a lunar landscape of massive boulders to the sandy desert. At Yuma I turned north off the freeway and headed for Quartzite along an empty road towards the Chocolate and Dome Rock mountains. The sun glared down without respite, torturing my eyes and rendering the architecture of the mountains almost invisible.

I climbed up a zig-zag road into the Central Highlands, and stopped at the old territorial capital, Prescott, an unexpectedly pleasant town with fine old painted Victorian buildings grouped round a shady green. At 5,000 feet it enjoys a healthy climate of dry air and cool summers, and is understandably popular among people with respiratory ailments. Its citizens looked healthy and spruce, with brown legs framed between white socks and cotton skirts or shorts. None of them seemed to be wheezing.

By the time I got to Grand Canyon, all the camp grounds were full. The village was aglow with giant RVs and mobile homes, whose curtained windows flickered with television. It was raining hard, so I pulled in at a parking place, despite a notice saying that overnight stays were forbidden. Two other RVs were already there. Nervous – as always – of authority, I tapped on one of their windows. An elderly Yankee lady with toughness and humour written on her features came to the door.

'If they try to run us out of town they're going to have to reckon with me!' she said. Impressed, I parked my wagon behind hers. Sleep was fitful, punctuated by slamming doors and the sounds of revellers practising their Indian war whoops. I got up at five to do the Bright Angel Trail, aiming to beat the sun and the other tourists.

My diligence was rewarded. For the first two hours I saw practically nobody, except some fellow-Europeans. Within fifty feet of the rim the trappings of tourism were invisible, and forgotten. I was in a four-dimensional world of vertical space and geological time, going back a million years with every foot. It was delicious to pass through the different climatic zones while dew was still fresh on the plants. One began in Alpine forests, passed through English country lanes with nettles, brambles and wild came to rest at Plateau Point after crossing a long flat stretch of cactus and sagebrush that could have been on some Greek island. From there I gazed down at the relentless, barren rocks where the river swirled, jade-green, among dark grey schist that looked as lifeless and forbidding as the arid mountains of Sinai.

All this, according to the geologists, represented a journey of a billion years, from the light sandy Kaibab limestone at the rim to the hard granular metamorphic Vishnu schist at the bottom, itself a reconstitution of even older shales and basalts dating from a time when the earth was half its present age, a desolate place of swampy lands and shallow waters punctuated by volcanoes and lava flows. The Grand Canyon is the scientist's Book of Genesis: much of the known history of life is recorded here, beginning with the fossils of algae that hide in the Vishnu schist, ascending through pre-Cambrian and Cambrian shales where lurk the traces of trilobites, brachiopods and worms, through cemeteries of crinoids and bryozoans, up to the layers of sandstone where slimy reptiles left their traces, if not their bodies, a mere 270 million years ago, and finally through the mammalian remnants of the upper strata; the whole great evolutionary edifice, of course, being topped by beer-bellied, sun-hatted, T-shirt-bearing *homo sapiens*, creation's crowning glory.

There was a kind of heroism in the creationist's insistence that all this was a mere 10,000 years old – just a millimetre or two from the top of the rim. Why would God have planted all those trilobites and brachiopods in the bottom layers? It brought to mind the argument of Philip Gosse, the English clergyman who tried to refute Darwin by claiming that God had deliberately planted misleading fossils to test man's faith. The creationists, of course, would never countenance the idea of such a deceitful, practical-joking deity, though the ancient Greeks wouldn't have put it past Zeus. The creationists' God was actually nastier than this: He did it by catastrophe. The trilobites and brachiopods were down near the bottom because of the great tectonic upheavals that went with the Flood.

I looked at the terraces, with their buttresses and pinnacles and cupolas rising in majestic tiers towards the rim. The early American topographers had named them ecumenically after different gods and sages: Wotan's Throne, Freya's Temple, Valhalla Plateau, King Arthur's Castle, Holy Grail Temple, Vishnu Temple, Apollo Temple, Jupiter Temple, Brahma Temple, Isis Temple, the Tower of Set, Osiris Temple, Shiva Temple, Confucius Temple. The only Christian reference in this pantheon were Angel Canyon and Angel Gate, Angel Window (a hole in the rock) and, of course, the Bright Angel Trail. It was fortunate that these enlightened men had arrived in time to claim the Canyon. The thought of biblical names (Ezekiel Point, Methuselah Tower, Zion Gate, Jerusalem Plateau) was too depressing to contemplate. But who knows? Was there perhaps an element of resentment among the Gishes and other fundamentalists who claimed a monopoly of religious wisdom, at this pantheistic appropriation of America's most famous natural feature? Was there wishful thinking in their catastrophe theories? If God had destroyed the world once in order to punish mankind (saving, of course, the few who deserved to be saved) He could do so again.

To contemplate the Grand Canyon is to utterly reject the catastrophe theory. Catastrophe produces chaos, a violent distortion of structure. The beauty of the Grand Canyon which enraptures so many visitors, turning good writers into bad poets (as my guide book caustically observed) lies in harmony, regularity and structural simplicity. The 'temple'-like pinnacles and cupolas are everywhere supported by great triangular buttresses which form the huge amphitheatres that lie between them. The pattern is repeated in the canyons and subcanyons, as it is among their myriad tributaries on different levels. The pinnacles are formed because the erosion has been greatest near the top, where wind and water have had more time to eat away at the rock. The splendour of the whole derives not from any soaring defiance of gravity, but rather the reverse. It is an expression of gravity, acting on water and rock. The human brain, programmed aesthetically to perceive regularities, can take it all in, while marvelling at its scale.

This may seem too obvious to be worth mentioning. But it told me something about the creationists and their geological colleagues, the catastrophists. The refusal to recognise the structure and order in nature came from something deeper than a simple attachment to biblical dogma – or rather, a particular interpretation of certain biblical texts. It came out of a religious fear of pantheism, of the possibility that God is part of, but not superior to, nature. The God they wanted had to be transcendentally superior to nature – able to inflict catastrophes by supernatural interventions – because he represented their will to power. They wanted a God who would punish their enemies, the godless atheists and secular humanists, the geologists, palaeontologists and biologists of respectable science whom they identified with everything they disliked in American culture.

It was the Mormon saga replicated in a different branch of science. The Mormons expressed their modern, intellectual identities by trying to defend archaeologies and anthropologies that were rejected by the scientific establishment. The creationists were playing the same game with biology and geology. For both groups a text – the Book of Mormon or Genesis – became their shibboleth or banner. But these were only badges: what they wanted was something deeper: recognition, even power. They were angry adolescents, intelligent *enragés*. Furious at their exclusion by the conspiratorial élite they considered responsible for America's moral and political decline, they took on society by attacking its conventional wisdom, beating it around the ears with their books. Eventually they would be forced to recognise that the forces they had taken on were much too big for them: evolutionary theory wasn't just a plot by a secular humanist élite: it represented the pooled knowledge of the whole human race. The Mormons, who had been seeking social acceptance for a century, ever since the Manifesto implicitly cast doubt on the authenticity of their prophet, were further down the road of accommodation, which was why their intellectuals sounded apologetic, almost pleading. The creationists, who came from a tradition of premillennial separatists who had until recently kept out of politics, were still full of rage. They still believed – or, at least, wanted to believe – in a vengeful God who would soon bring the world to an end, 'rapturing' the faithful and destroying everyone else.

Their counterparts in the Middle East, who had many of the same motivations, were preaching their gospel with bullets and bombs. It spoke well for the stability of America's institutions, its attachment to freedom of speech, its willingness to let people have their say regardless of how idiotic or nonsensical the message, as well as for the availability of funding for the most quixotic enterprises, that the terrorism of America's *enragés* was purely intellectual. In other parts of the world the Institute of Creation Research would have been a bomb factory.

The ascent was punitive. Like hell, the Grand Canyon is much easier to get into than out of. Halfway up I ran out of water. I began to melt around early Mississippian. By the time I got to early Permian – about 60 million years back – I had to beg a drink from a couple in a rest hut. When I finally made it to the top it was hailing and bitterly cold. I took refuge in the Bright Angel Lodge where I lunched on chicken and Californian champagne. It was my forty-fifth birthday.

Page Arizona, where I put up next day, is a dreary little town founded in the 1950s on Lake Powell, an artificial lake caused by the damming of the Colorado River. It consists of a few forlorn streets, a shopping mall, half a dozen garages, and a population, so a notice informed me, of 6,500. It had a dozen churches, all situated next to each other, on the hill leading down to the dam. The grandest was the Immaculate Heart of Mary – a one-storey building in terracotta stucco with air-conditioning units on the roof: nearby stood three First Baptist churches from different denominations; then tiny St

David's Episcopal in cheap pebbledash; Shepherd of the Desert Lutheran in hideous lavatorial brick; the small brick Reorganised Church of Latter Day Saints and the larger chapel of the official Utah Mormons; United Methodist, tastefully decorated with medallions representing loaves and fishes; the Church of the Nazarene in white brick; and the hall of the Jehovah's Witnesses, in nondescript brown. I felt sorry for those citizens whose denominations were not represented: life in Page looked only marginally more interesting than life in some Siberian settlement for political exiles. Apart from a single cinema and two or three dismal bars, Page seemed to have little but religion to offer.

I decided to stay at a motel, since I wanted to call my family in England and needed a shower. Before I had got out of the van the manager was at the window, urging me to take one of his rooms. He was bald and round-faced with a thin sandy moustache and a spreading gut overhanging his belt.

'British?' he said, recognising my accent. 'We Americans *love* your Mrs Thatcher. We do so admire her. Have you heard she's just dissolved Parliament, a year before time?' I hadn't. She wasn't my Mrs Thatcher anyway. I changed the subject to practical matters.

'Do you have 'phones in the room so I can call my family?'

''Fraid not, but you can use the office 'phone any time you like.'

I took the room which had the same composition walls as Delia and Ted's mobile home. I went to the office to register. A Gideon's Bible was prominently displayed on the counter.

'So you're from the mother country,' said the manager. 'We sure beat the hell out of her twice, but she's still our mother, I guess!'

He asked me what I was doing in America. I explained I was researching a book about religion. He looked uncomfortable and changed the subject. For a dollar he would let me use the motel laundry and dryer. I asked him if he owned the motel.

'No,' he said. 'I teach electronics and computers in the local high school. I manage the motel in the evenings.'

'How do you fit it in?'

'I stay till all the rooms are sold, and then I go home. I've just got one left this evening. Then in the morning I'm here between six and seven.'

'You mean I have to make my calls by seven.'

'Right on,' he said.

'That doesn't sound so good,' I said. 'My family will all be out. Can't I use the 'phone when you're out?'

'The owner doesn't allow it.' I swallowed my indignation, and went to do my laundry at the machines. He came up while I was loading the washing, and nudged me conspiratorially.

"Bout that book you're doing,' he said. 'What kind of viewpoint do you have? Do you have a personal relationship with Jesus as your saviour, who died for your sins?' This formula, invented by pietists in the last century as a reaction against formalised religion, had become the new fundamentalist shibboleth, the test of who was and who was not 'born-again' I acted dumb.

'Not really. I was brought up a Christian, and accept some Christian teachings. But I wouldn't say I had a personal relationship with Jesus – any more than with Muhammad, Buddha or any of the other great teachers of humanity.'

'That's very interesting,' he said, pausing for a moment. Then, while I loaded the washing, he came back at me. 'Haven't you taken Him into your heart, and let your spirit be lit by the Holy Ghost?'

By now I was thoroughly irritated. 'No. I don't think I've had that experience. I'm afraid I take a rather sceptical view of religion, specially in this country. I mean, look at Jim and Tammy Bakker. $1.6 million a year. Two homes. Sex with a *church secretary* in a motel. Hush money paid out of church funds. Then there's Oral Roberts on his Prayer Tower, trying to blackmail God into paying off his debts. What about the commandment, "Thou shalt not tempt the Lord thy God"? Most of these preachers are in it for the money. I've been travelling all over the country and I've only met one Christian' – he held out his hand with a stupid, self-satisfied grin, assuming I was referring to him -'and that was a Catholic priest on an Indian reservation who prayed for the sins of his Church. If you want to know my opinion, Christians are people who have straight dealings with others.'

'What do you mean?' he said, beginning to look alarmed. I had worked myself into a rage of godless indignation.

'I mean by not taking advantage of wayfarers. You lied to me about letting me use the 'phone whenever I liked just so you could sell me the room and get off to bed. Is that what you call Christian behaviour?'

The effect was electrifying. He grovelled. He would tell the cleaning woman to let me use the 'phone in the office, trusting me to leave the right money. He would finish the laundry himself, have it ironed, and bring it to me in the morning. He even asked me if I would like to come to his Bible class, an offer I politely declined.

I returned to my room in triumph, and turned on the television. It was the '700 Club' telethon. 'We've got to see before we finish this week an additional $20 millions,' Pat Robertson was saying. 'That will break down on a seven-month basis at three million a month. That's what's needed to catch up and move ahead . . . If you join with me and Ben, we're going to pray together over this!' The camera zoomed into Ben Kinchlow's suave, black, handsome face as he screwed up his eyes in prayer.

'By the power of the Spirit of the Living God in Jesus's name, touch these lives! Do miracles tonight!' he crooned, bringing his outstretched hand right up to the lens. 'Touch many hearts, Amen.'

'Now, Mr Director,' said Robertson, 'if you'd be good enough to set the clock for thirty minutes, I'd appreciate it . . . We're waiting for your calls from . . . NOW! We're going to have to have over $2,000 every single minute, so wherever you are, go to your 'phones with your pledges . . . '

A tall, elegant women in her thirties appeared on screen. Her little boy had fallen out of the window of their third-floor apartment. She had actually seen him falling and in the split-second available, had uttered a panic-struck prayer (who wouldn't?). The child had landed in soft dirt within an inch of a rock that would have smashed his head to pieces.

'If he had fallen straight outta the window he would have splattered over that rock,' said the woman. 'But in mid-air he was turned supernaturally to fall in the dirt. The Lord gave angels charge over him, and he missed that rock.' The woman did not explain why the Lord, or his angels, allowed the child to fall from the window in the first place. Nor did Ben Kinchlow.

'Ladies and Gentlemen, this is real, this is REAL!' he cried, screwing up his eyes in prayer, while the woman moaned softly, as in the throes of love. 'We know and believe and have experienced the power of God! Lord, in Jesus Name we thank you for evidence of your grace and mighty protection. In the name of JEE-SUS we ask for miracles! . . . '

Then a story came up about a couple whose business was about to go bankrupt. Despite their financial straits, they decided to pledge a certain amount to the '700 Club' every month. The miracle happened! Investments that had lain dormant suddenly rose up and showered them with money, like the rock that Moses touched with his staff. They were now saved financially as well as spiritually . . .

I drove to the Canyon de Chelly and parked near Spider Rock, a twin-towered monolith of red sandstone that stands at the edge of the valley like the crumbling wreck of some vast cathedral built by giants. The taller of the towers is higher than the Empire State Building. It has a flat top where a boulder the size of a house has lodged itself near the edge, waiting for an earth tremor to send it crashing down.

Spider Rock is at the centre of the Hopi Indian creation myths. In the Hopi version of Genesis – which is considerably more sophisticated than the Hebrew one – the Spider Woman Kókangwúti is the holy creatrix, helpmeet of Sótuknang, the first being and nephew of Taiowa the Creator. Mixing earth with her saliva, Spider Woman created the twins Pöqánghoya and Paloügawhoya who made the mountains and keep the earth rotating on its axis. Then she made the trees, the bushes, the plants, the flowers, the birds and the animals, moulding them from the earth and giving to each its proper name. Finally she created the four male beings, from red, yellow, black and white earth, in the image of Sótuknang, and four females like herself to be their partners.

The Navajo, more prosaically, say that the Spider Woman taught them how to weave.

The Canyon de Chelly makes an entirely plausible Eden. It is less majestic but more beautiful than the Grand Canyon, combining grandeur with intimacy, the sublime with the arcadian, the *ying* of landscape with its *yang* in perfectly balanced proportions. The great cliffs fall sheer and smooth, as if molten from wax, cascading into rounded terraces and ledges carved by the waters. The valley bottom, unlike the Grand Canyon, is utterly seductive. The river meanders through a park of luscious fields between gentle banks of cottonwood and blue-green Pacific willow. As the evening shadows began crawling up Spider Rock I watched a Navajo horseman herding ponies across the river a thousand feet below, making great gallumphing splashes and uttering war-whoops which echoed around the walls, pursuing and catching each other in rebarbative play. The spectacle made my spirits soar like the eagles that rode the thermals above the cliffs, looking for ground squirrels and other small creatures. The rider's rumbustious energy, the careless way he controlled his ponies wrenched at the heart, proclaiming a freedom uncorrupted by greed an Adam before the Fall.

I spent the night there and looked at Spider Rock as the moonlight cast its angular shadow across the valley. The silence was complete except for the rustle of small creatures and the distant sound of the river, amplified by the cliffs, as it quietly ate its way through the earth. In the morning I walked down the short trail to the bottom and waded across the river's shallow pebbles. A party of Navajo toddlers was splashing around in the water, utterly absorbed in play while their teacher, a slender beauty with silken black pigtails, sat demurely watching them, knees under chin, from the beach. Their shrill chattering bounced off the cliff along with the dappled light from the waters that flickered beneath its great protective overhang, as if twinkling at their merriment. It was a place of safety, a nursery where the children of the earth were free to play in peace.

The idyll was brutally shattered by the sound of a truck groaning its way up the track on the opposite side of the river. As the teacher nervously herded her charges into a disciplined row on the bank, the vehicle splashed across the ford in a rage of grinding gears and unloaded its cargo right beside us: a party of fat, sweating middle-aged white tourists with bulging bellies and pendulous dugs that wobbled like jellies as its owners staggered to relieve themselves at the public toilet hidden in a grove by the stream. I took my cue and left.

That evening I drove sixty miles west through the open grasslands to Hotevilla, near the three mesas or limestone escarpments where the Hopis have their villages. I camped discreetly behind some out-buildings before driving in the morning to Shipaulovi where, as luck would have it, the Hopis were holding a corn dance.

In their own estimation, the Hopis own the whole of the United States and a great deal beyond. In the 1940s, when the US government requested them to file any claims they might have to lands in the Navajo reservation, a group of Hopi chiefs politely informed President Truman that they had claimed the whole Western Hemisphere 'long before Columbus's great-grandmother was born' and would therefore not ask a white man whose ancestors only arrived recently for a piece of land that was already theirs. As well as refusing to allow their land to be used for oil prospecting, the Hopi chiefs rejected the North Atlantic Treaty on the ground that they were an independent nation of pacifists. 'Our tradition, religion and training,' said the chiefs, 'forbid us to harm, kill or molest. We therefore object to our boys being forced to be trained for war, to become murderers and destroyers.'

The Hopis – the People of Peace – are America's chosen ones. The secrets of the universe have been entrusted to them. They know that the world has already been created and destroyed three times, and is headed for a new cataclysm. The people of the First World were happy till they neglected the commands of Sótuknang and the Spider Woman to respect the Creator, and to use the vibratory centres of their bodies – the soft gap at the crown of the head which closes during childhood, the brain, the vocal chords, the heart and the solar plexus – for the purposes of worship. The People of Peace were saved by Sótuknang who led them to safety among the Ant People, deep in the womb of the earth-mother. The rest were destroyed by fire. In the Second World, newly created from the waters, the same thing happened. Most of the people neglected to respect the Creator, and the world was destroyed, this time by ice.

Again, the People of Peace were safe with the Ant People. But then the Third World was destroyed with the Flood, after the people had become corrupted by large and complex cities, an excessive worldliness and a tendency to use their reproductive organs for frivolous aims. This time the People of Peace were rescued by the Spider Woman, who taught them how to make rafts from hollow reeds and allowed them to drift, after months on the oceans, to the Fourth World, America.

The fortunes of the Fourth World are now at their nadir, with godless materialism, lust and power holding sway from the lower centres of the body, seat of the carnal appetites. But soon there will be a turning-point, perhaps after the next cataclysm has been brought about – who knows? – by man himself. Thereafter the human soul will graduate back through the higher centres, till at last the gap at the top of the head will open, allowing it to return to the cosmic infinite whence it came.

The Hopi villages have a charm all their own in a country starved of antique communities. Their flat-roofed stone and adobe houses tumble over each other like the hill towns of Palestine or Greece. Unfortunately they are much less tidy. The chosen ones are not renowned for their cleanliness. Leo Crane, the US agent from 1910 to 1919, described one Hopi village as a place where 'the sun broils down on the heated sand and rock ledges, on the fetid homes and the litter and the garbage and all that accumulates from unclean people and their animals'. Seventy years has, if anything, increased the squalor, adding modern rust and indestructible plastics to the organic waste of yore. Rotting motors perch on ledges which they are obviously destined never to leave, obscuring the view of the plains; while old-fashioned outdoor privies send pungent messages downwind, announcing banquets for flies. The lower slopes of the mesa, below the village, have become enormous rubbish dumps, with rusting cans, plastic containers, organic waste and paper jumbled promiscuously among the rocks. Proud of their antiquity and resentful of the modern world, the People of Peace have an aristocratic disdain for municipal order: their minds are permanently fixed on higher things.

I came into a small crowded courtyard at the top of the village where the corn dance was about to begin. The whole population was already assembled, seated on tubular steel and canvas chairs, on benches or on the low flat roofs surrounding the square. There were only half a dozen foreigners there, including myself. Our presence was accepted, without acknowledgement or hostility. The Hopis were dressed like any other Americans in summer, in jeans and T-shirts or cotton dresses. Many, especially the women, were conspicuously overweight. They sat matriarchally on their chairs looking like prehistoric fertility goddesses, all bosom, buttocks and belly, with small, pointed heads. Their complacency was justified: Hopi women own and inherit the land; all clan life revolves around them.

The masked dancers, all male, filed in. Two groups of spirits – kachinas – were represented. The first resembled pigs: they had green heads and red snouts, with eyes painted on the backs as well as the fronts of their heads. Their hats had four eagle feathers arranged horizontally at the quarter hour positions; they wore necklaces of herbs and aprons, fore and aft, that allowed underpants of a variety of colours to be revealed at the sides above knee-length moccasin boots and anklets with jingle-bells and other silver ornaments. The second group wore bird-like masks, with beaks and pobbles on their heads, and plain black aprons. The exposed parts of their bodies were painted with stripes or white circles, but otherwise the 'birds' had no decorative embellishments.

The chanting and 'dancing' began. The 'birds' formed the outer circle, the 'pigs' the inner one as the kachinas moved concentrically in opposite directions. The chant was low and monotonous, more like a hum than a song, consisting of only four notes (F-F-G-F-D-C-C-C if registered in C major). The rhythm was four square, but syncopated on the last beat, allowing for different permutations of movement. The dancers stomped with military precision with the bow-legged gait peculiar to Indians. For an hour they circled and stamped and chanted.

> Li-i-hi-la
> Li-i-hi-la . . .
> Oho Qho-wa
> Ihi Ihi-yi Hi-ho
> Oho Haya-nani
> Hiya-nani, Hiya-nani

The kachina spirits live in the San Francisco mountains, a range that rises to nearly 13,000 feet just north of Flagstaff. They remain there during the winter when there are no masked dances. In the summer they come to the villages, to dance and sing and bring all kinds of blessings, especially rain. The Hopis believe that the spirits of the dead go west, to return as clouds. If performed correctly, the dances will bring them back and make them water the land.

During a pause in the dance, the food was handed out. I had expected it to be carefully selected cobs of corn or other local products, like the sacramental foods of the Nez Percés, but it consisted entirely of things bought in supermarkets—popcorn, sweets, packets of biscuits and other sugary foods certain to rot the teeth and keep the Hopi soul chained firmly below the solar plexus. The children eagerly caught the packets and littered the ground with wrappers as the dancing recommenced. But then, quite suddenly, the powers above manifested their displeasure. A dust-devil struck the courtyard, enveloping everyone in litter and dirt, causing skirts and headgear to fly, even chairs to collapse. A pause was called and I struggled back to the camper, shielding my eyes, ears and throat against the blasting wind.

On to US 40, I stopped at Winslow for petrol.

'You sure oughta do sum'n'bout that tira yours,' said the garage hand. One of the extra fat rear tyres had become cracked and completely bald, except for some fibres that were beginning to work themselves through the rubber. The hot roads of Arizona had worn the threads smooth. The tyre was due to explode at any moment, like thousands of others one saw strewn along the freeway. The trouble was that I only had a spare for the standard thickness front tyres. There were no rear tyres of the right size to be had in Winslow or in neighbouring Holbrook. The nearest place was Albuquerque, 270 miles ahead.

I drove slowly, to reduce the amount of friction. The tyre became a haemophiliac with AIDS. Every pebble could be a bullet, every fragment a potential dagger.

I stopped at the Petrified Forest National Park. There were notices everywhere threatening severe penalties to anyone taking bits of petrified wood. The Visitors' Center had several showcases of specimens, with films and diagrams explaining how volcanic ash had preserved 60-million-year-old pines by replacing their cells with silica.

One of the showcases contained letters from people who had repented of their thefts, together with the returned fragments. Most of the letters, written in childish hands, reported the bad luck that had dogged the offenders. One of them was typewritten:

Take your piece with my blessing. Let me tell you a tale of woe. Took this thing of beauty and the following has happened in the last six months:

1) Wrecked auto
2) Broken bones
3) Dog got ran [sic] over
4) Four vehicle violations
5) Lost our house
6) Business lost over $15,000
7) Son almost flunked school
8) No jobs
9) Wife was abused
10) Fish have died
11) Wife has left me.

I can no longer afford to keep this around. All total it must have cost me around $50,000 . . . I am glad that I did not take a bigger piece as it may have cost me my life and that of my wife and my son. Nope, this belongs to you and I will rest easier now that it is gone.

The bottom of the page, with the sender's name and address, had been folded out of view. The young ranger I spoke to said this was deliberate, to protect the sender's privacy. No, he insisted, the National Parks did not have a special department where hard-luck letters were composed.

I drove to a parking place and walked up a small canyon where the volcanic ash had formed itself into wrinkled hillocks of mauves and russets the texture of elephant hide. There were great fallen logs and woodchips everywhere, as if a gang of lumberjacks had just been at work. Only, when you touched the chips they were stone. The temptation to pocket one was overwhelming, till I remembered the bald tyre and all the other disasters I didn't need at the moment.

I made it to Albuquerque, bought a new tyre for less than half the expected price, and drove on to Dallas.

XI

Among Believers

Oh, wretched man that I am! Who shall deliver me from the body of this death!

ROMANS 7:24

I came to Dallas in the night, after a two-day drive from Albuquerque along almost empty roads where all I saw was the occasional pickup or cattle truck. After the tinted sands and monuments of Arizona, the ordinary immensities of New Mexico, miles of rolling scrubland punctuated by water towers and occasional irrigated fields, came as a relief. Texas became evident with nodding donkeys and mud-spattered cattle corrals. The traffic thickened gradually. Just as the light was failing, the towers of Fort Worth, glowing with fire from the setting sun, beaconed into view. Then, too suddenly, it was dark, and I was drawn into the glittering orbit of the Metroplex freeway system, like a tiny satellite lured into the field of an unknown, futurist planet. Somehow, more by luck than design, I fetched up at a motel in Arlington, near Dallas-Fort Worth Airport.

The Dallas of the mind, as known to a hundred million viewers across the world, is a sparkling city of glass and steel offices and lavish ranch houses built on 10,000-acre estates. Here money and sex vie for supremacy over the souls of cowboys turned into corporate barons by the extraordinary chemistry of oil. It is a world of Venetian intrigue and Machiavellian politics, where men have the scruples of Renaissance princes and the women are both predatory and instantly desirable. The characters have the fixed, two-dimensional quality of the comic strip. The levers of their emotions are few and uncomplicated: lust, greed and the desire for revenge rule most of the time, occasionally pitted (especially in the women) against more inchoate longings for love and security. Conspicuous by its absence, though, is the stuff from which American culture in general, and Dallas's in particular, is made: the stuff of religion.

Absence of piety, conviction or personal virtue never kept anyone out of church, least of all in Dallas, where no one makes engagements on a Sunday morning out of the *politesse* that their friends are in church and not playing golf. Forty per cent of Americans go to church at least once a week – sixty per cent in the case of the evangelical Protestants who make up a high proportion of Dallas's population. The city is a powerhouse for fundamentalism, funding Bible colleges and born-again take-overs of school boards all over the country. If the Ewings are not to be seen attending church, there must be a reason: the most obvious is that *Dallas* is a national institution, like public education, the armed forces and the federal and state governments. Prayer on its screen, like prayer in schools, would be seen as a violation of the US Constitution. There would be riots, demonstrations, boycotts. Sensibly, the producers have spurned verisimilitude by leaving religion out of it.

On Memorial Sunday, when Americans honour their war dead, I got up early and drove downtown to the First Baptist Church of Dallas. It is one of the largest and wealthiest churches in America. It has 28,000 members and a staff of 300, including a private security force which patrols the whole block where the church and its affiliated institutions – the Criswell Bible College, the Criswell radio network and half a dozen other enterprises named after Dr Criswell or his friends – are situated. The head of this empire is the almost legendary pastor, the Reverend W. A. Criswell, pastor of First Baptist since 1944 and guru to a whole generation of new radical fundamentalists. It is not the sort of place you would expect to find the Ewings or other Texan 'oiligarchs'. Though some Southern Baptists are wealthy, most have blue-collar backgrounds or thinly-covered rural roots. I expected fire and brimstone from Dr Criswell, and I was not disappointed.

Even for the eight o'clock service the sanctuary was nearly full. Built as an auditorium, with oak pews and Tiffany glass windows, it only holds about 3,000 people, a fraction of the church's membership. The congregation was overwhelmingly white, young and well turned out. The women were neat, but never ostentatious, with cotton mid-length frocks or twin-piece suits with blouses. The men wore light summer suits of grey or beige. I was sure I was the only man there with collar-length hair. The children, however young, behaved impeccably. Racially and culturally the people were solidly

Anglo-colonial: the same as you would find in Salt Lake City or, for that matter, in New Zealand, members of that extraordinary human tribe which ruthlessly tames continents to make them fit for suburbia. There were jaunty hymns, old Baptist favourites, and a well-rehearsed psalm from the choir, accompanied by First Baptist's famous Hallelujah Brass Band.

A stocky, square-cut man wearing a flamboyant summer suit, Dr Criswell was well into his seventies. His aura was part showman, part elder statesman. The theme of his sermon, predictably, was the importance of the Bible, the necessity of underpinning the spirit of Christ with the authority of the Word. He read out a poem that had been found on the body of a young soldier killed in action:

> Look God, I've never spoken to you
> But now I want to say 'How d'ya do'
> You see, God, they told me you didn't exist
> And like a fool I believed all this
> Last night from a shell-hole I saw your sky.
> I figured then that they'd told me a lie . . .

. . . and so it went on for two dozen lines or more in similar vein.

Having put before us this rather cosy image of the deity, the pastor began to adopt a more fearsome, accusatory voice. 'At the final hour of judgement when we stand before Almighty God,' he intoned, enunciating every syllable with portentous clarity, 'who stands with us? Who defends us? And who c-o-n-d-e-m-n-n-s us?' The words rose from his throat like the sound of the last trump, filling every space in the chamber with their resonance. The silence that followed was even more portentous: not a cough from the audience, not a squeak from the children. And then the unexpected answer in a hushed, stagey whisper: 'Even those whom you love . . .'

'In my first pastorate sixty years ago,' he continued in a voice tinged with a faint, nostalgic tremble, 'in the Tennessee county where I had my first tiny church, there was a hanging. And it was a lad, a young man, very young. And before the hangman's noose wrenched his life away, they asked him, as they usually do, before the trap is sprung, 'Do you have any last word you would like to say?' And he said 'Yes, I'd like to speak to my mother.' And so they brought his mother to the hangman's platform. And the boy said unto his mother:

"'Mother, had you taught me the Word of God, and brought me to the Saviour, and had you brought me as a little boy to Sunday school and church, would I be here today, paying for my crime with my life?"

'What an a-w-e-s-o-m-e moment, what a-w-e-s-o-m-e pain. And that is just a small prefiguration of that grave and final, ultimate day when those who reject Our Saviour are cast into everlasting darkness and fire and damnation, and the children will rise and say to their parents: "If you had taught me the Word of God, and brought us to the Lord, we would not be facing an eternity of hell!"'

The images rose up starkly, as in a Western: the scaffold erected in the prison yard with governor, sheriff and hangman standing by; the young man's pale, pinched features; the mother's hollow, tear-stained cheeks. Then the sound of the trap and the wince on the governor's face; and the long-shot of the body swinging on the rope, silhouetted against the dawning sky as the music fades up: THE END. It was a world away from the Dallas that surrounded us with soaring angles of sheeted glass, muzak-soaked malls and shopping arcades with playing fountains, multi-level orbiting freeways and parking lots that overflowed with expensive limousines.

It was also a journey into the theological past. The dead soldier's poem reflected the modern, chummy image of God, addressed almost on terms of equality, like a senior business partner. This immanent, domesticated deity, frequently referred to as 'Friend', 'Companion', 'Helper', even 'Co-pilot', was a comparative newcomer to the evangelical repertoire. It contrasted starkly with the 'angry God' of Jonathan Edwards and his Puritan forbears, the transcendent upholder of divine sovereignty whose justice could be vindictive and pitiless. Yet the latter image was present, if not directly visible, in Criswell's story of the hanging, where he explicitly told his congregation that divine justice would be even harsher than the ultimate human penalty. The modern 'born-again' Christian seeks an intimate, *personal* relationship with God through Jesus. But lurking behind Him there stands the more menacing, punitive figure of the Father, a ghost from the crueller, more authoritarian past.

I was made forcefully aware of this contrast between the modern, born-again deity and his atavistic forbear at the Sunday school after the service. The woman next to me in church invited me to come with her and her family. There were hymns, struck out powerfully by a lady at the piano: and then we prayed, first for a member of the church who had cancer; then, rather more briefly, for a Spanish community in West Texas whose town had been destroyed by a tornado. Then came a long, rambling discourse from the Sunday school teacher, a tall Yankee lady in her sixties, based on a text from the psalms. She affirmed God's transcendence and sovereignty: but less in the punitive Old Testament mould (she said nothing about hell or judgement) than as a weapon in a diatribe against the New Age: 'He is transcendent, He is above and over and around His creation, but He is not so prevalent as to be pantheistic. God is not in every blade of grass or in every tree – that's what we're hearing in this New Age Movement. The Scriptures do not teach that. God is God, He is Transcendent, and Here he is right here in this Scripture,' she said with governessy certitude, stabbing her Bible with her finger.

'He knows He is God, and He knows man is man. But it's part of Satan's plan to convince man that man is God, and that's what Satan is doing today, through much of the music, through some of the leading people, John Denver for one, Shirley Maclaine for another, and some of this New Age philosophy that says: We're Gods, we're all gods.'

We prayed again, thanking God for our children, our spouses, our parents and grandparents. These were essentially tribal rites: there were no wider concerns expressed about the state of the world; its poverty and strife. Even the prayers about the unfortunate town of Saragossa had a self-congratulatory air – thanking God that First Baptist had managed to send some money and volunteers.

Though Southern Baptists spend millions on 'spreading the gospel', they are not particularly interested in charity, as compared with members of other denominations. According to a survey conducted in 1968, in which people were asked to determine the *sine qua non*'s of salvation, only 29 per cent of Southern Baptists included 'doing good to others' (as compared with 57 per cent of Methodists, 54 per cent of Episcopalians and 48 per cent of Presbyterians); by contrast 97 per cent of Southern Baptists regarded 'belief in Jesus as Saviour' as absolutely necessary for salvation. The less liberal the theology, the less the concern for social justice.

During the coffee break a small man in thick spectacles came up to me and asked where I worshipped in England.

'I was brought up in the Church of England. I suppose I'm what you call Episcopalian,' I said, ducking the question.

'I don't think what church you go to is important,' said the man, apparently missing the point. 'The important thing is whether you have a personal relationship with Jesus Christ. And you do have a personal relationship with Jesus Christ, don't you?'

'I'm not sure what you mean by personal,' I said, feeling like a Cathar under investigation by the Inquisition. 'I mean I was brought up to believe in Jesus Christ. But "personal" – well, that sounds kind of private, exclusive. Surely Jesus belongs to everybody?'

'Let me ask you something – what's your name, by the way?'

'Malise.'

'If you died, Malise, in the next two minutes, and stood before God, and He said: "Malise, why should I let you into Heaven?" What would you say?'

'I think I would say: "You're a kind and merciful God. You've seen my file. You know everything about my life, my vices and virtues. I rely on Your judgement."'

'And what if He says "Malise, what else?"'

'What would you say?' I asked, trying to look stupid, because I knew perfectly well what he was driving at.

'I used to be very worldly, and much involved in sin. As a youngster I had a religious experience. But I never had a saving knowledge of Christ. Then when I was in the First Marine Division in Korea I realised, for the first time in my life, Malise, that if I died I was going to go to hell. So I made a deal with God, I accepted Jesus as my personal Saviour.'

'You really believe that otherwise a merciful God would have sent you to hell? You actually believe that a God whom you consider to be good would sentence people to eternal punishment just because they don't believe in Jesus Christ?'

'Yup, the Bible says: "I am the way, the truth and the life. No one comes to the Father but by me." Jesus was nailed to the cross for our sins. He died for everybody, you, me, everybody. We must individually and collectively either accept or reject that free gift.' He made it sound like something that came with ten gallons of petrol.

'What about members of other religions? There are other holy books as well as the Bible. Are all the Muslims, Confucians, Hindus and Buddhists going to burn in hell?'

He retreated slightly. 'I choose to believe that the only way a person can get into heaven is through a personal relationship with Jesus Christ.' This was less than a wholly categorical statement. 'The only thing I can say for sure is that the minute I invited Jesus to come into my life my whole existence changed. I have a total peace I didn't have before.'

'So you're no longer worried about what will happen when you die?'

'I do worry. But you see, Malise, you and I as men, we're walking on this earth for a very little time – life is very short, OK? But eternity is very long, OK? If the Bible's true, and the only way into Heaven is through Jesus Christ, well then I choose to accept his free gift, OK? It's not worth taking a chance on it. All I have to do is confess that Jesus Christ is my Lord and Saviour, and then I'll be saved . . . '

He had backed another step away from total conviction. Now he was making a rational bet, like Pascal: *I believe just in case it's true – because if it isn't it won't matter anyway.* But there was an urgency about his manner that prompted me to observe: 'For a person experiencing total peace of mind, you seem remarkably concerned about personal survival. In Eastern religions people don't bother so much about that. We return to the One from whence we came, like drops of water meeting the ocean. Why are you so bothered about what happens to you individually?'

'The Bible says there are only two places,' he said. 'Either we're going to be in heaven, or we're going to be in hell. Forget about Islam, forget about Buddhism, forget about religion. Jesus Christ says there's only one way to heaven, and that's through Him, OK?' Having slammed the door on doubt, he handed me a tract and walked away.

A small, trim dark-haired woman came up, and after we had chatted a while she invited me to lunch at a nearby cafeteria where families were gathering after church. Her name was Bonnie. Only when she told me she had a son exactly my age did I guess she must be at least in her sixties. Before she found Jesus in 1954 Bonnie's life had not been especially happy. Her husband had been a salesman – a southern Willy Loman who found little satisfaction in his job, 'enduring fifty weeks of the year for the sake of a two-week vacation'.

'Things didn't go right in his work,' said Bonnie, with the understatement that accompanies failure. The difficulties spilled over into their married life. They joined a church, partly in order to meet people and partly to assuage anomie. Though active in the church, Bonnie was still unhappy because she found she could not live up to the moral standards of the people around her.

'I couldn't be what I wanted to be,' she said. 'I couldn't experience what I saw them experiencing. I was trying as hard as I could, teaching in Sunday school, going to church conferences, getting trained. But the others had a joy and a peace and a love for the Lord Jesus I just couldn't seem to get. I became increasingly aware of the exceeding sinfulness of my condition.

Looking at Bonnie's face, I thought anxiety rather than sin would be her problem.

'What did you feel to be sinful?' I asked. 'Your life doesn't seem to have been at all immoral.'

'Not particularly immoral,' she said. 'But I wasn't meeting the standards of the Sermon on the Mount. I didn't seem able to cope with the crises of my life – things like the kids' chickenpox, my husband's dissatisfaction with his job, the fact that he was out of work for a while which was traumatic for all of us. I remember going to the pastor and saying "Does God care about our jobs? Is it OK to pray for a job?" He assured me that it was, so I started praying. But however hard I prayed, my prayers didn't seem to get any higher than the ceiling. Then one day I was working as a volunteer secretary at the Church office, when I came upon a passage from Romans 7: "Oh wretched man that I am! Who shall deliver me from the body of this death?" I realised that what I was carrying around was just a "body of death" that could *never* be good enough, no matter what I did.'

'So now you don't have to worry so much about your conduct: you just put your trust in Jesus?'

'Right,' said Bonnie. 'I went straight into the sanctuary, fell on my knees and turned myself totally over to the control of the Lord Jesus. And very shortly I began to feel a sense of overwhelming peace. I became aware of the cleansing blood of the Saviour just as it says in the Bible.'

Later I interviewed several other members of Criswell's church. In every case the details were similar: a period of acute anxiety accompanied by feelings of abject inadequacy, followed by the experience of inexpressible peace upon taking Jesus as their Personal Saviour. A few of them confessed to having led 'sinful' lives in the formal sense of drinking or having sexual relations outside marriage. But the majority were already believers, like Bonnie, whose source of anxiety was not immorality, but their perceived inability to live up to the exacting standards set by Christ. The acceptance of Jesus as their *personal* Saviour absolved them of their feelings of inadequacy. God the Father remained in the background, still the implacable judge from whom no secrets were hid; but Christ relieved them of the burden of this God-induced anxiety and guilt by taking on the punishment Himself. Jesus 'made them feel good about themselves'.

Psychologically, if not theologically, born-again Christianity was closer to Robert Schuller's 'theology of self-esteem' than appeared at first sight. The same implicit narcissism was there, the same obsession with the good of the self. Only the vocabulary in which it was couched was different. Instead of talking overtly about 'self-esteem' in language muddied by its associations with secular psychology and – God forbid! – New Age psychotherapies, it presented itself in the traditional guise of American evangelicalism, in language that suggested, misleadingly, that the 'free gift' on offer was a return to the certitudes of the past. Actually, though there were elements of this 'traditionalist' discourse, much of the born-again message was modishly new. It addressed itself to the plight of the modern American soul, just like the other remedies, cults or panaceas.

All the born-again people I spoke to felt that their conversion had been part of God's 'plan' for them: in that sense they held to the traditional Calvinistic view that salvation comes by grace, not works. Bonnie was convinced that her educational career, which took off in her late forties, was part of this. Before her marriage, she had only completed high-school education; and though she had taught Sunday school and helped run the youth programme at the church she and her husband joined in Shreveport, Louisiana, where they had lived for some years, it was only when they came to Dallas and joined First Baptist that she was able to go on and earn a degree at South-Western Theological Seminary. She never mentioned the fact that it is not unusual for married women to improve their education when their children are grown-up.

The idea that God has a plan for each individual is, of course, psychologically comforting. Financial hardships, rejection or humiliation by employers, potential spouses or children, the struggle against debt, frequent changes of job and moves to strange cities and new suburbs – the whole restless nightmare that constitutes the American Dream for those who are insufficiently talented, ambitious, competitive, or just plain unlucky: all these things become more bearable if they are perceived as foreordained, or as 'tests' of fortitude as described in the Book of Job. In the fundamentalist mind, nothing is too trivial for God's attention. 'Almost anything, good or bad,' writes Nancy Ammerman, a sociologist at Emory University, Atlanta, who has made a study of modern fundamentalism,

> can be explained as God's doing. God keeps the dishes from breaking, locates things that are lost. He supplies friends and offspring. He makes sure cars get fixed at affordable prices. He arranges convenient overtime work schedules and makes hiring and firing more pleasant. He provides clothes and food when they are needed, as well as less essential items like tickets for a rodeo or a pet dog for the children.'

Above all, He provides an ordered mental defence against the threat of both social anomie and private chaos. He is therefore especially effective in solving matrimonial problems. Several of the men I interviewed believed their marriages had been saved by their conversions.

'Dallas is the divorce capital of the US,' said Bonnie. 'A marital crisis can really trigger conversion. I've seen it happen time and again. I've watched many people, and seen how the greatest Christian growth seems to come through personal crisis. I think it's because it's only when we realise how vulnerable we are that we turn outside ourselves for help.'

Sometimes it was the men who turned to Jesus, hoping their wives would become more docile. But often it was the women themselves, hoping to save their marriages. They expected to find order in adopting the traditional role of homemaker after the difficulties of trying to negotiate equality. 'Wives submit yourselves unto your husbands, as unto the Lord. For the husband is the head of the wife even as Christ is the head of the church' (Eph 5: 22–3.) The submission of wife to husband, perhaps after a lengthy struggle, was justified and made more acceptable by Scripture. Abandoning the uncharted and treacherous waters of women's liberation could be represented, not as defeat, but as a victory over sin perceived as 'personal wilfulness'. The 'saved' woman, of course, enjoyed undisputed power in her own territory, the home, probably more than she enjoyed before. But she could now duck out of larger responsibilities by deferring to her husband as 'head'. In return, she could expect the support of the church with its strong social and religious sanctions against divorce.

Increasing ease of divorce and its attendant contingencies, such as sex outside marriage, are the greatest sins in the evangelical book. In a 1983 survey of 'immoral behaviour' by religious preference, evangelicals rated extra-marital relations as the worst of sins with 96.7 per cent, even higher than abortion (95.3 per cent) and homosexuality (88.7 per cent); with 66.7 per cent opposed to divorce, they were also well ahead of Catholics (57.4 per cent). A typical evangelical tract blames the ills of society on the break-up of the family due to a falling off in religion:

We have crime, in large part due to youthful offenders. They commit crimes due to their lack of proper, balanced, godly upbringing. This springs from homes broken by adultery, alcohol, promiscuity and other sins. These problems arise due to a lack of proper upbringing. The circle completes itself and always comes back to failure to put God first in the family.

Later, Bonnie arranged for me to see Dr Criswell himself. His office was furnished with gilt mirrors, deep pile carpets, chandeliers and expensive-looking English and French antiques, like a show flat done up by Harrods.

'I'm a Calvinist in my theology,' the great man said. 'I believe that if a man is called, he will respond. If he's not called he will fall away.

Close-to his face was kindly, his voice mellifluous, his manner endearingly gentle. I knew his beliefs had to consign me a contumacious non-believer, to hell: but he would do it in the nicest possible way, as if to say 'No offence, brother, but you're going to burn . . . !' When I pressed him on the fate of other non-believers, he was careful to say that it was in God's hands, not his. I asked him about the Jews, knowing that Bailey Smith, a former President of the Southern Baptist Convention, had caused a national outcry by stating in public that 'God does not hear the prayer of the Jew.' He avoided the trap.

'Well, I'm not getting into the argument about whether the Lord hears the prayer of the Jew or not. I'm much in sympathy with Israel, very much so. I am very pro-Israel. All I know is, Christ came into the world to die for our sins, and *there is none other name under heaven given among men, whereby we must be saved*. What God does with the Jew, the Muslim, the Hindu lies in God's prerogative, not mine.'

There seemed an implicit *de facto* acceptance of religious pluralism here which conflicted with the Biblical text he quoted. There were similar openings in his remarks about baptism and biblical inerrancy. Although no one entered heaven without a personal experience of Christ, nine-year-old children could be baptised into the church, provided they had a knowledge of sin. This was getting near the Half-Way Covenant: born-again conversion was effectively institutionalised. As for the Bible, there seemed slightly more room for interpretation than I had realised.

'Not all of the Bible is of equal importance,' he said, in answer to my question. 'By "inerrancy" what we mean is that the Holy Spirit guided the authors of the Bible, and that what they wrote is correct. The doctrine is about what the authors wrote, not about the text that has come down to us which has been copied and recopied. It is only by comparison of the many copies that we come to an approximation of what the original author wrote.'

When I left him Criswell took my hand and held it for a moment. 'Are you married, young man?' he asked. I told him I was, with daughters of seventeen and eighteen. At this he flatteringly expressed surprise.

'I can tell you're a remarkable man,' he said, in tones that were meant to sound pregnant with spiritual insight. 'Tell your wife from me she's a very lucky woman.'

I knew better. But I expected that kind of thing won souls for Christ.

With 14 million members organised into 38,000 affiliated churches, the Southern Baptist Convention is America's largest non-Catholic denomination: purists avoid the 'protestant' label on the ground that though Baptist theology belongs to the reformed tradition, the Baptist churches which arose in England, Holland and New England in the seventeenth century were not reformist offshoots of Catholicism, but independent growths. The disestablishment of all colonial churches gave a huge boost to Baptism in the aftermath of the revolution: as religious free-marketeers *par excellence*, unencumbered by elaborate rules of church governance, they were better placed than any other denomination to take advantage of the new circumstances. Their relative lack of concern with theological orthodoxy (some were Arminian free-willers, others Calvinist determinists), their indifference to education and their emphasis on individual adult conversion were admirably suited to conditions on the frontier, especially in the Old South and West.

The classic Baptist minister was a licensed farmer-preacher, unpaid but financially independent, who moved with the people into new areas. He might be ordained in an existing church, or create one for himself, baptising new members and ordaining new missionaries. In this way 'the Baptists advanced in the wilderness, or moved back among the unchurched multitudes in older areas, without direction from bishops or synods, and without financial support from denominational agencies or special societies.'

The churches were organised into a relatively loose structure until the 1840s, when the slavery question began to divide them. Resentful of the zeal of Northern abolitionists who refused to appoint slave-owners to missions, the Southern Baptists organised themselves into a separate convention in 1845. The Southerners developed a tighter, more centralised structure in order to rein in their own abolitionists. Born in slavery, the Southern Baptist Convention has, despite its democratic, parliamentary system, retained a highly authoritarian mode of control.

With six seminaries and two universities (Baylor and Mercer) under their control, Southern Baptists were slower than other denominations to become embroiled in the controversies spawned by the new theologies of the nineteenth and twentieth centuries. The question of biblical inerrancy only surfaced occasionally in Convention-controlled schools and seminaries. In 1925 the SBC averted the possibility of a split by adopting a revised version of its confessional article; the *Baptist Faith and Message*. The relevant sentence stated that the Bible 'has God for its author, salvation for its end and truth without any mixture of error, for its matter'. Inerrantists were satisfied, while 'closet' liberals kept their heads down by arguing, somewhat tautologically, that it was the 'truth' of the Bible, not its text, the message rather than the medium, that was 'without any mixture of error'.

It was not until the late 1950s and early 1960s, half a century after most other denominations had already faced these issues, that the new theology, now taking the modified form of neo-orthodoxy, finally penetrated the Southern Baptist seminaries. A major furore occurred in 1961 when the seminarian Ralph Elliott came out of the closet with the publication of *The Message of Genesis*, in which he plainly declared that the stories of Adam and Eve, Cain and Abel, Noah's flood and others were non-historical parables intended to 'convey deep historical insight'. After protests the book was withdrawn by its publishers, the official Southern Baptist Sunday School Board, and Elliott was fired for refusing to give an undertaking not to publish it elsewhere. The warning proved salutary: moderates put their heads below the parapet again; they continued to teach, but were careful not to publish.

The moderate strategy worked fairly well. Although conservatives like Criswell were elected to the presidency of the SBC, the moderates remained entrenched, not only in the seminaries, but in the bureaucracy, enabling the denomination to broaden its theological appeal. A few liberal churches even had women pastors, while in 1976 a liberal politician and Sunday school teacher, Governor Jimmy Carter of Georgia, became the first Southern Baptist to win the Presidency of the United States, backed by the evangelical vote. Though a minority, the moderates underpinned their ascendency with education and patronage. Surveys reveal that as late as 1980 more than 80 per cent of Southern Baptist ministers were inerrantists; but those holding master's degrees were five times more likely to subscribe to moderate viewpoints, while students became less orthodox for every year they spent in seminary.

Any form of learning is, at heart, inimical to fundamentalist certitudes: for all critical methodologies, not only those of the exact sciences, inculcate the value of doubt. The patronage network was subtle, but all too palpable to those who found themselves excluded. The Convention has a comprehensive career structure for its clergy. Going to the right schools, getting on with the professors there and making the right friends assured the ambitious of recommendations to good churches or well-paid Convention staff jobs, with salaries of more than $100,000, plus tax-free clerical perks for some executives. A cosy atmosphere prevailed at many agency conferences, where 'trouble-makers', 'rednecks', 'hayseeds' and other outsiders definitely felt themselves excluded. For insiders, inerrancy was out: what Catholics call 'cardinal's scepticism' and Baptist moderates 'denominational diversity' had become the norm.

There was, however, a contradiction between the liberal commitment to enlightenment and the traditional Baptist task of saving souls. As the fundamentalists looked at other churches, they could find ample justification for their belief that liberal or neo-orthodox theology acted like a viral infection, undermining church growth. In the two decades between 1960 and 1980 Episcopal, Lutheran, Presbyterian, Congregationalist and United Methodist missionary agencies had declined drastically, with falls in conversion ranging from 79 to 46 per cent. Although comprehensive statistics were not available, *ad hoc* surveys of Southern Baptist churches revealed a similar picture. For example, a survey of churches in Louisville, Kentucky, conducted in 1984 showed that whereas churches with fundamentalist pastors were registering new baptisms at the rate of 1 per 34 church members, the ratio for those under moderate control was 1 per 138.

Two men decided to put things to rights. One was Paul Pressler, a Texas Appeals Court Judge from Houston. The other was Criswell's chief lieutenant, the Reverend Paige Patterson, President of the Criswell Center for Biblical Studies. Together they organised the campaign that would wrest the SBC from liberal control and restore it to the path of strict biblical truth. The task before them was enormous. But they had the energy and the political skills. First they would see that a full-blooded conservative was elected to the presidency of the Convention: then they would ensure that he deployed his powers effectively. This would mean appointing committees with fundamentalist majorities to ensure that the twenty-odd boards which ran the six Southern Baptist seminaries, and the various agencies, including the powerful Home and Foreign Mission Boards, came under fundamentalist control. Once these boards had fundamentalist majorities, time would do the rest. New posts would go to fundamentalists, while the liberals would in due course retire. It was a long-term plan: but eternity was its goal.

By ecclesiastical standards the war was dirty, more akin to the board/bedroom battles of J. R. Ewing and his cronies than the subtler forms of malice that usually prevails among Christian brethren. Liberal incumbents found themselves accused of alcoholism and general moral laxity, allowing evolution to be taught in SBC schools and tolerating R-rated movies, homosexual advocacy and other invitations to sin. Moderates replied with accusations of 'fascism' and a 'holy war', conducted by unholy forces that were seeking to hijack the denomination and its agencies. The fundamentalists replied, illogically, that the 'denominational fascists' were bent on wrecking the Southern Baptists by dispensing 'spiritual slop'. Moderate professors were accused of teaching universalism (the doctrine that all will eventually be saved, regardless of whether or not they are 'born-again') and – horror of horrors! – of behaving with Episcopalian arrogance.

Fundamentalist broadsheets revealed scandalous excerpts from liberal lectures surreptitiously taped by students. The President of Southern Seminary, Roy Honeycutt, had suggested that the burning bush seen by Moses might only be a vision, 'an inner experience the details of which had been drawn from the thought patterns common to his generation: thought patterns that embraced a literal angel of the Lord and a literal angel of fire.' To this Bailey Smith – notorious for his remarks about the Jews – gave the robust riposte 'Jonah was a literal person swallowed by a literal fish and was in a literal mess.'

What most outraged the fundamentalists was the liberal tendency to remove the miraculous from the Biblical narrative, in order to make divine intervention seem more rational. Here, for example, is an account of the Crossing of the Red Sea in Exodus by a former professor of Christian philosophy at Southern Seminary, Eric Rust:

> ...In one sense, what occurred might be dismissed as a natural phenomenon. A strong wind drove back the waters and provided a way of escape over the dry seabed. Its cessation made possible the return of the waters and the drowning of the Egyptians. But the miracle was not just a wind driving back waters from a reedy lake and marsh. The miracle was God *using a natural happening* to deliver his people and so guiding them and the forces of nature that they fulfilled his liberating purpose. This was no mere chance occurrence of nature. It was a mighty act of the Lord.

Intellectually, the fundamentalists had a powerful case: if one supernatural intervention was rejected, why not others, like the Virgin Birth or even the

Resurrection? By choosing to de-supernaturalise or even reject miracles, liberal and neo-orthodox theologians lay themselves open to the charge of subjectivism and inconsistency. The same applied when liberal scholars got into the game of allowing certain texts and rejecting others: the whole edifice was in danger of crumbling. As Adrian Rogers, the young pastor from Memphis who became the leading fundamentalist holder of the Convention presidency observed, 'When we admit error in the Bible in any area of history, cosmology or philosophy, then we put ourselves in the precarious position of having to decide by human subjectivity what is error and what is not. We then leave the door open to let in much worse error which will ultimately be the demise of the denomination.'

The campaign began in earnest in 1979. At the Houston Convention Rogers was elected by a decisive, though small majority (51 per cent) on the first ballot. The moderates cried 'foul', alleging bussing of unregistered messengers (as church delegates to Baptist conferences are called) and other irregularities. However, despite six consecutive wins by fundamentalist candidates to the presidency, the war was not finally won until the 1985 convention in Dallas. A key role in the 'Chattanooga' of the Baptist Civil War was played by Criswell himself, who sent out 36,000 letters to his fellow pastors urging them to bring every church messenger they could to Dallas to the Convention in order to help beat off a moderate counterattack by re-electing the incumbent president, the popular television preacher Charles Stanley. Criswell's circular produced a response that astounded even its authors: 45,000 messengers turned up at Dallas, more than twice the previous record. In the Convention Sermon they heard the seventy-five-year-old pastor proclaim that 'All Scripture is inspired of God. All of it. Not parts of it. If the Bible which is supposed to be written by the Holy Spirit of God contains errors, it is a work of men, it is not a work of God . . . If higher criticism continues to grow like a parasite in our universities, there will be no missionaries to hurt – they will cease to exist.'

'Amen,' roared the crowd.

Thereafter the moderate cause was lost, at least for the foreseeable future. A Peace Committee was set up, ostensibly to reconcile the two factions. However, since it was dominated by inerrantists, it became a permanent body designed to monitor the orthodoxy of professors of theology and Convention employees.

I myself witnessed the *coup de grâce* two years later. In June 1987 I flew to
St Louis to attend the Southern Baptist Convention.

By the time I had arrived at the Cervantes Convention Center, Adrian
Rogers had already been re-elected by a comfortable 60–40 majority. The
armies of the Lord filled the two enormous convention halls to overflowing.
There was a semi-festive atmosphere. Apart from officials and speakers,
many of the men wore shirtsleeves, the women pants or cotton dresses.
They were overwhelmingly white and, to judge from their manners, either
rural or if urban, from the lower income groups. They sucked soft drinks
through straws, munched hamburgers, popcorn and ice cream throughout
the proceedings. A high proportion appeared to be overweight. Many had
children with them. Only the front rows could see the platform in any detail. The rest watched on cinema-sized video screens and listened through
speakers that echoed round the hall. For three full days the messengers
filled every seat, listening intently to every speech, voting for fundamentalist nominees on the various committees and for resolutions condemning
pornography, abortion, and women who held jobs outside the home. A
$114 million budget – the largest ever – was approved. By the end of the
conference all but one of the seminary boards of trustees had come under
fundamentalist control, as had the important Home and Foreign Mission
boards.

The high points were the speeches, or sermons, of the star preachers.
The personable Dr Rogers announced unconvincingly that 'We Southern
Baptists are old fashioned Christians who believe that hell is hot, heaven is
sweet, sin is black, judgement is sure and Jesus saves.'

The messengers loved it, but it was hard to believe that such a suave,
clean-cut, good-looking man, who looked more like a banker or business
executive than a preacher, really held such primitive views.

The best-known speaker was Billy Graham, a paid-up member of
Criswell's Church, who preached a rousing sermon that was masterful
in its ambiguity, sitting carefully on the fence between pre-millennialism
and post-millennialism, fundamentalist and liberal theology. Graham's
phenomenal success depended – like Schuller's – on being all things to
as many people as possible. In a carefully veiled reference to the scandal
then raging round the Bakkers' ministry, he condemned the 'Elmer Gantry'
image as a trick of the devil designed to discredit good evangelists, without
making it clear if it was the fictional representation of the corrupt preacher
which was the devil's work, or its original in the form of Jim Bakker. Then,

papering over the theological fissures of a decade, he concluded with the practised enthusiasm of the seasoned professional that all that was needed was another great crusade for Christ. 'There's not a problem in this Convention or in any seminary that a Great Holy Ghost Revival wouldn't settle,' he announced with the voice of Charlton Heston on Mount Sinai. The audience loved that too.

But the star speaker was Jerry Vines, a pastor from Rome, Georgia, and former convention president. Vines's Convention Sermon was vitriolic and funny. He had them clapping, cheering and chuckling for forty minutes of a highly entertaining delivery. They split their sides when he mimicked the flabby liberal trying to convert an alcoholic:

> Go with us for a moment into the house of an unsaved man. The carpets are smelly, beer cans are littering the floor. His family is hanging together by a thread. He's an alcoholic. He's on drugs. His daughter is pregnant. And I say to him:
>
> 'Sir, I would like to share with you today some verses from the Epistle to the Romans, but before I do you know we're not quite sure that Paul really wrote these words, they may have been put in his lips by some of his disciples. And, sir, can I interest you in an existential encounter with the Spirit of Jesus that is alive and somewhere today?' I guess he'd say:
>
> 'No thanks. But if you've got the phone numbers of Drug Rehab, Alcoholics Anonymous and Planned Parenthood. I'd sure like to have them.' Brothers, if you don't believe in the Bible, you're out of business in the homes of lost people.

The messengers also loved it when Vines told an anti-Indian joke and gave a vivid description of how liberal theology took hold in the seminaries:

> At the turn of the century a thief stole almost unnoticed into this land. He had already done his damage in Germany, robbing them of scriptural authority and moral conscience. He is an old, ancient thief, because he had worked even as far back as the Garden of Eden, persuading Adam and Eve to question the accuracy and acceptancy of the Word of God. Very soon he began robbing and stealing in the North, so that in his trail there were faith-denying schools, bankrupt denominations, and powerless churches. He began to move steadily down the Eastern coast. He was very crafty and subtle. His intended goal was to take the Bible from the hands of the common people. He appealed to the innate pride and desire to be considered intellectual on the part of those who were scholarly men.

This old thief's name is Destructive Criticism . . . I'm talking about the kind of criticism that clips the wings of faith with the scissors of reason, that subjects the warm wonder of the Word to the cold, merciless analysis of unbelief. This old destructive critic is a demolition expert. He's got a heretical hammer, and with that hammer he drives into the canons of scripture the nails of anti-supernaturalism and the anti-miraculous, so that every supernatural event in the Bible becomes an example of puerile folklore . . . He's also got a cynical crowbar, and the purpose of that tool is to rip the Bible out of the heads and hearts of ordinary Baptist people . . . But I've got something to tell you [he added, pausing to turn to the imaginary thief] I'm here to tell you your hammer won't work on the Bible, because if you deny the supernatural in the Bible, you deny the very nature of the Bible itself. You can't kick God out of the Book any more than you can kick Him out of the universe.

The crowd roared its approval. All the favourite themes were there, xenophobia, Yankeephobia, racism, anti-intellectualism, wrapped up in vivid, Bunyanesque personifications – the authentic Baptist vernacular. It was a hate-inspiring speech, designed to excoriate the liberals and ensure that the voting went against them. To me it revealed more than anything what the Bible meant to the majority: not a record of spiritual truth, or even of God's revelation to humankind, but a totem or shibboleth, a flag to be waved at the forces of modernity, hated because deeply feared.

The climax of the Convention was the adoption of a report by the twenty-two-man Peace Committee. Dominated by fundamentalists, it gave no quarter to the moderates. A Statement on Scripture affirmed the inerrancy of the Bible 'in all realms of reality' and 'all fields of knowledge'. It insisted that most Baptists believed in the direct creation of mankind, and that Adam and Eve were real persons; that the named authors in the Bible did indeed write the books ascribed to them; that the miracles in scripture were actual supernatural events; and that the historical events described in the Bible occurred exactly as written. The convention voted to keep the Peace Committee in existence for another three years. It seemed quite likely that it would become a permanent organ of the Convention, designed to monitor orthodoxy. At a press conference President Rogers made it clear that while faculty members were entitled to their own beliefs, they 'would be expected to reflect in their teaching what those who paid their salaries [i.e. the convention majority] believed'.

Afterwards, I spoke to Glen Hinson, a leading moderate and professor of church history at Southern Seminary. A gaunt, gentle man with an air of saintly resignation, he looked predictably depressed.

'It amounts to converting the Peace Committee into a Holy Office or Inquisition,' he said. 'This is something that can only end up with the grossest perversion of truth. Truth does not lie with the mob. You have to see this as analogous to what happened in Germany in the Thirties.'

A woman taxi-driver drove me back to the airport. Though she had rather coarse features and a slightly pockmarked face, she was quite attractive, with chestnut hair and a full figure. There were a couple of scars on her forehead: I expected she had been in a fight or two, or been beaten up by one of the men in her life.

'I sure love to see all those Baptists hitting this town,' she said when I told her I was a journalist covering the Convention. 'Of course there are some shitty ones among them, but most of them are good Christians. I'm a Christian myself.' I presumed the shitty ones were moderates.

'When did you become a Christian?' I asked.

'Last November.'

'What difference does it make?'

'It's like a stone removed from your heart. I'm on my second divorce, and my finances are in one hell of a mess. I'm two months behind with the rent and electricity and it looks like my daughter's going to move in with her dad. But I'm not fussed about that. I know there's Someone there who loves me!'

'Have you changed your lifestyle, given up drink or anything like that?'

'I still like to take a drink or two, but I don't have one night stands any more: you know, saying goodbye to someone in the morning knowing you're not going to see them again. I mean it makes you feel used, and maybe they feel used too. It just doesn't add up to anything just part of the rat race. Same with money. Now I know who my real friends are. I can depend on them, and they can lean on me sometimes. There was this girl I know. Been on drugs. She hasn't been saved yet, but I stayed up with her all night. Saved her from doing herself in, maybe.'

I said I hoped the girl would get saved. I meant it sincerely. It was better than being on drugs.

XII

The Black Gospel

> And Ham, the father of Canaan, saw the nakedness of his father, and told
> his two brethren outside. And Noah awoke from his wine . . . And he said,
> Cursed be Canaan; a servant of servants shall he be unto his brethren.
>
> GENESIS 9: 22–25

> Servants, be obedient to them that are your masters according to the flesh,
> with fear and trembling, in singleness of your heart, as unto Christ.
>
> EPHESIANS 6:5

I left Dallas late in the afternoon, relieved to be heading east. There was
something depressing about the co-existence of such wealth with so much
bigotry, although it was not, I had come to see, illogical. For all the contradictions between science and scripture, Biblical literalism is the natural ally
of materialism, its theological counterpart. For members of the born-again
fraternity – lower-grade teachers, engineers, technicians – words must be
concrete and practical, like tools: spades are spades. They must find the idea
that truth can reside in myth inherently objectionable, because they live on
a two-dimensional semantic plane where things are either true or false, like
positive and negative charges.

I switched on the radio to while away freeway boredom. A Christian
counsellor was hosting a phone-in.

'That's a pretty heavy-duty triangle you're involved in,' he was telling
one man who was sobbing down the line. 'You and her had better make a
clean break of it.'

'That's what she told my wife she was going to do.'

The counsellor sounded outraged. *'She called and told your wife that you and
she had talked?'* The idea of collusion between the females involved evidently
offended the counsellor's sense of propriety more than the adultery itself.

'We'd like to join with you in prayer. Pause from whatever you're doing and join Don in prayer . . . '

The next caller was rendered inaudible by some high-tension cables. I just caught the end of the counsellor's reply. 'Sex isn't just a physical act, it's an emotional and spiritual one designed by God for procreation. *Somebody masturbating against somebody else's body in the elevator isn't emotional or spiritual. It's sick and perverted.* You've got real problems. Your head's in a mess and your soul's on the way to hell . . . Bob, you need to know God loves you. I'm going to pray for you now: in the name of Jesus Christ . . . '

The final caller's story was so bizarre it must have been true. He had recently come across evidence which gave him reason to suspect that the woman to whom he was married was his long-lost sister. The counsellor was stumped for advice when the caller revealed that his wife, still ignorant of the probable truth of their relationship, had been made miserable by her husband's sudden loss of ardour.

'You don't want to hurt her by telling her, but she thinks you're rejecting her as a woman,' said the counsellor. 'God knows the answer. Let us pray . . . '

None of the advice proffered, apart from admonitions to prayer, was distinctively Christian. I doubted if there really was any such thing as 'Christian' counselling. It was simply a way of packaging the same kind of commonsensical advice that ordinary agony aunts dispensed. The same went, by and large, for 'Christian' music, especially the 'Christian rock' churned out by many stations between sermons and Bible readings. The rhythms and the tunes were similar to those of the ordinary popular music they played on commercial networks. The only difference was in the words which were addressed to God rather than to some more sexually accessible love-object. But since the lyrics were usually inaudible, this difference was nugatory.

I spent the night at Rayville, beyond the Louisiana boundary, after dining deliciously on deep-fried oysters. I only slept four or five hours, setting off at dawn to escape the heat of the day. The countryside was lush, and pleasantly unkempt. It was densely forested with evergreens, except for an occasional clearing where tall grass all but concealed some tumbledown shack. The vehicles looked as poor as the countryside: rusting automobiles and trucks with precarious loads held together by string, the drivers everywhere black. After Dallas, it was reassuringly familiar, like Egypt or Ireland. The road crossed several muddy 'bayous' or bankless streams where the forest came straight into the water, as in a jungle: I knew I must be approaching the Mississippi.

I crossed the river at Vicksburg, site of Ulysses S. Grant's famous civil war victory. The town, built on high bluffs on the east bank, on one of the river's tortuous curves, had been the principal obstacle to Union control of the waterway. Its massive earthworks and fortifications on the landward side made it virtually impregnable. After two unsuccessful attempts to take it by storm, Grant sat it out for a siege which began on 22 May 1863, establishing batteries to hammer the fortifications and burrowing tunnels to undermine them with explosive charges. From the river a fleet of Federal ironclad gunboats cut off Vicksburg's communications and blasted the city with their cannon. After seven weeks, with supplies dwindling, no hope of relief and 10,000 of his men out of action through sickness, wounds or malnutrition the Confederate commander, General Pemberton, surrendered on terms that allowed the defenders the dignity of parole. The great earthworks, now thickly wooded, have been made into a permanent memorial to the civil war dead: 17,000 Union men are buried there in addition to the 5,000 Confederates interred in Vicksburg general cemetery.

Religious fervour had sustained the conflict on both sides in the war. The Northern crusade against slavery had partly been a by-product of the evangelical revival of the Second Awakening. Anti-slavers experienced conversion to Christ and the abolitionist cause simultaneously. Southern revivalists, equally fervent, directed their enthusiasm to less visible moral evils, learning to parrot the standard biblical texts concerning Negro inferiority and the acceptance of servitude. According to the testimony of Frederick Douglass, the half-white former slave who went on to become a leading abolitionist, Southern revivalism actively worsened the slave's condition. When his master became converted after attending a Methodist camp meeting, Douglass 'indulged a faint hope' that he might emancipate his slaves, or at least make him more kind and humane; in fact, said Douglass, it had the opposite effect on his master's character: 'Prior to his conversion, he relied upon his own depravity to shield and sustain him in his savage barbarity; but after his conversion, he found religious sanction and support for his slaveholding cruelty . . . The slave auctioneer's bell and the church-going bell chime in with each other, and the bitter cries of the heart-broken slave are drowned in the religious shouts of his pious master.'

Just as Northern crusaders had converted the anti-slavery question into an unstoppable juggernaut, so Southern clergy actively fanned the flames of secession. The spirit of revival increased intransigence on both sides, encouraging men to commit the issue to arms and the judgement of God. By the time the first shots were fired in the Civil War, nearly all the denominations had split. Social and political pressure forced the waverers to back their respective sides wholeheartedly. Thus by 1862 Southern Presbyterians, who had previously maintained that slavery was a 'political' question on which their church was neutral, were insisting that 'this struggle is not alone for civil rights and property and home, but also for religion, for the church, for the gospel, for existence itself.' Chaplains not only performed heroic services on the battlefield, tending the wounded and ministering to the dead. They held massive revival meetings in both camps, finding converts even among senior officers. Between one and two hundred thousand were born again during the war. Religion increased commitment on both sides, lessening desertions, prolonging the war and adding to human misery.

The outcome – one million casualties, 600,000 dead, a greater carnage than America would suffer in two world wars combined – was widely perceived in religious terms. For Northerners, victory was the judgement of God wreaked upon the slave-owning rebels, 'the ambitious, educated, plotting, political leaders of the South', as Henry Ward Beecher would call them. Southerners, just as sure that divine judgement would ultimately vindicate their cause, increasingly took refuge in pre-millennialist fantasy. Christ would return soon to punish the Nigger-loving Yankees.

The city of Vicksburg was scarcely more lively than the battlefield. Set on a hill with steep slanting streets, Vicksburg was a curious mixture of self-consciousness and neglect. The roads and the sidewalks were full of cracks, with tufts of grass growing out of them. The hedges were untended, cars were parked chaotically, while overhead the cloudless sky was obscured by confused thickets of electric cables and telephone lines. At eleven in the morning, the place was asleep. The railway shunting-yards and warehouses on the dockside were rusty as ancient shipwrecks. Yet here and there one encountered a porticoed villa in brick, with fresh painted shutters and balconies, as well as more substantial late-Victorian mansions fashioned in Tudor style. I knocked at the door of one of these dwellings, the Balfour House, which advertised itself as open to the public. It remained obstinately shut, an hour past its official opening time, and I abandoned it to some more hopeful visitors who seemed to think their persistence would be rewarded.

The courthouse museum was open. A grim granite building with classical columns, it dominated the town from its highest point. Built by slaves, it trod a delicate curatorial line between celebrating the society of the antebellum South and deploring its principal institution. A room devoted to the life and work of Jefferson Davis, first and only President of the Confederate States of America, with samples of his handwriting, pictures of his bride and similar mementoes was balanced by a room with manacles, bills of sale and other accoutrements of slavery. In case this induced a mood of irrepressible rage, or despair, someone had thoughtfully added a vignette devoted to good Mother Walker, whose home-brewed recipe for straightening out curly hair made her the first black millionnairess in America by the time of her demise in 1919. Here was the American dream, custom made for Southern blacks.

East of Vicksburg the forest became more coniferous. The road was littered with fragments of tyre and squashed armadillos and other small animals. Occasional clearings revealed idyllic meadows with grazing horses and cattle. Near the Alabama border I left the freeway and took the state road to Selma and Montgomery. The trees became more stately, the pastures richer with wild flowers and grasses. By the time I reached Selma it was dark.

The Union victory in the Civil War proved a false dawn for Southern blacks. The Emancipation Proclamation freed them from physical bondage, while in theory the Fourteenth and Fifteenth Amendments gave them the right to vote and equality before the law. However, once the Federal occupation armies had been pulled out, the clock was quietly but firmly put back. Just about every form of tyranny and discrimination, short of actual slavery, was restored. High poll taxes and 'grandfather' clauses (stating that no one was eligible to vote unless their grandfather had been a voter) effectively disenfranchised the black population; sharecropping arrangements tied black farmers to white landowners with bonds of debt scarcely less powerful than those of slavery itself. 'Jim Crow' laws allowing separate and thoroughly unequal facilities, upheld by the Supreme Court in 1896, enabled racial segregation to penetrate every area of ordinary life. It became illegal for blacks and whites to eat together in public, to sit next to each other in theatres, buses or trains, to use the same drinking fountains or toilets, to enter or exit public buildings by the same doors. For a century Southern whites exacted their revenge from the hapless people whose plight had caused them war and humiliation.

But while the state failed to fulfil the promise sealed in the blood of civil war, the church offered the hope of better things to come – and not just in the next world, though for many blacks it must have seemed that way. In their churches American blacks were inviolable. The black church, however poor, did not depend on the white community for its sustenance. Its branches, whether Baptist, African Methodist or pentecostal, nurtured black self-consciousness. It became the training ground for leadership and the place where the same biblical epic which had inspired so many other sojourners in the American wilderness was studied, disseminated and transformed into a programme of action. Like the Puritans and the Mormons, the American blacks became a People of the Book, whose understanding of their special destiny in the world was shaped by the Bible in general, and Exodus in particular.

In Montgomery I called in at Martin Luther King's old church on Dexter Avenue. A plain brick structure with gothic windows, built in the 1880s and only a block from the handsome state capitol where Jefferson Davis took the oath of office, it became a symbol of black aspirations long after the blacks had been pushed out of the downtown area. Its congregation, most of whom were doctors, college professors or prosperous business men, had arrived in automobiles: it was known to the poorer blacks as the 'big people's church'. King received the call to be pastor in 1954 at the youthful age of twenty-five, having impressed the congregation with the same combination of earnestness and rhetorical skill that made him the spokesman of his generation. An outstanding student, he had graduated from Crozer Theological Seminary in Pennsylvania before going on to Boston University for his PhD. He had familiarised himself with existentialism as well as modern theology, studying Jaspers, Heidegger and Sartre along with Tillich and Wieman. The dominant influences on his career, however, were Gandhi and the Social Gospel of Walter Rauschenbusch.

'I'm not concerned with the temperature of hell nor the furnishings of heaven,' he used to say, 'but with the things men do here on earth . . . Any religion that professes to be concerned with the souls of men and is not concerned with the slums that doom them, the economic conditions that strangle them, the social conditions that cripple them, is a dry-as-dust religion.'

The basement of the church – now renamed the Dexter Avenue King Memorial Baptist Church – is a shrine to King and the movement's other leading personalities. The main events are depicted in a crude but colourful mural that covers the whole of one wall. It begins with Rosa Parkes, the woman who launched the movement with what must be the least inflammatory statement in the history of social conflict: 'I'm tired.' Her refusal to give up her seat to a white and her subsequent arrest led to the Montgomery bus boycott, the first of King's successes. It ends with King's ascension into heaven where he communes with the Kennedy brothers, Mahatma Gandhi, Malcolm X, Frederick Douglass and numerous black martyrs to the Cause. The mural shows the pick-up stations where King and his fellow-organisers arranged for 40,000 blacks to get lifts to and from work every day; the parsonage where he lived with his family, bombed by white racists; the Birmingham Sunday school where four little black girls were killed in another bombing; the 'freedom rides' on inter-state buses with which the activists followed up their success in Montgomery; as well as many black faces, some familiar, like Jessie Jackson and Andy Young, two of King's chief lieutenants, and others almost forgotten, like Huey Newton, Stokely Carmichael and H. Rap Brown. It shows King's form on the balcony of the Lorraine Motel, Memphis, seen through the assassin's telescopic sights, and depicts the murderer – James Earl Ray – in accusatory proximity to the late J. Edgar Hoover, director of the FBI and the man who played devil to Martin's saint.

The smart young woman who showed me the mural went over its details with more pride than comprehension. She knew most of the facts about King's life and death but not, I suspected, their deeper resonances. But how could anyone understand the inner programming, the state of self-contempt induced by segregation laws without having experienced them directly? And how, without such experience, could they hope to understand the barriers, internal and external, that King's sense of absolute right, of God-given self-assurance, enabled them to surmount?

The pastor, Dr Branch, was in his office. He was gentle and thin with grey hair and a slightly world-weary air. I asked him how much things had improved for black people in the twenty years since Dr King's death.

'Only in the sense that you don't have to fight the law,' he said. 'The number of people below the poverty line has increased. Strikebreaking sets the tone. A few token blacks have benefited from the new opportunities. But here the authorities are dragging their feet on affirmative action. You know, they'll put in a token black as chairman of some committee – but he's what they call an Oreo Black, like Oreo cookies, chocolate outside, white inside. "Black" means much more than "coloured" or "Negro": it's a much more comprehensive term. It includes one's stance in life, one's self-understanding.

'You know,' the pastor continued, 'the culture of this country is becoming increasingly anti-religious. Although people don't talk about it, a lot of people object to the theistic understanding of the world. It shows up in the textbooks – more often by what's omitted than by what's included. Of course there are lots of nominal churchmen. But they do not really subscribe to the principles of Jesus. This country has come almost as close to economic determinism in its outlook as the Soviet Union.'

'But when you switch on the radio or television, most of the time all you get is preaching,' I pointed out.

'That's all a distortion of the Message,' he said, with a distant look. 'So many churches have become self-serving institutions, little more than social clubs.'

The telephone rang. Would Dr Branch accept a collect call? The caller was obviously phoning from jail, or the police station. 'You should insist on one call,' said Dr Branch. 'You have a right to one call. You can get his name from the directory. Tell them you know your rights. You have an absolute right to call a lawyer . . . ' He was still talking when I signalled good-bye and left him to his work.

I took the freeway to Atlanta, through cottonwoods, maples and swamps. I checked in at a motel near the airport. It was cheap, clean and featureless, and it had a swimming-pool. I slept fitfully, over-tired from the long drive in the heat.

Next morning was Sunday. I went to the early service at Ebenezer Baptist Church, where King was co-pastor with his father from 1959 until his death in 1968. The church was already full. Everyone was immaculately dressed, the men in dark suits, the women smart in twin-sets and hats. I was glad I had put on my only suit and tie, and felt smugly superior to the only other white people there, a middle-aged couple from Milwaukee – probably Jewish – whose shirtsleeves and slacks held the faint odour of liberal condescension. The service was as elegant as the congregation, with music, prayer and speech merging together in a seamless web that was highly professional without seeming insincere. In the fastness of their chapels, blacks had honed the crude Baptist liturgy with its yearning hymns and anthems into a work of art as polished as a Mozart mass and scarcely less beautiful. The words were rich in the images with which King had roused the American conscience.

Coming out of revival, we had been to the mountain top; but now it was time for us to go back down into the valleys, to do what the Lord had commanded.

'This morning,' crooned the handsome deputy pastor in a smooth velvety voice, 'we feel we're able to make it because we've got God on our side . . . This morning I feel good, because it is well with my soul.' We reached out and touched the hands of the persons next to us, and held them while the choir sang It Is Well With My Soul. The hand that held mine felt lean and capable. It had worked in the cotton fields, it had tied children's bows. Its owner, a small monkey-faced woman of sixty, made me welcome in a manner that stretched beyond politeness towards acceptance, community.

The theme of Pastor Roberts's sermon was community and urban anomie. A highly-strung, intellectual man, he paced to and fro across the platform with the restlessness of a caged panther. His discourse combined the whooping cadences traditional to black Baptists with the fastidious articulacy of a university professor.

"'O opulent city, standing beside great waters. Your end has come, your destiny is certain!'" he thundered the words from Jeremiah, pregnant with doom and destruction. The 'all rights', 'hallelujahs', 'amens' and 'praise the Lords' rose from the audience like birds in the forest.

'Now let me begin by positing some indisputable verities which I believe we can all agree to be beyond successful contradiction,' he continued professorially, coming to his second subject, an overview of urban sociology with erudite references to W. B. Yeats, Marshall McLuhan, Lewis Mumford, Emile Durkheim and a dozen lesser luminaries. The two themes were woven together in intricate homiletic patterns: the world of modern Atlanta, the brilliant capital of America's New South, where some blacks had achieved real power and prosperity, a city of 'glittering urban malls and shopping centres, with cultural plazas and pocket parks'; and that shining city of the soul, the New Jerusalem, for which his forbears, and those of his audience, used to yearn and which sustained them in their travails:

'Can't you imagine the saga of our people who in the midst of slavery were taken to the city and placed upon an auction block? *That's right!* Can't you imagine how a woman looked at her son or husband, realising she would never see them again? But she always said: "I know that even though there is slavery in the United States of America, God has another City! *Amen!* A New Jerusalem which one day shall be established. And the crooked places shall be made straight, and the rough places shall be made plain." *Amen! Hallelujah!'*

The panther voice maintained a steady crescendo, the lower frequencies now surging to a brassy growl while the whirling wind and strings soared to a climax of righteous passion: ' . . . .EVERY VALLEY SHALL BE EXALTED AND EVERY MOUNTAIN SHALL BE MADE LOW. *Amen! Hallelujah! Praise the Lord! . . .* I am a poor pilgrim of sorrow, I'm lost in this wide world of sin, I have no hope for tomorrow, I'm striving, just striving to get in!'

Then suddenly the professor was back, discoursing elegantly on downtown urban development and suburban gentrification, taking a swipe at the global village, pointing out that at heart Atlanta's brave new metropolis was cold and empty, with or without television. We sped back through 5,000 years of history, past the Tower of Babel, revisited the sites of Hebrew captivity in Egypt. Then we swooped forward to the Holocaust, to the rebellion at Treblinka where a few Jews escaped to tell the world what happened: 'We've got to tell the story of *our* struggle,' said the pastor. 'We've got to tell the story of how hard it's been for black people to make it.'

Then he returned to the Old Testament again, and the Exodus story. But there was no obscurantism in this discourse, no clinging bibliolatry that used Scripture as a tribal fetish, a symbol of lost supremacy. The Exodus myth, employed in the past by Puritans and now by Jews to justify the expulsion of indigenous peoples and the denial of their rights was here used – as it has ever been among blacks – as the sacred code that charted the course of emancipation. For blacks the Bible was an open book, a passport to their participation in American society. This was recognised, early on, by those who had been sold into slavery. In one of her poems, Phillis Wheatley, who had been brought from Senegal and sold to a Boston tailor in 1791, described her own enslavement, not as bondage but, paradoxically as deliverance:

> 'Twas not long since I left my native shore,
> The land of errors and Egyptian gloom;
> Father of mercy! 'twas thy gracious hand
> Brought me in safety from those dark abodes.

By the same token she recognised the right that Christianity gave her to equal treatment as an American:

> 'Twas mercy brought me from my Pagan land
> Taught my benighted soul to understand

> That there's a God, that there's a Saviour too.
> Once I redemption neither sought nor knew.
> Some view our sable race with scornful eye;
> 'Their colour is a diabolic dye.'
> Remember, Christians, Negroes black as Cain
> May be refined, and join the angelic train.

After the service, I walked up Auburn Avenue to the place where King is buried. The tomb – a white marble sarcophagus with the simple inscription 'FREE AT LAST' – stands in splendid solitude on a circular plinth of brick surrounded by water. A black couple from Virginia persuaded me to take their picture. They grinned happily, teeth flashing in tone with the tomb. I asked them what King meant to them.

'He gave us our freedom,' said the girl. It wasn't a platitude. Her manner was suddenly solemn. 'But we still have a long way to go. Our generation, the next generation, must keep the dream alive.'

'The dream of a country free from racial intolerance?'

'That and non-violence,' she replied. 'We have to go along that road. It's the only way to keep the world together.'

Further up the street the King family home – a two-storey wooden house with gables and balconies built in what Americans call the Queen Anne style – was open to visitors. It was dark and gloomy inside, furnished in dreary colours. The windows were fringed with lace, the settees with antimacassars. The ranger who showed me round, a lively, buxom young woman with braces on her teeth, was at pains to describe King and his siblings as ordinary fun-loving kids who loved football and roller-skating. But her ebullience failed to dispel the austere, patriarchal atmosphere.

'Daddy King' was in many ways as remarkable as his son. The second child of an impoverished sharecropper from Stockbridge, Georgia, who used to drown his sorrows in drink, Martin Luther King Sr left home at sixteen with his only pair of shoes slung over his shoulder, determined to get himself an education. This he achieved by taking odd jobs and going to night school. A large man physically as well as morally, he led the struggle against racial segregation in Atlanta from his protected position as pastor of an important metropolitan church. His personality shadowed Martin Luther Jr throughout his career.

The civil rights leader was strictly patriarchal, even 'male chauvinist' in his family relations, indulging in extra-marital affairs while expecting his

wife to be a perfect home-maker. He seems to have been fuelled as much
by guilt as by love of his fellow-human beings. 'He was so conscious of his
awesome responsibilities,' wrote his widow, 'that he literally set himself
the task of never making an error in the affairs of the Movement . . . though
he knew that as a human being he was bound to.'

Perhaps it was guilt that lent him the courage to face the martyrdom he
always expected. His faith gave him a strong sense of personal destiny as well
as belief in the Christian idea of redemption through sacrifice. The night
before his assassination he preached a sermon in Memphis which hinted
at foreknowledge: 'We've got some difficult days ahead,' he said. 'But it
doesn't really matter to me now: Because I've been to the mountain top.
I won't mind . . . I may not get there with you, but I want you to know
tonight that we as a people will get to the Promised Land. So I'm happy
tonight. I'm not worried about anything. I'm not fearing any man. Mine
eyes have seen the glory of the coming of the Lord . . . '

I lunched in the splendour of the Ritz-Carlton hotel, choosing a club sandwich, the least expensive item on the menu. The dining-room had pink
upholstered furniture and English hunting prints. Though most of the clientele was white, a number of smartly-dressed young black people were
seated at the bar or eating at tables – enough to provide visiting journalists
with evidence of Atlanta's 'miracle'. The city's half-million population was
about 60 per cent black. Since King had embarked on voter registration,
the political advance of Atlanta's blacks had been steady. Like Detroit,
Washington DC, Birmingham, Little Rock and nearly three hundred other
cities across the nation, Atlanta had a black mayor, in the person of Andrew
Young. He had vigorously pursued 'affirmative action', the key to which
was 'contract compliance', a policy whereby contractors were obliged to
have a black partner when bidding for the city's custom. Though bitterly
resented at first, it had produced impressive results. Black participation
in city contracts had been raised from one sixth of one per cent in 1970
to between 15 and 20 per cent. The rule, however, was 'racist' and was
eventually declared unconstitutional by the US Supreme Court. I drove
out from downtown towards the suburbs. A newspaper advertisement had
alerted me to the existence of a mosque in Decatur. For nearly an hour
I searched for it, driving through shady valleys where wooden bungalows
crouched under tall pine trees. The black areas were visibly less prosperous
than the white, but only by a few degrees. The homes were less pretentious,

but no less neat. Contract compliance had trickled down into well-kempt lawns and brightly painted children's bicycles.

The mosque was a bright new building of glass and polished wood, more like a modern school than anything in the Middle East. The car park exhibited ancient American limousines and modern Japanese compacts. A bearded brother whom I greeted with the Arabic 'Salam Aleykum' said it would be all right for me to sit in on the *talim* (instruction). The interior resembled a large gymnasium. The women, wearing colourful prints with scarves covering their heads and chins, sat at the back with the girls and infants. The men and boys, dressed normally or sporting African shirts, sat cross-legged on the floor at the front. Most of the men had beards. They looked serious – more Afro than American. Some were making their prayers, facing the *qibla* (prayer niche) directly in front of them.

A young imam, dressed in black, began reciting the *fatiha*, the opening chapter of the Koran, in the meandering, nasal tones peculiar to classical Arabic. The sound, in such an unfamiliar setting, was strangely reassuring. Muslims are mercifully unburdened with the mysteries of the Trinity, the doctrine of vicarious atonement, the absurdity of a God in human flesh. Islam is a religion with which – for all the political excesses committed in its name – the agnostic, rationalist or secular humanist may feel reasonably comfortable. Like Judaism, its focus is on this world rather than the next, though its demand for justice and fair dealing is underpinned by the traditional eschatology of the Day of Judgement. But, unlike orthodox Judaism, it is a supra-tribal religion, welcoming all comers, addressing humanity regardless of birth.

The imam's discourse was strictly in conformity with Koranic teaching. There were no supernatural events in Islam, except for the Koran itself, God's final revelation to humankind. God's miracles were manifest in nature, in the movements of sun, moon and other heavenly bodies, in the industry of bees and beavers. The world was created for man's benefit: even the angels bowed down to Adam.

Belief in Allah and the Koran reinforced an ordered, rational, view of life. Unlike Christians, Muslims did not have to go through their scripture making changes. The Koran had been revealed in its finality, once and for all. Its text was perfect.

'It is the same revelation that spread our religion throughout the Middle East and into Europe, and ignited the Renaissance,' the imam told us. 'It is the same revelation that established great empires in Africa. It is the same revelation that will establish us in America as a Muslim nation . . . I predict that by the year 2,000 Islam will have a predominant influence in the major cities of this country.'

This seemingly fantastic prognostication was greeted with cries of 'All right!' and '*Allahu Akbar!*' ('God is Greater!') from the audience. It was not difficult to see the appeal that Islam might have for blacks in the industrialised North, whence it was spreading south. Twice uprooted, first by slavery, then by migration from their churches and homesteads in the South, Northern blacks had disintegrated as a community. It was no accident that the leadership of the Civil Rights Movement had come from the South.

'One of the great tragedies of the African-American experience has been the inability of the race to re-establish a stable family life since being physically freed from slavery,' Wallace (Warithuddin) Muhammad, the American Muslim leader, has written.

> We should be disturbed knowing that we don't think of ourselves as a community or feel an obligation to be a community. We should be disturbed when we see our own people not measuring up to that structure or to community fulfilment. It should bother us knowing that we cannot manage two or three blocks or one little district. It should bother us if we are unable to be the responsible factor for the tax base, the moral and economic life or the cultural life in our community.

For more conservative Southern blacks the free churches established by evangelical Protestantism offered a high degree of community support. The Northerners, doubly deracinated, had travelled much further along the road of alienation. The Great Code of Exodus was too far removed from their culture to provide them with a passport to the Promised Land, their successful integration into American society.

Most black American Muslims came out of the tradition established by the Nation of Islam, a highly unorthodox blend of African nationalism, biblical eschatology and Islam ideas. Its origins can be traced to the African dreams of Bishop Henry Turner and the Jamaican-born Marcus Garvey, founder of the Universal Negro Improvement Association and first 'Provisional President of Africa'. A more direct link seems to exist with the Moorish Science Temple of America founded in 1913 in Newark, New Jersey, by Timothy Drew who published a pamphlet containing Islamic, Christian and Garveyite passages which he called the 'Holy Koran'. Drew's successor, Wallace D. Fard (Wali Farad Muhammad) evidently acquired a closer knowledge of

Islam than his master, having studied Sufism – Islamic mysticism – and visited Mecca. His most celebrated convert was Robert Poole, born in 1897 and the son of a Baptist minister in Georgia, who took the name Elijah Muhammad. Like the leaders of many Sufi brotherhoods in Asia and Africa, Elijah Muhammad claimed a direct mandate from Allah, communicated in a vision. However, he continued to teach mainly from the Bible.

Elijah Muhammad's message was overtly racist, preaching hatred for the 'white devil'. God had already arrived; there was no life after death; heaven and hell were merely two contrasting earthly conditions. The hereafter – which will begin around the year 2,000 – is merely the end of the present 'spook' civilisation of Christian usurpers. It will be followed by the redemption of the Black Nation and their glorious rule over the earth.

Elijah Muhammad's most influential disciple, Malcolm Little (Malcolm X) left the Nation of Islam after making the pilgrimage to Mecca, where he realised that racism of all kinds is abhorrent to Islamic teaching. 'You may be shocked by these words coming from me,' he wrote

> But on this pilgrimage, what I have seen and experienced has forced me to *rearrange* much of my thought-patterns previously held and to *toss aside* some of my previous conclusions . . . During the past eleven days here in the Muslim world, I have eaten from the same plate, drunk from the same glass, and slept in the same bed (or on the same rug) – while praying *to the same God* – with fellow Muslims, whose eyes are the bluest of blue, whose hair was the blondest of blond, and whose skin was the whitest of white. And in the *words* and in the *actions* and in the *deeds* of the 'white' Muslims, I felt the same sincerity that I had felt among the black African Muslims of Nigeria, Sudan, and Ghana.

Elijah Muhammad's son and successor, Wallace, continued the tradition begun by Malcolm X by bringing his Black Muslim followers into the mainstream of Sunni Islam. The racist minority in the Nation of Islam fell under the sway of Louis Farrakhan, a semi-literate demagogue whose attacks on whites and Jews have become notorious.

A remarkable feature of this evolution is the way it conforms to the historic patterns of Islamic development in Africa and Asia: the Sufi brotherhoods which brought Islam to backward and culturally undeveloped regions remote from Islamic centres of learning usually began by mixing Islamic ideas with local cults and traditions, gradually increasing their orthodox content. The dynamic of Islam, in contrast to that of Christianity, is centripetal: whereas Christianity, with its complicated theology and infinite variety of liturgies, tends to fragment towards sectarianism, Islam, with its emphasis on legal and ritual conformity, tends to draw eclectic converts into its universalist framework. The Prophet of Islam built up a community where the rule of religion transcended tribal particularism. For centuries his model worked for tribal societies in Africa and Asia, civilising them by bringing them into contact with the great centres of high culture in the cities. It was not impossible that this formula could work in the great urban ghettos of Chicago, Detroit and other cities of the north.

Where Christianity offered redemption and salvation for the individual, Islam offered a positive social discipline for the community. For radically-minded blacks trying to break free from a culture perceived as irredeemably contaminated by racism, Christianity projected the image of a God made flesh in the person of a 'white' Saviour. Islam abhorred such anthropomorphism, teaching that humans were created by God, but not in God's image. The idea of reducing the unimaginable Sustainer of the Universe to human proportions struck Muslims as a grossly arrogant impiety.

In the social and economic sphere the new, more orthodox Islam had considerable appeal for urban blacks. The young imam stressed what in fact were archetypically American values. Allah had taught that education was a sacred right and duty. The public schools were controlled by outsiders. Muslims must therefore build their own elementary schools, their own high schools and, eventually, their own colleges. They were creating their own business networks, redistributing wealth among themselves by the payment of *zakat*, the compulsory charity that is one of Islam's five obligations or 'pillars'. American blacks who had failed to adopt the Protestant work ethic were taking to Islam's co-operative traditions. Above all they were revolting against the tradition of welfare dependency which had taken hold, especially in the North. They perceived it as demoralising, sapping the African-American's will to succeed. Islam offered a mode of local redistribution outside the oppressive structure of the state. The Muslim blacks – no longer Black Muslims – would raise themselves by their own bootstraps.

I asked the imam why there were no whites among his flock. 'We co-operate with other Muslim groups,' he said. 'But we prefer our independence.'

Here in this polarised, racist city, integration was still a distant prospect. White Muslims might lend their support; outsiders – like myself – might attend as honoured guests. But for whites or Asians to join the *jama'at*, the mosque-community, would be to raise the ghosts of suspicion that they were trying to take it over, depriving the black Muslim of the significance of his choice, his conversion. Integration was admirable in theory. But its application would have to wait.

Listening to the imam expound the teachings of Wallace Muhammad, I ceased to find his claim that Islam would one day be the predominant influence in American cities entirely fantastic. The image of Islam conveyed by the media, its almost exclusive association with 'terrorism' and 'fanaticism', to the detriment of its more humanistic, more rational traditions, must ensure its continuing appeal for the alienated. The sober example of Muslim self-help, which Wallace Muhammad was promoting, lay squarely within the traditions laid down by generations of white immigrants. Many black Americans were still refugees in their own land. It was idle to expect that the United States would suddenly change its spots and embark on a massive programme of wealth redistribution which would bring black people to economic and social parity with other groups. The Islamic alternative seemed more practical. It seemed to be more in keeping with the social and political realities, with the American Way.

XIII

Holy Wars

'Put on the whole armour of God, that ye may be able to stand against the wiles of the devil. For we wrestle not against flesh and blood, but against principalities, against powers, against the rulers of darkness of this world, against spiritual wickedness in high places.'

EPHESIANS 5:11–12

Heritage USA, Christendom's Disneyland, was a few hours drive from Atlanta, through undulating hayfields interspaced with cottonwoods, maples and pines. Near Charlotte the trees turned to orchards with rows of apple and peach trees quietly soaking up the sunshine, preparing for autumn's abundance. At Rock Hill I ran into a thunderstorm. I stopped at a giant shopping mall to shelter from the sheeting rain and bought a new pair of shoes. I couldn't resist a T-shirt that was selling for ten dollars. It bore the smudged impression of a human face in gaudy pinks and mauves, with two spidery blobs for eyes and the legend: I RAN INTO TAMMY FAYE IN THE MALL. I asked the salesgirl if they sold the shirts at Heritage USA. 'I doubt it,' she said, unsmiling.

Pastor Jim Bakker and his wife Tammy Faye had been in the headlines for weeks, ever since Jim had left his ministry after confessing to a sexual encounter with Jessica Hahn, a New York secretary, seven years previously, and paying money out of church funds to keep her quiet. Founders and creators of the PTL ('Praise the Lord' or 'People That Love') television network, Jim and Tammy had long been familiar to Christian viewers through the *Jim and Tammy Show,* a nationally syndicated programme put out by Pat Robertson's Christian Broadcasting Network (CBN) and later through their own *PTL Club*.

Where Robertson, Yale graduate and senator's son, won souls for Christ through a combination of patrician charm and charismatic fervour, Jim and Tammy appealed by their apparent ordinariness and accessibility. Both were diminutive. Jim was a mere five foot four, with boyish good looks that belied his forty-nine years, a puckish smile and a trim shape enhanced by a wardrobe of well-cut suits and casual clothes appropriate to every occasion. Tammy, smaller and pudgier, had made her nondescript features into an icon of the Eighties, creating a porcelain doll out of make-up and wigs with stick-on lashes that nestled under painted brows like a pair of furry tarantulas.

Their ghosted biographies chart the Bakkers' rise to fame and fortune. Jim's father was a piston-ring machinist from Muskegon, a small foundry town in Michigan. An academic failure, Jim seemed set for decent obscurity until he ran over a child while skipping church in his father's Cadillac. The child miraculously recovered, and Jim got saved, dedicating his life to the Lord. He met Tammy Faye (four foot eleven, seventy-three pounds) at North central Bible College in Minneapolis, where both were studying to become preachers. He proposed to her on their third date. 'Even without make-up, she was a little doll,' he would write.

Tammy came from a Pentecostal family in International Falls, Minnesota. Her mother, a devout woman with musical talents, had been virtually ostracised from her church for having divorced her first husband, Tammy's father. The family was poor, without plumbing or hot water in their home. Tammy fell in love with Jim almost as soon as she met him. Since it went against college rules to marry, the couple dropped out and embarked on a career as itinerant evangelists.

At first the road was hard. Between prayer meetings, Jim worked at a restaurant. The couple were so hard up they had to redeem their Coca Cola bottles to buy groceries. Tammy got a kidney infection that made her wet her bed.

A visiting evangelist invited them to accompany him up the Amazon. Though he never showed up at the rendezvous – he turned out to be a fraud – the planned mission gave them their first experience of fund-raising. They used the money to buy a car. Then they prayed for more money, so they could have a trailer to live in. At the next prayer meeting, the collection plate was filled with hundred-dollar bills. They used the money to buy an RV, a thirty-foot Holiday Rambler of outmoded design. On their first trip the shaft came off, causing the trailer to write itself off on a telegraph pole.

The company admitted liability, so they got a newer and more expensive trailer for free. The Bakkers characteristically put their good fortune down to divine intervention.

One day, while shopping for groceries, Tammy spotted 'a Soakie bubble bath bottle with a cute little porky pig' on top. They gave the pig a little blond wig with freckles and eyelashes – just like Tammy's. They called it Susie Moppet, and started a Christian puppet show. Attendance at their meetings doubled and trebled. A man from CBN saw them and told his boss. Pat Robertson invited them to join his fledgling television channel at Portsmouth, Virginia. They found an apartment in the better part of town at a rent they could afford. 'God wants His kids to have the best and we were living the way the rich lived on $150 a week,' wrote Tammy.

The *Jim and Tammy Show*, aimed mainly at children, was an instant success. According to the Bakkers, it weaned many young souls off sex and violence and turned them on to Jesus. Then God used Jim to save CBN which, despite the show's popularity, was in severe financial diffi- culties. In November 1965 Robertson held his annual telethon, designed to raise funds for the following year. The station needed $120,000 to stay on the air – $10,000 a month. By Sunday night they were far short of their target. What was more, the station was $40,000 in debt. The staff had been given strict instructions not to mention the financial crisis, since it was thought this would undermine confidence. But Jim Bakker – prompted, he said, by the Holy Spirit – thought better. Near the end of the telethon, while still on camera, he began crying – a gift he would use during his career with increasing effectiveness.

'Listen, people,' he said, between sniffs. 'It's all over. Everything's gone. Christian television will be no more. The only Christian television station is gone, unless you provide us with the money to operate it.'

The phones began ringing. The pledges began pouring in. 'Soon all ten lines were jammed. People had been touched by the Spirit of God.' A new weapon, the Crisis Appeal, had been forged in the service of Christ.

When Pat Robertson launched the *700 Club*, named after his first telethon partners, Jim became its co-host, interviewing guests, telling folksy anec- dotes, introducing singing groups, denouncing secular humanism, perform- ing healings, and saving the unborn.

One evening in 1967, Jim Bakker relates, the Holy Spirit really filled the studio. The singers broke off weeping, and gave their testimonies. Then Jim heard the Lord saying 'Take off your shoes, you're on holy ground.'

Everyone in the studio, audience and technicians included, took off their shoes in obedience to God's command. Jim handed the mike over to Pat and stepped off camera, to worship the Lord in the Spirit. Pat kept trying to get him back, but Jim was 'lost in the heavenlies with Jesus'. Finally Pat looked into the cameras and said 'God has told me to get out of the way, and I don't know what to do or where to go. I don't want to block His power.' Then he handed the mike to Lee Russel, a singer.

> As Lee began to sing, the feeling of God's presence became so strong in the studio that people in every corner of the building began weeping. Two cameramen huddled arm-in-arm around a camera, weeping until a puddle of water formed under their feet . . . The people in the control booth were crying so uncontrollably they couldn't operate the equipment. They just set the controls on automatic. Cameramen couldn't see through the lenses of their cameras. Directors could no longer give instructions. There was nobody left to run the station's equipment and finally we had to go off the air. The last shot that night was a wide-angle view of the entire set – empty . . . The entire staff huddled on the studio's floor arm-in-arm and wept before the Lord. It was a genuine revival among CBN's staff, the likes of which nobody had ever seen.

However, according to Tammy, the devil had other plans. 'One of the greatest tools that Satan has is jealousy, and he doesn't care how or when he uses it.' Jim was presenting the *700 Club* three nights a week in addition to five weekly *Jim and Tammy Shows*. The punishing schedule led to a nervous breakdown. Jim just lay in bed for a month in the back bedroom with his Bible in his hand, begging God not to let him lose his mind completely. The doctor ordered a diet of milk and cream. 'You can't imagine how much milk is in a glass of milk,' observed Tammy.

None of the staff at CBN – except one person – came to see Jim. Satan had filled their hearts with jealousy. Then, as the couple cried out to God in their anguish, 'He spoke to Jim about his eating habits. We had been eating hamburgers, French fries, all that junk food, because we never had time to fix a meal – always on the run, between one show or the other. He spoke to Jim about vitamins and proper nutrition.'

Jim recovered and went back on the show. But Tammy was having problems as well. She had her first child after a difficult labour. The hospital was overwhelmed with telephone calls and gifts of clothing. But the medication made Tammy ill and depressed. She ignored the baby, saw spiders under the pillow. Jim became desperate, and urged Tammy to find a psychiatrist.

But then, according to Tammy, the Lord spoke to her. 'Let Me be your psychiatrist,' He said. Little by little, God began to restore her. Her child, Tammy Sue, became a real treasure. It wasn't long before she too was appearing on the *Jim and Tammy Show*.

But Satan was still at work in the studio, infecting members of the CBN staff. Tammy was constantly slighted by one of the women executives. Jim was reprimanded for refusing to take a late night shift – though when Jim threatened resignation, Pat Robertson secretly paid the fine himself to smooth things over. By now, however, the Lord was telling Jim it was time to leave CBN. Pat took this devastating news quite calmly, like a true Christian. 'If God has told you, I can't argue with that,' he said. 'You've got to do what God says. As much as I'd like to, I can't hold on to you.'

The couple were back on their own. After a period of freelance fund-raising for different Christian stations, they headed for Santa Ana in Southern California, where they started the Trinity Broadcast Systems with Paul and Jan Crouch, a couple with whom they felt a deep affinity. Paul and Jim, both pastors, had worked in television. Jan and Tammy liked all the same things. They both adored bargain-hunting at the local flea market. 'We would get our eye lashes and wigs there and all the things that girls need,' wrote Tammy.

It was here that *The PTL Club* – a late-night chat-show on the Johnny Carson model – was conceived. They wanted something that would be a code-name for the Christian world, without turning 'lost' people off, as Jim explained. Christians would know what the initials stood for; others wouldn't care.

Despite many teething problems, due to their technical inexperience, the show was a success, with dozens of people getting saved, baptised and healed with the Holy Spirit. Though desperately short of money at first, Jim's tearful appeals for contributions did not go unanswered. 'God began to bless,' wrote Tammy. 'The Holy Spirit was outpoured and thousands of dollars were pouring into the station.' But then Satan, she says, infiltrated himself again, driving a wedge between the Bakkers and the Crouches. A local pastor, invited by the Crouches, publicly criticised the show while taking part in it. After further disagreements, Jim was voted off the board and forced to resign.

At first, the couple were desperate. But then Tammy had a vision. The air was filled with angels flying back and forth, wearing large metal helmets with swords in their hands. Facing them, with his back to her, stood the

Lord Jesus. He too had a helmet and sword. He wore the most beautiful white gown with a blue sash that covered His shoulders and fell to the floor. Then He turned to her and said: 'Tammy, even as you are standing here, My angels are going forward to do battle for you – so you don't need to worry about anything . . . '

A Christian station in Charlotte invited them to do a telethon. Once again, their very presence brought a great outpouring of the spirit and a proportionate inflow of cash. Miracles fell as thick as dollars. Arthritis, kidneys, bad backs, eyes and ears were healed by the hundreds, cancers dropped off bodies, tumours vanished.

'The number of people accepting Christ was equally stunning,' wrote Jim. 'From late Friday night until Sunday night, more than five hundred people received Jesus. It seemed as if God had unleashed the bomb of his Holy Spirit on the metropolitan Charlotte, North Carolina area . . . '

The message was clear. God wanted Jim and Tammy in Charlotte. They leased a building on East Independence Boulevard, converting it to television studios. A series of telethons raised the necessary money, with hundreds of pledges pouring in. But Satan was still in the studios, spreading negative gossip, putting it about that, while masses of money was being raised, PTL wasn't paying its bills. Once more Jim prayed to God, and asked about leaving. 'I'm not going to require you to quit this time' said the Lord. 'This is the ministry I have established for you.'

As ever, God was as good as His word. 'Within days,' Jim modestly relates, 'the corporation's five-man board of directors voted to dismiss our business managers.' On examining the books, the picture turned out to be worse than expected. The ministry was virtually bankrupt. To stay on the air they needed to pay their station manager $70,000 within a month – more than three times their normal income. Jim prayed again. 'Give him what he asks,' said the celestial bank manager, 'and I'll do the miracle for you.' Jim had the first cheque for $20,000 made out on a Friday. His vice-president was horrified, and at first refused to counter-sign.

'We haven't the funds to cover it.'

'Trust the Lord,' said Jim. There wasn't time to raise the money on television. But the cheque did not bounce. On Monday, $30,000 came in the mail. 'It was the greatest miracle of concentrated giving I'd ever witnessed,' said Jim, 'totally inspired by the Lord.'

The following Friday Jim wrote another $20,000 cheque, although the balance, of course, was down to zero again. On Monday, contributions which more than covered the sum came in the mail; and so it went on, the following weeks, till all the debts had been paid. In total they amounted to more than quarter of a million dollars. The Lord was allowing them to see the debts in just bits and pieces, thought Jim, so they wouldn't get too discouraged.

By 1975 PTL had signed up forty-six stations, and was outgrowing its premises. There wasn't enough room for the studio audiences that were getting ever larger as the programme's popularity increased. They moved to a twenty-five-acre site off Park Road in south-west Charlotte, but soon even this proved too small for the plans that God had for Jim and Tammy Bakker. With the ministry growing at a phenomenal rate of 7000 per cent in eighteen months, a whole city was needed. In 1978 work began on Jim's greatest dream, his twenty-first-century Nauvoo: Heritage USA, a holiday camp for Christian families, where prayer could be fun.

The entrance announced itself with a row of fairy-lights attached to an avenue of young trees. At the check-in the computer refused to accept my London address, so I gave that of friends in New York – realising, too late, that the poor souls would probably be flooded with Christian pamphleture. I vowed that in future I would only give the address of people I really disliked.

I chose a site at the bottom of 'Praise Hollow' – my designated camp ground. It was much like other, secular, camp grounds, with tents, R Vs, campers, and ordinary limousines secluded among bushes and trees. A few people were barbecueing their evening meals, but the place was largely deserted – the faithful, I presumed, being mostly at their devotions. I walked up the hill to what looked like a castle with crenellated walls. It turned out to be an outdoor amphitheatre. A replica of Roman Jerusalem had been built upon the stage, with stylised temples and flat-roofed Middle Eastern houses. The performance of the Passion Play, however, had been cancelled on account of the weather.

I wandered into the Family Entertainment Center. A group of boys – several of them overweight – were playing basketball in an indoor court with a star-spangled ceiling. A couple of women – evidently parents – were sitting nearby knitting and watching a giant television on which two men in suits were discussing theology. 'I don't want to be contentious,' one of the men was saying, 'but we've got to tear down the walls, restore the foundations . . . '

The same discussion – piped from PTL's twenty-four hour cable service – was being carried by miniature screens in the Village Hobby House, which was still open for business, though it was now long past dark. The merchandise on offer bore the unmistakable imprint of Tammy Faye: there were puddleducks with hats, tea-cosy cottages, gnomes and windmills, souvenir platters. I was particularly struck by a family of anthropomorphised pigs done in hard glazed pottery, but made to look like leather with stitching. It was a fitting sample of Heritage kitsch: hardness imitating softness imitating life, an artefact twice removed from its original, an emblem of vicarious sentiment.

Nearby I came across a cottage where mechanised gnomes with wings and Santa Claus beards nodded in time to winking lights, while prayer music blasted from hidden speakers. Here tastelessness had been taken beyond the relatively benign realm of kitsch to enter regions of the mind that normally surface only in bad dreams, or during the nastier kinds of drug experience.

Along the esplanade the lake reflected the lights of the Mall in brilliant, shimmering colours that merged with the lurid blue of an artificial waterfall, lit from behind. By now the rain had stopped completely, and people were beginning to appear. The men – white, clean-shaven, short-haired and mostly fat – were casually dressed in shirts and trousers; the women wore slacks or midi-length polyester frocks in pastel shades.

Next morning I went to see Pastor Sam Johnson, the minister Jerry Falwell had put in charge of Heritage Village Church. While waiting outside his office next to the PTL auditorium I watched a procession of young people rehearsing for next Sunday's service. Most of them wore red gowns and mortar-board hats with tassels, like college graduates. They included a nut-brown maid in dazzling white accompanying an infant in a wheel chair – at least, I thought it was an infant till I realised it was a tiny homunculus, all head and practically limbless except for a pair of hands that protruded directly from the shoulders like fledgling wings. The hands were operating a battery of control knobs on the chair. From this I concluded that the creature was the celebrated Kevin, the seventeen-year-old victim of a rare bone disease, who had grown to a height of only twenty-two inches. Kevin had been one of Jim Bakker's most successful fund-raisers. In 1986 three million dollars were donated for 'Kevin's House', a gabled mansion with special wheelchair ramps built to accommodate disabled children. A year after it was opened, however, it still had only five occupants – Kevin, his two sisters and his adoptive parents, who happened to be cousins of the Bakkers.

Dr Johnson was young and friendly. He had a sandy moustache, wore a blazer and tie, and thumped me on the back several times, telling me how glad he was to see me. He told me he had been on the PTL staff until the revelations in the *Charlotte Observer* made him decide to resign. When Jerry Falwell took over PTL, he asked him back. I asked Dr Johnson what conclusions he drew from the Bakker scandal.

'I have been trying to address that question myself as the Holy Spirit has led me from Sunday to Sunday,' said Dr Johnson, who was evidently used to billing his sermons for the media, having recently been on *Good Morning America*. 'This Sunday I'm going to address the question of compromise. We have compromised our stand, we have compromised our ethical dealings, we have compromised our spiritual dealings. We must learn to render unto Caesar what belongs to Caesar, and to God what belongs to God. We're here to pay our taxes. We have to be honest citizens, and do our duty.'

I suggested the problem might be that the First Amendment protection afforded to churches enabled them to run their affairs without proper supervision. Wasn't there a case for more oversight by the state?

'I don't think so,' he said. 'Because we who are godly, we who are righteous will do what the government has no business doing and need not get involved in. We're big boys. We're bringing things back into line fiscally. The problem here wasn't financial or sexual: it was spiritual.'

'You mean the Bakkers didn't practise what they preached?'

'It's easy to shove your beliefs aside. The Bible says faith without works is dead. Talk about faith, talk about the goodness of God. But by your fruits ye shall be known. We preached platitudes. We preached missions, and took huge bonuses in salaries. We talked about helping the street people; at the same time we rewarded ourselves generously.'

'You mean you yourself knew what was going on?'

'I knew that Mr Bakker lived in a comfortable home. I knew he had some services provided for him. I knew that he must have a good salary. But to tell the truth I had no idea it was so far out of line. I guess that sounds incredible . . . '

'Didn't you ever see the books?'

'Oh no. Unfortunately I was stupid enough, I was foolish enough, if you like, to accept an assignment without having the brilliance to say: "OK, if

you want me to be an executive of the ministry I must have total access."
You see, I had a blind faith, a blind trust. As multiple hundreds of thousands
of people across America did. They believed without asking any questions.
Unfortunately, a lot of people are going to be left with scars, and doubts.
We're going to have to work through that.'

I visited the Upper Room, a replica of the room in Jerusalem where the
Apostles were supposed to have received the Baptism of the Holy Spirit. It
was empty, except for the guardian, a gentle woman with spectacles who
ushered me around. By the altar there was a perspex box full of letters,
snatches of which were legible:

> 'I pray for spiritual healing and future conversion of my son-in-law.'
> 'Pray for arthritis in knees.'
> 'Fred: back, hip.'
> 'Lillian – hip, knee, overweight. Richt [*sic*] arm.'

Some people had consigned the receipts for their donations to the box,
doubtless to gain extra merit: 'Dear Anna . . . Your $15 will be used to
touch the lives of hurting people all across this country . . . '

There were several screens to which people had affixed photographs of
themselves – at wedding parties, barbecues, in family groups, at high school
graduations, in uniforms as marines, majorettes, cadets. They were all ages,
sizes and races. I asked the woman about the letters.

'At first we used to read every one and pray for each separately, but
now we're too busy. We keep them a while, then burn them in the lake in
a Grand Holocaust to God.'

Beside the lake there was an enormous swimming-pool in a setting
of artificial rocks topped by a giant water-slide. There were rivers and
bridges, waterfalls and shallow pools for the younger children. The people
certainly looked happy; fathers descended the slides holding their children,
or bounced with them along shallow streams in giant rubber rings. The
attractions were obvious: whatever the sins of the leaders, this was a safe,
wholesome place which any parent must applaud. There were no drunken
youths roaming around with beer cans and bottles, no teenage girls flaunting
their sexuality, no bits of litter spoiling the ground.

The Mall, which was supposed to represent 'Main Street USA', consisted
of a covered street flanked by an eclectic melange of façades with pillars
and wrought-iron balconies of every shape and pattern, as if picked at

random from a book of Victorian architectural designs by a greedy child accustomed to having one of everything. The whole was enclosed under a blue, vaulted ceiling that added to the feeling of Hollywood unreality. Despite their recent fall, the Bakkers were much in evidence. Near a Gay Nineties restaurant with wrought-iron tables and Tiffany glass, stood the Bakkers Bakkery and the Tammy Faye Cosmetics and Nutrition Center, which, judging from the people inside, was still doing brisk trade, as were Noah's Toy Shoppe Victoria's Café, the Heavenly Fudge Shoppe and several pizzarias with coloured umbrellas. There was no hint of spiritual asceticism here: the message was eat, drink, consume, indulge – you're already in heaven!

At one end of the Mall a man was playing a medley of hymn tunes on a heavily gilded piano next to a pool. A bystander explained the pool was for baptisms, not swimming.

I stopped at Tony's Sidewalk Café and examined the menu. Among the treats on offer was a twelve inch high hamburger which had somehow escaped the Lord's strictures on junk food; and a 'Jim Bakker Special – the ultimate pan-pizza with nine delicious toppings: pepperoni, ham, mushrooms, onions, green peppers, black olives, beef topping and Italian sausage' – all for $13.40.

At a nearby stall a young man and a girl were offering Bibles to anyone signing up for a fifteen dollars-a-month partnership. I asked him if business had flagged as a result of the scandal.

'We don't have the figures yet,' he said. 'Everything's been up and down so much the past few months.'

'Didn't anyone know what was going on?'

'No idea. We were just here to support the ministry. All these things have been revelations to us, just like to everybody else.'

'Weren't you rather disillusioned?'

'If you were dependent on a single person it could be very disillusioning. But if you see this as a ministry, you hope and believe it's going to continue. The ministry is what this place is about. Fort Hope for street people, Heritage House for pregnant teenagers, so they don't have abortions, the Upper Room for hurting people . . . Individuals have problems, they fall from grace just like all of us. But we want to give hope and assurance that there's a Better Way.'

'What's your job here?' I asked, wishing to draw him further.

'I'm in marketing.'

'What are you marketing? Religion? Or goods and services?'

He recited his sales litany: 'Well, we're here to expedite any programmes that help spread the Gospel. We're a full-scope ministry designed for children, for families, for singles, for elderly people, for everyone – not just Christians. We hope that when people leave they take with them some belief that there's a God.'

I wondered how Tammy's glazed china leather pigs, or Jim's winged gnomes, could possibly inculcate a sense of the divine, but kept the thought to myself.

'Almost everything that's here,' the young man went on, 'Jim Bakker did. Without him, there wouldn't have been anything.'

'Where did he get the idea from?' I expected him to confirm its divine provenance, but his answer was more prosaic.

'He had dreams when he was young that there should be a place for Christians to come and enjoy themselves. He was very restricted as a youngster. He couldn't go bowling. He couldn't go to the movies. The camp meeting grounds he and his folks used to go to had old buildings, broken windows, stained mattresses. He wanted to create something Christians could be proud of, where they could enjoy themselves without getting involved in drinking or gambling . . . '

And sex, I presumed. The devil, as usual, had come in the shape of a woman. Poor Jim had been 'set up'. The story he told had been really pathetic.

'I was wickedly manipulated by treacherous former friends and then colleagues who victimised me with the aid of a female confederate,' he said in his official statement resigning as head of PTL. Jerry Falwell, to whom Bakker had 'temporarily' entrusted his ministry, produced further details, recounting what Jim had told him at their fateful meeting on 17 March. Back in 1980 Jim and Tammy's marriage had been going through a difficult patch, with Tammy having developed what she called an 'innocent crush' on Gary Paxton, the born-again country and western singer. Poor Jim needed solace, and wanted to make his wife jealous so as to win her back. A former colleague and evangelist, John Wesley Fletcher, had arranged for Jim to meet young Jessica Hahn, a secretary for a Pentecostal church in Massapequa on Long Island, at the Florida hotel where Jim was staying. As soon as the door to the room was closed, Jessica set to work and began undressing Jim. Bakker told one of his friends afterwards he was 'surprised that this gal was able to perform the way she did. She knew all the tricks of the trade.' Jim; however, proved unable to perform. Fifteen minutes later he was weeping and praying in the shower: 'O my God! I've been with a whore!' Tammy forgave Jim; so did God.

Falwell says he believed Jim's original version: but then other things began to come out, tales of fiscal irregularities, of wife-swapping and homosexuality, all of which Jim denied, but which Falwell claims he was reluctantly forced to believe. John Ankerberg, another Pentecostalist pastor, claimed on television he had affidavits from men to whom Bakker had made advances, including former members of the PTL staff.

The most powerful testimony against Bakker came in the story Jessica Hahn sold to *Playboy* for a reported one million dollars. Along with pictures of herself in various aquatic poses, Ms Hahn related in considerable detail her version of the encounter, casting Jim in a much blacker light. A pious virgin of twenty-one and PTL fan of many years standing, she had leapt at the chance of meeting the great Jim Bakker and his family, when invited by Fletcher, a friend of her pastor. But what promised to be a dream-come-true rapidly turned to nightmare. At first she was confused, not quite knowing what was happening – probably, she later suspected, because Fletcher had spiked the glass of wine he made her drink. But then Fletcher came to the point.

'Jessica, you're going to be doing something tremendous for God,' he said, as he left her alone with Bakker.

'Jessica, by helping the shepherd, you're helping the sheep,' said Bakker, as he pulled off her clothes and pounced.

Afterwards he just rolled over and said: 'I've gotta get back to my bodyguards. But you really ministered to me . . . Thanks a lot.' Then, while she was still dazed and drugged, John Fletcher came and forced himself on her.

'You're going to forget Jim, but you're going to remember *me*!' he said. When he had taken his pleasure, he tried to get her to go with another man. But by then she was beyond doing anything . . .

This traumatic sexual initiation had ruined Jessica's life, making it impossible for her to have a normal relationship with a man, if not for ever, then for a very long time. Not that Jessica was being vindictive. If Jim had made just one little gesture of appreciation, by presenting her with a bunch of flowers, or even a single rose, he might still be master of PTL. Needless to add, Jessica's decision to pose semi-nude for *Playboy* had nothing to do with money: it had been a form of therapy, enabling her to regain that sense of womanhood that Bakker and his friends had so cruelly taken from her.

This story of innocence betrayed gripped America. Nobody seems to have thought it odd that a virginal church secretary, who had been drugged and virtually gang raped, should have had such a clear and detailed recollection of what was supposed to have happened seven years before, or that a modest woman of deep Christian conviction should have agreed to pose naked in a magazine that stood for everything the Moral Majority had been set up to oppose. Ms Hahn's revelation so infuriated Jerry Falwell, guardian of Christian rectitude, that he revealed the details in public even before the *Playboy* story came out.

'It really made my blood boil,' he said. There could no longer, he announced, be any question of the Bakkers having their ministry back: 'I must tell you – solemnly – that much as I love and care for you and will pray for you, I would be doing a disservice to God and to the Church at large, to allow you to come back, now or ever . . . ' he told Jim Bakker on television.

But then there came a counter-attack – not on Falwell directly, but on Jessica Hahn. The *New York Post*, the *Washington Post* and other papers ran investigative tooth combs over Jessica's past, revealing that, far from being an innocent virgin, she had had numerous boyfriends before she ever met Bakker. Finally *Penthouse, Playboy's* lewder and more successful rival in the soft pornography trade, delivered a bombshell of its own. It exposed – along with pictures of lesbians implausibly making love in advanced yogic positions – the darker secrets of Jessica's past: secrets which tended to confirm Jim Bakker's original supposition. She had been, according to *Penthouse*, a professional prostitute, working for a 'Madam' on Long Island. She had specialised in oral sex and servicing 'kinky' men, less out of preference than laziness. 'With oral sex she could just spit it out,' said Jessica's former madam. 'The other way she had to go to the bathroom, wash and douche again, and that bothered her . . . Anybody . . . that was into kinky sex or weird sex – that would be a fast number and you made twice or three times the amount of money you would normally make just for a blowjob or something: she was right on to them, like a fly to shit.'

Jessica tacitly confirmed this version of her past: she didn't sue *Penthouse*, and while the storm was still raging she went to live with Hugh Hefner, the founder of *Playboy* and America's sexual godfather – hardly a decision that fitted the idea of a demure and traumatised church secretary. Moreover, she was certainly well paid for her brief encounter with Jim, whether it lasted an hour and a half, as she claimed, or a mere fifteen minutes, according to his version. Under the deal arranged through the Reverend Richard Dortch, Jim's deputy at PTL, and Paul Roper, a business consultant, and laundered through the books of Roe Messner, the PTL architect-builder, Jessica Hahn and her advisers were paid $265,000 from a special trust fund in exchange for keeping things quiet.

Fletcher, however, was not part of the arrangement; and it was through him that rumour of the affair reached the ears of Jimmy Swaggart, the fire-eating televangelist from Baton Rouge.

Though both were ordained ministers of the Assemblies of God, the main Pentecostalist denomination, the styles and content of Swaggart's and Bakker's preaching were significantly different. Where Bakker was light and frothy, raising laughs as well as tears from his audiences with jokes and folksy anecdotes, Swaggart – a large and powerful-looking man with a mop of straw hair and the face of a pugilist – was, in his own words, 'an old-fashioned, Holy Ghost-filled, shouting, weeping, soul-winning, Gospel-preaching preacher'. A first cousin of Jerry Lee Lewis, the singer, with whom he was brought up among poor Louisiana Protestants, Swaggart believed that the Baptism of the Spirit was not just a gift of the Holy Ghost, but essential to salvation.

'Praise God my family didn't stop with getting saved,' I watched him proclaim to one of his television camp meetings, as he strode up and down the platform like a pop star, microphone in hand, shirt unbuttoned, tie loosened, beads of sweat on his brow, exuding an animal, sexual potency, along with an ambiguously sexual choice of words: 'if they had, Jimmy Swaggart wouldn't be here today . . . I would probably be in some smoke-filled night-club, half drunk, sitting down at some broken down old piano . . . It's not God's will that you get saved and just get stuck there. You need power – POWER! *Let the Holy Ghost come right inside you!* Praise God my parents grew hungry for the Holy Spirit, and my Momma was the first one to receive. And she got the full dose – I mean the full dose: Hallelujah!' As he wound himself up, he broke down in sobs: 'O God, let it fall in every heart, in every life, in every soul, in every spirit . . . I ask it in the Holy Name of Jeeeeeee-zus!'

The organ gently started playing, arms went up, people in the audience began drifting somnambulantly towards the platform, along what in the days of the real tent revivals used to be called the 'sawdust trail'. They were touching and crying and hugging and healing as Swaggart drew them towards him like a hypnotist.

'Heavenly Father, I thank you for what you are going to do' – *sob* – 'How many of you in the audience know you're saved, but haven't been baptised with the Holy Ghost? Come on . . . you know you want it! – all you have to do is come and get it, because it's free. H E paid the price two thousand years ago!'

Swaggart's targets – Communists, homosexuals, abortionists, secular humanists and liberal theologians – included all the familiar demons of the religious right. But he went much further than these, giving vent to the prejudices poor Southern Protestants traditionally felt towards the 'sleazy' hedonism of New Orleans, with its predominantly Catholic and cosmopolitan culture. Sometimes he sounded anti-semitic – 'Don't ever bargain with Jesus. He was a Jew' – but outspokenly anti-Catholic as well. Catholics were poor, pathetic creatures whose lives were bound by 'superstition, heathenism and emptiness'. Even the saintly Mother Theresa would be damned unless she recanted her theological errors and was born again in the Blood of Christ. Swaggart's anti-Catholicism partly accounted, no doubt, for his immense success in Catholic countries, such as Guatemala or the Philippines, where the Roman church was associated with poverty, repression and political and economic failure. He was also vicious in his attacks on the milder forms of Protestant evangelism, including the 'feel-good' Christianity of Robert Schuller and the Bakkers: 'I'm gonna tell you what's wrong with you denominational people, and a lot of you Pentecostalists: you want the Holy Spirit, but you want Him only as a companion, and not chairman of the board. You want to retain the gavel yourself. And that's the reason your sermons are like a Betty Crocker mix – they're all just alike. They look alike, they smell alike, they sound alike, they start on time, they end on time – it's a spiritual Betty Crocker mix.'

Angered by such jibes, the ecumenically-minded Bakkers removed Swaggart's programme from the PTL cable network. This infuriated Swaggart: although he was top of the television league table, syndicated by 3,000 stations in 140 countries, he had no cable outlet. Jim Bakker's suspicions that Swaggart had designs on PTL were not unfounded.

To undermine Jim Bakker, Swaggart related the story of Jim's indiscretion to the Assemblies of God in Springfield, Missouri. The denominational authorities would, in any case, have heard about it sooner or later: facts were already known to the *Charlotte Observer*, which was preparing to run a major exposure of PTL's financial irregularities, including the secret payments to Jessica Hahn. Faced with the impending storm and the threat of being taken over by Swaggart with the likely approval of Assemblies of God, Bakker made an extraordinary, but possibly shrewd, political move. At a meeting in Palm Springs, California, where Tammy was undergoing treatment for dependency on prescription drugs, he asked Jerry Falwell to take over his ministry on a temporary basis. The Assemblies of God – he presumed – would ban him from preaching for a year or so, for a period of repentance and rehabilitation. Afterwards he would be able to have his ministry back. It was the best chance he had of saving his kingdom.

On the face of it, Falwell was an improbable trustee. Whereas Bakker, like Pat Robertson and Jimmy Swaggart, believed in miracles, healing and baptism of the Spirit, Falwell was a sober fundamentalist and strict inerrantist from the opposite end of the evangelical spectrum. Indeed Falwell had expressly forbidden his employees at Liberty University from appearing on the Bakkers' programme; and the doctrinal statement they were required to sign contained a paragraph denouncing the charismatic movement and disavowing any connection with it. Though an independent Baptist outside the Southern Baptist Convention, the content and style of Falwell's preaching was much closer to that of Dr Criswell than the 'showbiz' approach adopted by the other big televangelists. Falwell's *Old Time Gospel Hour* – syndicated to 350 TV stations nationwide, plus a million and a half homes via cable – was a straightforward video recording of the Sunday morning service at Thomas Road Baptist Church in Lynchburg, Virginia, the church Falwell had started himself, at the age of twenty-two, in a disused bottling plant.

Falwell preached from the pulpit, sticking strictly to the text; the choir, in gowns of heavenly blue, sung the Old Gospel favourites. There was nothing gimmicky about the *Old Time Gospel Hour*, no tears, no shouts, no hand-waving or healing. In contrast to other more flamboyant preachers, Falwell's manner was careful, considered, even hesitant at times, creating a receptive empathy in his audience: nothing could be more different from the aggressive emotionalism of Swaggart, the boyish braggadocio of Bakker, the unctuous narcissism of Schuller. Falwell's face was kindly, receptive, unglamorous: he would have made a perfect provincial doctor or bank manager – an avuncular, friendly man, to whom one could confide one's problems.

But he was also a man of formidable organisational skills. Having built up his church to 22,000 members, he created Liberty University, a fundamentalist college with 7,500 students. He went on to found the Moral Majority, the umbrella movement of the Christian right which helped Ronald Reagan to power in 1980. With the ear of the President and numerous other connections, Falwell was probably the one man in America with the political 'clout' to rescue Bakker's ministry.

The picture that emerged in the weeks after the new board took charge at PTL was far worse, according to Falwell, than he had expected. The debts amounted to more than $50 million. Although the contractor had not been paid for months, work was still proceeding on the 500-bed hotel and a Disneyesque 'Cinderella Castle', housing what was intended to be the world's largest Wendy's hamburger restaurant. PTL owed its TV stations $8 million to stay on the air, as well as $2 million on mortgage payments. Its 1,500 employees had to be paid. Yet the balance in its various bank accounts amounted to only $200,000. For Jim and Tammy, of course, this had been a familiar situation. 'We were always playing "catch-up",' they said when interviewed on television.

And this seemed perfectly true. The cheques would be signed, and the Lord would provide the cash. Falwell, no stranger to fund-raising himself, explained in his avuncular, reassuring way, that unless eight million dollars were raised immediately, PTL would collapse, with direful consequences for every Christian in America. The sum was duly raised, and hailed as the 'May miracle'. With six million visitors a year, Heritage USA was Christianity's showcase – the third most popular 'theme park' in the country, after the two Disneylands. Its demise or, worse, its sale to secular interests, was unthinkable.

What bothered Falwell and other evangelical leaders was not so much the revelations of human frailty that came out of the scandal – Tammy's dependence on pills, even Jim's alleged homosexuality – but the Bakkers' much publicised greed which, he believed, would lead to a drastic falling in religious giving generally. In 1986, the year before they resigned, the couple had paid themselves nearly two million dollars. While widows on fixed pensions scrimped and saved to find fifteen dollars a month as 'partners', Jim and Tammy had acquired several houses and limousines – plus an air-conditioned kennel for Tammy's dogs. On top of that they had had the effrontery, in the negotiations that led to Jim's departure, to make exorbitant demands: Tammy's 'shopping list', scribbled on the back of and envelope, had included a $300,000-a-year pension for her husband and $100,000-a-year for herself, along with numerous other perquisites.

The scandal indeed led to a massive falling off in contributions. According to Falwell, the losses amounted to about 20 per cent of the American church's annual charitable budget – about sixteen billion dollars out of an overall sum of eighty billion dollars: it affected not only television ministries, but church and church-related charities, including universities, schools, hostels, outreach ministries, even the Salvation Army.

Falwell was himself no stranger to financial difficulties; nor had his own fund-raising operations escaped official scrutiny. In 1973, for example, the Securities and Exchange Commission had investigated the Old Time Gospel Hour for allegedly issuing some $6.5 million worth of bonds with nothing but Falwell's own fund-raising talents as collateral; although the allegations of 'fraud and deceit' were eventually dropped, a federal judge placed the Gospel Hour in what amounted to receivership, under the supervision of a committee of six local businessmen. In 1976, after the committee had relinquished its oversight, Falwell re-entered the bond market and embarked on a series of expansion programmes that left his enterprises forty-one million dollars in debt. In 1986 an eighty-one-year-old widow sued the Gospel Hour for making unauthorised loans to itself out of a $120,000 trust fund she had been 'unduly influenced' into establishing, with the Gospel Hour as ultimate beneficiary. In an out-of-court settlement the fund was taken out of Falwell's hands and turned over to the care of a local bank, with Gospel Hour paying the legal fees. The same year a long-standing dispute with the State of Virginia over the tax-exempt status of Liberty University led to Falwell's owing some $1.4 million in unpaid property taxes.

To replenish his coffers, Falwell had been making appeals that were no less dubious than Bakker's. Like Bakker, he would go on television to claim that unless donations were immediately forthcoming, his ministry would have to close – whereas in fact increasing amounts of money were flowing in and being spent on capital projects. Another classic technique was known as 'bait and switch'. A heartrending letter solicited funds for refugees or starving Third World children; most of the money so raised was then diverted to other projects, such as Liberty University or the Old Time Gospel Hour, in accordance with 'small print' clauses attached to the appeal. Other methods verged on the fraudulent: for example, in 1982 Falwell sent out an urgent appeal for donations to replace a Gospel Hour transmitter that had been damaged by vandals, without mentioning that the tower in question had been fully insured. Similarly, a Gospel Hour appeal for funds to 'save one million starving Africans' in the Sudan failed to mention that the proposed airlift for food, medicine and other supplies had been blocked by the Sudanese government.

In 1979, in order to scotch mounting congressional and public criticism, Falwell and other television preachers founded the Evangelical Council for Financial Accountability (EFCA), an organisation designed to ensure the 'highest standards of integrity' among the larger ministries. By 1982, however, it had become clear that many of the complaints received concerned Falwell's own operations, and Falwell decided to withdraw. The letter of resignation from his board was couched in the language of Christian brotherhood and sacrifice:

> It is the opinion of our board that you will be constantly bombarded by our enemies and critics, demanding a great deal of your time, money and energy in responding to these attacks. This has been your experience in the past and, in our opinion, will intensify in the future as Dr Falwell steps up his activities in opposition to the nuclear freeze, normalisation of homosexuality, acceptance of pornography etc. We would prefer to wage these battles without saddling EFCA with the resulting flak and criticism.

By 1986 of the major ministries only Billy Graham's organisation, which was not regularly networked, remained on the Council.

Falwell's strictures on the Bakkers' financial dealings, offered 'more in sorrow than anger', with a weary shake of the head, was therefore as much sympathetic as judgemental. There but for God's grace, he must have known, went the *Old Time Gospel Hour*. It may have been to distance his own operations from those of the Bakkers that he went out of his way to emphasise the sexual element in Jim's crimes, accepting the testimony of Jessica Hahn and a spiteful fellow-preacher against the repeated protestations of his fellow televangelist, who proclaimed his innocence of everything but a brief, unhappy encounter with the secretary. Falwell certainly had enemies among the liberal establishment, and his every move had been closely scrutinised by the press. But no taint of sexual misconduct had ever attached itself to him. By emphasising Jim Bakker's sexual misdemeanours, and concentrating less on the financial aspects of the scandal, he hoped to divert public attention from his own ministry, avoiding the dangers that always face those who live in glass houses.

Jimmy Swaggart was clearly incapable of such subtlety. The Holy Pugilist publicly and noisily baited his own trap. Having been thwarted in his aims of taking over PTL, he denounced Jim's sin as 'a cancer that needs to be excised from the Body of Christ'. Yet his own standard of living – a large mansion, a private Gulfstream jet, and identical 'His' and 'Hers' limousines for himself and his wife – was no less lavish than that of the Bakkers, and his style of leadership no less authoritarian. His ministry, which earned $142 million in 1986, seems to have been run largely for the benefit of his own clan, with twenty-two members of his family on the payroll. His downfall was less a consequence, like Bakker's, of ordinary human frailty, but rather of vicious, Pharisaic vindictiveness. He had ignored that most central of Christ's commandments: 'Judge not that ye be not judged . . . '

In his quest for expansion Swaggart had deliberately destroyed the ministry of a rival pentecostalist television preacher from New Orleans, Marvin Gorman. After Swaggart had accused Gorman of 'immoral dalliances' and 'sins of the flesh', the Assemblies of God – to which Swaggart was a major contributor, donating $12 million annually – defrocked Mr Gorman, causing his ministry to collapse and forcing him into bankruptcy. Gorman, aware of rumours of Swaggart's own sexual indiscretions, hired a private detective to 'tail' him. The picture that emerged was even more pathetic than Jim Bakker's afternoon of sin. The great preacher regularly took his pleasure by paying prostitutes and women drug addicts ten or twenty dollars to undress in cheap motels while he touched their private parts and masturbated.

Jimmy's lachrymose confession at his Sunday morning service was seen by television audiences all over the world: from most of his followers it excited sympathy, falling as it did within the great Manichean drama of sin and redemption that he constantly acted out on his programme. In the primitive puritanical climate that still prevailed in America's evangelical community, the sins of the flesh were perceived as being worse than those of the soul, the narrowing strictures of Pauline righteousness having been accorded precedence over the liberating message of Christ. The true nature of Swaggart's sin – greed for money, lust for power and, above all, spiritual pride – went virtually unnoticed and unrepented.

XIV

The Power of Silence

'He who knows does not speak
He who speaks does not know'

LAO TZU

Next day I drove north to Lynchburg, seat of Jerry Falwell's empire. An appointment with the great man had been out of the question. His engagement book had been filled for months. In any case, an advance booking would not have guaranteed an interview. Even the best-known television anchormen only manage to see evangelical superstars when these eminences have something they want to communicate to the world. I was courteously received, however, by various underlings.

The campus was set on a hill outside Lynchburg, a medium-sized town in southern Virginia named after a hero of the War of Independence whose way with loyalists added his name to the lexicon of cruelty. The buildings of Liberty University were new and undistinguished. The best that could be said of them was that they were low, and looked solidly built. One was made unduly aware of their logistical paraphernalia – water tanks, TV aerials, satellite dishes – but at least they reflected a comfortable human scale. The students were mostly white, clean and energetic-looking. None would have looked out of place on the campus of Brigham Young University.

Actually, the Liberty rulebook – an eighty-page document published by the office of student affairs – is a good deal more restrictive than BYU's. The dress code is precise and severe:

MEN: Ties must be worn in all academic buildings until 4.30 pm. They are to be worn to all classes. Flannel and sports shirts with a tie are not acceptable . . . Hair should be cut in such a way that it does not come over the ear or collar. Styles related to the punk culture such as hair, clothing and earrings are not acceptable. Beards are not permitted. Mustaches must be neatly trimmed and may not extend beyond the corners of the mouth (no handlebars). Sideburns should be no longer than the bottom of the ear . . .

WOMEN: Dresses and skirts should be no shorter than two inches above the middle of the knees. Slits in dresses and skirts should be no higher than two inches above the middle of the knee. Anything tight, scant, backless and low in the neckline is unacceptable . . .

The Music code is equally strict:

> Liberty University takes a conservative stand in regard to music, endeavouring to maintain a standard conducive to a healthy Christian atmosphere on campus. Students are to refrain from listening to rock, Christian rock, or any music that is associated closely with this type.

The code of sexual propriety is positively Victorian: single students are not allowed to visit or entertain members of the opposite sex in their apartments unless there are three or more persons present. Nor may they stay overnight in the off-campus residences of other single men or women. They are barred from entering the residence halls of the opposite sex on pain of expulsion. The sexes are not even allowed to mix in academic buildings without staff supervision.

Lights in the dormitories have to be out by 11.30. Under no circumstances may members of the opposite sex meet after dusk 'in any unlighted area such as the ball field, the ravine, the parking lots etc'. Nor may they go home together without written permission from both parents. While written permission is not necessary for dating, students are expected to exhibit 'mature Christian behaviour in social interaction': 'there must be no personal display of affection. Such display is considered in poor taste and is regarded as immature behavior . . . '

It seemed odd that an institution created to preach a Gospel which constantly urged Christians to 'love one another' should forbid displays of affection. The ban on lengthy locks also seemed strange, given that Jesus is invariably depicted with shoulder-length hair. The short hair rule is justified in fundamentalist circles by reference to I Corinthians 11:14 – 'Doth not even nature itself teach you, that, if a man have long hair, it is a shame unto him?' When a student at another Christian academy where similar rules applied asked 'But didn't Jesus have long hair?' he was told that pictures of Jesus were just representations painted by sinful men. The Bible taught that long hair was sinful, and that Jesus never sinned. Therefore Jesus did not have long hair.

The students seemed visibly happy with the code. A 'joyful countenance' is in any case as much part of the 'Christian uniform' as a 'decent' appearance. They bustled about the campus purposefully, jogging or carrying books. Their lives were thoroughly regulated by the Lord. They had to attend chapel regularly and Thomas Road Baptist Church on Sundays and Wednesdays; graduate students who lived off campus were expected to be 'active in their local home church'. Students had to show proper respect for each other at all times, and to always address staff by their titles (Dr, Dean, Mr, Mrs, or Miss). They were expected to 'live above reproach' during the vacations and 'to maintain a strong Christian testimony while away from the campus'.

The staff I met were all under forty, enthusiastic and extremely friendly. Like the Mormons, they seemed to want to defy the world with one hand while desperately seeking its approval with the other.

My first meeting was with Dr Larry Haag, Director of Missions, an earnest young man with the air of a busy executive. He began by telling me about one of their projects in the Sudan. There had been difficulties because their ministry was so openly pro-Israel. The former Israeli Prime Minister, Menachem Begin, had awarded Jerry Falwell the Jabotinsky medal for services to the Jewish state – the only non-Jew ever to be so honoured. The Sudanese didn't seem capable of understanding that one could be pro-Israel without being anti-Arab. 'We love everybody,' said Dr Haag.

'Do you think you'll succeed in converting the Islamic world?'

'It's rather doubtful. There will be individuals that come to know the Lord, but not in significant numbers. Muslims are very strict adherents of their own religion.'

'Doesn't that suggest perhaps that there is more than one path to God?'

'Not really. Because the one path to God we believe in is not a religion. It's not Christianity, or Buddhism, or Islam or Hinduism. It's the *person* of Jesus Christ. He is the only Way, the Truth and the Life ... '

'OK. But unfortunately Muslims don't believe that. They don't accept the doctrine of vicarious atonement. So from your point of view they must be in error – all 1,000 million of them.'

'Exactly. That's why they are the objects of our missionary endeavours. As Christians who believe in Christ as Personal Saviour we have to accept that these people are already under the Wrath of God, already condemned. Muslims, Confucians, Mormons – they're all condemned.'

'But surely, Mormons at least accept the Bible?'

'We've found Mormons to be very aggressive. They're amassing quite a following. Good people. Family oriented. Very good people – at least outwardly.' His compliments were genuine, those of a businessman impressed by a competitor's performance. Aggression in the service of evangelism is valued in fundamentalist circles: one famous preacher, the Reverend Carl McIntire, had gone so far as to call aggression 'an expression of Christian love.'

'I guess they share the same values as most of the people in your Church?'

'Sure. But if you look into Mormonism, you'll find sooner or later that they teach that Jesus and Satan are brothers. That's certainly not in the Bible. We have Mormons in my wife's family. They don't broadcast it at first, but they teach it. They also deny eternal punishment, and other kinds of thing. That's where we come into conflict with them.'

'Does doctrine really matter if your main concern is with moral values?'

'A person can be moral, can be a good husband or father. But if he's not rightly related to Christ by the New Birth Experience, he's still under the condemnation of God.'

'Does the converse apply? Are people who take Jesus as their personal saviour but remain lax in their own morality still going to be saved?'

'If they've made a true commitment to Christ, they are saved. That's not a licence to sin, though. What happens, you see is this: when a person becomes a Christian, it changes their whole life . . . '

The issue of pluralism was highly sensitive. In the last resort, fundamentalists put doctrinal purity before moral rectitude. At heart, they were still sectarians: personal salvation, which depended on the correct theological formula, took precedence over private morality or social reform. At the same time, they had come to publicly share many political positions with other religious conservatives: opposition to abortion and sexual licence, a hatred of 'secular humanism'. The Moral Majority (the name had actually been changed to the more neutral-sounding Liberty Federation) founded by Falwell in 1979 had deliberately sought to paper over the theological cracks in order to construct a common front of religious conservatives that would include evangelicals, fundamentalists, Catholics, Mormons and Jews.

Their gains had been considerable, particularly in the struggle against hated 'secular humanism' and other liberal teachings in public schools. A law originally introduced by Orrin Hatch, the Mormon Senator from Utah, to protect students from having to reveal personal information in class, had been used by the religious right to inhibit discussion on a wide range of topics they found objectionable, including nuclear policy, population control, witchcraft, suicide, sex, alcohol and drugs. As for 'secular humanism' – the national ideology perceived as atheistic – attempts to give it a legally coherent definition have been compared with trying to 'nail jelly to a tree'. In practice this catch-all term – which originated in a Supreme Court decision extending First Amendment protections to adherents of non-theistic belief-systems – covered just about anything the religious right found objectionable: 'hit lists' of books which Moral Majoritarians tried to have removed from public school curricular included everything from *Huckleberry Finn* and *The Scarlet Letter* to *The Diary of Anne Frank* and *The Lord of the Flies*.

The fragility of Falwell's carefully constructed 'moral' consensus was revealed when it came to anything resembling Christian service. While Moral Majoritarians could all agree that people must stand on their own two feet, and must at all costs be prevented from obtaining abortions, secular humanism or welfare stamps out of tax payers' money, the ecumenical alliance broke down on the issue of poverty: 'What about the poor?' asked Falwell in 1981.

> We could never bring the issue of the poor into Moral Majority because the argument would be, Who is going to decide what we teach those people? Mormons? Catholics? No, we don't get into that. As private persons and ministers, we make a commitment if we feel convicted. But for Moral Majority, no! If we go in there, create jobs, raise funds, and get involved with the local pastors, the problem is, which pastors? If we say the Mormon pastors, the fundamentalists are gone. If we say the Catholic pastors, the Jews are gone, and so forth. *We just have to stay away from helping the poor* [emphasis added].

The shift to political concerns was nevertheless relatively new. Traditionally, fundamentalists had steered clear of politics, their aim being to rescue as many souls as possible before the Rapture and other events associated with the Second Coming. As late as 1965 Falwell had argued the traditional case for separatism in a sermon attacking the Civil Rights movement entitled 'Ministers and Marchers':

> [As for] the relationship of the Church to the world, it can be expressed as simply as the three words which Paul gave to Timothy – 'Preach the Word'. We have a message of redeeming grace through a crucified and risen Lord. This message is designed to go right to the heart of man and there

meet his deep spiritual need. Nowhere are we commissioned to reform the externals. We are not told to wage wars against bootleggers, liquor stores, gamblers, murderers, prostitutes, racketeers, prejudiced persons or institutions, or any other existing evil as such. Our ministry is not reformation but transformation. The gospel does not clean up the outside, but rather regenerates the inside ...

The change was partly prompted by the very success of the Civil Rights movement, in which ministers had achieved visible political success. If liberal clergy could bring God out on their side, so could their conservative counterparts.

The leading theological light behind this revolution was Francis Schaeffer, a Presbyterian theologian who ran, with his wife Edith, an international study centre at L'Abri in the Swiss Alps. In 1981 Schaeffer published his most influential work, *The Christian Manifesto*, which set out the new conservative position in stark, uncompromising terms. Secular humanism had imposed its will on America. Millions of people had become indoctrinated with an anti-Christian ideology that could only lead to moral chaos and social breakdown. Significantly, Schaeffer's tract contained no reference to pre-millennialist doctrines. He argued strongly against dividing the world into spiritual and material realms. His plea for the reform of society based on the restoration of God's Law rested squarely on the classic Calvinist doctrine of depravity.

As a fallen creature, mankind could not possibly be expected to regulate its own affairs, to formulate its own laws. Humanism and Christianity were irreconcilably opposed: liberal theologians who attempted to reconcile the two were simply secular humanists using theological terms to deceive people. Schaeffer buttressed his case for a return to America's 'Judaeo-Christian consensus' with de Tocqueville's argument that religion was essential to the functioning of American democracy. The whole social structure built on this consensus was being destroyed. Christians were duty-bound to restore it, first by all possible legal means; then, if necessary, by civil disobedience or even force. 'The bottom line,' wrote Schaeffer 'is that at a certain point there is not only the right, but the duty to disobey the state.'

There was a picture of Francis Schaeffer – an anguished bearded face with hair of a distinctly unChristian length – in Dr Haag's office.

'He was the one who challenged Dr Falwell to do something about moral consciousness,' said Dr Haag reverentially.

'How did Jerry Falwell come into contact with him?'

The story had the hallmarks of a holy lineage or apostolic succession. When Francis Schaeffer was in the Mayo Clinic in New York for cancer treatment, he watched the *Old Time Gospel Hour*: on television and was so impressed that he sent Falwell a cheque. When Falwell was told that a cheque had been received from the great Dr Schaeffer, he immediately got in his jet and flew to Miami where a great meeting of Christian minds took place. Thereafter the dying Francis Schaeffer was a frequent guest on *Gospel Hour* indeed, just before his death in May 1984, he had been scheduled to speak but had been too ill to come. Falwell picked up Schaeffer's mantle, and the rest was history.

I was given a mandatory tour of the Museum of Creation Science, where Christian palaeontologists were busily arranging whale-teeth and butterflies according to their proper positions in the Noachian hierarchy.

I was spared a visit to the Tomb of the Unknown Foetus. I had seen too many pro-Life commercials to find the idea appealing. They dubbed five-year-old children's voices over pictures of babies in utero with messages like 'Mommy, why won't you let me live?' They were enough to convert the most woolly agnostic on this question into a militant supporter of abortion-on-demand.

I moved on to the department of Business Administration, where the dean, Dr Jerry Combee, had been deputed to talk to me. Dr Combee's hair was thoroughly Christian, as was the rather loud striped tie that adorned his crisp, white shirt. To my surprise he immediately rejected any suggestion that the Bible offered prescriptions for political economy. 'The evangelical community,' he said, 'seems to want to be able to open up the Bible and find a one-to-one correspondence between scripture and economic principle. That's a serious mistake. Martin Luther made an important point when he said "As a preacher, I don't tell a tailor how to make a suit. Likewise I don't tell statesmen how to govern." The Bible is not a textbook in political science. Everything it says may be true and relevant. But most of the disciplines we teach here are exercises in *natural* revelation, not special revelation. That's not well understood in the evangelical community.'

Holy Writ for Dr Combee was Locke's *Second Treatise*: it was there that one found the relationship between religious and economic concepts. Locke's concept of natural rights – the chief of which, of course, was the right to private property – was a 'distinctly religious concept in its original formulation'. The Christian perspective in his faculty's teaching flowed directly from this.

'We're unabashedly free enterprise in our economic orientation,' said Dr Combee. 'To the extent that the Bible makes statements about politics and economics it is absolutely, infallibly true,' he continued. 'But it is not enough to generate understanding of contemporary situations. There's a section in the evangelical community here that seems to think that all you have to do is open up the Book of Leviticus and you'll have all the moral and political legislation you want. I find that extremely dangerous, and it's something I campaign against constantly.'

'So where does the Bible come in? Is it just a matter of inspiration?'

'That's right. The Bible is the inspiration part of it. In politics the key is the doctrine of the priesthood of believers. If you follow the logic of that, it means the end of the church – state merger, and it brings down the curtain on the divine right of kings.'

Dr Combee acknowledged that his world-view was firmly rooted in the eighteenth century. His science was unequivocally Newtonian: it was materialistic and mechanistic. It meant the world was created out of nothing by an infinitely rational God who expressed His rationality in His creation.

'The trouble with science today,' he went on, 'is that it lacks epistemological foundations. The very concept of natural law has been given up. The science of Newton and Galileo was a science that articulated laws that could be stated in mathematical language. Now all we're getting is statistical regularities. It undermines the presumption that there's an infinite, rational God behind the cosmos, telling it what to do – that gives you confidence that a law is a law, not just a statistical regularity. It's not just the absence of laws that bothers me. It's the logic behind material reality. In the Newtonian universe there was a logic 'out there' that corresponded to the logic inside our heads. Both were the same: God's logic and our logic. Once God is taken out of the picture, logic becomes a mere function of human subjectivity. And once you've accepted that, then the scientific way of looking at the world is not necessarily superior to the mystical way of looking at it . . . '

Combee's logic seemed impeccable. He was fighting a desperate rearguard action on behalf of Christian civilisation. The Transcendental God – that extraordinary creation of the semitic mind – had sought to impose a primitive human logic and order on the cosmos. That order was now being undermined by Eastern mysticism and subatomic physics. Laws were going out. Statistical regularities – or even mere probabilities – were coming in.

Despite appearances, the God of the West was dying. The frantic activism of some Muslims, Christians and Jews, the rage with which they were terrorising society physically or intellectually, showed that somewhere in the depths of their souls they were becoming dimly aware of it.

This did not mean, of course, that all the gods were dead. The divine was re-emerging in eastern, mystical modes, in the dematerialised energies of the sub-atomic world, where appearances were continuously elusive and laws merely probable, not absolute. The mechanical materialistic god of the West (and that included Islam, which is largely Judaic in spirit) was still sovereign in the 'zone of middle dimensions' – the realm of daily experience where classical physics continued to be applicable. The dull, over-fed spirits of Middle America, with their garrulous, narcissistic preachers and complacent matriarchs, would survive for the present. But their zone was shrinking. Like the rest of America, they were living on borrowed time and borrowed money. The mystical currents of the East were penetrating the culture, just as its artifacts were penetrating the market. Eastern religions, like Japanese products, were better attuned to the age.

'Why are you so worried,' I asked Dr Combee, 'if the perceptions about reality of Hindus and Taoists match those of sub-atomic physics?'

'What disturbs me is the new scientific premise that the cosmos is in chaos. It is not an ordered rational whole, the truth of which can be found in the exercise of reason, according to the laws of logic. That's very disturbing. Remember, Einstein said "God does not dice with the universe!"'

'Einstein believed in the god of the philosophers, the god of Spinoza, not a personal god who concerns himself with human affairs.'

'I think we go too far in my circles in thinking of God as a buddy, who we walk along with and slap on the back, and tell jokes to, and think of that as a personal god. To me the god of Hegel coming to self-consciousness through the process of history – that's a personal god. What do we mean by person? Person comes down to self-consciousness. If God is consciousness, He is a Person. I believe I have a personal relationship to God, but that doesn't mean I play cool with Him, that doesn't mean that I would hold His hand while I walk down the street.

'When I talk about a personal relationship to God it means little me has a relationship with the infinitely rational intelligence that made the world out of nothing. When I try to conceptualise that God I keep going back to the eighteenth-century evangelicals. The best they could do was to say "He's a bright, pinpoint of pure, perfect light." That bright pinpoint of light did incarnate itself as a human body and did sacrifice Itself on the Cross and did rise from the dead. But the essence of It is that it's a bright pinpoint of light.'

'How did you become converted?'

'Through personal Bible study and discussions with Christians. But I had been led down the road by the study of Hegel. I was prepared by Hegel.'

'In a different social context might you not have found your Hegelian deity in Yale Divinity School?'

'I've had conversations with the products of Yale Divinity School. They fundamentally deny that Hegelian deity. I'm the only Hegelian Evangelical in the world, so far as I know – except for a couple of my students.'

'You mean liberal theology has gone too far down the road of subjectivism?'

'Yeah.'

'But it seems to me you're stuck somewhere between the subjectivism and situationism of the liberal theologians, and the positivist literalism of the fundamentalists . . . '

'It may seem that way to you. But if you really want to know where I am, I'll tell you. I'm Jonathan Edwards. That is who I am. He arrived at exactly the same view of God as I have. He was a Hegelian before Hegel. That's me. Jonathan Edwards. Updated with $E=MC2$.'

The snake church was situated in the Poor Valley, near the Cumberland Gap where Virginia pushes a westerly limb into Tennessee and Kentucky. It was out of the way, but there were still a few days to go before I had to be in London. Pastor Joseph Short, recommended by a helpful sociologist, had muttered something down the 'phone before I ran out of quarters. I barely understood his accent, but gathered it would be OK if I came along Saturday night. As the services only took place twice a month, the chance seemed too good to miss.

I set off early, taking the freeway to Wytheville then, with time to spare, branched on twisting country roads leading west. As I approached the Appalachians, the country became more rural and intimate. The rolling fields of the east gave way to idyllic little hill farms with Dutch barns and loaf-shaped haystacks. The smallholdings, hacked out of the forest by settlers generations ago, were growing an enticing mixture of hay with wild 'lowers, tobacco, potatoes and Indian corn. The homes were pleasingly rustic: rough-hewn structures of planed logs with real rocking chairs in their porches: there are pockets of America that preserve a past that Europe has lost.

West of Wytheville the hills began building up into steep wooded ridges in the classic Appalachian pattern, forming great petrified waves that ran absolutely parallel to one another, as on a vast geological ocean. The more distant ridges had the deep purple haze that gave them their Cherokee name, *Shaconage* 'the place of blue smoke', or Great Smokies.

The chapel was a plain red brick hall up a secluded woodland track some way from the village. The pastor was already there. He was a thin middle-aged man with a countryman's sun-weathered face and kindly crowsfeet round the eyes. He sat me in a pew while he continued his preparations.

The interior was plain and utilitarian, without cross or altar. There was a raised platform at the front, with a piano on one side and a lectern on the other. As the people began arriving, they vigorously shook hands with Pastor Short and with each other, sometimes two or three times: this was evidently part of the ritual. The men were clean-shaven, and wore open-necked logger shirts and plain trousers, some with braces. Several were immensely fat, with blubber bellies rolling over their belts. Three of them arrived carrying plywood boxes inscribed with crosses and fitted with grilles through which tiny beady eyes could be seen. The men placed the boxes near the lectern, and went and sat in the pews.

Most of the women were also large, except for the very young girls. They wore calf-length dresses in cotton or polyester, printed in pastel colours. There were a dozen young children, several of them extremely pretty, with angelic golden curls. The men and women sat apart from each other, separated by the aisle. When praying they knelt with their backs to the platform, propping their heads on the seats.

The pastor introduced me, explaining that I was writing a book about 'all the religions in America' and that God had sent me specially to join them that evening. He spoke in a peculiar, high-pitched voice which made it difficult to follow his words. So far as I could gather, he related Jesus's story of the rich man whose wedding guests failed to turn up at the feast. He moved on to the Passion and the dangers of dropping dead without having known the Lord.

An elderly white-haired man sitting next to me began to testify, using the same high-pitched sing-song voice, warning the younger members of the congregation to heed the pastor's words. His admonitions had no effect whatsoever on a group of adolescent boys sitting directly behind me, who continued to talk, fidget and giggle throughout the service.

But the Spirit began to move among the adults. They started ululating individually, each one winding up separately to the same high-pitched monotone as Pastor Short, like a group of motorbikes tuning up before a race. Their imprecations – 'O-o-o-o-o-o Ma Lord Come Down!' 'Hallelujah!' – created a tremendous cacophany, against which I could only hear snatches of the pastor's discourse. This was uniformly grim and minatory, consisting mainly of anecdotes about people who had died unsaved: ' . . . he took a seizure and died, just a young man smiling at God in his casket . . . Death is gonna catchup wi' ye. Ye ain't gonna escape, Hallelujah! Don't wait till it's too late for yourself and your children . . . '

While this was going on, the musicians took their place on the platform. There were five of them: a pianist, two guitarists and two women with tambourines. They played a blend of country, rock and gospel music in a martial, four-four beat, with much yelling and stomping of feet, as if marching to heaven in leaden boots. One of the tambourinists was a strikingly beautiful woman with russet, Pre-Raphaelite locks. As she gazed in the middle distance, shaking her instrument and stamping her foot, eyes fixed above the congregations, her features acquired a beatific radiance: she was definitely having visions.

The music started and wound down spontaneously, with no apparent direction from Pastor Short. When it stopped, he began preaching again in the same high-pitched 'funny' voice. This was not glossolalia or 'speaking in tongues' in the full sense, since the words were evidently understood by the audience. It was something more subtle – a discourse delivered in a special voice to indicate that it was the Spirit, rather than the pastor himself, who spoke. As the service wore on, the intention became clear: in a small farming community critical or hurtful remarks seen as coming from Pastor Short himself would arouse resentment. Delivered in the shamanistic 'semi-glossolalia' style they would be received, not as personal opinions, but as articulations of the Holy Ghost.

The pastor harangued his flock individually: 'I'd like to see ya pray, Carl . . . What 'bout you, Jermy?' When the latter remained obstinately glued to his pew, Pastor Short fixed his sightless gaze on me: 'Now you know this man there writin' a book 'bout all the religions in the United States . . . I wonder, friend, what your gonna tell 'em 'bout our worship tonight? I'm not ashamed of my God. I believe in Holiness from the top of this head to the bottom of this heart . . . '

One of the men sitting near me began to witness at me:' . . . if he's gonna keep outta hell, he'll have to get Holiness. I dunno if they've gotta a holiness church like this where he come from, but he ain't gonna keep outta hell without the Spirit . . . '

I thought this might be a cue for me to testify – a prospect that filled me with panic, as, even if I could think of something to say, I knew I couldn't manage the special voice. Inspired by Jermy's obduracy, I decided to take the proceedings at their face value: if the Holy Spirit chose not to alight upon me, that was its problem.

The music started up again, and this time Pastor Short brought out one of the snakes – a fat rattlesnake three or four feet long which coiled itself stiffly round his arm. As the reptile hissed and reared, bewildered by the music and shouting, my phobia gave way to indignation. There was something obscene about using animals as props in a religious ritual. This was not the spirit of St Francis, whose sanctity wooed the birds off the trees, but a bravado circus act, or worse: for while the lion-tamer achieves some kind of rapport with his beasts, the snake handler seemed to have no relationship with the reptile beyond mutual incomprehension and terror.

After the service the men brought out the two other snakes, a copperhead and another rattlesnake, for my benefit. This hardly fitted the theory that immunity from harm was contingent on the operations of the Holy Ghost, since the latter, I presumed, was no longer with us. The pastor explained that the snakes were absolutely wild, having been caught in the mountains. They rarely survived for more than three or four months in captivity.

God had not been kind to snakes. First the Father had cursed them for what was essentially human weakness. Now the Holy Ghost was subjecting them to this. Not that its operations were always consistent, or predictable.

'You absolutely have to be a believer,' Pastor Short explained. 'You either have to be insane or believe in God. A rattlesnake will take your life. But God will keep you from hurting. I've been bit several times: bit and hurt, and bit and not hurt.'

'What happened when you were bit and hurt? Did you get medical help?'

'No. I never bin to the doctor. I was bit on the thumb by a rattlesnake. It got as black as shoe leather. Somebody told me, if you don't take that scab off, you'll lose your thumb. But I left it on and it came off by itself.'

'Do you keep a snake kit in church?'

'No, sir. We don't believe in doing nothin'. If you come here and get snake bit, you're on your own. We had a person die from snake bite. Very unpleasant situation. He was from Indiana. Came down one week-end. He was down a-praying, like we were tonight. He came in the building and took a serpent and was already snake-bit afore I even knowed he was in the church.'

Snake bites were rare, but they certainly happened. In two hundred services observed by two sociologists, three people were bitten, none of them fatally. In one case, during their first attendance at a snake church, the sociologists saw that a young man had been bitten on his hand. The snakes were put away, while the victim ran round the pulpit and altar; there was ecstatic dancing, then a healing, with laying on of hands. Two women appeared to go into trances, and had to be helped. About half an hour after he was bitten, the young man walked out of the church, washed the blood off his hand, and then returned to his seat, while the service continued.

Although *ad hoc* serpent handling may have occurred at Holiness revival meetings during the nineteenth century, the first man to introduce it as a religious rite seems to have been George Hensley, of Sale Creek, Tennessee, in 1909. Hensley took as his text two verses from the last chaper of Mark: 'And these signs shall follow them that believe. In my name shall they cast out devils; they shall speak with new tongues; they shall take up serpents; and if they drink any deadly thing, it shall not hurt them; they shall lay hands on the sick and they shall recover.'

In the 1920s and 1930s newspapers occasionally reported snake bites sustained during services; and as the practice spread, mainly in the south-east, it was denounced by the more respectable Holiness churches, including the Church of God and the pentecostal Holiness Church. Responding to public concern, several Southern state legislatures outlawed the practice. Most of these states, including Virginia, treat snake-handling as a misdemeanour, punishable by a fine or six months' imprisonment; but in 1941, after a seven-year-old girl was bitten by a rattlesnake in a case that aroused much publicity, Georgia made snake-handling a felony that under certain circumstances was punishable by death. The Georgia law proved so severe that no jury could be found to convict. It was repealed in 1968.

Pastor Short was unperturbed by the fact that the Virginia law was still on the statute book. He had been arrested several times, along with other people during the 1950s; but the arrests caused the authorities so much trouble that they eventually gave up. Nowadays the sheriffs knew when not to drive too close to the chapel.

'Did you start handling snakes when you got saved?' I asked.

'No. I guess I'd been a Christian two or three years before I handled a serpent. I was in a church in Kentucky. My grandmother – my daddy's mother – had serpents ever since I was a kid. So I thought when I got saved I could just take 'em up. But it didn't work out that way.'

'You tried and got bit?'

'No. I was afraid. I couldn't overcome it. I was afraid of the serpents. I'd sit in the back. It takes the Lord to take the fear out of you.'

A second experience of grace, an act of sanctification: I wondered what Wesley would have made of the use to which his doctrine had been put.

Pastor Short allowed me to camp by his church, so I set off at dawn the next morning. I drove through the Cumberland Gap, the key pass between the Potomac and Ohio valleys. The place was virtually unknown to Europeans until Daniel Boone and his famous party of axemen cut the Kentucky Trail in the 1770s. Kentucky was virgin ground. The Cherokee Indians had used its rich wooded pastures for hunting, but had never settled there. The whites who began to arrive around 1800 could not believe their luck: acres and acres of good rich land, stretching to eternity. The Cherokees were deported to Oklahoma; those who survived that terrible journey were eventually permitted to settle in a small reservation at Qualla in the mountains.

Kentucky was Methodist country. Wesley's movement was admirably suited to the frontier, with its widely scattered and highly mobile population, especially after the Revolution had severed its ties with the Anglican church. His optimistic Arminianism, contrasting with the older Calvinist teachings, appealed to the individual: God's grace was free for everyone to accept or reject; the 'justified' sinner, with the help of the Holy Spirit, had only to strive towards perfection, by avoiding deliberate sins, including alcohol and slave-holding. The Methodist bishop, once elected, enjoyed near-autocratic powers: he appointed the preachers, designated the 'circuits' where they rode, and chose the elders who supervised the districts. Above all, Methodist preachers, like Baptists, spoke the language of the frontier. They scorned an educated ministry. Peter Cartwright, the most famous of the circuit riders, considered a theological training a positive hindrance in preaching the gospel. While other Protestant ministers were only 'lighting matches', arguing about pews, or music, or their salaries, the illiterate Methodist preacher was actually 'setting the world on fire'. The results were remarkable. By the mid-1840s Methodism had become the largest denomination in the United States, with more than a million members. West of the Appalachians their numbers had increased from around 2,600 at the turn of the century to 175,000 in 1844.

The day brightened, and the country opened up as a pleasing landscape of small farmsteads, with hay fields, Dutch barns and rough-hewn cabins gradually taking over from the forest. As I approached Lexington the landscape became increasingly tidy, with stone walls and neat wooden fences. The suburban dwellings of Bourbon County proclaimed their allegiance to the cult of the horse: the lawns displayed horses in moulded plaster, there were china horses on window-sills, horse mascots on cars and pick-ups, jockeys instead of gnomes in the garden rockeries. Occasionally I passed a real thoroughbred or two grazing sleekly in long grass that was disappointingly green. Its famous blue tint must come later in the season.

In 1800 this immaculate country was raw frontier. The backwoodsmen – as the first settlers were known – were brutal and primitive. The English traveller, Fortescue Cuming, described them as being

> very similar in their habits and manners to the aborigines, only perhaps more prodigal and more careless of life. They depend more on hunting than on agriculture, and of course are exposed to all the varieties of the open air. Their cabins are not better than Indian wigwams. They have frequent meetings for the purpose of gambling, fighting and drinking. They make bets to the amount of all they possess. They fight for the most trivial provocations, or even sometimes without any, but merely to try each others prowess . . . Their hands, teeth, knees, head and feet are their weapons, not only boxing with their fists . . . but also tearing, kicking, scratching, biting, gouging each other's eyes out by a dexterous use of a thumb and finger, and doing their utmost to kill each other, even when rolling over one another on the ground.

Into these men and their womenfolk the preachers put the fear of God, or more specifically, the fear of hell. The camp meeting was from the first an inter-denominational event, though pioneered by Presbyterians. It was the Methodist circuit in reverse: the people arrived to hear the preaching and camped on the spot in their wagons or tents. Camp meetings were social as well as religious occasions: at a time when the people were mostly illiterate and widely dispersed, they provided entertainment and an opportunity for getting together.

In the August of 1801 Barton Stone, Bourbon County's young Presbyterian minister, announced that a great meeting would be held by his little log church on Cane Ridge near Lexington. A maverick with only four or five years education, Stone had informed his presbytery that he would only abide by the Westminister Confession – the official Presbyterian doctrinal statement – so long as he thought it consistent with the Word of God. He called on Methodist and Baptist preachers, as well as fellow-Presbyterians, to help with the revival. The response astounded everyone. The crowd was estimated at between ten and twenty-five thousand – this at a time when the population of Lexington was only two or three thousand. They came from all over the state, from Ohio, Tennessee, Virginia. People travelled for days to get to Cane Ridge; they remained until the food and fodder ran out.

What astonished people even more than the numbers were the manifestations of the Spirit – if that was what it was, and not, as some observers thought, the work of the devil, or mass hysteria. As the preachers declaimed from the wagons, tree stumps, or crude makeshift platforms, the people responded with violent bodily movements: some (Stone wrote in his autobiography) would emit 'a piercing scream' and 'fall like a log on the floor, earth or mud, and appear as dead'. Others were afflicted by 'the jerks', violently moving their heads from side to side or even their whole bodies, oscillating 'backward and forward in quick succession, their heads nearly touching the floor behind and before'. The jerking was usually accompanied by 'barking' or grunts induced 'from the suddenness of the jerk'. This would often be followed by the 'dance': 'Such dancing was indeed heavenly to the spectators; there was nothing in it like levity, nor calculated to excite levity in the beholders. The smile of heaven shone on the countenance of the subject, and assimilated to angels appeared the whole person.'

Some people laughed 'a loud hearty laughter', which induced no laughter in others; others tried to escape from the 'bodily agitations' by running away, 'but it commonly happened that they ran not far, before they fell . . . ' The most moving manifestation, according to Stone, was the 'singing exercise': 'This is more unaccountable than any thing else I ever saw. The subject in a very happy state of mind would sing most melodiously, not from the mouth or nose, but entirely in the breast, the sounds issuing from thence. Such music silenced everything, and attracted the attention of all. It was most heavenly. None could ever be tired of hearing it.'

The sceptics (and there were many) interpreted these proceedings less decorously, noting a greater increase of lust than spirituality, and claiming that during the six nights and seven days of this spiritual Woodstock – the largest religious gathering to occur in North America during the whole of the nineteenth century – 'more souls were begot than saved'.

For the believers, however, scepticism was no defence against the Spirit: 'There were those that came to scoff but stayed to jerk,' wrote one observer complacently.

The results of Cane Ridge were far reaching. The camp meeting, with its ecumenical overtones, became the major instrument of revivalism, not only in the West but in other parts of the United States; translated into the urban context it saved the cities as well.

Stone's spiritual progeny lasted well into this century. Dwight Moody brought religion into the urban wilderness, selling a sentimental brand of American optimism and evangelical Arminianism. His partner Ira Sankey supplied the music – the old-style hymns that set the people on fire and had them humming in the streets. Billy Sunday, who died in 1935, was less a salesman, more a vaudeville artist who specialised in smashing furniture to the accompaniment of a torrent of verbiage: what the Church needed – he would say – was fighting men of God, not 'hog-jowled, weasel-eyed, sponge-columned, mushy-fisted, jelly-spined, pussy-footing, four-flushing, Charlotte-russe Christians'. The targets of his invective were socialites, politicians, liberal preachers, trashy immigrants and above all the 'booze traffic'. He is the most direct forbear of Jimmy Swaggart.

In 1804 Stone and his associates parted company with the Presbyterians. In writing the 'Last Will and Testament of the Springfield Presbytery', Stone stated that in future the Bible would be his only authority, and that he and his followers would be known simply as 'Christians'. In 1832 the Stoneite Christians merged with Thomas and Alexander Campbell and their followers to form the Disciples of Christ.

Stone's old wood and plaster church is now enclosed in a stone super-structure to protect it from the elements. The interior has been restored to its early nineteenth-century condition, with plain glass windows and a slave balcony, entered by a ladder from outside the building. I was lucky enough to find it empty. The pastor-cum-caretaker, Franklin Dwyer, told me they had 10,000 visitors every summer, six or seven hundred a week. Most of them were Disciples, but Baptist groups came as well. The shrine had apparently retained its reputation as a source of fecundity, spiritual or otherwise: it was very popular for weddings.

'I insist that they bring their own ministers,' said Mr Dwyer. 'I refuse to do any weddings myself – I don't want this place to get the reputation of a marriage parlour where they can just come out and get the whole package.'

We talked about the great events of 1801.

'What amazes me,' he said, 'is how all those people managed to get anything done. How did they farm? How did they keep up with their trades? The meeting only stopped because they ran out of provisions – food for people and grass for the horses. You can't tell how long it would have gone on if they had been properly stocked.'

I asked him if he thought modern revival meetings were part of the same phenomenon. Did they have the same fervour?

'Well, I'm not a revivalist,' said Mr Dwyer. 'I never go to the things. Except when I've gotten caught in a situation where it was necessary to put in an appearance, for political reasons, if you know what I mean. I'd have to think for quite a while before I could recall meeting anyone who was ever seriously affected. Undoubtedly there are people who have been "converted". But to what, I'm not at all sure . . . '

Towards Bardstown the land seemed familiar, English, like the Cotswolds or the Blackmoor Vale. The Abbey of Our Lady of Gethsemani was just a few miles away, in a secluded valley among rolling woods and fields of brown and green. Founded in 1848, it belongs to the Order of Cistercians of the Strict Observance, known as Trappists.

The rule is probably the most rigorous in Christendom. The monks rise at 2 a.m. for Vigils: this is followed by meditation before Lauds, then private masses, then meditative reading. A light breakfast is taken before Prime at 6:15, followed by Chapter, when the brothers gather for a spiritual discourse by the Father Abbot and confess their faults against the rule; then more meditative reading, before Tierce and the Conventual Mass, which is always sung in full. Two hours of manual labour are done in the morning, followed by the office of Sext and then Dinner. Trappists are restricted to milk, cheese and vegetables, unless they are sick, when meat, fish or eggs are allowed. In the afternoon there are two or more further hours of manual labour. The monks make cheese, which they sell, split wood and grow vegetables. They are bound by a strict rule of silence: they never converse with each other, and speak only to their superiors when necessary. In the evening they return to their reading, and then chant Vespers and Compline before retiring at 7 o'clock 'along with the birds'.

It was the strictness of the rule that attracted its most famous adherent, Thomas Merton to the order. The son of a New Zealand father, and an American mother who died of cancer when he was six, Merton, like many saints before him, led a wild and dissipated youth before dedicating his life to God. Having grown up in France and been largely educated in England, he was drawn to the Roman Church by its culture – he must be the only Catholic in history to have been converted, at least in part, by reading James Joyce – its antiquity and by his need for authority and family (his father had died when he was young).

A psychiatrist would probably conjecture that the morbid self-loathing he experienced before his conversion – which he describes in his celebrated autobiography, *The Seven Storey Mountain* – was largely, if not entirely, due to unconscious childhood feelings of guilt at the death of his mother. His account of his adolescence is fraught with an obsessive, neurotic anguish. He gives no details of the 'sins' he too readily admits to having committed, so the reader gets no chance of judging what factual basis, if any, there was to his self-contempt. An inverted narcissist and obsessive penitent, Merton found that his desire for self-mortification could not be satisfied by the relatively comfortable regime of the Franciscans, whom he first approached with a view to joining. 'Becoming a Franciscan,' he wrote, 'meant absolutely no sacrifice at all.'

In Our Lady of Gethsemani Merton found his Mother and, with Her, his peace of mind:

> The embrace of it, the silence! I had entered into a solitude that was an impregnable fortress. And the silence that enfolded me spoke to me, and spoke louder and more eloquently than any voice, and in the middle of that quiet, clean-smelling room, with the moon pouring its peacefulness in through the open window, with the warm night air, I realised truly whose house that was, O glorious Mother of God!

Here, in the womb-like silence, he began to climb the spiritual ladder that led, beyond ego-transcendence, to an experience of enlightenment that seems to have been both Eastern and Western, universal yet distinctively Catholic.

Merton's spirituality was complex, not to say convoluted: nothing could have been further removed from the glib, simplistic formulas of born-again evangelism. His first, most significant step, was to distinguish between the two selves: the 'true self in God' and the 'false self of egocentric desires': 'To say that I was born in sin is to say that I was born into the world with a false self. I was born with a mask.'

Sin became not so much action as identity, its focus shifting from the realm of morality to that of being. All sin sprang from the false self – from 'the assumption that the self that exists in egocentric desire is the final reality of life to which everything else in the universe is ordered'. The ladder to God, to enlightenment, depended on repossessing the true self by 'liberation from anxiety and fear and inordinate desire'.

The ascent was far from easy: since the two selves appeared to be so similar, the quest for true selfhood by means of prayer and contemplation could be very hard to distinguish from the religiosity of the false self: Merton was constantly trying to guard against confusing the two – the false self of spiritual pride that congratulated itself on its own piety, its own humility, and the true God-oriented self that was so elusive as to be barely aware of its existence:

> The inner self is precisely that self which cannot be tricked or manipulated by anyone, even the devil. He (the true self) is like a very shy wild animal that never appears at all whenever an alien presence is at hand, and comes out only when all is peaceful, in silence, when he is untroubled and alone. He cannot be lured by anyone or anything, because he responds to no lure except that of the divine freedom.

It was this conundrum of definition, this spiritual problematic, that drew Merton towards the study of eastern mysticisms, especially Zen Buddhism where the paradoxes of enlightment are stock-in-trade. Allowed by his abbot to make contacts among Eastern gurus, he died, absurdly, in Bangkok in 1968, when an electric fan fell into his bathtub.

It was six in the evening by the time I arrived at the Abbey. The sun, shorn of its ferocity, was casting lengthy shadows from the tree-lined avenue. The buildings looked drab and utilitarian – like the dreary convents one finds in Ireland on the outskirts of middle-sized towns. Ugly buildings, wrote Merton, were 'a false orientation of the monastic spirit'. He had been fortunate to arrive at night when the little steeple shone 'bright as platinum' in the moonlight, lending the place an air of mystery. But only an eye already transfigured – or corrupted – by faith could see in this jerry-built, concrete priest-factory a worthy descendant of Rievaulx or Slaney.

Brother Bruno was manning the office, which privileged him to speak to visitors. He was tall and looked quite young in his white cowl and brown cape, with his shaven head and bottle-glass spectacles that hid a pair of watery pale blue eyes from the world's gaze. I asked him how things had changed since Merton's day. He spoke gently, with weary resignation: 'We were a large monastery at that time, several times larger than now. We had about 300 monks, over a hundred novices. Now there are only three novices, and a couple of postulants. There are plenty who come but – well, you know, the problem today is commitment.'

'You can't find people to make a commitment?'

'When you look at married life, it doesn't surprise me. Fifty per cent divorces.'

'But in that case you might expect more children of divorced parents to opt for celibacy.'

'A vocation comes from home. The family usually has a lot to do with it.'

'Thomas Merton's family life was pretty tumultuous.'

'But he was an extraordinary person. How many parents nowadays want their children to devote themselves to God? There's only one supreme god in America – the dollar. It's destroying our country.'

We discussed PTL, the confounding of money and power with spirituality, the way in which churches had become caught up in the materialism they denounced.

'It's just shocking,' he said, with what I suspected was the nearest he could muster to rage. 'I hope I'm not pretending to be a prophet of doom, it's just so ghastly . . .'

He let me have some postcards, for which he refused to accept payment. Directing me to the graveyard he requested me not to stray beyond the point where visitors could go.

The enclosure was empty. There were some pine trees and a few palms, along with a couple of broken chairs and a procession of plaques representing the Stations of the Cross. The graves were grouped together, near the chapel. There were half a dozen of them with plain crosses, without headstones. That of Father Louis – to give Merton his monastic name – was among them.

The discipline of Gethsemani appears to have made him happy. Henri Nouwen, who met him there for the first time, described him as an 'earthy man dressed in sloppy blue jeans, loud, laughing, friendly and unpretentious'. He took prayer seriously, but not in a solemn way.

But whatever inner peace his soul may have found, there remained a profound tension – not to say contradiction – between his role as a monk and that of a writer, between Father Louis and Thomas Merton. Aware of his value as a Catholic propagandist, his Superior – prompted by Rome – had allowed him to resume writing – at least for a time, until his attacks on the Vietnam War began to upset the hierarchy. After that, Merton published his views in *samizhdat* typescripts. The privilege accorded to Merton caused Father Louis considerable spiritual anguish:

> But then there was this shadow, this double, this writer who had followed me into the cloister. He is still on my track, he rides my shoulders, sometimes like the old man of the sea. I cannot lose him. He still wears the name of Thomas Merton. Is it the name of an enemy? . . . And the worst of it is, he has my superiors on his side. They won't kick him out. I cannot get rid of him. Maybe in the end he will kill me, he will drink my blood. Nobody seems to understand that one of us has got to die.

How can we be certain which voice is speaking, that of Louis, the contemplative, or Thomas, the writer? The voices are usually, but not always, distinguishable: 'To be consciously or willingly committed to the worldly power struggle in politics, business and wars is to founder in darkness, confusion and sin,' says the monk, adopting the apocalyptic mode. The saints, he continues, are not part of this struggle. Instead they must 'trust in God to work out their destiny and rescue them from their final destruction, the accidents of which are not subject to their control'.

But then Merton the writer and advocate of non-violence takes over, urging 'direct action' against nuclear tests in the Pacific, supporting the Berrigan brothers in their protest against the Vietnam War, not to mention Martin Luther King's Civil Rights movement. None of these positions would necessarily be inconsistent with the pastoral role of a 'secular' priest. But Merton's vocation had drawn him beyond priesthood to what he calls 'the Mystery of divine silence' where the Church 'by her prayer gains strength from the Apostles themselves, so often harassed by the monster'.

He tried, it would seem, to get the best of both worlds – the visible world of matter and the unseen world of the spirit. While others were out on the front line facing the stones and tear gas, battling for peace and justice, Merton sat in his cell in Gethsemani pronouncing anathemas on the evil forces that threatened the world with destruction, a silent Savonarola who spoke only with his pen.

Merton the pacifist proclaimed the Catholic's overwhelming duty to work for peace. In this age of napalm and the bomb, he argued, the old Augustinian notion of a 'just war' was dead. Since most of the victims of war were civilians, modern wars were inherently unjust. For too long Catholics – and Christians generally – had blithely rendered part of God's portion to Caesar in order to protect the wordly, institutional structures of the Church, to the point when they eventually acquiesced in war, the ultimate obscenity.

It is not hard to guess what Merton would have made of the warmongers in the contemporary evangelical community, advocates of a 'Christian' America that must needs maintain its moral supremacy by remaining at the front of the arms race. He deplored 'the more or less complete identification of God with "Western civilisation" and "Western society"' which led, he thought, to a situation where the crisis of Western civilisation necessarily became 'a crisis of Christianity and of Christian faith'. In the ensuing 'state of insecurity and frustration', he continued,

> You can now find the most ardent Christians lined up in the most ridiculous, regressive, irrational parades. If they were concerned only with flying saucers and conversations with the departed it would not be so bad: but they are also deeply involved in racism, in quasi-Fascist nationalism, in every shade of fanatical hate cult, and in every semi-lunatic pressure group that is all the more self-congratulatory in that it is supported by the affluent as well as by the clergy . . . In such a situation, who needs atheists? *The unbelief of believers is amply sufficient to make God repugnant and incredible* [emphasis added].

Since Merton was writing in the Sixties, before the American airwaves had become saturated with biblical junk-preaching and scriptural gobbledegook, his words have a prophetic ring. Whether or not he was a good monk, or a great mystic, his value for ordinary, fallen, confused and unbelieving mortals is that he understood, and drew strength from, the meaning of silence in a cacophanous world where language – including religious language – has become corrupted by militarism, advertising, politics and the Almighty Dollar.

In a fallen world, the revelations through which the God may appear to manifest Himself cannot approach even the barest approximation of truth. The one, universal and truly inerrant Scripture is written in the Language of Silence.

The bell was tolling for Vespers. I took my place at the front of the visitors' gallery so I could watch the choir below. Light shafted down in regular bands that shone on the polished pews and lecterns, illuminating some of the monks in their cowls and capes, casting others into deep shadow. Theirs were American, Yankee faces, purged of pride and complacency, grown lean in the struggle for freedom over the tyranny of the flesh, of the world. The words they uttered were ancient, Latin, incomprehensible; the plainsong monotonous, but deep and warm and subtle, like the colours of medieval glass or gothic patterns carved in antique oak.

The chant was the same as I had heard one summer's evening in the chapel of Mont Saint-Michel, after the tourists had left, when all was suddenly quiet. It made me nostalgic for the cathedrals and cities of Europe, for the patina of my continent.

I was happy to be nearly home.

Epilogue

Half-way up the wooded slopes of Monticello, near Charlottesville, Virginia, where Thomas Jefferson built his delightful Palladian villa, lies the burial plot of the Jefferson family: a half-acre of flattish ground, fenced by iron railings, which, like the twenty-odd miles of roadway crossing the estate, was hacked and grubbed from the virgin mountain by some of the slaves he failed to liberate. The most prominent of the tombstones conforms precisely to his instructions: 'a plain die or cube of 3 f[oot], without any mouldings, surmounted by an Obelisk of 6 f height', each fashioned from a single piece of coarse stone 'that no one might be tempted hereafter to destroy it for the value of the materials'. The inscription is justly famous:

> Here was buried Thomas Jefferson
> Author of the Declaration of American Independence
> Of the Statute of Virginia for religious freedom
> And Father of the University of Virginia

In Jefferson's estimation these achievements ranked higher than any others in his career, not excluding the offices he held – minister to France, delegate to the Continental Congress, governor of Virginia, Secretary of State, Vice-President and President of the United States.

The Virginia Act, adopted by the state legislature in 1786 after years of effort by James Madison, embodied the most ringing proclamation of religious liberty ever made – and that in a former colony with an Anglican establishment, where heresy had carried the death penalty: 'No man shall be compelled to frequent or support any religious worship, place, or ministry whatsoever, nor shall be enforced, restrained, molested, or burthened in his body or goods, or shall otherwise suffer, on account of his religious opinions or belief; . . . all men shall be free to profess . . . their opinions in matters of religion.'

Years later, in his autobiography, Jefferson recalled that the Virginia assembly had rejected a proposed reference to Jesus Christ in the preamble to the bill 'in proof that they meant to comprehend within the mantle of its protection, the Jew and the Gentile, the Christian and the Mahometan, the Hindoo, and infidel of every denomination'. Madison summed up the feelings of the majority when he wrote afterwards: 'I flatter myself [that we] have in this country extinguished forever the ambitious hope of making laws for the human mind.'

The key provisions of the bill, of course, were later written into the Constitution of the United States. Article Six prohibits religious tests 'as a qualification to any office or public trust under the United States'. The First Amendment contains the famous 'establishment clause', which forbids Congress from making any law 'respecting an establishment of religion or prohibiting the free exercise thereof'. In a letter to the Danbury Baptist Association in 1801, Jefferson – now President – promulgated what has become the basic doctrine governing religion in the United States. The Constitution, he wrote, had wisely erected a 'wall of separation between Church and State'.

Jefferson was no atheist. He believed firmly in the God as creator and author of the universe; but he rejected the idea of personal immortality or the notion of a god who intervened in the natural order. Though he supported his local Anglican church, his religious outlook was Unitarian, denying the Trinity and godhood of Christ, but accepting the teachings of the Gospels. He saw in Jesus the ideal Jeffersonian democrat, a social reformer who died in an unsuccessful struggle against church and state, an early victim to the 'jealousy of the altar and the throne, entrenched in power and riches'. 'Christ's principles,' he wrote, 'were early departed from by those who professed to be his special servants and perverted into an engine for enslaving mankind, a mere contrivance to filch wealth and power to themselves.'

Jefferson had no doubt that American society would eventually follow him along the deist path: indeed he expected the whole nation to be Unitarian by about 1830. Yet if nearly two centuries later Unitarianism is one of the smaller denominations, a bland, uncontroversial strand in a Protestant tradition full of exotic new growths like Mormonism, Christian Science and Pentecostalism, the responsibility is partly his.

The disestablishment clause, that 'wall of separation' between church and state, had very different consequences from those intended by its architect. The institutions he designed in order to free reason from the shackles of superstition and state-enforced religious conformity turned out to be as William Lee Miller points out 'an encouragement less to Enlightenment rationalism than to aggressive Biblical pietism'. The enlightened society he envisaged was much slower in coming to the New World than to the archaic religiously-based tyrannies that had dominated the Old.

From the strictly rationalist standpoint, the structure was flawed from the start. The wall of separation was actually constructed by two entirely different sets of builders: the aristocratic democrats of the Enlightenment, led by Jefferson himself; and the Baptists with their sectarian allies, including the Quakers and some Methodists and Presbyterians. The latter, like Jefferson, saw the state as an instrument of coercion, a threat to individual liberty. But their reasons were primarily religious: heirs to Roger Williams, they were first and foremost advocates of Christian pietism, the 'voluntary way' in religion. During the first fifty years of the republic, this unlikely combination of pietists and rationalists finally triumphed. They overcame the views of those, including John Adams and Patrick Henry, who had argued in favour of a modified form of establishment, in which the established churches would continue to be supported out of taxation, retaining their place in the public sphere. American religion was firmly set along Williams's 'voluntary way'.

The contrast with Europe is striking. There, after centuries of religious conflict, the emergent nations achieved an accommodation between church and state in which the church was subordinate but nevertheless remained part of the public realm. Its dignitaries, who claimed to represent the nation's moral conscience, had the right to speak out on moral issues, engaging in public debate in the knowledge that they would, at least, be heard as *churchmen*, as members of an estate of the realm. In so doing they were forced to adapt themselves to a reasoned discourse: however fervently they upheld the claims of divine revelation from the pulpit, they lacked the authority to impose these claims on society at large without the help of secular government. The very fact that such help had to be won by persuasion and argument diluted the 'religious' or revelational content in their case: in West Germany and Italy, for example, Christian Democracy was simply political conservatism; in Britain the Church of England came to be seen as the Tory Party at prayer.

It is true, of course, that in America clergy engaged in politics: 'reverends' of different denominations have sat in Congress and several, including Father Charles Coughlan, Gerald L. K. Smith, Martin Luther King Jr and Jesse Jackson, have been leaders of popular movements. But however effectively they have employed the language of the pulpit, they have spoken as citizens rather than as men of the cloth. In multi-denominational America the Church sings with too many discordant voices to act as a convincing source of moral authority, of collective wisdom.

The wall of separation erected to protect the state from ecclesiastical tyranny has had the complementary result of protecting any group which organises itself into 'church' from embarrassing scrutiny by the state. Though nothing so overtly theocratic as the Nauvoo Charter now exists, the latter-day prophets and gurus of our era nevertheless enjoy – under constitutional protection – a freedom of opportunity, of organisation and of action that would be hard to imagine in other, more crowded, more tightly administered regions of the planet. Many of these movements, of course, have found supporters elsewhere, including Europe, among the confused, the deracinated, the health-conscious, the unhappy or the merely curious. But it is difficult to see how they could have become rooted in Europe during the delicate 'nursery' stage of development. The commitment to religious pluralism implicit in the Constitution, the tax exemptions granted to churches, the First Amendment freedoms of speech and worship, provide fertile soil in which new religions can grow. Even in the aftermath of the Jonestown tragedy in November 1978, when 900 members of the Reverend Jim Jones's People's Temple – including many children – committed mass suicide in the forests of Guyana, the state has refrained from a major clamp-down on cults and new religions. Anti-cultism has been left in the hands of the private sector – to evangelical or parent-funded groups which operate in the free market, like any other group.

The key to this development is *denominationalism*: the ideology of pluralism. The denomination is a uniquely American creation: in Will Herberg's words it is 'the non-conformist sect become central and normative'. It differs from the European idea of the Church 'in that it would never claim to be *the* national ecclesiastical institution'; but it also differs from the sect, in being 'socially established, thoroughly institutionalised and nuclear to the society in which it is found'. In the American Church the 'fringe' is the centre.

Non-conformism rendered central and normative is, of course, a type of conformity: but it is one in which an overarching pluralism – the general condition of religious toleration – acquires a value that is superior to any particular sect's claim to absolute truth. Absolutisms thus relativised lose their power to infect society. The small utopias that flourish behind church walls not only counter-balance each other: they also drain secular politics of seriousness, taming passions, reducing conflict, keeping the civil peace. It is only when denominational boundaries are overspilled in great moral crusades like Abolitionism, Prohibition and Civil Rights, that the political status quo becomes seriously threatened. In 1860 this led to civil war; in 1920 to institutionalised gangsterism; in the 1960s to unprecedented social turmoil. But these were exceptional occurrences. Unlike most of Europe – including Eastern Europe – where the state has tried more or less successfully to appropriate or suppress the powers of the church, the United States makes religious competition a condition of secular, bourgeois government: it is a policy, not of crude 'divide and rule', but of allowing divisions in order to govern minimally, in a manner most conducive to the requirements of business.

Denominationalism increases religious competition, diversity, and inno-vation – all of which, as every retailer knows, tend to enlarge the size of the market. With its increasingly mobile and heterogeneous society, religious America has become a divine supermarket where a church can be found, adapted, or invented, to suit almost any taste – from Yoga to Nazism, from stolid Bible-reading to 'holy rollering', from High Anglican 'smells and bells' to concerts where the faithful 'rock for Jesus'. In the divine super-market atheism is almost unknown, and agnosticism is rare: according to the most recent survey, 98 per cent of Americans believe in some form of God.

The First Amendment is a two-edged sword. The disestablishment of religion is the condition of its free exercise. Freedom of worship means freedom, not just from the coercive power of the state, but from public scrutiny – freedom from anything resembling religious quality control. The path from Monticello to Jonestown may be overgrown, but is clearly discernible, as are the paths from Monticello to Salt Lake City, Hayden Lake and Heritage USA. Freedom of worship – American style – means freedom to shut out the corrosive effects of Enlightenment: a paradox which Jefferson, with his optimistic belief in human progress and perfectability, can hardly have anticipated. While the light of reason born by educated divines may have penetrated the divinity schools of Harvard, Yale or New York, the wall of separation helped keep Dallas Theological Seminary and the Moody Bible Institute in the dark.

De Tocqueville, as is well known, regarded religion as indispensable to the functioning of American democracy. Religious authority, he argued, acted as a moral counterweight to political freedom, mitigating the natural selfishness that comes with equality. 'The chief concern of religion,' he wrote, 'is to purify and regulate, and to restrain the excessive and exclusive taste for well-being which men feel at periods of equality; but it would be an error to overcome it completely, or eradicate it. Men cannot be cured of the love of riches; but they may be persuaded to enrich themselves by none but honest means.'

Writing in the nineteenth century from a Catholic perspective, de Tocqueville was unaware of how easily Protestantism would change its message to suit the needs of the occasion. In the hands of self-selecting, self-ordaining, self-educated, partially educated or wholly uneducated preachers a text as rich and varied as the Bible could sanction every conceivable political or social attitude. Unconstrained by Catholic education and traditions of poverty, obedience and natural justice, Protestant sectarians had no difficulty in espousing almost any ideological position, from socialism to 'prosperity' theologies or full-blooded racism; and while it was certainly true that American Protestantism has inspired private philanthropy, anti-slavery, the Social Gospel and the civil rights movement, it has been equally efficacious in shoring up slavery and defending the rights of the rich. The cult of the Bible provides not a uniform or coherent ideology, but a common vocabulary and set of symbols through which political and ideological positions are articulated.

Even the Roman Catholics, who arrived in America in large numbers in the decades after Jefferson's death, succumbed to the prevailing Protestant culture. Aware of the vulnerability of their flocks to the attacks of nativist Protestant bigots, Catholic bishops eventually became champions of the American, Jeffersonian way, seeking protection behind those very pluralist walls which the Papacy was fighting against in Europe: not surprisingly, relations between Vatican and the American hierarchy have been constantly strained and fraught with misunderstandings.

With 28 per cent of the population, Catholics comprise the largest single group of religious adherents in the United States; yet from the time of Anglo-Saxon settlement the Roman Church (which, of course, is the oldest in North America, having been established by the Spaniards in New Mexico and Florida in the sixteenth century) has been progressively *denominalised* – which, in effect, means protestantised, not in terms of dogma, but of church government. In the free religious market that came into being after the Revolution, the Roman church had to compete with other denominations without any special claims to the loyalties of the faithful (saving, perhaps, the sentimental ties attached to ethnicity, a wasting asset). There is no Concordat between church and state, as in European countries with Catholic histories; nor can the Church, as in Poland, lay claim to the status of official ideological opposition; nor, as in England, to the status as a historic minority with a special claim on group loyalty. It is simply one American denomination – albeit the largest – among others.

In many respects Jefferson's wall proved an immense boon to Christianity – or rather, to its Protestant version. Freed from governmental responsibilities, the free-flowing structures of Protestantism were able to expand westward along with the shifting frontier. This applied especially to the Methodists, with their horse-borne circuit riders, and to the Baptists, with their itinerant evangelists: in the aftermath of the Revolution both denominations rapidly overtook the more tightly organised denominations – the Anglicans, Congregationalists and Presbyterians. For frontier-dwellers the revival meeting which could last days, even weeks, became the most important and lively of all social events. Like Islam in the shifting territories of Africa and Asia, Protestant evangelism became a process of socialisation and acculturation which operated independently of state power.

A consequence in both cultures has been a state that is weak in relation to society. For energies that might otherwise be devoted to socially beneficial ends – energies still channelled in Britain by a much-maligned class of public servant – are drained in the sawdust trail, wasted in the quest of 'souls for Christ'. Not the least of the ironies flowing from Jefferson's wall is that a disbeliever in personal immortality, a cultivated epicurean and advocate of the virtues of the Roman republic – quintessentially 'public' virtues – should have fathered a system that so explicitly favours personal salvation above the public good, that pays for its 'private affluence' with 'public squalor' in both spiritual and material realms.

Yet that irony embraces less than half the story. Jefferson's wall has its sunnier side. It protects the state from the weeds and the bigotries that flourish in its shadows. While it is true that the crasser versions of

Protestantism, the absurdities in Mormonism, the corruption of personality cults, the rampant idiocies of Creation Science, and the distortions of Schullerism would find it harder to entrench themselves in a Europe with established priesthoods manned by worldly professionals, those bigotries, those idiocies counteract each other. They could almost be said to cancel each other out.

Most religions are absolutist. Claims to revelation militate against rational argument and compromise. In this sense all religions contain totalitarian possibilities; for totalitarianism, which welds the state into a single body 'knit together as one man' (to borrow Governor Winthrop's phrase) is really the religious impulse, the worship of leadership and ideology, the cult of Person or Book, directed towards secular ends. That dream of Protestant America, the Holy Commonwealth, contained the possibility of totalitarianism, of a state which abolishes the individual will, just as surely as Prussia or the empire of the Tsars. Anyone who doubts this is unlikely to have witnessed the *apparatchiks* of Utah obediently voting for their geriatric 'prophet' or the storm-troopers of the Southern Baptist Convention baiting liberal theologians.

A state religion can prepare a nation for a totalitarian ideology: one need look no further than Iran to see how easily religion can ally itself to the politics of terror. In Russia Orthodoxy 'right teaching' prepared the ground for Marxist-Leninism: in the 1920s Joseph Stalin, the ex-seminarian, was able to draw tears from rural Communist Party delegates by using Old Slavonic, the liturgical language of the church; in Germany the Nazis drew on centuries of Christian anti-semitism – Lutheran and Catholic – in creating the enmity that helped bring them to power. The public language of America is suffused with terms like 'manifest destiny', 'one nation under God', 'In God we Trust' that hark back to the heroic age of the Holy Commonwealth. It is not inconceivable that, but for the foresight of the Founding Fathers in separating church and state, a very different kind of nation might have come into being, one in which the intolerance and bigotry which still exist behind church doors could have been politically sanctified. Those anti-intellectual forces – what Richard Hofstadter called 'the paranoid style' – have, of course, periodically erupted into the public realm: they generated Prohibition and reappeared with Senator Joe McCarthy. They were mobilised in the late Seventies and Eighties when Jerry Falwell and the Moral Majority spearheaded the New Christian Right. But their gains have been limited. Prohibition was repealed; the anti-Communist hysteria subsided. The campaign against 'secular humanism', bugbear of the New Christian Right, has done little more than persuade some educational publishers to withdraw or modify certain schoolbooks; it falls far short of the original aim of 'bringing God back into the classroom', of restoring the United States to the status of a 'Christian nation' in the white Anglo-Saxon Protestant sense of the term.

The movement's most signal successes – the anti-abortion campaign and the defeat of ERA (the proposed constitutional amendment granting equal rights for women) – have also revealed its essential weakness: for those successes could never have been achieved without the help of Catholics, conservative Jews, Mormons and even some liberal churchpeople, forces from outside the community of Protestant evangelicals, which would never join with the New Christian Right in its wider attacks on religious pluralism and 'secular humanist' values. Falwell's decision in 1986 to change the name of his 'Moral Majority' to 'Liberty Federation' underlined this weakness by tacitly admitting that the overarching pluralism of the Constitution took precedence over Biblical truth. No longer would his organisation claim to speak for the unconsulted, unheard 'Christian' majority. It was now just a pressure group demanding the same 'liberty' to lobby and organise as other pressure groups, including those it most disliked such as civil libertarians, activist blacks, feminists and homosexuals.

Utopian dreams, millennial yearnings and other irrational manifestations of the religious spirit all tend to undermine democracy, whose principal moral resource is reasoned discourse. All these things flourish in America as surely as in other parts of the globe, including the world of Islam. They thrive on the same insecurities, embracing as they do the same paranoid responses to the moral uncertainties and social disruptions of modernity. But in America their destructive force is gravely weakened by Jefferson's wall, which acts as a kind of breakwater, draining their emotional appeal by denying them religious legitimacy and sanctifying power in the political realm. For that America, and the world, must be grateful.

For the European, American political life often seems bland, corrupt and dull: smelling of palm grease, pork barrels, smoke-filled rooms. The passions that enliven European politics, the clash of interests tied to rival ideologies, are notable by their absence, except on those occasions when some great evangelical movement like Prohibition, Civil Rights or anti-abortion temporarily overwhelms the public agenda. In normal times the regional, social and ideological divisions that could tear the nation apart (a nation that did tear itself apart little more than a century ago) find an outlet in religion – in the salvation of souls. For the non-believer this must seem a peculiar way to expend so much time, talent and energy. But if that is the price of peace, the price that must be paid for American democracy, for preventing the world's most powerful nation from going down the path Russia, Germany, China or Iran have taken in our time, so be it.

Let the Soul of America rest in peace! Let it remain forever where it belongs, not in the corridors of power, but in the place Thomas Jefferson prepared for it: the aisles of the Divine Supermarket!

A Note on Sources

As this is an impressionistic not a scholarly work, I did not wish to distract readers with detailed references. However, such knowledge as I acquired about religion in America was not entirely based on personal experiences and interviews. The most important general works consulted were Sidney E. Ahlstrom, *A Religious History of the American People* (Yale, 1972); George C. Bedell, Leo Sandon Jr. and Charles T. Wellborn, *Religion in America* (New York, 1972); George Gallup Jr. and George O'Connell, *Who do Americans say that I am?* (Philadelphia, 1986); Edwin Scott Gaustad, *Historical Atlas of Religion in America* (2nd ed., New York, 1976); Winthrop E. Hudson, *Religion in America* (3rd ed., New York, 1976).

Other works consulted include the following:

Chapter 1. Sacvan Bercovitch ed., *The American Puritan Imagination: Essays in Revaluation* (Cambridge, Massachusetts, 1974); Richard L. Bushman, *From Puritan to Yankee: Character and Social Order in Connecticut* (Cambridge U.K., 1967); *Chronicles of the Pilgrim Fathers* (Everyman edition, London, 1936); Cotton Mather, *A Christian at His Calling* (Boston, 1701); Perry Miller, *Jonathan Edwards* (New York, 1949), *Roger Williams: His Contribution to American Tradition* (New York, 1953), *The Puritans: A Source Book* (New York, 1953); Perry Miller and Thomas Johnson, *The Puritans* (London, 1938); G. Mourt, *The Journal of the Pilgrims at Plymouth in New England in 1620* (New York, 1848); Chard Powers Smith, *The Housatonic: Puritan River* (New York, 1947); Henry David Thoreau, *Cape Cod* (1864).

Chapter 2. Edward Denning Andrews, *The People Called Shakers* (New York, 1953); Priscilla J. Brewer, *Shaker Communities, Shaker Lives* (Hanover and

London, 1986); Catholic pamphleture from Auriesville, including Angus T. Macdougall ed., *Martyrs of New France* (n.d.), Thomas Coffey, S. J., *Blessed Kateri Tekakwitha – America's Marvellous Maiden* (n.d.), and *Lily of the Mohawks*, Vol XL, Nos 3, 4, 6, 16, 17, 19; Whitney R. Cross, *The Burned-over District: the Social and Intellectual History of Enthusiastic Religion in Western New York, 1800–1850* (Ithaca, 1950); Lawrence Foster, *Religion and Sexuality* (Urbana, 1984); Paul E. Johnson, *A Shopkeeper's Millennium: Society and Revivals in Rochester New York, 1815-1837* (New York, 1978); *Sunstone* magazine (Salt Lake City, July/August 1980).

Chapter 3. The Book of Mormon: Another Testament of Jesus Christ (Salt Lake City, 1986); Fawn M. Brodie, *No Man Knows My History: The Life of Joseph Smith the Mormon Prophet* (2nd ed., New York, 1985); *Dialogue* magazine (Salt Lake City, Summer 1969); *Doctrine and Covenants* (Salt Lake City, 1987); Roger D. Launius, *The Kirtland Temple: a Historical Narrative* (Independence Missouri, 1986); *Sunstone*, January/February 1981; Mark Twain, *Roughing It* (1872); Dan Vogel, *Indian Origins and the Book of Mormon* (Salt Lake City, 1986).

Chapter 4. Leonard T. Arrington, *Brigham Young: The American Moses* (Chicago, 1975); Brodie, *op cit.*; Robert Bruce Flanders, *Nauvoo, Kingdom on the Mississippi* (Urbana, 1975); Linda King Newell and Valeen Tipps Avery, *Mormon Enigma: Emma Hale Smith* (New York, 1984); Dallin Oaks and Marvin S. Hill, *Carthage Conspiracy: The Trial of the Accused Assassins of Joseph Smith* (Urbana, 1975).

Chapter 5. Arrington, *op. cit.*; Brodie, *op. cit.*; Richard E. Burton, *City of the Saints* (London, 1861); Kate B. Carter *Heart-Throbs of the West* (Salt Lake City, 1939); *The journal of William Clayton from Winter Quarters to Salt Lake Valley*, compiled by Kate B. Carter (Salt Lake City, 1944); Wallace Stegner, *The Gathering of Zion: The Story of the Mormon Trail* (New York, 1964).

Chapter 6. Ed Decker and Dave Hunt, *The God Makers: a Shocking Exposé of what the Mormon Church REALLY Believes* (Eugene Oregon, 1984); Robert Gottleib and Peter Wiley, *America's Saints: The Rise of Mormon Power* (New York, 1984); Robert Lindsey, *A Gathering of Saints: a True Story of Money, Murder and Deceit* (New York, 1988); Steven Naifeh and Gregory White

Smith *The Mormon Murders: a True Story of Greed, Forgery, Deceit and Death* (New York, 1988).

Chapter 7. Robert Ignatius Burns, S. J., *The Jesuits and the Indian Wars of the North-west* (Moscow Idaho, 1966).

Chapter 8. Robert Balch, *Money and Power in Utopia* (1986), paper kindly made available to author; Frances FitzGerald, *Cities on a Hill: a Journey through Contemporary American Cultures* (New York, 1986); *Oregon* magazine, Portland, Oregon, 'The Rajneesh Files 1981–86', ed. Win McCormack; Bhagwan Shree Rajneesh, *Above All, Don't Wobble* (Poona, 1976); *Blessed Are The Ignorant* (Poona, 1979) Swami Subhuti (David Waight), *Bagwan's American Dream*, unpublished ms (1986); D. T. Suzuki, *Essays in Buddhism* (London, 1975).

Chapter 9. Martin Gardiner, *New York Review of Books*, Vol. 34, 9 April 1987, pp. 16–19; Shirley Maclaine, *Dancing in the Light* (New York, 1987); Benito Reyes, *Conscious Dying* (Ojai, 1986); Pat Rodegast and Judith Stanton, *Emmanuel's Book* (New York, 1985); Robert Schuller: *Tough Minded Faith for Tender-Hearted People* (New York, 1979, 1983), *The Peak to Peek Principle* (New York, 1980), *Self-Esteem: The New Reformation* (New York, 1982), *Tough Times Never Last But Tough People Do* (New York, 1983), *Be Happy Attitudes* (New York, 1985), *Be Happy You Are Loved* (New York, 1986).

Chapter 10. Niles Eldredge *The Monkey Business: A Scientist Looks at Creationism* (New York, 1982); Frank Waters, *The Book of the Hopi* (1960); A. Kennard, *Hopi Kachinas* (New York, 1983); Hal Lindsay, *The Late Great Planet Earth* (Chicago, 1970); Henry Morris, *Scientific Creationism* (New York, 1974).

Chapter 11. Nancy Tatom Ammerman, *Bible Believers* (New Brunswick, 1987); Steve Bruce, *The Rise and Fall of the New Christian Right* (Oxford, 1989); James Hunter, *American Evangelism* (New Brunswick, 1983); James C. Hefley, *The Truth in Crisis: the Controversy in the Southern Baptist Convention* (2 Vols., Dallas, 1986; Hannibal, 1987).

Chapter 12. Coretta Scott King, *My Life With Martin Luther King Jr.* (New York, 1970); Malcolm Little, *The Autobiography of Malcolm X* (New York,

1966); W. Deen Muhammad, *An African American Genesis* (Calumet City, Illinois, 1986); Benjamin Quarles ed., *Narrative of the Life of Frederick Douglass An American Slave* (Cambridge, Massachusetts, 1960); W. Sollors, *Beyond Ethnicity: Consent and Descent in American Culture* (Oxford, 1986).

Chapter 13. Jim Bakker with Robert Paul Lamb, *Move That Mountain!* (Charlotte North Carolina, 1985): Tammy Bakker with Cliff Dudley, *I Gotta Be Me!* (Charlotte North Carolina, 1985); FitzGerald, *op. cit.*; J. K. Hadden and C. E. Swann, *Prime Time Preachers: the Rising Power of Televangelism* (Reading Massachusetts, 1981) *Penthouse* magazine, January 1988; *Playboy* magazine, November 1987.

Chapter 14. Ammerman, *op. cit.*; Fritjof Capra, *The Tao of Physics* (New York, 1977); Harvey Cox, *Religion in the Secular City* (New York, 1984); Kirk Elifson and Peggy Sullivan, untitled paper on snake handling kindly made available to the author; Jerry Falwell, *Strength for the Journey* (New York, 1987); James Finley, *Merton's Palace of Nowhere: a Search for God through Awareness of the True Self* (Notre Dame Indiana, 1978); FitzGerald, *op. cit.*; Thomas Merton: *The Seven-Storey Mountain* (New York, 1976), *The Silent Life* (New York, 1957), *The Non-Violent Alternative* (New York, 1980); Francis A. Schaeffer, *A Christian Manifesto* (1981).

Epilogue. Daniel J. Boorstin, *The Lost World of Thomas Jefferson* (Chicago, 1981); William Lee Miller, *The First Liberty: Religion and the American Republic* (New York, 1986); Frederick D. Nicols and James A. Bear Jr., *Monticello: A Guide Book* (Monticello Virginia, 1982); Charles B. Sanford, *The Religious Life of Thomas Jefferson* (Charlottesville, 1987).

Longer citations. Pages 12, 13: Bercovitch, p. 82; page 22: Calvin *Institutes*, Bk. III, Ch. 2, page 25: William Sargant, *Battle for the Mind* (London, 1957), p. 151 citing Jonathan Edwards, *A Narrative of the Revival of Religion in New England* (Glasgow, 1829), pp. 301–3; page 26: *Memoirs of the Rev. Jonathan Edwards* by Samuel Hopkins, revised and enlarged by John Hawksley (London, 1815), pp. 53–4; page 31: Foster, p. 42; page 49: *ibid.*, p. 91; pages 60–1: *ibid.*, p. 296; pages 62–3: *Book of Mormon*, p. 491; page 71: Launius, p. 186; page 78: Brodie, pp. 477–8; page 100: Stegner, p. 82; page 106: Clayton, p. 245 (22 May 1847); page 107: *ibid.*, p. 254 (29 May 1847); page 117: Burton, p. 366; pages 225–6: Ammerman,

p. 48; page 227: Hunter, p. 105; page 232: Hefley, Vol. I, p. 34; page 240: Quarles, pp. 84–6; page 248: Sollors, p. 45; page 249: King, p. 185; page 251: Muhammad, p. 31; page 252: Little, p. 341; page 258: Jim Bakker, pp. 72–3; page 274: archives of People for the American Way (Washington D.C., 1987); page 281: Cox, p. 230; page 282: FitzGerald, p. 129; page 293: Ahlstrom, p. 430; page 297: Merton, *Seven-Storey Mountain*, p. 321; page 298: Finley, p. 91; page 300: Merton, *op. cit.*, p. 410, *Non-Violent Alternative*, p. 37; page 301: *ibid.*, p. 206.

I would like to thank the authors and their publishers for permission to quote from these works.